Saving Special Places

Saving Special Places

A Centennial History of
The Trustees of Reservations:
Pioneer of the Land Trust Movement

Gordon Abbott, Jr.

THE IPSWICH PRESS
Ipswich, Massachusetts 01938

Photo Credits

The author expresses his great thanks for the following photographs made available through the courtesy of institutions, corporations and individuals: page 2, Copley Square, The Bostonian Society; page 3, Charles W. Eliot, Assistant Professor of Mathematics, Charles Eliot, class photo, 1882, Harvard University Archives; page 4, Frederick Law Olmsted in the 1880s, Society for the Preservation of New England Antiquities; page 11, Governor William E. Russell, Society for the Preservation of New England Antiquities; page 19, General Francis Walker, The Bostonian Society; page 20, Charles Eliot, age 35, Charles Francis Adams, first President of the Metropolitan Park Commission, Society for the Preservation of New England Antiquities; page 21, Charles W. Eliot, President of Harvard University, Harvard University Archives;

Also, page 22, Sir Robert Hunter, Octavia Hill (from a portrait by John Singer Sargent), and page 23, Canon Rawnsley, *The National Trust, Past and Present* by Robin Fedden, 1968; page 27, Charles W. Eliot II, 25th reunion photo, Harvard University Archives; page 36, Bradford Williams, Harvard University Archives; page 54, Thomas Hutchinson from a painting by John Singleton Copley, *The Life of Thomas Hutchinson, Royal Governor of the Province of Massachusetts Bay* by James K. Hosmer, Houghton, Mifflin & Company, 1896; page 58, Club House at Misery Island, photo from report entitled *The Misery Island Club, Incorporated July 6, 1900*; page 62, Abbott Lawrence Lowell, Fabian Bachrach; page 68, The Mission House, Haskell; page 70, Naumkeag, Clemens Kalischer;

Also, page 71, Chinese Garden, Naumkeag, Paul E. Genereux; page 98, The Bear's Den, Robert A. Clark; page 105, Harriet Backus, Underwood & Underwood; page 123, Monument Mountain, K.T. Sheldon; page 129, the "Marble Palace," Manchester Historical Society; page 132, Dr. Catherine Coolidge Lastavica, Bradford Bachrach; page 213, Norton Q. Sloan, Bachrach; page 240, interpretive booklets, David Stotzer; page 241, Paul Brooks, Kranzler; page 283, Frances Fairchild Bryant, miniature portrait on ivory, artist unknown, New York Historical Society.

Copyright © 1993 by The Trustees of Reservations. All rights reserved.
IBSN 0-938864-19-X

Manufactured in the United States of America
by Bradford & Bigelow, Inc.,
Danvers, Massachusetts 01923, and published by

The Ipswich Press
Box 291
Ipswich, Massachusetts 01938

Printed on Recycled Stock

Table of Contents

Foreword

Saving Special Places is the remarkable success story of the world's oldest regional land trust. As such, it will be encouraging reading for the growing number of people who care about natural, scenic, and historic areas, and who, as private citizens, are determined to tackle head-on the challenge of their preservation.

Saving Special Places talks about the land, but it is above all a book about people—a series of delightful anecdotes, warmly told, highlighting that "small association of generous men and women" who have rallied to Charles Eliot's clarion call since 1891.

The author, though, has failed to do justice to one of the brightest lights in The Trustees of Reservations' illustrious history—himself! In his 18 years as director, Gordon Abbott did more than any other individual since Charles Eliot to make the first one hundred years a success. Under his tenure (1967-84), The Trustees grew dramatically. Twenty-three reservations and 75 conservation restrictions were acquired, bringing the total acreage under protection from 10,000 to over 20,000. Abbott started a membership program and a formal annual appeal, and launched the organization's first capital campaign. The value of the endowment funds grew six-fold. Interpretive programs were initiated and scores of publications produced. He reorganized the volunteer governance structure and professionalized the staff, setting statewide standards of property management that have become the hallmark of the organization.

Abbott's most remarkable achievement is not easily quantified. His own limitless enthusiasm for the work of The Trustees has inspired literally hundreds to join the organization, many to get actively involved as volunteers, and more than a few of us to follow his example and make careers in conservation.

All of us who believe that conservation is best served when it is local, voluntary, and privately administered owe Gordon Abbott an enormous debt of gratitude. He has shown just how well it can work. It is entirely fitting that Abbott should be the one to memorialize in print The Trustees of Reservations. No one knows the organization better. No one loves it more. And no one has been more responsible for its success.

FREDERIC WINTHROP, JR.
Director
The Trustees of Reservations

Preface

Writing this book has been a labor of love. It has enabled me to recall in detail the happy and fulfilling memories of nearly 18 years with The Trustees of Reservations. Most important, it has provided me with an opportunity to relive the pleasures of working with a group of remarkable people — staff members, board members, members of local committees, benefactors and Federal, State, and community resource officials — for a cause to which all of us were devoted. It has also enabled me to recapitulate the early years of the organization, remarkable for their dedication and persistence, during the decades when the preservation of open space was not a major priority in American life and the struggle for recognition and accomplishment was never-ending.

As readers will soon realize, the book does not tell the story of every property of The Trustees of Reservations. This I have left to the *Guide* published by the organization as a handbook for visitors. My task has been to select those properties which I believe best illustrate the varied activities and responsibilities of The Trustees throughout its long and distinguished history.

I owe special thanks to former officers of The Trustees with whom I spoke at length about the past. They include Charles W. Eliot II, Laurence M. Channing, Theodore Chase, David C. Crockett, Roland B. Greeley, Arthur N. Phillips, and John M. Woolsey, Jr., as well as senior staff member Nathan W. Bates. The memories of most stretch back at least into the 1950s; one into the 1920s.

I also had the good fortune to be able to ask at least a few of those who took part in many of the activities described to each review an initial draft of the manuscript. For their comments, corrections and contributions, I am immensely grateful to the following: former Chairman of the Standing Committee Preston N. "Sandy" Saunders; former Deputy Director William S. Clendaniel; Regional Supervisors Thomas D. Foster, Wayne N. Mitton and Stanley I. Piatczyc; and especially Wesley T. Ward, Deputy Director of Land Conservation and Director of the Land Conservation Center. I also wish to thank former Deputy Director for Public Information Eloise W. Hodges for suggesting in the first place that I write a history of The Trustees of Reservations to celebrate its centennial, and for guiding me along the way.

The book, of course, could not have been completed without the enthusiastic and continuing support of Director Frederic Winthrop, Jr., who has constantly cheered me on, as well as members of the Standing Committee who approved its publication. Absolutely invaluable has been the encouragement and immediate involvement of the present Deputy Director for Public Information, Lisa McFadden, whose editing skills polished the manuscript and made it suitable to set in type. I am grateful also to three other key members of the publishing team: Charles Getchell, publisher of The Ipswich Press; Michael A. Milgroom of Milgroom Design Associates, who is responsible for the book's graphic design; and Jonathan Labaree, who transformed the final copy with its revisions and numerous illustrations into camera-ready copy.

I wish to thank as well scores of volunteers and other members of the staff of The Trustees of Reservations, both at Headquarters and in the field, who shared their recollections of events and helped me find vital information in the files. To everyone who loaned photographs, I send thanks as well, and, in this area, I am especially appreciative of the efforts of Sean M. Fiske, an archivist at the Metropolitan District Commission, for his assistance.

Finally, I want to thank my dear wife Katharine, who read and edited the original manuscript, and, as always, provided valuable comments and suggestions which improved its content and its style.

Any errors and omissions can be blamed only upon the author. As in every work of this sort, there are sure to be some, and for these I apologize in advance.

G. A., Jr.

Manchester-by-the-Sea
Massachusetts
July 1993

1

The Early Years

1

In the Beginning — There Was Boston

At the end of the nineteenth century, Boston was rightly known as the "Athens of America."

Its new public library, elegantly designed by architects Charles McKim and Stanford White, was under construction at Copley Square. Its symphony orchestra, founded by music-loving philanthropist Henry Lee Higginson, was about to celebrate its tenth anniversary and shortly would have a new home of its own as well. And, as if not to be outdone, its Museum of Fine Arts was planning a courageous move westward to the just-landscaped Fenway, where it would have room for a structure ample enough to display its rapidly growing collection.

Boston's literary heritage, too, was still legendary despite the death of many of the major figures of American letters who had called it home. The number and quality of educational institutions which it claimed — even though two of the giants, Harvard and the Massachusetts Institute of Technology, were across the Charles River in Cambridge — were not to be rivaled anywhere in the nation. And its hospitals, pioneers in medical research and teaching, had set standards for achievement admired throughout the world.

Industry had brought a new prosperity and wealth to an increasing number of Bostonians. More than a third of the country's woolens and almost half of its shoes were manufactured in Massachusetts. And Boston had shared in the impressive growth of railroads, insurance and banking which had taken place across the nation.

But despite the glitter of its accomplishments, the city had a darker side as well, less visible from the smart, four-story brick townhouses on Beacon Hill and in the newly-settled Back Bay. For in what Mark Twain satirically called "The Gilded Age," Boston and other metropolitan areas were becoming increasingly populated by the destitute, the diseased and the dispossessed. Many were foreign-born, but many also, were members of families who had escaped from decaying farms and country towns throughout New England and had come to the city to seek employment.

They lived, these newcomers, for the most part, in a degraded level of poverty, which today is difficult to imagine. And their dark and overcrowded tenements and narrow, trash-strewn alleys, contrasted harshly with the properous sections of the city.

This was a time also, especially in the Northeast, which marked the beginning of the end of a predominantly rural America and the emergence of the urban era. By the turn of the century, more than 67 percent of Massachusetts' nearly three million residents would live in cities. Since the end of the Civil War, Boston had grown into the nation's fourth largest manufacturing center. Iron works, glass factories, foundries — hundreds of industrial plants large and small, workshops and "sweatshops" — had sprung up everywhere. There was an abundance of jobs to be had and tens of thousands of people poured into the city to find them.

This massive demographic movement had enormous social consequences. Living conditions in the cities were deplorable. In slum neighborhhoods, food supplies and shelter were inadequate. Sanitation was nonexistent. Sewage and garbage were everywhere. And disease — cholera, typhus and typhoid — was rampant.

Copley Square, 1889. Boston's new public library is under construction. The early Italianate building at right is home to the Museum of Fine Arts, which later moved to the Fenway. Left is the new Old South Church. Architect H. H. Richardson's handsome Trinity Church is the centerpiece of the photo.

There was another factor as well which contributed to the desolation and despair of Boston's new residents. For they were in large part, whether from Europe or closer by, a rural people who had exchanged the autonomy and freedom of agricultural communities for life in a crowded, hectic and busy city away from the rhythms of the seasons and the beauty and tranquility of the countryside. Theirs was also, now, not a farm but a factory economy, which demanded a host of unfamiliar restrictions and controls to maximize efficiency and to benefit production. The contrast was overwhelming.

There was little doubt that the challenge of the nineteenth century was the challenge of the city. In earlier decades, conservationists had focused on how to prevent the pillage of the natural wonders of the American West. Now, efforts turned to ways to mitigate the continuing destruction of human resources, particularly in the densely-settled, urban environments of the East. One of those dealing with these troubling issues was a young landscape architect by the name of Charles Eliot.

Charles W. Eliot, Assistant Professor of Mathematics, Harvard University

2

Charles Eliot: the Man and the Idea

Born in 1859 as the country stood on the threshold of its great Civil War, Charles Eliot was the son of a then Assistant Professor of Mathematics at Harvard. His father, Charles William Eliot, was later to become President of the University and one of the most respected and beloved educators of all time. His mother was descended "from a line of Lymans," as his father wrote, who in three successive generations had been citizens "useful" to society and "successful in their endeavors."

Although blessed with wealth and comfort, young Charles's life, like those of so many Bostonians of his time, is a remarkable story of how a sense of civic consciousness and public responsibility developed among old Yankee families at the end of the nineteenth century. Brahmanism may have seemed standoffish, even affected at times, but out of its mold came some extraordinary human beings who accomplished great and unselfish things for the world in which they lived.

Not all of these, of course, could be credited to any single person, but the record of achievements in Massachusetts at the time is impressive. It includes the first kindergarten in the nation; the first vocational high school; the first employers' liability law; the first women's college (Mount Holyoke); the first garden

Charles Eliot, class photo, Harvard 1882. "A quiet man of rare, spiritual qualities..."

cemetery (Mount Auburn); the first State Department of Public Health; and the first organization of its kind in the world devoted to the preservation of open space for public purposes, The Trustees of Reservations.

Charles Eliot grew up in a loving household where culture flourished. His parents had the money and the time to appreciate art, literature and music as well as science and engineering, so important to America's emerging industrial society. They took special pains to see that their children (Charles's brother Samuel later became a distinguished Unitarian clergyman) read good books, learned about the history of their country, and studied English and mathematics. And they placed important emphasis as well on the appreciation of the simpler things in life, such as an association with nature and the out-of-doors and upon experiences which build character and self-reliance.

As a child in Cambridge, Charles played happily in nearby Norton Woods, even mapping it with a friend with tape and compass, identifying various characteristics of the landscape and marking appropriate sections "Public Park" or Public Reserve." He loved walking, too, and as he grew older he explored the still open countryside which then surrounded Boston, taking the train with friends to various destinations and hiking home. These were all experiences which were to stand him in excellent stead later as he began to develop a system of parks and open spaces for the metropolitan area.

By the summer of his graduation from Harvard in 1882, he had chosen his profession. He knew no ordinary business would provide him satisfaction, but he had heard from his uncle, Robert S. Peabody, an architect, about the field of landscape architecture. Mr. Peabody, a resident of Brookline, had worked from time to time with a near neighbor, Frederick Law Olmsted, the celebrated environmental planner who had won world acclaim for his success with New York's Central Park.

Everything in Charles's life to date made the choice of landscape architecture a natural one, and that fall, at the age of 23, he entered the Bussey Institution, a part of the Department of Agriculture and Horticulture at Harvard. The following year, Charles was asked by Mr. Olmsted himself to join his office in Brookline as an apprentice. His professional career had begun.

Frederick Law Olmsted in the late 1880s

3

Parks: An Antidote for the Ills of Urban Life

The influence of Frederick Law Olmsted upon the thinking of the day was immense. The great architect of so many spectacular urban designs and open spaces was, at heart, a social reformer and idealist. He believed that the purpose of his public projects was to improve the quality of life in the nation's cities where most of its people were to live in the years to come.

With his friend Parke Godwin, son-in-law of William Cullen Bryant, who later took over from Bryant as editor of the *The New York Evening World*, Olmsted became a Utopian Socialist and a devotee of Charles Fourier, the French writer and social critic. Fourier's concepts and ideas led in 1841 to the establishment of Brook Farm, a cooperative community located in West Roxbury, Massachusetts, whose supporters included such literary lights as Ralph Waldo Emerson and Nathaniel Hawthorne.

It is said that Olmsted's life was "a constant search for means by which human ideals could be translated into environmental forms." The public park was to be the center of a new kind of community where people of all walks of life could come together for recreation and refreshment.

Charles Eliot was 24 years old when he first joined the Olmsted office (FLO was 61), but his apprenticeship soon ended and he left for what was to be a year's concentrated study and travel in Europe, one of the most valuable experiences of his young life. His interests ranged from public parks and gardens to private country estates, from newly-established suburban developments to trees, shrubs and flowers native to each region. He explored the origins of his new profession both in England and on the Continent and his voyages took him to the major cities of the Old World, where he was able to see at first hand the parks and playgrounds which put them far ahead of their American counterparts.

In October 1886, Eliot returned to Boston and opened his own office at the corner of Beacon and Park Streets. There he offered his professional services as a landscape architect, as he wrote, to "owners of suburban and country estates, trustees of institutions, park commissioners, hotel proprietors, and persons or corporations desiring to lay out or improve villages, suburbs and neighborhoods, and summer resorts."

Throughout all of his activities, he continued to maintain a close personal association with Frederick Law Olmsted. The older man had taken quite a shine to him and thought highly not only of his architectural knowledge and accomplishments, but of his abilities to express himself in writing.

"I have [had] no such justly critical notes as yours on landscape architecture matters from any traveller for a generation past," Olmsted told him. "You ought to make it part of your scheme to write for the public, a little at a time, if you please, but methodically, systematically." It was advice that was well taken and well used in the years ahead and a skill which considerably extended Charles's influence and reputation, especially with the public sector.

In papers, speeches, letters and reports, he perpetuated and extended Olmsted's and his own belief that parks and open spaces were vital to the physical and psychological well-being of urban residents. In one of his talks, he quotes a doctor from Boston who declared: "a few hours' exposure of a child on a mother's lap to the freshness of a park will produce a sleep such as never follows opium, chloral or ether and will yield a chance for health such as no drug can give." In another he proclaimed that "a crowded population thirsts for the sight of something very different from the public garden, square or ball field.

"The new electric street railways which radiate from the Hub carry many thousands every pleasant Sunday to the real country," he wrote. "Hundreds out of these thousands make the journey for the sake of the refreshment which an occasional hour or two spent in the country brings to them."

What was urgently needed in cities everywhere, Eliot declared, were public parks of 50 acres or more where visitors could enjoy "the subtle influence which skies and seas, clouds and shadows, woods and fields, and all that mingling of the natural and human which we call landscape sheds upon human life.

"It is an influence," he continued, "which has a most peculiar value as an antidote to the poisonous struggling and excitement of city life. Whenever a busy man is over-worried, the doctor prescribes the country; and whenever any of us are brought into depression by care or trouble, our cure is the sight of our chosen hills."

There seemed, indeed, to be a symbiosis between the quality of life in an urban community and its ability to offer opportunities to enjoy a proximity to nature and open space. "The rich," Eliot said, "satisfy [these desires] by fleeing from town at certain seasons, but [the needs] of the poor are only to be met by the country park."

"Country parks," however — "lands intended and appropriated for recreation. . . by means of their rural, sylvan, and natural scenery and character" — were not to be found in Boston. According to a census survey of 1880, the city was last on a list of 26 cities throughout the nation reporting parks of 50 acres or more in size.

In fact, its 3,424 persons per acre of park land was only just behind New York City, but trailed smaller cities throughout the nation such as Macon, Ohio, or New Britain, Connecticut by a wide margin.

It was Eliot's opinion, because of the costs of acquisition and management, that the establishment of a series of "country parks" of significant size must wait for the appointment of a special state commission. That was to come later. Meanwhile, however, he proposed a plan which would allow the private sector to act immediately to provide a collection of smaller open spaces for the health and pleasure of Boston's rapidly growing population.

"Within 10 miles of the State House," he wrote in January 1890, in a letter to the periodical *Garden and Forest*, "there still remain several bits of scenery which possess uncommon beauty and more than usual refreshing power. Moreover," he added, "each of these scenes is characteristic of the primitive wilderness of New England, of which, indeed, they are surviving fragments."

As examples he mentioned a steep moraine in Waverly "set with a group of mighty oaks" (now preserved by the Metropolitan District Commission), and a site where the Charles River narrows in Sherborn and flows between ledges crowned with shaggy hemlock (which today is owned and protected by The Trustees of Reservations).

Most of the areas were located in different communities and along town borders outside of the city itself. And thus to acquire and protect them he urged the establishment of "an incorporated association" whose board would include representatives from "all the Boston towns."

It "would be empowered by the State," he wrote, "to hold small and well-distributed parcels of land free of taxes, just as the Public Library holds books and the Art Museum pictures — for the use and enjoyment of the public.

"If an association of this sort were once established," he declared, "generous men and women would be ready to buy and give into its keeping some of these fine and strongly characterized works of Nature; just as others buy and give to a museum fine works of art."

As Bostonians united to establish their art museum, he urged, "so her lovers of Nature should now rally to preserve for themselves and all the people, as many as possible of these scenes of natural beauty which, by great good fortune, still exist near their doors."

The Trustees of Reservations, the first private organization in the world devoted solely to the preservation of open space, was on its way to becoming a reality.

Unique as the idea seemed, however, there were other organizations of a similar bent which had come before. Four of them were right here in Massachusetts. One was the Laurel Hill Association, the nation's first village improvement society, founded in

Stockbridge in 1853. It acquired its first public open space in 1854. A second, was the Ravenswood Park Trust, established under the will of Samuel Sawyer in 1889 to preserve what ultimately became some 600 acres of woodland in Gloucester (now held by The Trustees of Reservations). Another was Mount Auburn, America's first garden cemetery, established in 1825, where, according to its founders, the dead might lie in restful repose and their survivors might find solace and consolation surrounded by the beauties of nature. A fourth was the venerable Appalachian Mountain Club, founded in Boston in 1876, which was to play a major role in the establishment of The Trustees, and which today continues to support preservation of the natural environment as well as maintaining and expanding opportunities for outdoor recreation, especially in the forest lands of the eastern United States.

But the concept of a statewide organization, independent of government, established solely to protect special "bits of scenery" for the health and well-being of an urban population was unique. What was needed next, Eliot knew, was a special blue-ribbon committee which could support the idea, give it credibility, and carry it forward.

4

A Unique Concept Catches Fire

The Appalachian Mountain Club, or "AMC," as it is affectionately known today, was a most appropriate place to start discussions about a new organization designed to preserve selected areas of open space. Charles Eliot was a member of its ruling Council and for many years had served as its Councillor on Topography.

In a letter to the President and the governing board, he asked for the names of 10 club members who "would make good fathers to such a scheme." The response was immediate and enthusiastic and AMC Council representatives agreed to ask Eliot to "draw up an invitation to societies and individuals to meet and consider a plan for preserving natural scenery."

To test the idea further, Eliot also wrote to a series of "influential persons" throughout the Commonwealth. Ever practical, he recognized in his letter a major issue which haunts land trusts everywhere today. "Funds for the maintenance of particular reservations," he explained, "would have to be provided at the same time that lands were given." The concept was to have far-reaching consequences in the years to come.

The letter itself struck a popular nerve. It seemed that sentiment for the establishment of an organization such as Eliot proposed already existed, and some 400 encouraging responses poured in. Middlesex Fells had long been eyed as an area which should be preserved — perhaps this was the opportunity — and Lynn Woods, some 2,000 acres, already established as a reservation by the City of Lynn, had set an example which others could follow. And, it was readily agreed, much more was needed in the way of land conservation throughout the metropolitan region.

On Saturday, May 24, 1890, some 100 persons gathered at the Massachusetts Institute of Technology, which was then located in the newly-filled Back Bay on Boylston Streeet. Eliot had done his homework well. Henry R. Sprague, President of the Massachusetts Senate, presided.

There were letters of support from Governor Brackett; from the editor of the Boston *Pilot*, John Boyle O'Reilly, beloved and respected by both Irish and Brahmin alike; from the "Autocrat of the Breakfast Table" and former Dean of the Harvard Medical School, Dr. Oliver Wendell Holmes, by that time 81 years old; from historian Francis Parkman, author of *The Oregon Trail;* and from John Greenleaf Whittier, the Yankee poet who captured the simple spirit of New England in "Snow-Bound." It was an impressive list.

Eliot himself advocated the special legislation. "Scattered throughout the State," he declared, "are many thriving historical and antiquarian societies. . . some of these societies have already accomplished the saving of memorable or striking spots. The Essex Institute has purchased the Great Boulder in Danvers called Ship Rock; the Old Colony Historical Society owns Dighton Rock and the Worcester Natural History Society owns a part of the shore of Lake Quinsigamond." Let these societies unite, Eliot urged, and ask the legislature to create "one strong Board of Trustees" with the power to hold selected properties throughout the state.

Following a series of supporting remarks, the chairman was asked to appoint a committee. Its purpose: "to promote the establishment of a Board of Trustees to be made capable of acquiring and holding, for the benefit of the public, beautiful and historic places in Massachusetts." They were the words which would be incorporated into legislation establishing what was to be called The Trustees of Reservations.

5

A Small Association of Public-Spirited People

Henry P. Walcott, chairman of the committee which proposed establishment of The Trustees of Reservations

George Wigglesworth, Treasurer of The Trustees from 1891 to 1920

Committee members (and there were 29 in all from Williamstown and Lenox to Salem and Fall River) included Dr. Henry Pickering Walcott of Cambridge, Chairman, and George Wigglesworth of Boston, Treasurer. Charles Eliot served as Secretary.

Henry Walcott was born in Salem in 1838. He attended Harvard and studied both there and at Bowdoin College in Brunswick, Maine, from which, in 1861, he received his degree as a doctor of medicine. His primary interest was the field of public health and during his lifetime he served as Chairman of the Massachusetts State Board of Public Health, and of the Metropolitan Water and Sewer Board. At one time as well, he was acting President of Harvard University.

George Wigglesworth was also an establishment figure. A graduate of Harvard College and Harvard Law School, he began practice in Boston in 1879. Like other successful attorneys, he was involved in a wide variety of business activities, serving on the board of directors of numerous corporations and as a trustee of a variety of charitable institutions.

Both of these men were to play major roles as well in the success of The Trustees of Reservations. Henry Walcott served as Chairman of the Standing Committee, its governing board, for 23 years, from 1903 to 1926, and as Vice President from 1926 to 1932. George Wigglesworth served the organization as Treasurer for 29 years, from its founding in 1891 to 1920.

Both were also typical of the kind of individuals who, at the time, would have been involved in such a cause. They were leaders of their community, and in those days the characteristics of community leadership were easy to identify: a patrician background with a genealogy which often included ancestors who were instrumental in the establishment of the country; marriage to a woman of equal genealogical qualifications; a degree from Harvard College; a religious faith which was Unitarian or Episcopalian; recognized success in whatever field was chosen as a profession; wealth, not ostentatiously displayed, but enough to quietly reflect intellectual tastes in literature, music and art, and to allow for some measure of personal indulgence such as a summer house or yacht; an involvement in public life in an appointed or elected position, usually at the state level — for this generation thought it important to serve one's community actively in government (and almost always as a member of the Republican party); service also on a number of charitable boards; and last, but by no means least, membership in one or more "acceptable" Boston clubs such as the Somerset or the Union.

Theirs was a small, tight society of people who went to school together, worked together and played together. They knew one another well and, guided by that ever-present Yankee conscience, they accomplished great things for all walks of people in the world around them while still enjoying a style of life and leisure which was never to be seen again.

The committee also included three women: Sarah H. Crocker and Marion Talbot of Boston, and Elizabeth Howe of Cambridge, for at the end of the nineteenth century, women were becoming increasingly important to the conservation movement. The tradition happily continues today at The Trustees of Reservations, where, in recent years especially, women have played a major role in the organization's activities and accomplishments.

However distinguished the committee may have been, it is clear that what progress was made to promote the establishment of The Trustees must be credited primarily to the spirited dedication and skilled staff work of Charles Eliot. It was he, as Secretary, who provided the horse and drove the wagon. He drafted the minutes, wrote the resolutions, drew up the circulars which rallied political support, raised money to aid the cause and spoke frequently around the region about the critical need for open space.

6

Chapter 352 of the Acts of 1891

Charles Eliot also took no chances that there would be a lack of enthusiasm for the measure demonstrated at the hearing before the Judiciary Committee scheduled for March 10, 1890. He sent notices to more than 700 persons who had expressed interest earlier, and asked members of the original study committee to write letters to their own and to other State legislators. According to Eliot's handwritten account of the proceedings, "about 50 ladies and gentlemen were present. None spoke in opposition."

The bill passed both Houses easily and was signed into law as Chapter 352 of the Acts of 1891 by Governor William Eustis Russell on May 21. True to form and in keeping with earlier proposals, the legislation established a corporation "for the purpose of acquiring, holding, maintaining and opening to the public, under suitable regulations, beautiful and historic places and tracts of land within [the] Commonwealth. . . ."

It declared that The Trustees could "acquire and hold by grant, gift, devise, purchase or otherwise, real estate such as it

William E. Russell, 34-year-old Democratic Governor of the Commonwealth, signed legislation creating The Trustees of Reservations.

may deem worthy of preservation for the enjoyment of the public. . . ."

And it stated that all lands held by the corporation and open to the public "shall be exempt from taxation."

There were caveats. One was that the total amount of land held by The Trustees should not exceed $1 million in value. The figure was increased to $10 million in 1963, and, as the land prices rose in recent years, the legislature acted to remove the restriction altogether. Another was (and is) that lands held that were not open to the public within two years would be subject to taxation. Both requirements seemed more than reasonable at the time.

Thus was The Trustees of Reservations born. It was nine months after the first public meeting at which the concept had been originally presented.

In each of his proposals to establish the organization, Eliot referred continually to the need for a "respected Board of Trustees" modeled after other successful charities such as hospitals, colleges, libraries or art museums. A "trustee" was and is a person or agent holding legal title to property in order to administer it for a beneficiary, in this case, the public. And it was Eliot's belief that once integrity and trust were established, "lovers of Nature and History [would] rally to endow [the organization] with care of their favorite scenes." Such has been the case now for just over a century.

For its first 63 years, the organzation was called "The Trustees of *Public* Reservations," for so it was named in its Act of Establishment. In 1954, however, because of the continuing and frustrating perception that it was a State agency supported with taxpayer funds, with the permission of the Legislature, the word "public" was dropped. But the complications of the name itself haunted the organization from its very beginnings as times changed and the words "Trustees" and even "Reservations" grew less and less familiar to younger generations.

Many attempts were made to switch to something which better described the purpose and activities of "The Trustees." It was not out of sentiment that they failed. It was simply that no other name could be found which met universal favor. Actually, in the mid-1930s, only a vote or two kept the organization from becoming "The Massachusetts Trustees for Places of Natural Beauty or Historic Interest," a phrase borrowed directly from the full name of The National Trust of England.

Finally, as its centennial approached, it was agreed universally that too much history was at stake to merit a change in title, and it was decided to capitalize on the turn-of-the-century nature of the name by urging prospective members to join as "Trustees" in the crusade to secure and safeguard special features of the Massachusetts landscape.

Members of the corporation whose vote actually controls the destiny of the organization are now known as "Corporate Trustees."

7

A Choice of Leaders: the Key to Credibility

As with its organizational committee, the choice of persons to serve as members of the new corporation's governing board was of immense importance to its credibility and success. And here Charles Eliot was particularly fortunate. Corporators held their first meeting on June 26, 1891, in Boston at the offices of Frederick L. Ames of Easton. United States Senator George Frisbee Hoar of Worcester agreed to serve as President.

U.S. Senator George F. Hoar of Worcester, first President of The Trustees of Reservations

An old-line, Harvard-educated Yankee, Senator Hoar was the living symbol of the then-dominant Republican Party of Massachusetts. His grandfather had fought at the Battle of Concord Bridge in 1775. His mother was a daughter of Connecticut's Roger Sherman who helped draft both the Declaration of Independence and the Constitution. A staunch abolitionist, Hoar himself was considered somewhat of a radical, supporting black civil rights and a thorough reconstruction of society in the South. As a liberal, he also worked for women's suffrage and voting rights for former slaves.

Vice President of the new organization was William Steele Shurtleff of Springfield. A much-admired judge of the Probate Court of Hamden County, Mr. Shurtleff was famous for his love of walking in the out-of-doors. It was a pastime he enjoyed each Sunday and one which, with his professional abilities and personal stature in Western Massachusetts, brought him to the attention of Charles Eliot.

Once, with a friend, according to a more than three-column obituary which appeared in the *The Springfield Republican*, the Judge walked "from the mouth of the Connecticut River to its source," a significant distance, discovering along the way "good inns" as well as cozy lodging places offered by local residents. A person of many interests and abilities, the Judge was, by his own proud admission, "an all-around man." He was a published poet, an orator and a collector of books and manuscripts. He was congenial with people from all walks of life and beloved in his court as "a friend of the widow and orphan."

Most important for The Trustees of Reservations (which even then the confused writer called the "state board of public reservations"), Judge Shurtleff was hailed "as an active worker for the preservation of places of historic interest and natural beauty throughout Massachusetts."

Other members of the original committee were Philip A. Chase of Lynn, who was known as the "Father of Lynn Woods," then the largest urban park in the nation; Dr. Walcott; George Wigglesworth; Charles Eliot, of course; and Charles Sprague Sargent of Brookline.

Philip Chase, unlike many of his contemporaries, did not spring from the Harvard mold, nor was the pathway of his life smoothed by wealth or social connection. His choice as a member of the governing board, however, showed, once again, Charles Eliot's political genius as well as his admirable insistence that The Trustees of Reservations be constituted to serve and represent all the people of the Commonwealth.

Board members and corporators were chosen with an eye to geography — they represented cities and towns from Berkshire County to Cape Cod — but, most important, they were selected, as they are today, because of their proven interest and involvement in efforts to maintain and improve the quality of the environment. Philip Chase certainly satisfied these criteria completely.

His father and grandfather had operated a painting business in Lynn for nearly a century. He was educated at public schools and upon graduation, went directly into the business that had made his city famous — shoe manufacturing. A pioneer in the introduction of shoe machinery, he soon became a rich man, and in 1877, at the age of 43, his fortune guaranteed and his professional life providing both stability and fulfillment, he began a commitment to public service.

As Chairman of the city's Park Commission, he all but single-handedly raised $31,000 from public subscription, quite a sum in those days, to initiate the preservation of Lynn Woods. He also served as Chairman of the Metropolitan Parks Commission, resigning only when the major purchases and takings of land had made the system a reality. He was a man who saw the needs of society and who could get things done efficiently and effectively. As such, he served as the first Chairman of The Trustees' governing board from 1891 to 1893.

Charles Sargent was a very different human being but no less dedicated to the cause. A man who turned a passionate hobby into a distinguished profession, Sargent graduated from Harvard in 1862. Following service as a major in the Union Army, he returned to Boston after the war to develop his own garden, which soon became known as one of the best in the region. In 1872, Sargent was asked to become a Professor of Horticulture at Harvard. A year later, he began a life-long career as Director of

Philip A. Chase of Lynn, father of Lynn Woods and first Chairman of The Trustees of Reservations

the newly-established Arnold Arboretum. Editor and publisher also of the weekly periodical *Garden & Forest*, to which Eliot had directed his first letter about The Trustees, Sargent awakened a broad interest in arboriculture and forestry throughout the country.

There were other giants on the list as well whom Eliot persuaded to join as members of the fledgling corporation. Among them was Nathaniel S. Shaler of Tisbury, Martha's Vineyard, one of America's most renowned geologists. He was also the progenitor of Seven Gates Farm at Tisbury and Chilmark. Originally conceived as an agricultural community of more than 2,000 acres where a limited number of houses were sited so that no one could see another, it provided inhabitants with a perfect rural setting.

Seven Gates Farm is still much in existence today. It is primarily used as a summer colony, but, as building opportunities are controlled, it retains its original concept and with it a landscape remarkable for its beauty and diversity. The Trustees of Reservations holds conservation restrictions or easements protecting more than 1,250 acres of its ocean shoreline, fields and woodland.

Besides Shaler, the first corporators included Frederick L. Ames of Easton; Christopher Clarke of Northampton; Charles R. Codman of Cotuit; Elisha S. Converse of Malden; John R. Russell of Plymouth; George Selden of Deerfield; Daniel D. Slade and Leverett Saltonstall of Newton (the latter, Collector of the Port of Boston and, unlike other members of his distinguished family, a leader of the State's Democratic Party); Joseph Tucker and George H. Tucker of Pittsfield; and General Francis A. Walker of Boston.

8

The Work Begins

The first meeting of the Standing Committee, or board of trustees, took place on July 1, 1891. Philip Chase of Lynn was elected Chairman. A seal was adopted which showed the new corporation's name and the year it was founded in a circle surrounding a native white pine (*Pinus strobus*) which once adorned the flag and a coin of Massachusetts. Committee members then addressed the business at hand.

Perhaps in anticipation of the founding of The Trustees, Mrs. Fanny H. Tudor had recently suggested to a number of board members that she would like to give the new organization some 20 acres of mixed woodland in Stoneham between Spot Pond and the Medford town line. It was to be a memorial to her daughter Virginia, who had died in an accident, riding horseback in England. The tract, to be called "Virginia Woods," was, the Standing Committee reported, "divided by a hollow containing a brook; possessed many fine specimens of hemlocks, pines, oaks, and other trees, and [was] capable of serving as a delightful retreat for the large population which the opening of the proposed Stoneham railroad will bring into its neighborhood." The land met two of the organization's primary criteria: it was "beautiful" and it offered significant opportunities for public enjoyment.

The committee, however, wisely decided to postpone acceptance of the property until an endowment of $2,000 could be raised, the income of which could pay for its continuing maintenance and protection. This was soon accomplished, thanks primarily to the efforts of public-spirited citizens in the nearby towns of Melrose, Malden and Medford. The board then agreed to make Virginia Woods its first reservation.

In keeping with the philosophy of both Olmsted and Eliot, which called for the protection of outstanding portions of natural landscape, the property was, indeed, a "reservation" and not a park. In wide use at the end of the nineteenth century, the word "reservation" meant literally land that was "kept back or withheld" from development and "reserved" as public open space.

Blue Hills Reservation, Middlesex Fells Reservation, and Stony Brook Reservation, for example (now each a property of the Metropolitan District Commission), were all acquired and named in the 1890s. On the national level, the Forest Reserve Act, passed

20-acre Virginia Wood, Stoneham, first property of The Trustees of Reservations. "Is not a religiously guarded living landscape a finer monument than any ordinary work in marble or stained glass?"

by Congress in 1891, gave the President power to "set apart and reserve" forest lands as "public reservations." And, of course, lands identified by the Federal government for the use of Indian tribes were also called "reservations." The Trustees of Reservations continues today to attach the name to many of its properties, while public resource agencies prefer to call theirs national or state "parks" or "forests."

Meanwhile, as Eliot predicted, there was no shortage of suggestions about which areas should be preserved. The piles of letters grew until The Trustees were forced to issue a special statement to describe reality. "The Board possesses no magical powers," it read in part. "With all the other lovers of scenery and the history of Massachusetts, [it] must hasten to imitate those admirers of the fine arts who have so liberally endowed the public art museums. Maintenance funds as well as purchase funds will be needed."

Money and the lack of it, either for endowment or for purchase, was, and would continue through the years to be, one of the major roadblocks to acquiring and protecting all of the land the organization was either offered or sought to preserve.

9

Public Lands: a Call for Government to Act

There was another consideration as well, however, which matched in importance The Trustees of Reservations' direct acquisition and protection of specific sites. It related to a broader issue: the lack of publicly designated open space throughout the Commonwealth and the need for government to become involved in efforts to acquire it.

Impressed with the favorable political climate which resulted in the enthusiastic approval of legislation to create The Trustees, the Standing Committee decided to move next in each of four directions.

First, it would study and list the number of public open spaces presently existing. Second, it would "collect and publish" the laws of Massachusetts relating to public open space. Third, it would seek a joint meeting of members of park committees within the Metropolitan District to see what could be done collectively to acquire land for open space. And fourth, it would ask for a more comprehensive study of the whole matter by the Great and General Court.

Despite a lack of adequate funding, what was done was remarkable. It included two landmark publications, one entitled "The Province Lands Report." The other, a narrative inventory which described "The Public Holdings of the Shore Towns of Massachusetts." And, perhaps most important, action by the Standing Committee led to the formation of a coalition which ultimately resulted in the establishment of the first system of metropolitan parks in the nation.

The recommendations of the Province Lands Report resulted in the completion of a detailed map of the area, legislative approval of a management program and the appointment of a paid superintendent to oversee the state's some 4,000 acres, its largest conservation property. A remarkable area of outer Cape Cod which included sand dunes, beaches and fresh water ponds, the Province Lands in those days were suffering from much the same kind of abuses from human use that are found in the area today.

"Half of the Province land is already a treeless waste," The Trustees' report stated. ". . . Beach grass planted by the government seems to have stayed the destruction of the ridges in some measure; but the wheels of [horsedrawn] carts continually crossing the sand-drifts in the direction of the worst gales, soon broke the grassed surface so that the wind got hold, 'blew out' great areas, and dumped the sand in such steep drifts in the edges of the woods, that many cart paths became impassable, so that new routes were sought, where the operation was repeated." How familiar this is today to all who are concerned with the impact of motorized four-wheel, all-terrain vehicles on the beach and dune environment.

Included also in The Trustees' management recommendations, which were adopted by the General Court, was a proposal that responsibility for the Province Lands be placed in the hands of the already established Board of Harbor and Land Commissioners.

The inventory of "The Public Holdings of the Shore Towns of Massachusetts" showed with dramatic intensity the need for public access to the coast to meet the demands of a growing population for water-based, outdoor recreation. Development was, indeed, rapidly privatizing shorelines everywhere and preempting public enjoyment of a precious natural resource.

The studies were a first of their kind in what was to become the field of recreation planning. And, indeed, they were the first of a long line of productive planning projects initiated by The Trustees of Reservations throughout its history. They proved conclusively the axiom that identification of specific sites and a description of their environmental values is a vital first step in the process of open space preservation.

10

Another First: A Public Park Agency for Greater Boston

It was the meeting, however, called by The Trustees of Reservations in December 1891 of the coalition of park commissions and park committees from Boston, that, within a few years, revolutionized the acquisition of open space within the metropolitan area.

Boston Park Commissioner General Francis A. Walker (also a member of the corporation of The Trustees of Reservations) served as Chairman of the gathering, with Charles Eliot in his accustomed role as Secretary. The arguments for action were persuasive. First, maps showed dramatically that Boston not only lagged far behind other major cities of the world in the amount of open space it offered its residents, but also that the city lacked adequate public access to rivers, lakes and ponds, as well as to the region's extensive seashore and beaches.

Second, it was clear that except for a single effort in the Fells, which had been frustrated by what Eliot called a "ridiculous town boundary difficulty," no steps had been taken to "secure even one water basin from pollution" to protect Boston's supply of pure drinking water.

General Francis A. Walker, president of M.I.T. and chairman of the Boston Park Commission

Third, it was evident that "present methods of securing open space [were clearly] too slow and inefficient" and, therefore, that "some sort of joint or concerted action [was] advisable at once." Thirteen of those present declared steps should be taken immediately, and a committee was appointed to contact legislative leaders. Its Chairman: Philip A. Chase of Lynn, also Chairman of the Standing Committee of The Trustees of Reservations.

Committee members did their homework well. A resolution was sent to the General Court stating the problem and asking for a legislative study to determine what action might be taken. Petitions signed by several thousand citizens and public officials were submitted in support of the study. The result was the appointment of a "Joint Special Committee on Public Reservations" which held its first hearing on March 8, 1892.

Again, key to the success of all of these early efforts of The Trustees of Reservations was the careful preparation provided by Charles Eliot. At times, however, despite his commitment to whatever cause he initiated or was involved with, and his continuing record of success, there were moments of understandable frustration, as there were prior to a hearing scheduled by the Committee on Public Reservations.

"Yesterday," he wrote to his wife Mary, in early 1892, "my committee meeting was a farce, nobody agreeing with anybody

Charles Eliot at age 35, a year after he led the way to the founding of The Trustees of Reservations.

Industrialist and author Charles Francis Adams, first president of the Metropolitan Park Commission

else, and [it] finally resulted as usual, namely, in an appeal to me to invite speakers to appear at the hearing on March 8, to speak myself, and to make sure of an attendance by sending out post cards." But his irritations were temporary. He invariably did all that he knew had to be done to accomplish the larger purpose.

His remarks at the hearing, as always, crystalized both the problems at hand and the proposal to solve them "Now," he declared, "the park act limits the field of action of our park commissioners to the bounds of their respective towns and cities, while it is self-evident that these boundaries bear no relation to the scenery of the district they divide." The solution? A *Metropolitan* Park Commission which could act regionally to acquire and manage open spaces for the benefit of residents of all greater Boston communities. It would be the first of its kind in the nation.

As he had on so many previous occasions, Eliot presented a draft of a bill and, once again, the legislature responded favorably. The measure to create a regional park agency was enacted by both the House and Senate and signed into law by Governor Russell on June 2, 1892.

Charles Francis Adams, grandson of John Quincy Adams, sixth President of the United States, was appointed chairman of the newly-formed commission. A former president himself of the Union Pacific Railroad (1884-1890), Adams was nationally known and widely respected. He was a perfect choice to provide the commission with the standing it needed to accomplish its mission.

Eliot, too, could take personal pleasure in the accomplishments, as his father wrote, "of one public-spirited, well-informed and zealous young man who, working with public sentiment and the support of community leaders, managed to do much good for his community." He was not one, however, to rest on his laurels. The work went on. And in August 1892, Charles Eliot, then age 32, was appointed landscape architect for the new park commission.

Immediately, he began work on a comprehensive survey and maps of specific properties and areas of open space within the metropolitan region which he believed should be preserved as public reservations. A look at the record of the commission 10 years later shows its accomplishments were considerable.

In 1902, newly protected areas, each proposed by Eliot in his report, included the following: an enlargement of Middlesex Fells and the acquisition of Spot Pond as a storage reservoir; the preservation of Prospect Hill, Waltham, which became a city park; the acquisition of Stony Brook Reservation and Blue Hills Reservation (some 4,858 acres in all); protection of key portions of the shores and marshes of the Mystic, Charles and Neponset Rivers; the acquisition of seven miles of shore and beach between Winthrop Great Head and Point of Pines (except Point of Pines

itself and about one and one-third miles of shoreline between
Grover's Cliff and Crescent Beach); the protection of some two
miles of the westerly half of the shore of Quincy Bay; and at
Newton Upper Falls, the acquisition of Hemlock Gorge and
Beaver Brook with its grove of ancient oaks.

By 1902, the commission also had acquired three properties
which were not recommended a decade earlier in Eliot's report.
They were King's Beach and Lynn Shore at the northeast edge of
the district, and Nantasket Beach outside of the district to the
southeast, which required a special act of the legislature.

By December 1901, according to President Eliot's account of
the commission's accomplishments, "the total expenditure for
metropolitan reservations, including Nantasket Beach, was
$7,049,256, of which more than two-thirds ($5,087,237.40) was
paid for land, the rest being paid for construction, maintenance,
care, interest, and sinking-fund assessments during the eight
years." Statistics show that by 1902, 9,248 acres of public open
space had been secured as well as 26.3 miles of public parkway.
The average price paid per acre was $550. Even at the time, it
seemed like an extraordinary bargain.

The most expensive reservations purchased were Revere
Beach and the Charles River, which cost nearly half (or $2,439,307)
of the total amount paid for all other properties together. Still
awaiting implementation was Eliot's massive proposal for the
improvement of the Charles River Basin, which was not only
designed to provide waterfront parks, but to solve a sanitary
problem of some dimension. But it was to come later.

All in all, the initial accomplishments of the Metropolitan
Park Commission were remarkable. And the concept of a regional
park district for a major metropolitan area became a model for
other cities throughout the country. Charles Eliot and The Trustees of Reservations could take considerable pleasure in the
knowledge that, as President Eliot wrote, "it is impossible to
imagine a more purely beneficent expenditure of public money, or
one more productive of genuine well-being and healthy
happiness."

*Charles W. Eliot served as
president of Harvard
University for 40 years and is
widely regarded as one of the
nation's greatest educators.*

11

Showing the Way at Home and Abroad

Meanwhile, as the nineteenth century neared its end, England,
too, faced with increasing pressures to develop portions of its
magnificent landscape, began a movement to establish "a Land

Sir Robert Hunter, first chairman of The National Trust

Octavia Hill: her inspiration was invaluable

Company formed. . . with a view to the protection of the public interests in the open spaces of the country." The proposal, made initially by Sir Robert Hunter, honorary solicitor of the Commons Preservation Society, won support as early as 1884 but grew in strength markedly when Hunter's cause was joined by two others.

One was a redoubtable lady by the name of Octavia Hill. She had made a national reputation for herself in housing reform and believed passionately in the protection of selected portions of the landscape as "open air sitting rooms for the poor." The other ardent advocate of open space preservation was Hardwicke D. Rawnsley, Vicar of Crosthwaite and Canon of Carlisle. A colorful figure with a legion of interests, he was an orator and author whose persuasive skills were considerable. Above all, he was the nation's leading spokesman for the preservation of his beloved Lake District.

By 1893, with the Lake District under siege, the three agreed that the time had come to establish a "National Trust," an idea that had long been talked about, as a repository for special portions of the landscape which, for the sake of the nation, deserved to be protected. In January 1895, "the infant association was duly registered under the Companies Acts. . . as 'The National Trust for Places of Historic Interest and Natural Beauty.'"

That the existence of The Trustees of Reservations played a major role in the establishment of England's National Trust there is no doubt. As a history of its beginnings states, "The Trust in its early days was also surprisingly sensitive to the achievements and importance of the New World. Probably, this is to be explained by the prestige of The Trustees of Reservations of Massachusetts. Founded in 1891 to hold land in the public interest, it was the senior body of its sort and its constitution deeply influenced that of the Trust."

In its Annual Report in 1896, The National Trust observed that it was in part "suggested by, and follows the lines of, an American Institution, 'The Trustees of (Public) Reservations, Massachusetts,' a body which had nominated Professor C. S. Sargent, one of its most prominent members, to the Council of the Trust." Indeed, until its reorganization in the 1970s, The National Trust, under its by-laws, continued to invite a representative of The Trustees to serve as a member of its governing Council.

England's Trust, being national, soon eclipsed the accomplishments of The Trustees. It was especially gratifying, however, to realize that a small organization in Boston had contributed so importantly to the creation of a similar association in what was to many still the "Mother Country." And, of course, it was a special feather in the cap of Charles Eliot.

Through the years, the relationship between The National Trust and The Trustees of Reservations has remained warm, cordial and productive. There have been visits back and forth by

The Trustees' chosen representatives to the Trust's Council. And in 1966, Lord Antrim, then Chairman of The Trust, was selected guest of honor as The Trustees of Reservations celebrated its 75th anniversary with an elegant luncheon at Naumkeag in Stockbridge.

In recent years, both organizations have participated in a regularly-scheduled series of international conferences of national trusts from around the world. The Trustees of Reservations was host at such a one here in the United States in 1981.

There have also been instructive exchanges of administrative personnel both with The National Trust of England and with The National Trust for Scotland, founded in 1934. Since 1973, when The Royal Oak Foundation was established as an American charity to seek support for The National Trust throughout the United States, Gordon Abbott, Jr., who served as Director of The Trustees from 1967 to 1984, has been an honorary member of its board of trustees.

Canon Rawnsley, eloquent defender of the Lake District

In 1990, in anticipation of The Trustees of Reservations' 100th anniversary, a delegation led by Standing Committee Chairman Herbert W. Vaughan and Director Frederic Winthrop, Jr., toured properties of the Trust and were feted at a special dinner. Hosted by Dame Jennifer Jenkins, Chairman of the Trust's Council, the dinner was attended by a number of English dignitaries including the Under Secretary of State for the Environment.

And in June 1991, as The Trustees of Reservations celebrated its centennial with a gala evening at Castle Hill, Ipswich, Angus Stirling, Director-General of The National Trust, was present in

Angus Stirling, left, Director-General of England's National Trust, congratulates Frederic Winthrop, Jr., as The Trustees of Reservations hails its 100th anniversary at Castle Hill.

person to present congratulations.

Most exciting, Stirling carried with him a special message for The Trustees from Her Majesty Queen Elizabeth, the Queen Mother, Patron and President of The National Trust. On Clarence House stationery it read:

"The Centenary of The Trustees of Reservations (Massachusetts) is an occasion for celebration in the United Kingdom as well as in the United States.

"The founding of The Trustees of Reservations in 1891 preceded that of our National Trust for Places of Historic Interest or Natural Beauty by four years. As the senior body of its kind to hold land in the public interest, the prestige and high reputation of The Trustees quickly became known on this side of the Atlantic. For this reason it was natural that the constitution and purposes of The Trustees of Reservations should have a strong influence on the way those of The National Trust of Britain were drawn up and subsequently enacted by Parliament.

"The enduring success of both organisations since those pioneering days is a tribute to the wisdom and foresight of your founders and those of The National Trust.

"On the Centenary of the Foundation I send my sincere congratulations on all that has been achieved in the first hundred years and offer my very warm good wishes for the continuing fulfillment of your endeavours in the years ahead."

It was signed "Elizabeth R."

12

So Short a Life: 1859-1897

By 1893, Charles Eliot was well established as a landscape architect. His activites and accomplishments in both private and public sectors had won him wide respect and admiration. That year, too, an invitation came to join the Olmsted office in Brookline and despite a genuine inclination to remain on his own, it was an offer he could not refuse. A month later, now soon to be the father of a fourth little girl, he was made a partner of Olmsted, Olmsted & Eliot.

For the next four years, he continued his work for the Metropolitan Park Commission, for municipalities and for individual clients, expanding and extending his professional reputation. But it was while engaged in the development of Keney Park in Hartford, that he returned home feeling, as his father writes, "as if he had taken cold. . . . At first the disease was [thought] to be the grippe; but the consulting physician summoned on the third day immediately recognized it as cerebro-spinal meningitis, an inflammation of the lining of the brain and spinal cord."

He lingered for seven days and died quietly on March 25, 1897. Born in late 1859, he was 37 years old. "So ended abruptly," his father declared, "and to human vision prematurely, a life simple, natural, happy and wholly beneficent."

Father and son were unusually close, and, as Henry James writes in his biography of President Eliot, "this blow which fell without warning was almost prostrating." The older man, often reserved, "had been watching Charles's rapid advance in the new profession of landscape architecture" with a "respect which might justly be called reverent." It was apparent, James wrote, "that Charles's death submerged him in grief."

The loss to the community, too, was great and expressions of sentiment and condolence poured forth from individuals and from institutions. Among the most eloquent was the resolution passed by the Standing Committee of The Trustees of Reservations the day after his death. It read: "Charles Eliot found in this community a generous but helpless sentiment for the preservation of our historical and beautiful places. By ample knowledge, by intelligent perseverance, by eloquent teaching, he created organizations capable of accomplishing his great purposes, and inspired others with a zeal approaching his own."

Although death had ended prematurely what surely would have been an extraordinary career, what was truly remarkable was what Charles Eliot accomplished in so short a lifetime. Today, parks, boulevards and magnificent open spaces in Boston, as well as in other cities and towns throughout New England and the nation, owe their inspiration, scope and design to the work of Eliot himself and to the Olmsted firm of which he became a partner. Regional planning has come of age and is now widely recognized as the fundamental way to deal with critical issues involving the future of both urban and rural environments. His concepts of land conservation are as meaningful today as they were when he first proposed them. And the organization that he established a century ago has created a model that the world has followed and expanded on.

How was Charles Eliot, so young a man, able to be so successful in his endeavors? It was his unusual ability to draw people together and to persuade them to his point of view. "It resulted," his father explained in his affectionate biography, "from a mastery of his subject and clearness in presenting it, from fairness in argument, and from a pleasantness, modesty, and gentleness in which there was no trace of weakness."

Surely, he deserves to be ranked among the great figures of his time.

Planning for Preservation

1

A New Generation Takes the Helm

By 1918, The Trustees of Reservations, then 17 years old, had preserved for public use and enjoyment eight properties totaling more than 500 acres of land. World War I had just ended and the United States was a world power.

Few on the Standing Committee had been called to the colors. The answer was that they were all overage. Charles Sargent, for example, served with distinction in the Union Army during the War Between the States. Treasurer George Wigglesworth, born in 1853, was 64 years old in 1917. Charles Rackemann was 60 and Henry Pickering Walcott, Chairman of the Standing Committee, a hearty 79 when President Woodrow Wilson signed the Congressional resolution declaring war on Germany.

Herbert Parker, who was to serve as President of The Trustees of Reservations in the mid-'30s, was a member of the Massachusetts State Guard. And Henry Channing, father of Laurence M. Channing (President and Chairman of the Standing Committee 1960-1966), was turned down for the Army for medical reasons and spent two years in Washington as a dollar-a-year man with the War Industries Board.

Many of the founding fathers had died: Philip Chase, William Shurtleff, Senator Hoar, and, of course, Charles Eliot. But there was a new generation in the wings, members of which served their country with distinction. Charles W. Eliot II for example, nephew of the organization's founder, who was to become its first Field Secretary, joined the American Red Cross Ambulance Service on the Italian front and was awarded the Croce al Merito di Guerra for bravery. He was just out of Browne & Nichols School at the time.

Charles Sumner Bird, who was to become Chairman of the
Standing Committee, served as a captain in the Field Artillery.
Fletcher Steele, future Chairman of the vitally important Reserva-
tions Committee, was with the American Red Cross in France and
Russia. Dr. John Phillips, benefactor of The Trustees and a key
member of its governing board, went overseas with the Harvard
Medical Unit and later commanded a Field Hospital. And William
Ellery, who was to serve as a member of the Standing Committee
for 27 years, was appointed overseas director for the Army's
Quartermaster General, with the rank of colonel.

By 1921, new names also had begun to appear on the list of
members of the corporation: Abbott Lawrence Lowell, later to
become President of Harvard as well as donor of Lowell Holly
Reservation; Frank A. Waugh, who in 1903 founded what is now
the Department of Landscape Architecture and Regional Planning
at the University of Massachusetts at Amherst; William Roger
Greeley of Lexington, a leading Boston architect who was to
become President of The Trustees in the late 1950s; and Arthur
Lyman of Waltham, who was to make major contributions to
conservation not only with The Trustees but as the
Commonwealth's Commissioner of Natural Resources.

But it was Bird, Eliot and Robert Walcott — whose father was
Chairman of the Standing Committee from 1903 to 1926, and who
himself was to serve as President for 18 years — who were to play
leading roles with the organization in the years ahead.

Involvement with The Trustees of Reservations has, throughout its history, been a tradition with many families in the Boston
area. Sons have followed fathers on the Standing Committee, as
have nephews and cousins, not because of any special efforts on
the part of the Nominating Committee, but because, in the best
traditions of New England, family members as individuals have
shared an interest in and commitment to one charity or another
for many years. Such was the case with the Walcotts and the
Frothinghams, the Wigglesworths and the Channings, the Guilds,
the Greeleys, the Phillips, and, of course, the Eliots.

From his birth in 1900, it was assumed that Charles William
Eliot II, would carry on the work of his uncle, whose promising
life had ended so tragically and unexpectedly at age 37.

Graduating from Harvard in 1920, Charles fulfilled every
expectation. He spent the next three years at Harvard's Graduate
School of Landscape Architecture surrounded by family and
living at home in Cambridge. His grandfather, the retired President of the University, was still alive. His father, the Reverend
Samuel A. Eliot, was President of the American Unitarian Association with offices in Boston (he later became rector of Arlington
Street Church).

In 1923, much like his uncle, Charles traveled to Europe on a
fellowship, working in England, and visiting Germany, Italy,

*Charles William Eliot II at the
time of his Twenty-fifth
Reunion at Harvard College,
1945*

Holland and Belgium. When he returned in 1924, he opened his own office and began practice as a planner and landscape architect. Imbued with vision and a liberal mind, a righteous commitment to his own high ideals, great professional abilities and boundless energy, he was a man interested in action and accomplishment. Like his uncle, he was a master of the artful use of logic and persuasion, but no one would deny that, through the years, his greatest assets were persistence and tenacity. If the cause was just, he never tired in his efforts to support it.

During his career, he worked for the Roosevelt Administration as Director of the National Capital Park and Planning Commission and later as chief of the National Resources Planning Board. In 1955, he became the Charles Eliot Professor of Landscape Architecture at Harvard's Graduate School of Design, remaining on the faculty until his retirement in 1968. Throughout his professional lifetime he also served as a planning consultant for scores of communities, large and small, from California to Vermont.

A political activist, he was, even in his 90s, passionately engaged as a volunteer member of numerous state commissions or, as an individual, in countless efforts to improve the quality of life and the environment and to advance programs, particularly in the public sector, which lead to the preservation of additional open space.

But it was in the mid-1920s, as a young man, that his special abilities and interests, and his devotion to The Trustees of Reservations and its mission, revived the organization's earlier recognition of the critical importance of planning in efforts to preserve selected areas of open space within the Commonwealth.

After he had left for Washington in 1929, the Standing Committee expressed its appreciation for his achievements. It was he, the Committee declared in its minutes, who had helped to change the direction of The Trustees from one "mainly limited to acting as custodian for suitable public areas conveyed to it, to [taking] a more active part in the solution of the problem of open spaces, first, by investigation to determine the most suitable and beautiful areas available for acquisition, and, next, to taking the necessary steps to acquire for the public such of said areas as might be possible for it to acquire."

Throughout its first 100 years, The Trustees of Reservations has been a pioneer in the field of open space planning. What follows is the story of some of these planning programs and the people who made them possible.

2

'The Needs and Uses of Open Spaces' — a Blueprint for Progress

By 1925, 34 years had passed since the founding of The Trustees of Reservations. Great strides had been made throughout the Commonwealth in the acquisition of public park lands. In cities and towns across the state, numerous other organizations, both public and private, had been established to protect open space.

In 1925, the Massachusetts Department of Conservation, another offspring of The Trustees, listed in its possession seven State Reservations, eight refuges for wildlife, and more than 100,000 acres of State Forests. There was much more to do, however, but first, it was agreed, environmental organizations should get together to decide how to do it.

Thus in May 1925, The Trustees of Reservations, with the support of 10 "other societies," sponsored a conference on "The Needs and Uses of Open Spaces in Massachusetts." The result was a landmark agreement to appoint an executive committee to promote "cooperation among existing organizations and government departments interested in the provision, distribution, development and maintenance of open spaces."

Chairman of the committee was Charles S. Bird, Jr., Vice Chairman William Roger Greeley, and Secretary, Charles W. Eliot II, then also Secretary of The Trustees of Reservations. Already the younger generation had taken over, and new directions and new accomplishments lay ahead. What the committee hoped to achieve would provide the Commonwealth with its first comprehensive plan to meet the "needs and uses of open space" in the years to come.

Cooperating organizations represented at the conference besides The Trustees included the Appalachian Mountain Club, the Boston Society of Landscape Architects, the Federation of New England Bird Clubs, the Massachusetts Audubon Society, the Massachusetts Civic League, the Massachusetts Federation of Planning Boards, the Massachusetts Federation of Women's Clubs, the Massachusetts Fish & Game Protective Association, the Society for the Preservation of New England Plants, and the Society for the Preservation of New England Antiquities.

Committee chairman Charles S. Bird, Jr. was the scion of a patrician family from East Walpole. Just 41 years old at the time of his appointment, he was a vice president of the family firm of Bird & Son, which manufactured roofing and building materials used throughout the world. A graduate of Harvard College with the class of 1906, Bird was a man of many interests and the means to

Charles S. Bird of East Walpole and Ipswich, chairman of the Standing Committee from 1933 to 1956

enjoy them. He was a great horseman and rode extensively both at "Waldingfield," his summer home in Ipswich, and later at his country place in Ireland. He was married to the former Julia Appleton, which tied him to one of the earliest landowning families in America. (A part of Appleton Farms in Ipswich, which was conveyed to Samuel Appleton in 1638, is now protected by The Trustees as Appleton Farms Grass Rides.)

An avid lover of history, especially of England and America, Bird was a leader in efforts to preserve Washington Old Hall, the ancestral home of the nation's first President, located near Newcastle, England. Wonderfully gregarious and always with a twinkle in his eye, he was immensely generous and deeply committed to the work of The Trustees. No better testimonial of this exists than his 23 years of service as Chairman of the Standing Committee, from 1933 to 1956.

The report of the Committee on the Needs and Uses of Open Spaces was presented to Governor Alvan T. Fuller in 1929. It had taken four years to complete and $25,000 — raised by The Trustees of Reservations — to publish. It was a major milestone in efforts to protect the rural character and natural charm of the countryside of Massachusetts. And it emphasized the critical importance of the need to identify and describe the qualities and characteristics of specific areas if they are to be preserved. It was open space planning at its best. It followed, also, the traditions and objectives of earlier plans completed by The Trustees at the end of the nineteenth century, such as the study of the Province Lands at Cape Cod and the inventory of public open spaces in the shore towns of Massachusetts.

The report included the State's first map of existing and proposed open spaces from Berkshire County to Cape Cod and the islands of Martha's Vineyard and Nantucket. In calling for additions to the state park system, it emphasized not only the economic values of recreation, estimated in those days to be some $300 million annually for all of New England, but the importance of adequate open space to the health and well-being of the citizens of Massachusetts, an amount valued in general, the report declared, "considerably in excess of the sums which she [New England] spends in acquiring and maintaining these health-producing facilities."

The increased demand for outdoor recreation experiences, because of a new mobility provided by a rapidly growing number of automobiles, was also cited. And its statistics ranked Massachusetts eighth on a list of eight states selected which showed the acreage of "organized public reservations per thousand of inhabitants," despite Boston's pioneering establishment of its historic Common as early as 1634.

New York finished first with 207 acres per thousand residents. It was followed by Minnesota, Wisconsin, Pennsylvania, and

Michigan. Even Vermont with 87, and New Hampshire with 65, far less populous states, outranked Massachusetts, which could muster only 23 acres of parkland for each 1,000 of its people.

Major recommendations of the report dealt with specific properties which the committee urged be acquired. They were classified according to use: forestry, water supply, outdoor recreation, wildlife conservation, wilderness camping and motor camping. Included were Salisbury Beach, Duxbury Beach (which never became state property but today is open to public use), and Westport Beach.

Nine new state forests were proposed including Berkshire County's October Mountain as well as forest lands in Wendell, Sharon, and Miles Standish and Yarmouth on Cape Cod. Thirteen new State Parks were called for from Bash-Bish Falls and Sage's Ravine in western Massachusetts to Dogtown Common in Gloucester.

The committee also identified 10 new sanctuaries for wildlife to be located from Boxford and Sudbury to Neponset, Barnstable and the moors of Nantucket Island. All were composed primarily of marsh, swamp or wetland. It was suggested as well that the Appalachian Trail be extended to northern New England and that in Massachusetts a Watatic Trail be created in the vicinity of Mount Wachusett.

Finally, the report urged state legislators to establish a Division of Parks within the Commonwealth's Department of Conservation. A bill had already been filed — thanks to the efforts of The Trustees of Reservations — for a special agency was urgently needed to take specific responsibility for a growing number of public open spaces.

Today, nearly every site then recommended by the committee has been protected for public purposes, either by a state or federal agency or by a non-profit organization such as The Trustees of Reservations. And its selection of the great salt marshes of Newbury and Rowley as areas to be preserved played a major role in the defeat of a proposal in 1932 which called for the construction of a highway from Ipswich to Salisbury. It would have traversed a part of Plum Island, and crossed Plum Island Sound and the Merrimack River with two drawbridges.

In a poignant conclusion to the report, the committee pleaded for greater recognition for The Trustees of Reservations. "This group," it stated, "would be more effective if [its] purposes were better appreciated."

Just how this was to be achieved was not explained. But public awareness of the organization and its mission was a problem that had stalked it since its beginnings and would plague it for years to come.

3

The Bay Circuit

A major portion of the Report of the Committee on the Needs and Uses of Open Spaces dealt with a magical idea. It called for the creation of what would be known today as a major "greenway."

Because 3.5 million of the state's then total population of 4.5 million people lived within 40 miles of the State House, the committee urged that "a series of connected reservations [be established] in a semi-circle about midway between Worcester and Massachusetts Bay" following "a wide parkway [from] Duxbury Beach to the South, via Charles River Narrows, Walden Pond, Bedford Meadows and Boxford, to Plum Island and Salisbury Beach to the north."

The area, the report stated, was composed of "land of comparatively low value [and thus could be] gradually developed without undue expense." The route of the proposed greenway already included "nine public tracts and nine out of 32 projects" recommended by the report. It was called the Bay Circuit, and it was to be an extension of the original plan for the region's system of metropolitan parks, first proposed by The Trustees in 1891.

The area also abounded with both natural features and historic sites. Among them were Duxbury Beach and Saquish Neck; Fowl Meadows and the upper course of the Charles River; the Sudbury and Concord Rivers; Walden Pond (a glacial kettle

Celebrating enactment of The Bay Circuit with Governor Christian A. Herter in August 1956. From left: William Roger Greeley, President of The Trustees of Reservations; State Representative Howard Russell; Governor Herter; Professor Charles W. Eliot II, member of the Standing Committee of The Trustees; and State Representative James De Normandie

hole as well as the site of Henry Thoreau's hermit cabin); as well
as Pilgrim memorials in Plymouth; the Battle Ground, the North
Bridge and homes of literary figures in Concord; and the Timothy
Dexter House and such landmarks as the Chain Bridge in
Newburyport.

The Bay Circuit, which an original copy of the report states
was "first suggested by Henry M. Channing, Secretary of The
Trustees of Reservations," also called for a connecting parkway,
now often mistaken for Route 128. The new road was to be farther
to the west. With the completion of Route 128, however — the
"Golden Semicircle" — and the construction of superhighway
Route 495, the original parkway was never built. It would have
been located about half-way between the two. Open space areas
along the Bay Circuit are instead linked by local roadways which
drivers still can follow from the South Shore to the North.

The plan fell victim to the Great Depression in 1929 but was
revived in 1937, only to be shelved again because of the arrival of
World War II. With the assistance of Governor Christian A.
Herter, however, the Bay Circuit won administrative approval in
1956, but it was little more than lip service as no funds were
appropriated.

Finally, in 1980, 51 years after it had been originally proposed,
the Bay Circuit was awarded $3.5 million as part of a major open
space bond issue which The Trustees of Reservations had worked
to support. Land prices had risen dramatically, however, and it
was sad to think what that money could have purchased and
preserved in 1929. It might have done the whole job. Nevertheless,
the Department of Environmental Management made imaginative
use of the funds, using matching grants in 28 communities to
acquire key parcels. Sadly, a state budget squeeze in 1988 put an
end to funding once again.

Throughout its history, The Trustees of Reservations has been
instrumental in efforts to revive the Bay Circuit. Charles Eliot II
persistently carried the banner for 61 years unitl his death in 1992.
And staff members of The Trustees from Lawrence Fletcher to
Nathan W. Bates and Gordon Abbott, Jr., have served on Bay
Circuit Advisory Committees.

Today, despite a lack of State funding, the Bay Circuit is alive
and well. Recognizing the appeal of a trail accessible to the public
and circling the metropolitan area, the National Park Service has
contributed technical assistance and the Appalachian Mountain
Club and The Trust for Public Lands have urged the formation of
a Bay Circuit Alliance.

A new, non-profit organization, the Alliance is helping to
establish local Bay Circuit Committees designed to work in their
own communities with private landowners to secure a defined
trail corridor. To generate public interest in the work of the

Alliance, The Trustees of Reservations has sponsored trail walks and has designated special routes where the Bay Circuit passes through its own properties.

The original concept of a broader, open space corridor or greenbelt has not been forgotten, but the idea of a trail has already demonstrated that it has immense popular appeal. And, who knows, perhaps some day, when governments are solvent again, new opportunities will arise to complete the dream.

4

Laurence Brown Fletcher

Laurence B. Fletcher, Executive Secretary of The Trustees of Reservations for 29 years

When Charles Eliot II left for Washington and the National Capital Park and Planning Commission, his place as Secretary of the Committee on the Needs and Uses of Open Spaces was taken by the President of the Federation of the Bird Clubs of New England. His name was Laurence Brown Fletcher and in March 1929 he became The Trustees of Reservations' first full-time Executive Secretary.

A former Boston bank clerk and stock broker, Fletcher's real loves were ornithology, natural history and the out-of-doors, and when offered the job he leapt at the chance. For the next 29 years, his remarkable spirit and selfless dedication were to carry the organization through some of its most difficult and yet productive decades.

His beginning salary, which was finally set at $2,500 a year plus expenses (as Fletcher was a bachelor this seemed enough at the time), was paid for, in part, by the generosity of individual Standing Committee members — primarily Charles Bird, who provided office space for The Trustees at 50 Congress Street, Boston.

Throughout his career, Fletcher, an excitable personality, but a man of boundless energy and enormous enthusiasm for the task at hand, focused not only upon acquiring new properties, but upon expanding recognition of The Trustees and its mission with the public, with the press, and with politicians. He enjoyed the job and he was good at it, although it must be admitted he was not always popular with everyone. Opinionated, somewhat vain (he took special pains to be a natty dresser and was known playfully to some as the "Crown Prince"), he enjoyed immensely the prestige of his position and the access it gave him everywhere. When he wanted, he could converse with and charm people from every walk of life. He was equally happy and at home at society

teas, in farmhouse kitchens or with small town Boards of Selectmen. But he was at his best with older ladies, who must have seen
in him the elegance and joie de vivre of an earlier era.

His schedule was prodigious. He often spent as many as four
to five nights each week attending meetings or lecturing and
showing films about The Trustees to people around the state.

A resident of Cohasset, he had a house at Lilly Pond, where
more than one now retired Standing Committee member recalls
sipping dry martinis and watching hummingbirds at Fletcher's
feeders. Always in demand for his knowledge of natural history,
he was a member of the boards of directors of the Massachusetts
Audubon Society, the Society for the Protection of New England
Wildflowers, the Nutthal Ornithological Society and the Society
for the Preservation of New England Antiquities.

(In earlier days with a smaller constituency of environmental-
ists, there was considerable overlap as interested and influential
individuals served as members and even officers of a number of
different organizations. Robert Wolcott, for example, was at one
time President of the Massachusetts Audubon Society and of The
Trustees of Reservations.)

But through the years, it was Fletcher's dedication to The
Trustees and what it stood for that is most impressive. He was a
single man, and The Trustees took the place of wife and family.
He gave selflessly and continously of his time, far beyond that
expected or demanded of him, to lead the organization forward
through nearly three decades. His relationships with key members of his board, especially with his chairmen and his presidents
(of which he had few because of the length of service in those
days), were very close, and there is a friendship evident in memoranda and correspondence which is touching and which obviously made things work easily from day to day.

In 1934, Fletcher initiated The Trustees' Conservation Award
with its accompanying annual ceremony. His field trips to western Massachusetts were famous and once included 21 vehicles
with a State Police escort. On other occasions he would hire
busses and serve sandwiches and champagne for lunch. He also
began the organization's interpretive programs, encouraging the
publication of informative literature about selected properties,
such as an early history of Nathaniel Hawthorne at The Old
Manse.

During his tenure, The Trustees of Reservations increased its
holdings from nine to 34 properties and from 693 to more than
4,400 acres of land. His struggle was The Trustees' struggle with
finances, and during his 29 years of service there was the agony of
more than a few annual operating deficits. But his spirit never
wavered and his optimism was always contagious.

He died very much in harness in 1958, but not until after he
himself had received The Trustees of Reservations' by-then

prestigious Conservation Award. It was bestowed at an Annual Meeting luncheon with a host of accolades, a wonderful feeling of warmth, and an affection and respect which were justly earned and well deserved.

5

Bradford Williams and the Massachusetts Landscape Survey

Landscape architect Bradford Williams, author of the 1933 Massachusetts Landscape Survey

By the early 1930s, The Trustees of Reservations, aware of the growth and importance of the automobile, and fearful for the future of the region's scenic roadways, had commissioned and published another report. This time the author was the nationally-known planner, environmentalist and "Father of the Appalachian Trail," Benton MacKaye.

Entitled "Highway Approaches to Boston, a Wayside Situation and What to Do About It," it urged planning for open space along major highways in the "hub, rim and spokes" of the Bay Circuit to alleviate "wayside fungus" on modern "freeways" (a word that had just been coined), as well as to improve the efficiency of transportation routes and enhance the safety and enjoyment of the motoring public. But it was Bradford Williams' "Landscape Survey of Massachusetts" in 1933 that broke still newer ground in the field of open space planning.

While the report of the Committee on the Needs and Uses of Open Spaces was designed primarily to urge action by public resource agencies whose responsibilities included a mix of natural resource protection, such as forestry, wildlife preservation, and outdoor recreation, the Landscape Survey dealt solely with the identification and classification of scenic areas and thus was of special interest and concern to The Trustees of Reservations.

A landscape architect himself, Williams, who was to be one of the most productive but least predictable members of the Standing Committee, began his career by sharing offices, if not clients, with his graduate school classmate, Charles W. Eliot II.

The years of the Depression were not easy ones for landscape architects, and thus the opportunity to be of service, even at a relatively low level of remuneration, was welcome. Indeed, as one member of Williams's team reported, "that year the woods were full of landscape architects, who, with their 'flivvers' parked by the roadsides of the Commonwealth, were eagerly noting areas which deserved protection."

The purpose of the project, sponsored jointly by The Trustees of Reservations and the American Society of Landscape Architects, was to identify and locate scenery "believed to have special character or outstanding value"; to state the reasons such scenery ought to be preserved; and to suggest what kinds of use might best be made of the areas "without destroying their landscape values."

The study warned that in the years ahead there would be "unprecedented growth of the 'open space habit' with increasing leisure time"; that this would occasion "ever greater wear of our countryside by weekend and holiday crowds"; and that because of these coming pressures on the landscape, action to protect selected areas should be initiated at once by The Trustees of Reservations as well as other resource agencies and organizations.

For purposes of the survey, Williams created an imaginative process which divided the landscape into categories. They included ocean beaches and dunes; moor and seashore upland; scenic highway roadsides; mountains, valleys and gorges; woodland, beautiful for its foliage canopy and texture; and flooded lands in the coastal plain. Other sites were also to be a part of the inventory: "the Historical: areas perhaps of landscape beauty, but chiefly significant in the history of man; the Curious or Unusual: scenic areas causing surprise and a desire for their intimate exploration and understanding; and the Restful: landscapes offering the enjoyment of natural scenery without exertion."

As no organization alone could accomplish all that was asked, the study also called for a statewide program in cooperation with the Massachusetts Department of Conservation which would "awaken local interest, knowledge and pride" in the natural beauty of the Commonwealth.

When it was completed, the Massachusetts Landscape Survey included a list of more than 70 specific sites of scenic and historic interest which should be protected. Wherever possible the owner was identified as well as the feature's location and a suggestion relating to the kinds of recreational use which were in keeping with its preservation. All in all, it was a remarkable job.

Most important, the Landscape Survey led ultimately to the preservation of an extraordinary number of selected sites. The list is well worth a review. It included Castle Neck and Crane Beach, now held by The Trustees; Duxbury Beach, open to the public and held in trust by a private, non-profit association; Monomoy Island, now a U.S. National Wildlife Refuge and Massachusetts' only designated Wilderness Area; and Cape Cod Headlands, now a part of the National Seashore, owned and managed by the National Park Service.

Also included were the Mohawk and Taconic Trails, scenic roadways now protected in large measure by the State's Depart-

ment of Public Works and the Department of Environmental
Management; Mount Everett, Mount Race and the Holyoke
Range, each now owned and operated as State Parks; the upper
Ipswich River, protected in large part by the Massachusetts
Audubon Society and Essex County Greenbelt Association; the
scenic corridor of the upper Charles River Valley, protected by the
U.S. Army Corps of Engineers' Natural Valley Storage Program (a
flood control measure), and by the Massachusetts Audubon
Society, the Charles River Watershed Association, The Trustees of
Reservations and local land trusts; and thousands of acres of salt
marsh in Ipswich and Essex, now protected by the State's Coastal
Wetlands Act, by Essex County Greenbelt and by The Trustees.

Other sites listed were Windsor Jambs, now a State Park;
Sudbury marshes, now a National Wildlife Refuge; Chesterfield
Gorge, Bartholomew's Cobble, and Rocky Narrows, all presently
owned by The Trustees of Reservations

All agreed that the Massachusetts Landscape Survey was an
extraordinary piece of work. Its recommendations were subjec-
tively arrived at, to be sure, but history shows there need be little
doubt about their validity.

A tireless and committed worker, Brad Williams was active
with The Trustees for more than 25 years. Upon the retirement of
Charles S. Bird as Chairman in 1956, Williams thought that Roger
Greeley should take over the position. When he declined to serve,
Williams apparently believed that his own record of service
qualified him for the job. And when on a four to three vote, the
chairmanship went to Maurice Osborne, Williams resigned from
the Standing Committee. It was a tragic decision, for it deprived
The Trustees of a man of considerable talent whose work was
widely recognized and applauded and who had contributed
immensely to the success of the organization as it neared its
fiftieth year.

Ironically, as Williams wrote later in a letter to Laurence
Fletcher, one of the four votes for Osborne was his own, as he
thought it "improper to vote for myself in what I regarded as a
test of confidence."

6

A New Professionalism and the Environmental Years

Awakened by the Report of the Committee on the Needs and Uses
of Open Spaces and the Massachusetts Landscape Survey, envi-

ronmental organizations throughout the Commonwealth swung
into action.

During the next three and one-half decades, The Trustees of
Reservations alone increased its holdings from 12 reservations to a
total of 50. Massive strides were made as well by the State Department of Natural Resources, which significantly increased the
number of state parks and forests. By then, the Federal government had acquired Cape Cod National Seashore and wildlife
refuges from Plum Island and the Sudbury marshes to Monomoy.

By the late 1960s, the first Earth Day had taken place and the
environment and the preservation of open space were considered
national priorities. Outdoor recreation was a major pastime of
hundreds of millions of Americans. With the emergence of the
suburbs, the growth of the automobile and a new federal highway
system, the countryside was under greater pressure than ever,
and The Trustees of Reservations decided it was time to take
another look at the challenges that lay ahead.

In 1968, too, the organization had just celebrated the 75th
anniversary of its founding, and, equally important, it had a new
Director, Gordon Abbott, Jr., who had taken over as chief administrator a year earlier.

Abbott had joined The Trustees at a propitious moment.
Interest in the environment was at an all-time high. And the
organization had just received a major addition to its endowment
— income from a legacy of $4.1 million left by Lieutenant-Colonel
Arthur D. Budd with the bequest of Notchview Reservation in
Windsor.

*At Great Point, Nantucket,
Director Gordon Abbott, Jr.,
left, talks with Robert W.
Sziklas, a donor of Coskata-
Coatue Wildlife Refuge*

A former journalist, Abbott had developed his interest in open space preservation, land use and regional and municipal planning as Editor of *The Gloucester Times* and *The Beverly Times*, two small-city dailies on the North Shore of Massachusetts. A third-generation resident of Manchester, whose parents and grandparents had been active in the campaign to preserve Misery Islands, he had an abiding love of nature and the out-of-doors.

His position was a new one, with new executive authority, and his charge was to develop and implement a new system of management and new directions for an organization whose financial resources had all but doubled overnight.

When he joined The Trustees in early 1967, its Annual Report listed as preserved 44 reservations totaling 9,305 acres of land. When he retired 17 and one-half years later, the organization had acquired in fee 75 properties totaling 17,488 acres and 35 conservation restrictions or easements protecting an additional 5,245 acres. A series of preservation projects also underway and pending bequests were to further increase the amount of land protected in the years just ahead.

The Trustees of Reservations also was prepared to deal with every opportunity to continue its mission. It had two full-time professionals assigned only to land conservation. Its affiliate, the Massachusetts Farm & Conservation Lands Trust, was able to deal with the latest and most innovative techniques in preserving open space, many of which it had pioneered itself. A professional management team for the properties was now in place with some 60 full-time field and head office employees. A comprehensive process of master planning, designed to provide each property with policies which would balance the highest possible levels of resource protection with public use and enjoyment, was underway.

The organization's embryonic interpretive program had been greatly enlarged and expanded. Scores of booklets, pamphlets and folders had been published and displays erected, all designed to tell visitors the stories of specific properties.

A professional revenue-raising office with a staff of five was in existence. The Trustees had a full-fledged membership program and an Annual Appeal which added up to a half-million dollars in income yearly. And the organization had raised more than $6 million in its first formal capital fund-raising program. Endowment principal had increased some $4 million to $9.7 million, and an independent investment counsel had been employed to manage The Trustees' investment portfolio.

It was Abbott's belief that the mission of The Trustees of Reservations could best be accomplished if volunteers and the professional staff worked together in harmony as a single unit. Utilizing the time-tested system of committees and sub-commit-

tees, both at the level of the governing board and in the field
within each of The Trustees' new management regions, the
organization pulled together the largest collection of committed
volunteers in its history and a professional staff that was second
to none anywhere.

Certainly, it was this remarkable collection of personal
energies and talents that made the accomplishments of more than
a decade and a half possible. The beneficiaries, of course, were the
people of the Commonwealth wherever they lived in cities and
towns from Berkshire County to Massachusetts Bay.

7

The Governor's Advisory Commission on Open Space and Outdoor Recreation

In 1968, the Metropolitan Area Planning Council had just completed an open space and recreation study of Boston Harbor and
the three major rivers of the Boston Basin: the Charles, the Mystic
and the Neponset. To help celebrate the 75th anniversary of the
founding of the Metropolitan Park System, The Trustees of
Reservations decided to host a Parkland Conference to introduce
the study and its far-reaching recommendations.

Out of the conference — which was attended by Governor
John A. Volpe, key members of the Massachusetts legislature and
top natural resource officials as well as hundreds of dedicated
citizens — came the appointment of the Governor's Advisory
Commission on Open Space and Outdoor Recreation. Its members
included the names of many associated with The Trustees of
Reservations: John M. Woolsley, Jr., a former Chairman of the
Standing Committee; planners Charles W. Eliot II and Peter L.
Hornbeck; real estate executive Robert Livermore, Jr.; and newly-
appointed Director Gordon Abbott, Jr., who served as Secretary.
The Commission's charge was to take a new look at open space
and recreation needs throughout the Commonwealth and to make
recommendations for the future.

Its report, which was presented to Governor Francis W.
Sargent in late 1969, was another landmark in the process of
planning for the preservation of open space. (Sargent himself,
deeply committed to the environment, had been a member of the
Standing Committee while he was Commissioner of Fisheries &
Wildlife in Massachusetts a few years earlier.) Its recommendations, many of which were later adopted, centered not only on the
protection of specific sites, but brought into focus a new dimen-

sion: the critical role that a statewide system of community-based, comprehensive land use planning could play in protecting significant open spaces and the traditional character of the Massachusetts landscape.

The Commission's report called for a reorganization of state government to permit one Office of Environmental Affairs; the establishment of a Land-use Planning Division in the Executive Office of Administration & Finance which would propose a series of statewide land use policies in connection with state and Federal spending programs and would promote, in cities and towns, positive forms of development planning that incorporated amenity values and environmental considerations into the private planning and development process.

The Commission also urged that local planning agencies encourage a higher concentration of housing, schools and utilities to make more efficient use of limited land resources; that an Enabling Act be approved by the State Legislature to permit cities and towns to utilize planned unit or cluster development; that the Governor appoint a Task Force on the Retention of Agricultural Lands; and that open space acquisition funds be used first to meet the needs of urban areas. It recommended that the linear park concept, now called "greenways," be adopted as a policy guide in state land protection programs; that wetlands preservation be accelerated; that ponds, streams and rivers be classified according to their scenic value as well as for the quality of their water resources and recreation potential; and that environmental science be made a required subject in Massachusetts schools.

Finally, the Commission called for public ownership and control of the islands of Boston Harbor; for protection of the scenic and environmental values of the Charles, Mystic and Neponset Rivers, and for a program to protect other rivers of the Commonwealth; for support of a National Recreation Area along the Connecticut River; and for the acquisition of South Cape Beach, which the Commonwealth had once held but had returned to private ownership.

Preservation of the islands of Boston harbor presented a special problem. At the time, federal acquisition funds, which were critically important to the success of what was to be a huge project, could only be used by a statewide resource agency, then the Department of Natural Resources. The islands, however, were owned by the Metropolitan District Commission, whose jurisdiction was regional.

A special meeting was arranged, attended by MDC Commissioner Howard Whitmore, Jr. and Robert L. Yasi, Commissioner of the Department of Natural Resources, as well as by Governor's Advisory Commission members Chairman Thaddeus Beal, John Woolsey and Gordon Abbott. In view of the importance of the project and the opportunities at hand, parochial considerations were swept aside and it was agreed, unanimously and enthusiastically by all present, that every necessary step, including transfer of ownership, would be taken immediately to permit the Department of Natural Resources to apply for federal funds to purchase the harbor islands. It was a remarkable example of inter-agency cooperation.

Today, Boston Harbor Islands State Park, a precious resource, is owned and administered by the Department of Environmental Management, while the Metropolitan District Commission holds title still to three major island areas: Georges Island, Lovell Island and Peddocks Island. All publicly held island parks are operated and protected by both agencies with a coordinated management program.

Happily, the report's other recommendations were to be adopted as well, although some years later. A reorganization of state government in 1973 did result in the establishment of a cabinet-level Executive Office of Environmental Affairs.

In 1975, during his first term, Governor Michael S. Dukakis created an Office of State Planning which soon completed an outstanding and long-needed Growth Policy Report for the Commonwealth. The planning process it employed began from the bottom up, with a Local Growth Policy Committee in nearly every one of Massachusetts' 351 cities and towns. Each committee developed a series of recommendations for the future of its own community. These were then sent to state planners who wrote the comprehensive report.

The Governor's Advisory Commission on Open Space and Outdoor Recreation presents its report to Governor Francis W. Sargent in 1969. At the Governor's left is Commission Secretary Gordon Abbott, Jr. Other Commission members active with The Trustees of Reservations were Charles W. Eliot II, Peter L. Hornbeck, Robert Livermore, Jr., John W. Pierce, and John M. Woolsey, Jr.

In 1974, Martha's Vineyard set an example for the Commonwealth, giving birth to its own planning and regulatory agency called the Martha's Vineyard Commission. It was followed in 1990 by the Cape Cod Commission. Each was established by legislative action. Today, efforts continue, promoted by both public and private sector organizations, to expand the process of regional, comprehensive land use planning in other sections of the Commonwealth as well, such as Berkshire and Franklin Counties, by replicating the concept pioneered by Martha's Vineyard and Cape Cod.

A Scenic Rivers Act also exists, the Agricultural Preservation Restriction Program has preserved thousands of acres of top quality farmland, and, thankfully, South Cape Beach is once again in public hands.

8

Landscape and Natural Areas Study — 1970

Out of the work of the Commission on Open Space and Outdoor Recreation also came a commitment by The Trustees of Reservations to initiate new and intensive efforts to protect special features of the Massachusetts landscape, and, as a first step, to bring the 1933 Massachusetts Landscape Survey up to date. The planning proposal followed a familiar and successful path. Here within the Commonwealth, The Trustees declared, "we must be able to identify which areas and features should be preserved. We must be able to describe what environmental qualities they possess, and we must be able to list what priorities for preservation they should be assigned."

Work began in earnest in 1970, thanks to the interest and efforts of former State Commissioner of Natural Resources Charles H. W. Foster, then President of the New England Natural Resources Center, who, at one time, served as a member of The Trustees' Advisory Council. Following initial conversations with Foster, the project was wisely expanded to include not only Massachusetts but every New England state and, on those terms, funding was acquired from the New England Regional Commission. Each state, however, was responsible for conducting its own survey and in Massachusetts, The Trustees of Reservations chose the Research Office of the Department of Landscape Architecture at Harvard University to undertake the task.

The Landscape and Natural Areas Study for Massachusetts was finally completed with the assistance not only of professionals, but of scores of knowledgeable volunteers across the state, many of them members of Conservation Commissions. It identified more than 2,400 sites of environmental and ecological importance. Because of The Trustees' special interests, Massachusetts had the only statewide study which included an evaluation of the scenic qualities of each area.

Many of the properties mentioned were already protected, others were newly inventoried; 535 were listed in the final report. Forty-four percent were located on public lands, 56 percent on private. Their approximate area totaled 279,000 acres. Accompanying data included the location of the site, its size and elevation, ecological characteristics, visual values, significance, ownership, access, and integrity. Each site was then assigned a rating in its own category.

One goal of the study was to computerize the information so that it could become a part of the state's data bank and thus would surface in planning studies where development was proposed, providing notice of the existence of an unusual or unique natural feature. But its major purpose was to provide data which would lead to a comprehensive program which could provide protection for significant natural areas throughout New England.

Garland F. Okerlund, project chief, Landscape and Natural Areas Study for Massachusetts

The regional report produced by the New England Natural Resources Center linked the studies in each state and recommended the creation of a New England Natural Heritage System. Responsibilities for the protection of natural areas were to be assumed both by private organizations and public environmental agencies, thus creating early on the kind of "partnership" between government and the private sector which is so commonplace today.

The New England Natural Heritage Program led in turn to the formal establishment of a Natural Heritage Program for Massachusetts sponsored in the mid-1970s by The Nature Conservancy. The Conservancy's program, a national one, dealt with its own special interest: protecting rare and endangered species. There are Natural Heritage Program offices now in nearly every state of the union. In Massachusetts the program is administered by the Division of Fisheries & Wildlife.

The landscape and natural areas inventory also helped focus land conservation projects throughout the Commonwealth. Funds for open space acquisition were then, by today's standards, plentiful. And Land and Water Conservation Fund monies on the federal level, and a well-funded Self-Help Program within the State, enabled Conservation Commissions to acquire hundreds of critical acres of environmentally significant land. In many cases, their choice of sites was guided by the results of the landmark study proposed by The Trustees of Reservations.

9

Special Planning for Strategic Conservation Areas

In its efforts to accelerate its campaign to protect "beautiful and historic sites" throughout the Commonwealth, The Trustees of Reservations also initiated a series of special preservation projects in strategic conservation areas. These included the tidal estuaries and salt marshes of Ipswich and Essex; Tuckernuck Island, Nantucket; Jacob's Hill, Doane's Falls and Long Pond in Royalston; the East Branch of the Westport River, Westport; hill farm landscapes surrounding the Bryant Homestead in Cummington and the corridor of the Upper Charles River from Needham to Bellingham.

The Charles River project was a model preservation planning program. Initiated in 1972, it included a series of eight maps and overlays of the project area, showing its topography, vegetation, hydrology, existing land uses and visual values. Other environmental qualities such as the area's geology, wildlife, botany and archeology were also documented, as were sites already protected as open space.

One important overlay showed the boundaries of every property, both public and private, within the defined area of the watershed. Each was numbered and keyed to notebook pages which contained the name and address of each land owner, the size of the parcel and the assessed value of the land and (if they existed) buildings. Finally, the project committee assigned priorities to those parcels whose protection was vital to the goals of the program: to preserve the scenic and enviromental qualities of the corridor of the Upper Charles River.

Through the years, thanks primarily to a wonderfully cooperative relationship with the U.S. Army Corps of Engineers and its Natural Valley Storage Flood Control Program, the Massachusetts Department of Environmental Management, the Charles River Watershed Association, and the Massachusetts Audubon Society, the Upper Charles River Protection Project has been a huge success. Within the area, The Trustees of Reservations alone now preserves in fee, 1,126 acres of land, while an additional 417 acres are protected with conservation restrictions. Today, work still continues with the job not yet complete.

The Corps of Engineers' Natural Valley Storage Area, which won the enthusiastic support of The Trustees of Reservations and other environmental organizations, is still a unique national example of what can be accomplished to control flooding without the use of dams or other "hard" structures. Many of its details were worked out in discussions with The Trustees and with the Charles River Watershed Association.

The acquisition of wetlands — natural storage areas for water — finally totaled 8,103 acres. The Corps acquired fee title to 3,221 acres. Flood easements, also held by the Corps, protect an additional 4,882 acres. The total cost of the project was $8.3 million. Some of the land the Corps owns in fee is managed as wildlife habitat by the Massachusetts Division of Fisheries and Wildlife.

The project did include the construction of a new dam at the mouth of the Charles in Boston, a replacement for the old one built in 1910 to prevent the intrusion of tidal salt water into the river. Unlike the old dam, however, which relied on gravity flow to release water at low tide, the new structure is equipped with pumps which can discharge as much as 630,000 gallons of water each minute when the river is in flood stage. The dam, now operated and maintained by the Metropolitan District Commission, also includes navigation locks to permit passage of increasing numbers of pleasure boats.

The Charles River Natural Valley Storage Flood Control Project was authorized by Public Law 93-251. Its objectives are successfully multi-purpose, providing not only an effective and environmentally-sensitive way to deal with rising floodwaters, but also preserving valuable open space, and creating opportunities for recreation and fish and wildlife management.

10

A New Study Meets the Needs and Conditions of the 1980s

Both Director Gordon Abbott, Jr., and Robert D. Yaro, then Chief of Planning at the Department of Environmental Management (DEM), had long been fascinated with the concept of a study which would focus on the identification and ultimate preservation of larger scenic landscapes, reflecting not only the Commonwealth's outstanding natural resources but its cultural heritage as well.

The result, in 1982, was the completion of the "Massachusetts Landscape Inventory, A Survey of the Commonwealth's Scenic Areas." Funded by DEM, it was developed by a special 12-member Concept Committee which included Yaro, Abbott and such luminaries as Professor Hugh Davis of the Department of Landscape Architecture and Regional Planning at the University of Massachusetts, Dr. Ernest Gould, Jr. of the Harvard Forest;

DEM planners Christopher Greene and Katharine Preston; Valerie Talmadge, Executive Director of the Massachusetts Historical Commission (now a land protection specialist with The Trustees of Reservations); and Professors Norton Nickerson and Frank Thibodeau of Tufts University. DEM Landscape Architect Harry Dodson was chosen as project manager. He was assisted by DEM planner Mark S. Finnen and Neil Jorgensen, geologist, teacher and author of "A Guide to New England's Landscape."

The report was designed for its times. As it declared in its introduction, "thanks to [earlier] efforts, many of [the state's] most spectacular landscapes — its large beaches and dramatic mountain tops [for example] — have been protected. But the extensive areas of pastoral scenery: the rolling farmlands, winding country lanes and fields lined by stone walls, so common in [the 1930s], have been largely consumed by development and forest succession. What remains of the Massachusetts landscape has become rare and valuable not only for its scenic beauty but for its agricultural, historic and environmental qualities as well."

The goals of the study were not only to catalog visual values but to suggest an approach to preservation which also matched the climate of the future. It thus chose to swap the traditional acquisition of large parcels of land for an innovative program which would mix the use of conservation restrictions, transfer of development rights, visual easements, siting and design guidelines, zoning regulations, and public education as a way to protect the charm and character of the landscape.

Rather than areas of pristine beauty, so magnificently preserved in earlier eras, landscapes identified in this latest report are, as the text states, "places where man and nature have struck a careful balance, where human activity has complemented rather than destroyed the natural environment. They are beautiful not just because they are visually stimulating, but because they are healthy, invigorating places to live in or to visit."

Again, the determination of visual quality was based upon the subjective interpretation of trained experts, but with clearly defined physical criteria. The results, which were identified on topographic maps in the 268-page report, include only areas larger than a square mile, containing consistently high visual quality. "Distinctive" and "noteworthy" landscapes were found to make up about four percent and five percent, respectively, of the Commonwealth's land area.

Implementation of the report's recommendations obviously depends upon the establishment of a system of regional planning akin to what is happening on Cape Cod. There, as mentioned earlier, the Cape Cod Commission, a planning agency with regional powers and public support, is attempting to balance the need for development with the preservation of what gives the

Cape its charm and character — its traditional landscape, a mix of magnificent open spaces and small town centers.

The moves afoot to create other planning commissions as well, perhaps modeled after Cape Cod, both in Berkshire County and in Franklin County, are encouraging. But until they are in place, it is unlikely, in these times, that any major regional efforts aimed at preserving scenic landscapes on a larger scale can be successful.

11

Planning Shapes the Goals and Ambitions of The Trustees of Reservations

There is little doubt that through the years planning has played a major role in the success of every attempt to protect key areas of open space. Indeed, without its efforts to identify and describe special features of the landscape and offer recommendations for their protection and future use, it is likely far less would have been accomplished. That much has been, is the best testimonial to the continuing need for planning if open space preservation is to persevere and prosper in the years ahead.

Today, The Trustees of Reservations' planning procedures have carefully and realistically identified the organization's own goals and criteria in land conservation. In summary, they call first, for the acquisition or protection of "in-holdings," those parcels of land whose preservation is essential to maintain the integrity of existing reservations; second, for the protection of lands which could link one open space area with another; third, for the preservation of additional "beautiful and historic places" especially in the following geographic areas: Manchester, Essex and Ipswich; the upper Charles River valley; Cohasset and Hingham; Westport and South Dartmouth; Martha's Vineyard; northern Worcester County and within a 20-mile radius of the City of Worcester itself; Deerfield and Sunderland; Cummington and Worthington; South Williamstown; and south Berkshire County.

Each of the regions has a significant share of scenic countryside, as well as the ingredients which offer opportunities for active and successful land conservation programs.

Land Conservation

1

Heart of the Matter: the Properties Themselves

By 1905, The Trustees of Reservations was the proud protector of
five properties totaling some 665 acres of land. Among them
were Rocky Narrows in Sherborn, long recommended for preservation by Frederick Law Olmsted, Jr.; Mount Anne Park in
Gloucester; Petticoat Hill in Williamsburg; Monument Mountain
Reservation in Great Barrington; and Governor Hutchinson's
Field in Milton. As Charles Eliot had predicted in the beginning,
each property had come to The Trustees as a gift. This was to be
the primary pattern for the next century.

There were those acquired during an owner's lifetime as well
as those received as legacies or bequests. At times, donors
interested in a particular parcel would purchase it themselves
and transfer ownership, with the approval of the Standing
Committee, to The Trustees of Reservations. In recent years, most
of the organization's conservation restrictions have been donated
as well. However history measures The Trustees of Reservations
during its first century, it is safe to say that none of its accomplishments would have been possible without the great generosity of the men and women who so loved their properties that
they set them aside for the benefit of future generations. For some
with greater means, it was easier than for others, but for all it was
the satisfaction of knowing, as one donor declared "that you, The
Trustees of Reservations, have helped me save my lovely land
from ruthless and insensitive exploitation."

Coupled with this, of course, was a real feeling for the
spiritual values of the world outdoors and an incontrovertible
belief in the wonders of its powers of restoration. In his essay on
Nature published in 1836, Ralph Waldo Emerson put it best. "To
the body and the mind," he wrote, "which have been cramped by

noxious work or company, nature is medicinal and restores their tone. The tradesman, the attorney, comes out of the din and craft of the street, and sees the sky and woods, and is a man again. In their eternal calm, he finds himself.

"The health of the eye seems to demand a horizon. We are never tired, so long as we can see far enough. . . [and] in other hours, Nature satisfies purely by its loveliness. . . give me health and a day and I will make the pomp of emperors ridiculous. . . ."

2

The First Few: 1897 to 1905

The preservation of Rocky Narrows, some 21 acres on the north bank of the Charles River, popularly known as the "Gates of the Charles," was made possible in 1897 by the generosity of Augustus Hemenway, a member of the corporation and a resident of Canton. The south bank, opposite the reservation, was and still is owned by the Commonwealth. It was first a part of Medfield State Hospital. Later, thanks largely to the efforts of The Trustees, it became Medfield Charles River State Park.

Legislation to transfer the land to the Department of Environmental Management was petitioned for in 1972 by Standing Committee member Thomas B. Williams of Dover, Chairman of the special committee to coordinate the Charles River Protection Program, and committee member Charles W. Eliot II, also a member of the Advisory Council. The measure was enacted by the legislature and signed by Governor Francis W. Sargent a year later.

Standing Committee member Thomas B. Williams, chairman of the Upper Charles River Protection Program

Through the years, Rocky Narrows, with its granite ledges, tall hemlocks and small meadow known as the "Dingle Hole," has been the keystone of The Trustees of Reservations' program to preserve the scenic and environmental values of the upper Charles River, one of the great resources of the Boston Basin.

The year 1897 was a vintage one for the six-year-old organization, for it also marked the acquisition of Mount Anne Park in Gloucester. Now some 87 acres of land, the property, named for Queen Anne of England (1702-1714), includes the summit of Thompson Mountain with its magnificent views of Cape Ann, the shores of Ipswich Bay to the north, and to the east and south the settlements of Gloucester and Magnolia. The Reverend Samuel Thompson, minister of nearby West Parish Meeting House who died in 1724, is buried nearby. The gift of four brothers, William, Charles, Robert and Laurence Minot, in fulfillment of their

Henry Davis Minot, in whose memory Mount Anne Park was dedicated in 1897

father's wish, Mount Anne was a memorial to another son and brother, Henry Davis Minot, who died tragically in a railroad collision near New Florence, Pennsylvania, in 1890. Just 31 years old at the time, he was President of the Eastern Railroad which ran from St. Paul, Minnesota, to Superior, Wisconsin, and the youngest railroad president in the country.

An avid naturalist, Henry Minot was a Harvard classmate and intimate friend of Theodore Roosevelt. Frail in his youth, he took to birding and soon became widely respected for his knowledge. Indeed, when he was only 17, F. W. Putnam Company of Salem published a collection of his essays entitled *The Land Birds and Game Birds of New England*. Nineteen years later, it was republished by Houghton Mifflin as a classic in its field. The town of Minot, North Dakota, was also named for him as a tribute to his career as leader of industry.

In 1954, Mount Anne Park (its donors specifically stipulated that it be preserved as a "wild park") was rededicated by members of the Minot family. A handsome bronze bas-relief head of Henry Minot (Hilda Scudder Manning of Boston was the sculptor) was installed as part of an inscription on the face of a granite ledge which tells the story of the property and for whom it was named. The bronze head, unfortunately, was stolen in the late 1960s. At the time of rededication, the family also generously increased the original endowment from $1,000 to $20,000.

When Route 128 to Gloucester was constructed after World War II, a parking facility was established at the entrance of the reservation. The Standing Committee was enthusiastic about providing public access to Mount Anne and readily gave the construction its approval. But as the years passed, use and then abuse of the property grew and, fearful of jeopardizing the quality of the water supply for Dykes Meadow municipal reservoir (Mount Anne is a major portion of its watershed), the City of Gloucester and The Trustees of Reservations sadly asked the State Department of Public Works to close the parking area. Today, Mount Anne is inaccessible to the public.

Petticoat Hill, in Williamsburg, was given to The Trustees of Reservations in 1905 by Mrs. Martha W. Nash as a memorial to her husband Edward B. Nash of Boston who had "spent at least a portion of his childhood within sight of the reservation." It was named for the sight of freshly washed petticoats drying on the clotheslines of distant farmhouses, for in those days enough of the area was still in agriculture to keep it in pasture and cultivated land. Without trees, views from the hilltop of the surrounding countryside were magnificent. Today, alas, this is not the case. With the disappearance of family farms, the area is all but totally forested and petticoats, of course, are no longer in fashion.

In the early years of the century, Petticoat Hill was easily reached from the city of Northampton, some seven miles to the

Bronze bas-relief by sculptor Hilda Scudder Manning highlights the memorial inscription at Mount Anne

south, by a ride of about an hour on an electric street railway. From its beginnings, it was a popular reservation, but never more so than on one September day in 1921. Then more than 7,000 people, if written reports can be believed, visited the property, picnicked there and enjoyed the fresh waters of its spring as the First Congregational Church of Williamsburg celebrated its 100th anniversary. Today, Petticoat Hill, wisely endowed by Mrs. Nash, totals some 60 acres.

An early photo of Rocky Narrows, "Gates of the Charles"

3

Hutchinson's Field: the 'Finest Prospect' of All

Once a fruit orchard and a part of the estate of Thomas Hutchinson, the last Royal Governor of the Massachusetts Bay Colony, Governor Hutchinson's Field in Milton was acquired by The Trustees of Reservations in 1898. Given in part by John M. Forbes and his sister, Mrs. Mary F. Cunningham, the remainder was purchased by The Trustees with $31,250 raised from public subscription.

Endowed by Mrs. Cunningham and later, in 1983, by the Jessie B. Cox Charitable Trust, the property now totals 10 acres. Although, as an early report states, "its sides and eminences are

Thomas Hutchinson, last Royal Governor of the Province of Massachusetts Bay

covered with the houses of fortunate people," Hutchinson's Field remains today a picture window for the public with spectacular views of the Neponset River, the city of Boston and Boston Harbor beyond. It is passed by thousands of commuters daily.

Born in Boston in 1711, Hutchinson devoted his life to public service. A former Speaker of the House and Chief Justice of the Bay Colony, he sought refuge from the capital city and the cares of government in Milton. His presence in a dwelling designed and built for him in 1743 soon "gave a prominent character to the society of Milton Hill." Earlier, the area was best known as the site of Neponset Mill and a place where the Reverend John Eliot had preached to the Indians at Unquity.

"My house," wrote Governor Hutchinson in a letter to his Sovereign, King George III, in 1774, "is seven or eight miles from town, a pleasant situation and many a gentleman from abroad say it has the finest prospect from it they ever saw."

A gardener of imagination and taste, Hutchinson spent much of his time "with his men setting out and grafting trees." Behind his house he built a formal garden and, with documents and plans surviving from Hutchinson's day, a survey was prepared in 1919 which reproduced its design and character.

All that physically remains of the estate today is the field itself and the "Ha-Ha" (a sunken stone fence designed to separate garden from pasture land where animals graze), which formed the western boundary of the formal garden. The fruit trees, shrubs and plants have gone, as have the many elms, chestnuts and sycamores he planted. But the descendants of the copper beech and cheerful scilla which the Governor is said to have introduced from England still exist on the top of Milton Hill.

In June 1774, six months after the "unhappy affair" since remembered as the Boston Tea Party, Governor Hutchinson went into exile. Walking down the "Lower Way," now Adams Street, he departed, stories say, "nodding and smiling to his neighbors on this side and that, whether Whig or Tory, for he was good friends with all." He took a carriage to Dorchester Point (South Boston), and a boat to the city, where he boarded the vessel "Minerva" and sailed to England. He died in June 1780, and is buried in a church yard at Croyden, some 10 miles south of London.

His property and effects in Milton were sold at auction. The house, ironically, soon became the home of James Warren, whose wife, Mercy Otis Warren, was the brave polemist whose satiric sketches and accounts of the war circulated throughout the colonies during the Revolution. Owned by several families through the years, the house served as quarters for the American Red Cross in Milton during World War II. It was razed in 1946. Governor Hutchinson's writing desk remained and is owned today by the Milton Public Library.

4

Chesterfield Gorge: a Speedy Solution Saves the Day

Since its acquisition of Petticoat Hill in 1905, The Trustees of Reservations had found the going slow. For 23 years — from 1905 to 1928 — no new reservations had been added to the list. But with the completion of the report of the Committee on the Needs and Uses of Open Space in 1929, things began to pick up again. Within the next few years, a number of areas mentioned in the report had been preserved. They included the William Cullen Bryant Homestead in Cummington, which became The Trustees' first historic house and property with land in active agriculture; Misery Islands in Salem Bay; and Chesterfield Gorge in West Chesterfield.

Work on the Bay Circuit, too, was begining to bear fruit. At Plum Island, Newbury, more than 800 acres of ocean beach, sand dunes and salt marsh had been acquired by the Federation of Bird Clubs of New England. Negotiations with landowners in the area, primarily conducted by The Trustees' Laurence Fletcher, indicated by 1931 that as many as 3,000 acres of remarkable wildlife habitat might be preserved. The result was the establishment of a Federal Wildlife Refuge at Plum Island. Massachusetts Audubon Society was also an active partner in the project.

As it has pursued the preservation of open space throughout its history, The Trustees of Reservations has used its "good offices" to work cooperatively and quietly behind the scenes with both public resource agencies and other private environmental organizations to accomplish its goals. The results speak for themselves.

By the late 1930s, for example, The Trustees had assisted with the preservation of 17 major conservation areas besides those reservations it held itself. They included the Harvard Forest in Petersham; Willowdale State Forest in Ipswich and Topsfield; Boxford State Forest; Georgetown-Rowley State Forest; Roland C. Nickerson State Forest in Agawam; Wattatic Mountain in Ashburnham; Willard Brook State Park in Ashby and Townshend; and Gore Place in Waltham. Many of the properties had been offered first to The Trustees of Reservations. But because of their size and lack of endowment — so necessary for maintenance purposes — they were reluctantly, but responsibly, refused by the Standing Committee, but with the understanding that they would go to a public resource agency. This, however, was not to be the case with Chesterfield Gorge.

Always a spectacular sight for both residents and travelers alike, the beauty of its deep canyon, sided by granite cliffs and topped by tall hemlocks and spruce, was once in danger of destruction. As early as 1914, the recreation potential of the Westfield River was discovered by canoeists. From Boston, they came by auto over narrow country roads, or by train on the Massachusetts Central Railway. An early leader of expeditions to the Gorge was Alexander Forbes of Milton, a member of the Appalachian Mountain Club, who, with many others, took part in the adventure of running the river in canoes and kayaks.

In spring, the rough water of the Gorge itself remained unconquered until 1922, when Raymond Emerson of Concord (later a member of the Local Committee for The Old Manse) ran it in a covered kayak. It was the first time the feat had been accomplished.

But it was in May 1929 that the beauty of the Gorge was threatened by destruction. The group in canoes and kayaks had paused as usual in the river above West Chesterfield, then swept down towards the narrows.

"Our coming when we did," wrote Alex Forbes in *Appalachia*, journal of the AMC, "proved providential. To our horror, we saw a lumber gang at work in the woods hard by the head of the Gorge, constructing a bridge across it on the site of the old Boston to Albany Post Road. . . . Inquiry revealed that they were planning to strip the entire east side of the Gorge where pines and hemlocks, nearly a hundred feet high, standing on the very edge of the cliff, rendered it the most striking bit of natural scenery in Massachusetts.

In summer, following their spring turbulence, the waters of the Westfield River run placidly through Chesterfield Gorge.

"Immediately on our return to Boston, we got in touch with the Standing Committee of The Trustees of Reservations. A long-distance call to Westfield halted the cutting one day before the slope was to be stripped. . . . In a few days, negotiations had resulted in the purchase of the land and its transfer to The Trustees. . . who will henceforth hold it inviolate." The action was a perfect testimonial to The Trustees' reasons for being.

Today, that initial acquisition has grown to a total of 161 acres. The Massachusetts Division of Fisheries & Wildlife and the U.S. Army Corps of Engineers now also protect a significant portion of the river downstream from Chesterfield Gorge Reservation.

As for the half-completed new bridge, it was removed as well, leaving only a single abutment of an earlier span built in the eighteenth century. In 1777, it provided an escape route for the red-coated soldiers of General Burgoyne's army. Following their defeat at Saratoga, they marched east, crossing the wooden planks on their way to Boston and the ships that would take them home to England.

Later, the bridge enabled the first regular stagecoach service to New York State to cross the river in ease and comfort. A toll gate was established at the east end of the High Bridge, as it was known, and the gatekeeper's house became the center of a small settlement. Known as The Gate, its shaded burying ground, stone walls and cellar holes remain today.

The Great Flood of 1835, however, spelled disaster for the bridge and for much of the town as well. Its roaring torrent destroyed everything in its path including grist mills, saw mills and carding mills. Although the bridge was rebuilt, the Turnpike Company found it could not compete with competition from canals and the new railroad. It soon declared bankruptcy and the toll gate disappeared forever.

Today, stories of the coaching era are still told on summer evenings by the river. And when the moon is low and the night is dark, if you use your imagination and listen very carefully, you might just hear a four-horse stage crawling slowly up the tortuous hill, pausing at the crest, and then thundering down the steep and rocky track, wheeling with a roar of clattering hoofs onto the wooden planks of the High Bridge, and disappearing in the distant dust on the way to Albany.

5

Great Misery Island: Open Space or an Oil Tank Farm?

Great Misery Island, some 80 acres in size, is located in Salem Bay only a mile or less from the Gold Coast of the North Shore — Prides Crossing, Beverly Farms and Manchester-by-the-Sea.

The modern history of Misery (and Little Misery Island, some five acres, only yards from its larger sister) begins in 1630 with their mention in the log of the *Arbella*. The 350-ton vessel, which brought the Governor of the Massachusetts Bay Colony, John Winthrop, and 300 settlers to the New World, was bound for Salem.

Just how Great and Little Misery got their names is still a mystery. They were referred to in the early records of the Colony as "Morton's Misery" and "Moulton's Misery." Robert Moulton, the records show, was a master ship's carpenter sent over by London adventurers in 1629 to encourage shipbuilding. All of the islands of the bay in those days were heavily wooded and specu-lation has it — although there is no evidence that Moulton owned the islands at any time — that he could have leased them for a supply of timber, easily rafted to the nearby shore. Heaven knows the problems he may have endured.

The Club House at Great Misery Island in the early 1900s with the caddie house and third putting green

At one time, the land on the islands was farmed and during the nineteenth century summer houses — some elegant, some modest — were built on Great Misery.

The islands also served as the site of a fertilizer plant until about 1900, when they were purchased by the Misery Island Club as a summer resort. During its brief heyday the Club flourished. A restaurant, a skeet-shooting range, and a nine-hole golf course added to its attractions. Steam launches ran regularly from West Beach Pier. And with bungalows and homes filled with happy families, the islands became a thriving summer colony.

A commemorative mug discovered some years ago in an antique shop, shows that at least one nineteenth century Harvard College class celebrated its 25th Reunion at the club house. But the venture was not a financial success and the building was destroyed by fire in 1926.

That fire, started accidentally when a caretaker burning brush in the fall lost control of the blaze, also swept the length of the island. It claimed most of the private homes.

But it was a proposal to locate an oil tank farm on Great Misery in 1935 that shocked residents of the region and spurred them to action. Angry and concerned, many of them owners of shorefront property which looked directly out at the islands, they banded together as the North Shore Associates and proposed purchasing the property with contributions, the size of which, ingeniously, would be in direct proportion to their own real estate tax payments.

The appeal was an immediate success. The 68 acres, acquired for a reported $15,000, were given to The Trustees of Reservations with a promise that an endowment would follow. Some years later, Little Misery Island was also purchased and preserved.

During World War II, the islands were "occupied" by the U.S. Coast Guard to prevent saboteurs from landing there and on the mainland and were off-limits to visitors. Slowly, through the decades, fire claimed all of the remaining houses, now abandoned by their owners. But there are grown men and women today who remember, as children, the romance and adventure of exploring the properties, the fascination of furnishings that had been left behind, reading old magazines in the attics, and even playing a piano which remained in one of the last houses to go.

The Trustees now owns all but three acres of land at the north end of Great Misery, still in the hands of a family which has held it for generations. In marked contrast to what was paid for the island as a whole in the mid-'30s, in 1987 The Trustees of Reservations found itself faced with the need to purchase a critical half-acre "in-holding" which was about to be sold for development. Thanks to the efforts of Standing Committee members Ralph Vogel and Mary Waters Shepley, both long-time residents of the

North Shore, 522 people contributed $120,000 in less than three months, more than enough to buy the property and to endow its upkeep. Such is the appeal of the islands.

During the spring, summer and fall months today, Great and Little Misery are more popular than ever. Vistors use them for picnicking and walking, and on summer weekends scores of boats lie at anchor in their coves.

Some six miles to the west, at the entrance to Marblehead harbor, another island property of The Trustees of Reservations lies only a few yards off Peach's Point.

Crowninshield Island (also known as Brown's Island or Orne's Island) is named for Louise DuPont Crowninshield, who, with her husband, was a summer resident of the Point for many years. A great collector and one of the nation's leading advocates of historic preservation (a Louise DuPont Crowninshield Award is presented each year by the U. S. National Trust), Mrs. Crowninshield gave the island to The Trustees of Reservations in 1955.

A gem, only five acres in all, it includes some woodland (oak and pine), a rocky headland, a sandy beach, and a small salt marsh. From its 50-foot height, there is a sweeping view of the entrance to Marblehead Harbor, Salem Bay, the Beverly shoreline and Baker's and Misery Islands. Each summer weekend, hundreds of white sails sparkle on the waters nearby.

During the years prior to World War II, when Marblehead was the yachting capital of America, more than 400 boats would gather for Race Week. They included classes of Q-boats, Eight meters, R-Boats, two divisions of 30-square meter boats, MB's, U.S. One-Designs, Indians, the community's famous Town Class, and Brutal Beasts. Often moored in the outer harbor would be Herbert M. Sears' schooner *Constellation*, 134 feet overall, and near her, the Crowninshield's 109-foot schooner, *Cleopatra's Barge II*. Both flew the burgee of the Eastern Yacht Club, their shiny black hulls mirroring the dancing water around them, and their polished brass glistening in the summer sun.

Frank Crowninshield was fond of the island he owned. It offered a pleasant view from his bathroom, and, during the 1940s, he asked his caretaker to put a few goats on the property so that he could see them in the morning while shaving. The man did as he was bid, but the goats refused to cooperate. Each day as Mr. Crowninshield looked eagerly out of his window for them, they were on the other side of the island, munching contentedly on anything, including poison ivy, that appeared in their path.

Whether the goats were there at all soon became a question in Mr. Crowninshield's mind, and the caretaker, frustrated by the animals' unwillingness to behave as their owner wished and with the complaints he was receiving, decided to take matters into his own hands.

In the barn one day, out of wire and screen laths and concrete, he fashioned a full-size, model goat — horns and all — with its head down, eating grass. Then, one foggy day, he installed it on the right side of the island.

There were no more complaints. Mr. Crowninshield, whose eyesight admittedly was failing with advancing years, happily assumed that the white blob he saw was, indeed, one of the goats. And, if tales told about the incident are to be believed, he never did find out how his caretaker solved the problem. The remains of the concrete "goat" were still on the island in the late 1960s.

6

Lowell Holly: a Peaceful Peninsula on the Cape

Some 130 acres in Mashpee and Sandwich, Lowell Holly Reservation came to The Trustees of Reservations by bequest in 1943 with an endowment of $10,000. The property, which includes an outstanding collection of native American holly as well as a forest of beach trees, plantings of rosebay and catawba rhododendron, and several beaches of soft, white sand, is located on Cataumet Neck, which divides Mashpee and Wakeby Ponds, two of the largest bodies of fresh water on Cape Cod.

Lowell Holly Reservation divides the waters of Wakeby Pond (here) and Mashpee Pond, two of Cape Cod's largest freshwater ponds.

Abbott Lawrence Lowell,
president of Harvard
University and donor of Lowell
Holly Reservation

Lowell Holly was received as a legacy from the late Abbott Lawrence Lowell, who for 24 years (1909 to 1933) had been President of Harvard University. Dr. Lowell, who maintained a summer home in nearby Cotuit (during the winter he lived at 169 Marlborough Street, Boston) used to visit the property nearly every day in the warmer months by horse and wagon during his retirement. He enjoyed its peace and solitude as well as the beauty of its trees and shrubs. With friends and family he cleared a series of cart roads which still exist today.

"While the men worked hard chopping," a young cousin of Mrs. Lowell's recalls, "the women and the children walked, made paths and went swimming. Sometimes there were as many as four carriages or Cape-wagons, which travelled up there in the middle of summer, returning hot and dusty to a very late lunch."

President Lowell purchased the property from John E. Rothery, who had acquired it earlier from Fred Jonas, a Mashpee native and a Wampanoag Indian. When Rothery sold the land, his daughter Agnes recalled, "we flocked around him gleefully. 'All that money! We're rich now, aren't we?' Papa John looked at us thoughtfully. 'Yes [he said], I've sold it. The catheral grove — the beaches where you liked to bathe. And I have a big check for it. But I want you children to understand this: I feel distinctly poorer.'"

Lowell Holly is much the same today as it must have been 50 years ago. Thankfully, as well, some 500 acres of land bordering the reservation to the north were purchased by the town of Sandwich for conservation and recreation purposes in 1976. The Trustees of Reservations aided in the acquisition.

7

In-holdings: Piecing the Puzzle Together at the Ward Reservation

Of all of The Trustees of Reservations' priorities in land conservation, none rates higher than the acquisition of "in-holdings," those parcels of land whose protection as open space is imperative if the integrity of a reservation is to be kept intact. Small or large, they exist everywhere — on the borders of properties or even in the middle — privately-owned parcels which, if developed, as many could be, would destroy the very reason a reservation was preserved in the first place. The opposite bank of a stream or pond. The side of a hilltop. A strip of land in the midst of a magnificent view. Or a portion of barrier beach, swamp or field.

Although dealing with "in-holdings" is a continuous activity, no better example of how to address the problem exists at the Ward Reservation in Andover and North Andover.

Charles W. Ward (1859-1933), was a resident of Brookline for most of his working life. But in 1917, to escape the confines of the suburbs during the hot summer months, he purchased land in Andover known as the old Holt Farm.

The house itself was built in the early eighteenth century. Its views across the still rural and primarily agricultural landscape were magnificent. Indeed, Charles Ward so loved the place that he wrote in his will that he wished "to have a portion of the property, and all of it eventually, used in some suitable manner to benefit some deserving organization." Seven years after his death in 1940, his widow deeded some 107 acres of land to The Trustees of Reservations. An endowment was added later.

Through the years, thanks primarily to the interest, energies and patient persistence of John Ward Kimball, Mrs. Ward's grandson, numerous parcels have been added to the property. Today the Ward Reservation totals more than 640 acres.

The job was not easy. Fortunately, Dr. Kimball, a scientist, university professor and the author of several college texts, occupied the Holt house with his wife and children and thus was on the scene. Preliminary planning identified more than two dozen parcels of land, each with a different owner, which needed to be acquired to provide adequate protection for the remainder. Most would have to be purchased. Thankfully, none were built upon but this meant that the project must get underway immediately.

Teacher, scholar and author Dr. John W. Kimball, Chairman of the Local Committee for the Ward Reservation, Andover and North Andover

An exciting challenge came in 1967 when the Trustees of Phillips Academy offered to give some 64 acres to the reservation if it could be matched on a two-to-one basis. The Trustees of Reservations committed $14,000 to the project. The rest would have to be raised as needed.

That first year, four parcels were acquired totalling 32 acres. One, Dr. Kimball reported, represented "the culmination of several years of negotiations." The following year, five acres of wetland were added. And so it went, year after year, until, in 1973, the goal of 128 acres had been achieved and Phillips Academy had made good on its promise. But the patient work went on. An additional 35 acres, a vital hilltop, was purchased in 1974. And land was added later both by gift and by purchase.

When the in-holdings acquisition project began in 1967, the Ward Reservation totaled 340 acres. When the intensive portion of it ended in 1976, the property included 597 acres, an increase of 257 acres or 75 percent of the original land area. No parcel acquired exceeded more than 35 acres in size.

But the project should not be measured in numbers. What it really accomplished was the addition of orchards, woodland and open field as well as the preservation of spectacular views — to the south of the Boston skyline, and to the north of Mount Monadnock. And, most important, it had eliminated the threat of development which could have seriously jeopardized the character of the reservation and the beauty of its natural landscape forever.

Acquiring in-holdings is often time-consuming, unglamorous and expensive, but however it is characterized, it is an essential part of the process of land preservation.

8

Old Town Hill: Dream of a Lifetime

West of Plum Island across the tidal estuary of the Plum Island River stands Old Town Hill. A pastured drumlin, it offers spectacular views of the salt marshes of Plum Island Sound, the narrow strip of Plum Island itself, the mouth of the Merrimack River at Newburyport, and Ipswich Bay. A lone elm at its top for years had been a landmark for early mariners, and its branches had offered shelter for religious gatherings.

In 1929, the southern half of the hill was acquired by Stephen P. Hale, an elderly gentleman of admittedly limited means. But he so loved the property that, despite a malady which left him crippled, he is reported to have climbed the hill every day of his

Posts called "staddles" supported stacks of salt hay cut by farmers on the Newbury marshes at Old Town Hill Reservation many years ago.

life.

Hoping some day that Old Town Hill would become a park so that others could enjoy it as much as he did, he had repeatedly refused to sell his land to speculators despite offers as high as $15,000. In 1952, however, he offered his 25 acres to The Trustees of Reservations for $5,000. Tragically, a few days after the deed was signed and his dream of a lifetime had been realized, Stephen Hale shot and killed himself.

Old Town Hill Reservation today totals more than 372 acres. The primary benefactor of the property, besides Stephen Hale himself, was Mrs. George Bushee, for many years owner of neighboring Newman Farm. It was she who made possible the original purchase, added many acres of land, and provided an endowment.

A noted horsewoman who, in the mid-1930s, became famous for driving her coach-and-four from the Waldorf Astoria Hotel in New York to Atlantic City, New Jersey, in record time, Mrs. Bushee was a woman of considerable wealth and a generosity to match. The daughter of William Robie Evans, a former president of the Boston Five Cents Savings Bank, she was married twice, ultimately to George Bushee, a retired minister who had served in Congress.

Besides her farm, whose show horses had won her many blue ribbons and silver trophies throughout the U.S. and Canada, she took great interest in the historic character of her community, preserving open space, and restoring three seventeenth century houses on Newbury's Lower Green. Although childless herself, she assisted scores of children with their educations. Her name today is synonymous with the success of the reservation.

Other benefactors of Old Town Hill include Elliott and Mary Perkins of Cambridge, who loved to escape the city to their place on Hay Street overlooking the property and the surrounding countryside of Newbury with its winding tidal estuaries and its sweeping expanse of salt marsh. Perkins, a professor of history at Harvard and Master of Lowell House for many years, combined a Puritan formality and the intellectualism of academia with a temperament which enjoyed hugely the life and people of the out-of-doors. It was a characteristic which may have come from a year he spent in his youth as a cowhand on a Wyoming ranch. He mixed as well with neighboring farmers and fishermen as he did with fellow faculty members and enjoyed them all for what they had to offer of life. His home at Little River, Newbury, was a beloved sanctuary. It is thanks to his and his wife's generosity that future generations will be able to enjoy the wild beauty around it as much as they did. Others donors of land include Mrs. Mary P. Barton and Dr. Storer P. Humphreys.

Today, the reservation gives pleasure to scores of visitors annually, and there are those in the area who still fondly remember it as Hale's Old Town Hill.

Master of Harvard's Lowell House and donor of land at Old Town Hill, Professor Elliott Perkins, left, and his wife Mary look over maps of the area with Wayne Mitton, Supervisor of The Trustees of Reservations' Northeast Management Region.

9

The Mission House and a Grander Presence in Berkshire County

By 1948, it was clear that with 24 reservations to care for and a deficit operating budget, no new properties should be acquired without endowment. Happily this was not a problem when, in October, Miss Mabel Choate offered The Trustees of Reservations a gift of the Mission House in Stockbridge. For not only was it an historic property of national importance, it was accompanied by a most generous contribution of $103,000, the income from which, it was deemed, would make it satisfactorily self-sufficient.

Mabel Choate was the daughter of Joseph Hodges Choate, a lawyer of international renown whose accomplishments and abilities led him to be appointed the last U. S. Ambassador to the Court of St. James's during the reign of Queen Victoria.

A resident of New York City, he was born in Salem, Massachusetts, in 1832, nephew of another celebrated attorney, Rufus

Choate, who himself was born in the Choate House at Hog Island, Essex — now a part of The Trustees' Cornelius and Miné S. Crane Wildlife Refuge — and later served in Congress and in the U.S. Senate.

Early in his career, one of Joseph Choate's partners, Charles F. Southmayd, persuaded him to come to Stockbridge for the summer to escape the heat of New York. Finally, after renting in the village for a decade, he and Mrs. Choate purchased 49 acres of land at Prospect Hill.

It was a difficult sloping site, but there in 1885, with the assistance of the brilliant young architect, Stanford White, and a pioneer in landscape design, Nathaniel Barrett, the Choates built Naumkeag in the great shingle style of the Gilded Era. It was the Indian name for Salem (meaning place of rest), the city of his birth.

Choate's wealth, which was considerable (although his was certainly not one of the large fortunes of the era), enabled his daughter Mabel, who never married, to summer comfortably at Naumkeag for the rest of her life. She took a great and generous interest in the community, transforming the old Stockbridge Casino into the Berkshire Playhouse and art gallery, and, in 1929, moving the historic Mission House to Main Street, restoring it, furnishing it and opening it to the public.

The Mission House was built in 1739 for the Reverend John Sergeant, first missionary to the Stockbridge Indians, and his wife, the former Abigail Williams, whose half-brother, Ephraim, Jr., was the founder of Williams College.

There was no doubt that Sergeant, a graduate of Yale, a student of the great Jonathan Edwards and a deeply devout man, was there to bring Christianity to the Indians. But Abigail had different ideas. It was she, with a few others, who "civilized" Stockbridge, turning it from a humble missionary settlement into an expanding English town.

The Mission House was a symbol of her quest for sophistication on what was then the western frontier. Not one to live in a log cabin or in the village with the Indians, Abigail, who history has it was vivacious, pretty and of a practical turn of mind, wanted a house on the hill with more than a touch of elegance. With its two chimneys and handsomely carved front doorway, its pine-paneled interior and stone fireplaces, she got it in the Mission House.

In private hands for nearly two centuries, the property was all but derelict in 1927 when Mabel Choate bought it and decided to move it off the hill to Main Street where it would be more accessible as a monument to the town's history. The house was disassembled and numbered, piece by piece. A site was selected on the west end of Main Street, only a stone's throw from where John

Sergeant, prior to his marriage, had lived with the Indians in a log cabin.

In need of professional assistance, Miss Choate called upon the services and imagination of Fletcher Steele, a landscape architect of national distinction (and at the time, a member of the Standing Committee of The Trustees of Reservations), and between them they restored the house itself and created around it the kind of an environment which they imagined might have existed in the eighteenth century. They added a grape arbor; a well; a low, shed-like building which houses a small collection of Indian artifacts; a barn, which also included an apartment on its second floor; and, as a highlight, herb and flower gardens featuring species of plants from the Colonial era.

The interior was filled with an admirable collection of period furniture and as much Sergeant memorabilia as Miss Choate could find, including documents, books, and a New England armchair used by Sergeant himself.

The process of rehabilitating the structure — including its move to Main Street — and readying it to serve as a house museum, although it may have differed markedly from what might have been done today, was much in keeping with the thinking of its time.

Generous with her praise of Steele's role in the restoration, Miss Choate wrote John D. Rockefeller, Jr., who had visited the house in 1943 and admired it greatly, that "it was Fletcher Steele who did the whole thing except the furnishing of the interior.

The Mission House in its early years. Main Street in Stockbridge was lined with an impressive collection of handsome American elms, as were so many streets in New England country towns.

"I am afraid if it had not been for him," she wrote, "I should have painted it white with apple-green shutters and put umbrellas on the lawn and made it altogether horrible; but through his knowledge and inspiration, I learned what really should be done. It was his research that gave us the proper color for the rooms."

Steele was at the height of his career at the time and could claim to have designed some of the nation's finest gardens. Artistic, individualistic, and aristocratic, he mixed an unerring eye for design with a practical knowledge of plant materials and was often seen on the blade of a bulldozer directing it hither and yon as it sculpted the ground beneath it. He had attended Harvard's School of Landscape Architecture for two years, but never received a degree. "Throughout my life," he said, "I've learned more from experience than from formal education."

From 1929 to 1948, when the Mission House became a property of The Trustees of Reservations, it was administered by the Stockbridge Mission House Association, a committee (with Miss Choate as Chairman) of local residents and friends. But its transfer to The Trustees, with Miss Choate getting on in years and her doctor suggesting that she "slow down," made sense. It also provided the organization with the first property in its collection that was adequately endowed.

That Fletcher Steele was in large part responsible for the acquisition there is little doubt. Indeed, the Standing Committee recorded a formal vote thanking him for using his "good offices" so effectively.

The Mission House clearly fit The Trustees' commitment to preserve sites of "historic interest," and, although its acquisition was a departure from an early emphasis on open space, a precedent had been set by the purchase of the Old Manse, and the acceptance of the Bryant Homestead and the Great House at Castle Hill.

As costs escalated, however, the Standing Committee was to grow increasingly apprehensive about acquiring houses or buildings of any sort. Yet the Mission House, with its significant endowment, seemed to be one that could be managed effectively. It was also the precursor of another property which was to come from Miss Choate as well.

Miss Mabel Choate: "a natural friendliness, generous to a fault, she gave patronage meaning, respect, and understanding. . . "

10

Naumkeag: Another Gem from the Hand of a Great Benefactor

Even before discussions about a transfer of the Mission House to The Trustees of Reservations were complete, letters indicate that Naumkeag was to be next on the list. It was generally agreed that it should come by bequest, to exemplify, as Miss Choate wrote in 1947, 11 years before her death, "life and living conditions at the end of the nineteenth century. . . a sort of a place they call in The National Trust [of England], a 'country house museum.'"

Although the proposal had the enthusiastic support of certain members of the Standing Committee, including Chairman Charles S. Bird, when the news reached the ears of Sheffield resident Walter Prichard Eaton, Chairman of the Local Committee for Bartholomew's Cobble, a different point of view was expressed.

Eaton, a professor at Yale and a distinguished figure who had served as chairman of the university's Department of Drama, wrote Laurence Fletcher that he was "struck speechless by the idea. What on earth do The Trustees want of the Choate place?" he asked. "It isn't an old house, it isn't a beautiful house, and it has one of the most horrendous gardens in the Commonwealth."

Not one to be reticent, he continued: "Choate had no connection with the Berkshires except as a summer resident. . . He was a witty and able lawyer, who might have been a great man, per-

Naumkeag and the Afternoon Garden pleasantly shaded from the heat of summer by a gigantic elm. Like so many others, it fell victim to Dutch elm disease.

haps, but [he] certainly missed the opportunity. I really can't see why The Trustees should take over this white elephant of a house. The Mission House, yes. Maybe that is what you mean," he concluded. "I hope so." Eaton was not alone in his opinions, but a majority of the Standing Committee felt differently and discussions about the ultimate acquisition of Naumkeag endured.

Understandably, of particular concern was the size of its endowment. The sum sought was one which would yield an annual income of some $16,000. As Miss Choate wrote to Charles Bird in the summer of 1947, "You probably know that [I] have a trust. . . amounting to $20,000,000. . . I have already two small trusts for individuals in this pool. . . and I am hoping to make another for the Mission House.

"It seems doubtful whether I could make such a big one as this must be during my lifetime, but I could have this done in my will. . . . I am delighted that you yourself feel as you do about it [Naumkeag], and I do hope we can come to some agreement." Again, one of those who would be most helpful in reaching an accord would be Fletcher Steele.

There was no doubt about it, Steele had a special charm. Fun-loving, sophisticated, and delightfully entertaining, it was true that most of his clients became his friends as well. But there was a mystical side to him, too, as Steele's biographer Robin Carson of Amherst explains.

"Fletcher Steele made gardens as playgrounds for people's imaginations," she writes. "Wealthy women in the '20s and '30s had given up a large part of their inner selves in order to function

Fletcher Steele, master designer of the landscape at Naumkeag

Blue tiles, brought back from the Orient by Miss Choate in 1935, brighten the roof of the temple in the Chinese Garden, while dragons guard its Spirit Walk.

in society. . . . They were dominated by their husbands, they had to belong to certain clubs, dress in a certain way. Then Steele would come in — this passionate and dashing bachelor — and try to peer into their deepest and most private self and give them landscapes in which to dream. The making of a landscape was an adventure. . . like a drama unfolding. And the client had a major role to play."

Naumkeag was a fascinating reflection of this lavish and imaginative world of dreams, from the secret romance of its Chinese Garden, its birch walk and stairways with cascading water and its tree-shaded Afternoon Garden surrounded by colorful Venetian pilings, to its rose garden with serpentine pathways of pink marble chips, its elaborate topiary, and its soft terraces with their magnificent views of the distant Berkshire hills.

Ten years passed all too quickly and by December 1958 Mabel Choate was dead at 88 and the curtain had rung down on a golden age. Naumkeag did come to the The Trustees of Reservations with an endowment that seemed generous at the moment, more than $600,000. And as time passed, and others of the Great Houses of Berkshire County were sold and transformed, the idea that preserved Naumkeag grew more important each year.

As for Mabel Choate, she was to be remembered with affection and respect and sorely missed upon the streets of Stockbridge. For despite her wealth, she had, as *The Berkshire Eagle* declared in an editorial following her death, "a natural friendliness that her neighbors responded to instintively. It was no boughten response, although she was generous to a fault in her support of all village activities and Berkshire enterprises. It came from the manner of her giving and the warm encouragement she gave to any endeavor, especially in the field of fine arts and conservation. . . .

"The age of the patron is fast waning and Miss Choate was South Berkshire's last important one. In cultivating those areas where only personal, purposeful beneficence can bring forth flower and fruit, she gave patronage meaning, respect and understanding."

The editorial was written by Lawrence K. "Pete" Miller, editor and later publisher and owner of the *Eagle,* who had worked with Miss Choate on many worthy Berkshire causes and who served with great distinction himself as a member of the Standing Committee.

Certainly, Miss Choate was one of The Trustees' great benefactors and the properties whose preservation she made possible are two of the gems of its collection.

11

Bartholomew's Cobble: a 'Rock Garden' of Rare Distinction

As early as 1920, Berkshire resident S. Waldo Bailey, who was to become one of the country's most noted naturalists, visited Bartholomew's Cobble in Sheffield. It was, he reported, "a pleasure to find such a rare rock garden." In the years that followed, thousands of others were to echo his remarks, especially representatives of The Trustees of Reservations.

For Bartholomew's Cobble, orginally a cow pasture of some 20 acres of land bordering the Housatonic River, has become a mecca for botanists and birders from around the world because of its unique geological and topographical characteristics.

Although early Cobble custodians reported with some amusement that visitors have approached with a pair of worn shoes in their hands, a "cobble" in reality is a rocky hillock or stone island rising from alluvial bottom land. "Bartholomew" was the name of an early owner of the property.

Naturalists, from Professor C.A. Weatherby at Harvard University's celebrated Gray Herbarium, to Bailey himself (who later became the reservation's much-beloved Warden), have catalogued more than 740 plants at the Cobble, including 52 species of ferns. Ornithologists also have identified some 235

The quiet waters of the Housatonic River reflect the trees and ledges of Bartholomew's Cobble, milk cows graze on meadowland nearby.

different species of birds, which even the great Roger Tory Peterson found "surprising for an inland area." One September day, for example, watchers at the Cobble counted 4,300 migrating broadwinged hawks.

The Trustees of Reservations, which had its eyes on the area for many years, was finally able to purchase the property in 1946. Funds for the purpose were raised from public subscription and, thanks to Miss Mabel Choate, provided by a grant from the Founder's Fund of the Garden Club of America.

Because of its unique characteristics, the Cobble immediately attracted a special following. Author and essayist Hal Borland, winner of the John Burroughs Award for the best in nature writing and a resident of nearby Salisbury, Connecticut, became an active member of the Local Committee. He was joined by Boughton Cobb, a New York architect best known for his *Field Guide to the Ferns*; ecologist John Storer, whose landmark publications *The Web of Life* and *Man and the Web of Life* are considered two of the best texts ever produced on the balance of nature; Amy Bess Miller of Pittsfield, founder and president of Hancock Shaker Village; and Morgan G. Bulkeley, farmer, naturalist, and author of "Our Berkshires", a weekly newspaper column about the natural world of Berkshire County. With such luminaries at the helm, the Cobble prospered as a living museum of natural history.

Its worth was recognized by the National Park Service and, in 1971, it was designated a National Natural Landmark. In the early 1970s as well, as a result of a major campaign to raise a regional

Morgan G. Bulkeley, long-time chairman of the local committee, confers with Warden-Naturalist Howard T. Bain at Bartholomew's Cobble.

record $167,500 from public subscription, additional lands were added. Today the area includes nearly 280 acres. They vary from wetland along the Housatonic to a hilltop pasture with spectacular views of the mountain ridges of the Taconic Range to the west, and of Monument Mountain up the river valley to the north.

The campaign also included the acquisition of the Colonel John Ashley House located nearby, the oldest house (1735) in Berkshire County. The Ashley House is now a part of Bartholomew's Cobble Reservation, as the land itself had been a part of Colonel Ashley's original grant. Famous as the site of the "Sheffield Declaration," a petition against British tyranny written in 1773, the Ashley House also was home to the slave "Mum Bett," who won her freedom in a celebrated legal decision that established an enduring precedent in human rights.

As time passed, the Cobble yielded new treasures: Indian artifacts from arrowheads to stone tools which may be seen today in the collection at the Waldo Bailey Museum, established in his memory some decades ago. Geologists continue to marvel at the property's 500-million-year-old rocks that settled as sediment from the Permian and Ordovician inland seas. And visitors still seek out the rare Scott's spleenwort and, in season, admire, as botanist Rutherford Platt did, "a greater variety of prized wild-flowers than I have seen anywhere else in a single square mile."

No one is more responsible for what the Cobble is today than Morgan G. Bulkeley, who served as chairman of the Local Committee for nearly a quarter of a century. There were those in 1972 who doubted that Berkshire residents would subscribe to a campaign to buy conservation land in a county where open space seemed so plentiful.

But it was the combination of local history and a growing concern for the Berkshire's beloved but fast-disappearing agricultural landscape, both often mentioned in Bulkeley's weekly columns in *The Eagle*, that caught the imagination of the region and its residents and incited their generosity.

The $167,500, which included a moderate endowment for the Ashley House, was raised within three years. Of vital importance to the success of the campaign was the commitment of its committee. It included Honorary Chairman Lawrence M. "Pete" Miller, then publisher of *The Berkshire Eagle*; celebrated author and naturalist Hal Borland and retired Yale University Professor Arnold Whitridge, both of whom represented interests in Connecticut; and, of course, Morgan Bulkeley who, as Chairman, worked tirelessly with General Headquarters of The Trustees of Reservations and directed activities locally from his home in Pittsfield.

Not only did Bulkeley's energies, devotion and leadership add new dimensions to the Cobble, they provided for its protection in perpetuity and insured forever its reputation as a reservation of national prominence and distinction. In honor of all of his accomplishments, Bulkeley received The Trustees of Reservations' annual Conservation Award in 1972. The ceremony took place at a special luncheon at Bartholomew's Cobble on a warm October day. It was attended by more than 220 people.

12

Redemption Rock: Symbol of a Woman's Courage

Redemption Rock, with its one-quarter acre of land, is the smallest property of The Trustees of Reservations. Its size, however, is made up for by its historic importance and by the extraordinary account which accompanied its preservation.

As Frederick Lewis Weis wrote in 1930, "the famous *Narrative of Captivity and Redemption* by Mary Rowlandson, devout helpmate of Lancaster's first ordained minister" tells the hair-raising tale of her capture by a band of marauding Indians and her later release.

"First issued from the press in 1682," Weis continued, "it is an eloquently pathetic record of grave perils bravely encountered, and terrible sufferings patiently borne with an unswerving faith in the wisdom and mercy of an overruling Providence." The story itself begins at sunrise on the winter morning of February 10, 1675, in the frontier town of Lancaster, Massachusetts.

"Hearing the noise of guns," Mrs. Rowlandson begins, "we looked out: [there were] Indians in great numbers; several houses were burning, and the smoke ascending to heaven. . . . At length they came and beset our own house. . . the bullets seem to fly like hail. . . [the] house was on fire over our heads. . . [and there were scores of] Indians before us with their guns, spears and hatchets"

By the end of the day, of the 50 families in town, 23 members had been killed and an equal number taken captive. Among the latter was Mary Rowlandson, wounded herself by a bullet in her side; an older daughter; her two sons, age 13 and 10; and Sarah, age six, who, like her mother, had been shot and injured in the massacre.

News of a possible uprising had come 20 days earlier from a Christian convert of the Nashaway tribe employed by the English as a scout, but colonial officials failed to heed his warning. It was only when another Indian scout confirmed the report that authorities began to move. Unfortunately, however, too little time remained.

Just before midnight on February 9, the scout, exhausted by an 80-mile journey through the wilderness on snowshoes from New Braintree, arrived at the house of Major Gookin in Cambridge with the news that the tribes were on the warpath and the assault was to take place on the following day.

Quickly, the Major dispatched a messenger to Concord and Marlborough, ordering military companies there to assist the garrisons at Lancaster. Captain Samuel Wadsworth received the message at daybreak and, with his command of some 40 men, he hurried to help the community, already under siege, some 10 miles to the west.

A few days earlier, as rumors of the pending attack had swept settlements throughout the Nashua River valley, Lancaster's minister, the Reverend Joseph Rowlandson, and Lieutenant Henry Kerley, the chief military officer of the town, as well as a number of other leading citizens, had journied to Boston to seek assistance. Alas, they were to be too late. By the time aid arrived, the town was a smoking ruin and the dead and dismembered lay everywhere.

The gripping story of Mary Rowlandson's capture and suffering, told in her own words, has impressed generations of readers with her bravery and fortitude.

"I had often before this said," wrote Mary Rowlandson, "that if the Indians should come, I should choose to be killed by them, than [be] taken alive; but when it came to the trial, my mind changed; their glittering weapons so daunted my spirit, that I chose rather to go along. . . than [at] that moment to end my days."

For more than three months, until she was ransomed in the spring of 1675, Mrs. Rowlandson endured the most unimaginable hardships and exhibited the most extraordinary courage. Her daughter and two sons were missing and her youngest child lay slowly dying in her arms. As the Indians left Lancaster and moved out into the wilderness to escape the English militia, they offered their prisoners little comfort.

"It quickly began to snow," Mrs. Rowlandson reported, "and when night came on, they stopped. . . now I must sit down in the snow by a little fire. . . with my sick child in my lap, and calling for water, being now [because of her wound] in a violent fever. My own wound also growing so stiff that I could scarce sit down or rise up; yet so it must be that I must sit all this cold winter night upon the snowy ground with my sick child in my arms. . . still the Lord upheld me. . . and we were both alive to see the light of the next morning."

On foot and on horseback, Mrs. Rowlandson was driven north and westward by the Indians. After eight days, Sarah died and was buried by the trail and although she saw her other children on occasion, she never knew if either of them would survive. Her own wound she cured with a poultice of oak leaves while the Indians, still pursued by English troops, took her through the forests and swamps of Princeton, Barre, Petersham and Northfield to the Connecticut River and finally, to New Hampshire and Vermont.

She learned to eat what little food was offered — tree roots, ground nuts, gruel or raw meat — constantly feared for her life, and suffered the taunts and beatings of her Indian captors. "My head was light and dizzy, my knees feeble, my body raw by sitting day and night. . ." Throughout her ordeals, she reported, only her Faith sustained her.

When the Indians discovered she could sew, she fared somewhat better. In the Connecticut River valley she met the great eastern chieftain King Philip "who spake to me about making a shirt for his boy, which I did, for which he gave me a shilling." Philip had just returned from his winter quarters on the Hudson where, with more than 1,000 warriors, he had sought powder and shot from the Dutch and had hoped to lead the Mohawks and Canadian Indians in a campaign against the colonists of Massachusetts.

Meanwhile, however, the Reverend Rowlandson was hard at work on a plan to free his wife and children and as many other captives as he could. Assisted in his efforts by two Christian Indians who acted as messengers, he finally sought help from a Concord resident by the name of John Hoar, who he knew was held in great respect by Indians throughout the region.

By May, the Indians had set up camp on the west side of Mount Wachusett and it was here at an isolated granite ledge in

Historic postcard shows "Old Hunter and Trapper Joe W. Mason" pointing to the legend at Redemption Rock, Princeton. According to the card, the Worcester-to-Gardner bus passed the site daily and "refreshments were served at the Rock."

Princeton, now named Redemption Rock, that the final negotiations took place. Despite threats to his own life, Hoar finally succeeded in freeing Mary Rowlandson for 20 pounds and a "pint of liquors."

Both escaped to Concord and traveled to Boston where Mrs. Rowlandson was joyously reunited with her husband. Not long afterwards, thanks to the continuing efforts of the Governor of the Bay Colony and its Council, other prisoners, including the Rowlandson children, were set free as well.

"It was but the other day," Mrs. Rowlandson concluded philosophically, "that if I had the world, I would have given it for my freedom. . . . I have learned to look beyond the present and smaller troubles, and to be quieted under them. . . "

In 1879, U.S. Senator George Frisbee Hoar of Worcester, descendant of John Hoar and later first President of The Trustees of Reservations, purchased Redemption Rock and had the following legend inscribed upon its face:

> *Upon this rock May 2nd, 1676 was made*
> *the agreement for the ransom of*
> *Mrs. Mary Rowlandson of Lancaster*
> *between the Indians and John Hoar of Concord.*
> *King Philip was with the Indians*
> *but refused his consent.*

Redemption Rock was given to The Trustees in 1952 by John Hoar and John Hoar, Jr. It borders watershed lands protecting the water supply of the city of Fitchburg. Mid-State Trail runs through the property to the summit of Mount Wachusett. Leominster State Forest is also nearby.

(The discrepancy in dates — 1675 and 1676 — is due to the fact that the Gregorian Calendar was not adopted until 1752. Previous to that, the new year began in March. Thus the destruction of Lancaster is recorded as February 10, 1675-76.)

13

Agassiz Rock: the Story of a Christening

Agassiz Rock in Manchester has been recognized as a scenic and scientific landmark of Essex County for more than a century. The huge glacial boulder, now a part of 104-acre Agassiz Rock Reservation, draws its name from Harvard University's famed Profes-

Early visitors pose for a stereoscopic slide photo of Agassiz Rock, a giant glacial erratic. Note the ladder which offers access to the top of the rock and a view of the ocean off Manchester.

sor Jean Louis Rodolphe Agassiz (1807-1873), who first recognized its scientific interest.

Agassiz Rock was formally christened in 1874 by Salem's Essex Institute, which itself, some years earlier, had preserved Ship Rock in Danvers, another huge glacial boulder. Miss Frances L. Burnett, widely-respected North Shore naturalist and historian, who, for many years served as Chairman of the Local Committee for Agassiz Rock Reservation, discovered the story of the naming of Agassiz Rock in *The Beetle and the Wedge*, a periodical published in Manchester in 1875.

The Bulletin of the Essex Institute, dated October 1884, describes the formal vote. "In reply to a call for the account of the large boulder in the Manchester woods which had been visited by the party, the Secretary, Mr. John Robinson, stated that he had taken great pleasure, during the morning, in visiting the curious boulder in the woods on the road to Essex.

"After a pleasant but difficult walk through woods and clearings," the Bulletin continued, "and finally by a scramble to the summit of the hill upon which many boulders rest, they came to the rock designated. It is about half the size of Ship Rock, so justly celebrated, and in the shape almost of a cube, of perhaps twenty feet on a side, one end resting upon the ledge which forms the hill, and the other propped up about two feet by a wedge-shaped rock, the sharp end downwards; the base of the thus inverted wedge is against the underside of the boulder. Beneath is room for two persons to crawl, and the glacial scratches upon the ledge, being so well protected, are nearly perfect, while a sidelong glance shows the surface of the ledge to be quite smoothly polished.

"Mr. Robinson, after speaking of the importance of such characteristic boulders in demonstrating the glacial theory, and of the interest expressed by the late Professor Agassiz, while visiting this rock some years since, made, at the suggestion of some residents of Manchester, the following motion, which was unanimously accepted, after being seconded by Mr. Lewis N. Tappan, who offered some remarks on the subject, including reminiscences of Professor Agassiz' visit on the spot.

"'Voted, that the boulder visited during the morning by the party from the Essex Institute Field Meeting held in Manchester, Oct. 2, 1874, be named and hereafter known as *Agassiz Rock.*'"

Swiss-born Louis Agassiz, appointed Professor of Natural History at Harvard's Lawrence Scientific School in 1848, was the leader of the natural history movement in America. A vigorous, stimulating personality, he lectured to thousands throughout the East. Agassiz also began the collections which later became the Harvard Museum of Comparative Zoology.

His influence as a teacher was immense. Perhaps his most distinguished writing appears in his *Contributions to the Natural*

History of the United States. Its four volumes were published between 1857 and 1863 and include his *Essay on Classification*, which opposed Charles Darwin's process of natural selection.

Agassiz' wife, Elizabeth Cary Agassiz, was a founder of Radcliffe College and served as President from 1894 to 1902. In 1885, she wrote a two-volume biography of her husband.

Just when Professor Agassiz first visited the boulder is not known. However, Miss Burnett reports that "Mrs. William Hoare of Manchester [once] told me that her grandfather, Mr. Frederick Burnham, guided Professor Agassiz to the rock."

Agassiz Rock Reservation also includes a second glacial boulder, located in a wooded swamp, known as "Big Agassiz." Beneath the area's hemlock, beech and maple, are ledges carpeted with mosses and lichens, bearberry, ground pine, blueberry and huckleberry. The view from Beaverdam Hill looks out over Beaverdam swamp and the rooftops of the town to the waters of Massachusetts Bay.

Initial purchase of the property by The Trustees of Reservations in 1957 was made possible by the generosity of Arthur W. Stevens of Boston, a summer resident of Manchester for two generations. Additional parcels land have been donated as well as purchased.

Today, Agassiz Rock Reservation is part of an historic area of open space which stretches for more than half a mile along School Street and Southern Avenue in Manchester and Essex.

In the early days, all of the area in both communities was cut to provide timber for shipbuilding and for firewood. Records

Discussing what steps to take following an infestation of hemlock looper at Agassiz Rock Reservation in the mid-1970s. From left, Standing Committee member Robert Livermore, Jr.; Deputy Director Garret F. VanWart; Chairman of the local committee Frances L. Burnett; Treasurer Richard L. Frothingham; and Forester Hugh Putnam, now Executive Director of the New England Forestry Foundation

show that as early as 1710, a series of wood lots was parcelled out to residents of Chebacco Parish, Ipswich, which later became the Town of Essex. In much the same way, land was subdivided into wood lots for Manchester residents as well.

Late in the last century, the woods were immensely popular as a place to drive carriages. However, a number of citizens were concerned that logging practices would destroy the beauty of the area. In 1879, they banded together to form the Woodland Park Trust to purchase property on either side of the roadway to preserve it as forest land. Included in the Trust's acquisitions was Cathederal Pines in Manchester.

In recent years, thanks to the efforts of the Manchester Conservation Trust, a major portion of the surrounding woodland has been protected as well. And although there are still some inholdings of private property, the land looks much the same as it must have to carriage riders in the 1890s.

And if you ask an old-timer about the place today, you might hear the story of Bishop's Grave, a stone marker which identifies the site where a resident of Essex died while walking in the woods a century ago; or of Baby's Rock, where a child was found deep in the forest after it had wandered away from its parents who, perhaps, were gathering firewood to heat their home.

14

The Pierce House: General Headquarters for 27 Years

Although in January 1899 the Standing Committee regarded Governor Hutchinson's Field as "the most important and valuable [property] historically and intrinsically yet received," more than half a century later there was little doubt in anyone's mind that the view, at least, was better from the Pierce House next door. And this, as well as a series of other factors, led to its being accepted by The Trustees of Reservations in 1958.

The house and some six acres of land, had been left to the corporation as a bequest of Henry L. Pierce with the provision that it be offered first to The Trustees of Reservations. If refused, it was then to go to the Town of Milton, and, if refused again, to Mr. Pierce's sister.

The recommendations of the special committee appointed to study the proposal (Standing Committee members Charles W. Eliot II and Fletcher Steele, both landscape architects) were clear. Number one, was to agree to accept "the whole property —

including the house" despite misgivings by some members of the board about the expense of acquiring another structure.

"From the house on the very top of the hill," Eliot and Steele wrote in their report, "the axis of the Neponset River is directly in the center of the outlook. And land and ocean lie beyond in an unrivalled combination of city and ocean beauty. It is finer than anything seen from Governor Hutchinson's Field. . . if we let the house go, the best of all goes with it."

The site also has its own relationship to history as a bronze plaque, placed on the stone wall bordering Adams Street by the Milton Historical Society in 1908, attests. "Opposite this tablet," the inscription reads, "stood Milton's first Meeting House built prior to 1660." Nearby, another sign, erected by the Massachusetts Bay Colony Tercentenary Commission in 1930, proclaims "Churchill's Lane — Indian Trail. When the Indians sold their land near the mouth of the Neposet River, they removed to the territory south of the Blue Hills which they called Ponkapog, sweet water."

From the beginning, it had been suggested that the organization move its headquarters from rented offices at 50 Beacon Street to Milton. Commuting for the staff, then Executive Secretary Loring Conant, Nathan W. Bates, Coordinator of Reservations, and one secretary, would be significantly easier. Conant was a resident of Dedham; Bates of Cohasset.

There would be ample room for parking, and more than sufficient office and storage space. The living room, with its gorgeous views, could be used for conferences and seminars. Access to Boston in those days for meetings of the Standing Committee was simple, a mere 20-minute drive. The wing of the house could provide living quarters for the secretary and her husband. And, finally, the property was within easy reach of Route 128 and the Massachusetts Turnpike and thus to other reservations throughout the state.

Operating costs for offices in Milton were estimated to be about the same as they were for Boston, but the former won out for convenience and a character much more in keeping with the role and responsibilities of The Trustees of Reservations.

A variance to the zoning by-law was needed to permit the operation of an office within a single residence area, but with the support of the community it was soon acquired, and The Trustees of Reservations moved its headquarters to the newly-christened Pierce House at 224 Adams Street, Milton, on February 28, 1959.

Earlier, while discussions about its future continued, the house, much to the concern of the Standing Committee, stood vacant. But a use was soon found which would give it memorable distinction. For Sir Anthony Eden, and just-retired Prime Minister of the United Kingdom (1955-1957), and later the Earl of Avon, had come to Boston for special surgery.

Milton,
Massachusetts.

April 30, 1957

Dear Mr. Fletcher,

My husband and I both want to thank you and the Trustees of Reservations to much for the beautiful flowers you sent us, which have given us the greatest pleasure. We are so much enjoying staying in this lovely house.

Yours sincerely,

Clarissa Eden

Laurence B. Fletcher, Esq.,

A letter from Lady Eden, wife of the former Prime Minister, thanks The Trustees for its hospitality while Sir Anthony was recovering at the Pierce House.

Searching for a place for him to convalesce after the operation, his staff was informed that the Pierce House, whose status was still in limbo, was empty and available. There he resided quietly for some weeks before returning to England. A letter from Lady Eden to The Trustees of Reservations thanking it for its hospitality and for the roses the organization sent to Sir Anthony to celebrate his successful recovery was framed and hung for many years in the office of the Director. The room had earlier served as the former Prime Minister's bed chamber.

Those years were also turbulent ones internally for The Trustees of Reservations. Veteran Executive Secretary Laurence Fletcher had died in July 1958 and former Standing Committee member Arthur T. Lyman had agreed to serve as his successsor. His appointment, however, was short-lived. For Lyman, who had served successfully as Massachusetts' Commissioner of Conservation for many years, was soon asked to continue in public service, this time as Commissioner of Corrections.

With Lyman's departure, Loring Conant, who had been appointed Executive Secretary in June, 1958, and Nathan Bates, took over administration of The Trustees of Reservations and stability returned. Seven months later, the two moved to Milton. From 1959 to 1966, the Pierce House was home to three full-time employees, but in February 1967, following the appointment of Gordon Abbott, Jr., as the organization's first Director, things began to change.

As Conant retired, Garret F. VanWart joined the staff as Deputy Director. And, as momentum increased in the campaign

Built in 1950 overlooking the Neponset River, and designed by architects Bradley & Hibbard, the Pierce House at 224 Adams Street, Milton, served as General Headquarters of The Trustees of Reservations for 27 years.

to preserve World's End, another secretary was hired. Bookkeeping was later transferred from the Bank of New England in Boston, also requiring additional staff.

Fundraising activities expanded as well, as did efforts to professionalize the organization's land conservation programs. By the early 1980s, with a $10.1 million dollar Capital Fundraising Program underway, the building's single large living room, three bedrooms and two-car garage had been partitioned to accomodate offices for a full-time staff at General Headquarters of 13 men and women as well as space for files, records and an IBM computer. The Pierce House was clearly too small to deal with all it had been asked to accommodate. Abbott initiated a comprehensive study to see what might be done.

There were three general alternatives: expand the Pierce House; move to another property of The Trustees of Reservations (Long Hill, Beverly, was considered the best site); or rent quarters somewhere else. To further complicate matters, looming on the horizon also was the pending bequest of Cherry Hill in nearby Canton, a magnificent property which would have served superbly as General Headquarters.

A fine reproduction of a Charleston, South Carolina, house of the early 1800s, Long Hill was designed by architect Philip Richardson and built after World War I for Mr. and Mrs. Ellery Sedgwick of Boston. Sedgwick was editor of the city's distinguished literary magazine, The Atlantic Monthly. *Since 1986, Long Hill has been headquarters for* The Trustees of Reservations.

The study included financial and architectural considerations as well as those which might affect personnel. Finally, after much discussion, it was decided, at least for the moment, to stay in Milton. But in June 1984, when Abbott retired, the die was cast. With Frederic Winthrop, Jr., coming aboard as Director, it was time to begin a new era. And Winthrop and the Standing Committee wisely chose to move General Headquarters to Beverly. Remaining at the Pierce House was simply untenable. To continue its mission effectively, The Trustees of Reservations needed more room.

It was proposed that the Pierce House be sold as a single residence protected with restrictions preserving its existing architectural character as well as its use as a single family dwelling; that the land between it and the Neponset River, bordering Hutchinson's Field, be retained by The Trustees as the Pierce Reservation; and that funds from the sale be used to endow it.

The deed of gift gave The Trustees the right to raze the house. An appeal to the courts was made for further flexibility. It was granted with one proviso: that Mr. Pierce's sister, orginally named as the third alternative recipient of the property, be awarded a portion of the sale price.

For a year, under the leadership of Acting Director William C. Clendaniel, General Headquarters remained in Milton. But by the spring of 1986, it had moved to Beverly. There was no looking back. The Pierce House had served its purposes well for 27 years. The only regret was the loss of several members of a dedicated and hard-working staff who, as South Shore residents, understandably chose not to commute an additional hour to Long Hill.

15

Notchview: the Colonel's Choice Opens a New Era

A part of the Hoosac Range of northern Berkshire County in the Town of Windsor, most of the land at Notchview Farm is 1,900 feet or more above sea level. The air, even on the hottest summer days, is clear and fresh. And in winter the snow piles deep around the edges of the fields and woodlands, and the wind·rattles the windows of the houses.

The land where Notchview is today was first settled in the mid-1700s. Hunted by the Mahican Indians during the summer months, it came to support sheep and cattle, lumbering and charcoal-making, a saw mill, an ax factory, a butter-maker, and even a country school. Its residents have included dozens of hardworking men and women, whose dwellings now are marked by cellar holes and old stone fences, as well as a prominent jurist and two distinguished soldiers. One of these was General Alfred E. Bates, a veteran of the wars against the western Indians in the late nineteenth century. The other was Lieutenant-Colonel Arthur D. Budd, United States Army.

Colonel Budd, who lived at Notchview from 1932, when he retired from the service, until his death in 1965, loved the land and put together over time a collection of small farms to make a property of significant proportions which today measures some 3,000 acres.

Among the many decorations received by Lieutenant-Colonel Arthur D. Budd was the Distinguished Service Cross with two citations. Budd was also honored by a number of foreign governments.

Despite the winter weather, life at Notchview was more than comfortable, for Budd had married well (his first wife, who died in 1953, was the former Helen Gamwell Ely). There was a large gambrel-roofed house which looked south onto Route 9; a full-time farmer, Warren Drew, who managed the timber assets of the property as well as a small collection of cattle; and two maids who cooked, cleaned, and waited on table.

Despite its size, the Colonel insisted that the house be heated by wood, and Drew, who later became Superintendent of Notchview for The Trustees of Reservations, remembers stoking many a furnace fire at midnight or after when the winds howled and temperatures, as they often did in January, dropped far below zero.

A graduate of West Point with the Class of 1904, Budd had a distinguished military career cut short, in part, by an accident which left him without sight in one eye. Said to be one of the most decorated American soldiers of his era, he served first in the Philippine Insurrection and later in World War I where, as an infantry commander, he missed only one of the major American engagements.

Among his awards for valor were the Distinguished Service Cross and the French Croix de Guerre, both with two citations. He also received the Papal Order of St. Benedict with the rank of Commander as well as numerous other decorations from foreign governments.

During World War II, he was recalled to duty as a military observer and was in Copenhagen when the Germans invaded Demark, and in Paris when the city surrendered. Hitler provided him safe conduct through Spain to Gibraltar, where he was able to find a ship to take him home to the U.S.

Obviously well-traveled, he was a connoisseur of food, fine wines, and spirits. He was wonderfully generous as well with his hospitality, as many Standing Committee members of the era happily recall. Late in life, he married Dorothy Frances Whitney, who, like himself, had been widowed some years earlier.

Without children to inherit the property, the Colonel began as early as 1960 to consider organizations which might preserve Notchview, as he wrote, as "a wildlife refuge and woodland area for public enjoyment." There were three candidates: the Massachusetts Department of Natural Resources, the Episcopal Church and The Trustees of Reservations. It was also envisioned that Smith College might make use of the main lodging. Accompanying the legacy was to be a sizable endowment.

The courtship continued for five years. There were numerous Standing Committee visits for lunch to Windsor, where Budd loved to entertain. Former Treasurer Richard D. Frothingham recalls he was asked whether he would like whiskey or champagne with the meal. "I hesitated a moment in answering," he said, "whereupon the Colonel declared, 'never mind, we'll have both!'"

Loring Conant, Executive Secretary of The Trustees from 1958 to 1967, saw the property for the first time in 1961. He was also a beneficiary of the Colonel's largesse. Following a meeting at Notchview, he wrote to express his thanks for his host's "generous gift of butter, a bottle of rye, and, as an added surprise, a tank full of gasoline."

On at least two occasions, the Standing Committee reciprocated with an invitation to lunch at the Union Club in Boston. The Colonel was delighted. "The [food] was excellent," he wrote, "and although I hadn't been in the Union Club for nearly 50 years, it didn't seem changed at all."

Finally, it came time to decide the future of Notchview. Those in the running seemed to be The Trustees and the Common-

Christening the Arthur D. Budd Visitor Center in the early 1970s. From left, Philip Dater, member of the corporation and Chairman of the Local Committee for the Bryant Homestead, Mrs. Budd, Mrs. Dater and Director Gordon Abbott, Jr.

wealth, but, as Colonel Budd wrote, "what with all the state scandals, [I] will probably adhere to [the] plan with your group." And that he did.

Shortly after his death in September 1965, the organization was notified it was the owner of Notchview Farm. With it also The Trustees of Reservations became a residual beneficiary under the Arthur D. and Helen Budd Trusts in the amount of more than $4 million. The income, after caring for Mrs. Budd who still lived on the property, amounted to more than $220,000 per year.

Smith College also received an interest in the main house, which the Colonel hoped some day might become an "academic retreat." When the moment arrived, however, following Mrs. Budd's death in 1988, it declined, agreeing to a settlement of $500,000 of endowment principal.

Today, Notchview is enjoyed annually by hundreds of hikers and cross-country skiers. A building has been converted to the Arthur D. Budd Visitor Center. And, in keeping with the Colonel's interest in woodland management, Hume Brook Demonstration Forest with its interpretive trail and literature helps private owners of forest lands understand the benefits of scientific forest management and programs that will preserve and improve the scenic values of a woodland; increase the numbers and kinds of wildlife; and grow trees for timber harvest and other uses that can meet the economic and social needs of a community or region.

In the early 1970s, managment plans and programs for the property called for the elimination of several derelict buildings, including the remains of the Bates house, a sizable poultry barn, and a collection of smaller structures. It was agreed with community officials that the most effective and efficient way to accomplish their removal would be by initiating an annual program of "controlled burnings" which would also provide fire-fighting experience for the members of Windsor's Volunteer Fire Department.

In appreciation of the department's services, each June for a number of years The Trustees of Reservations hosted a cookout at Notchview for firemen and their families. Picnic tables were spread out on the lawn. Steaks were brought from Rocky Woods Reservation in Medfield and "Master Chef" Mario Pederzini, Superintendent of Rocky Woods, would work his magic on the grill.

A solitary skier traverses the eastern pasture on a spring day at Notchview Reservation, Windsor.

The project not only succeeded in eliminating a series of dilapidated and dangerous buildings, it also brought The Trustees of Reservations and key members of the community together and helped establish a new understanding and appreciation of the role and purposes of Notchview.

Gift of the property to a charitable organization had eliminated a significant annual real estate tax payment to the town.

Loring Conant, Executive Secretary from 1958 to 1967, was widely-acclaimed for his lectures about the activities of The Trustees of Reservations.

Initially, quite understandably, this had created some antagonism. But after one of the last picnics with fire department volunteers, a member of the board of selectmen told then Director Gordon Abbott, Jr., "You know, nowadays you can hear the bulldozers and the sound of builders' hammers working their way up here from Dalton. All of us ought to thank the Colonel for what he's done for Windsor."

Although it is always said with good reason in Standing Committee circles that the wit and charm of Mary Channing, wife of then Chairman Laurence M. Channing, who often sat next to the Colonel at luncheon, was instrumental in his final choice of The Trustees of Reservations, no story of the acquisition of Notchview is complete without recognizing the role of Executive Secretary Loring Conant. Appointed in 1958, following the death of Laurence Fletcher, Conant was a wool broker whose real love was the out-of-doors. As he wrote in 1950 in his 25th Anniversary Report for Harvard, "after twenty-odd years in the wool business, I am still in search of Golden Fleece." He found at least a part of it with The Trustees of Reservations.

A self-taught but wonderfully knowledgeable naturalist, he was a birder and a fly fisherman of considerable skill. At The Trustees, he was probably best known for his lectures, illustrated with his own color slides, which told with wit and imagination the story of the organization and its properties to audiences everywhere. Most important, his considerable personal charm made him an excellent ambassador for the Standing Committee as it dealt with landowners throughout the state.

During the decade he served as Executive Secretary, the organization acquired 15 new properties and protected an additional 5,000 acres of open space, including 3,000 acres at Notchview. It also more than doubled the assets from which it received endowment income, from just less than $3 million in 1965 to more than $7 million in 1966.

Throughout his career, Conant's patient attention to detail and continuing contacts with landowners played a major role in reassuring if not convincing many, including Colonel Budd, to select The Trustees of Reservations as a fiduciary for their funds as well as for their properties. He retired in 1967.

Warren Drew served as Superintendent of Notchview Reservation and of the six properties in the Windsor Managment Unit for 17 years, retiring in 1983. A man with virtually unlimited skills in every area of property management, Drew not only helped establish the demonstration forest at Notchview, but turned an old farm house into the attractive and much-appreciated Budd Visitor Center. He also built the barn now used as the unit's maintenance headquarters. In the mid-1970s, he all but single-handedly restored the structural integrity of the Bryant Homestead, as well as its cottage, barn and outbuildings.

Superintendent of the Windsor Management Unit, Warren A. Drew

16

World's End: More Than 1,800 People Help Make a Dream Come True

The acquisition of Notchview and the unprecedented and unrestricted cash flow from its endowment, which far more than met the needs of the property itself, meant that for the first time in its history The Trustees of Reservations was, at least momentarily, free from financial worry. It also meant that the organization could engage itself in new and exciting directions in the field of land conservation, confident that it could take some risks if the benefit to the public was judged to be worthwhile. There was little doubt that it was when it came to the preservation of World's End, two drumlins or glacial hills which formed a spectacular peninsula of land in Hingham.

The property, some 250 acres in all, with more than five miles of shoreline facing Hingham Harbor and the Weir River, had been farmed for decades. But at the end of the nineteenth century, it was tentatively planned as a 176-lot subdivision. As landscape architect for the project, the owners chose Frederick Law Olmsted. Not one house, however, was ever built. But many of Olmsted's winding roadways following the contours of the land were constructed from 1886 to 1900. Lined on either side with English oak, Norway maple, green ash, and, in those days, American elm,

View of World's End, the outer drumlin, from Planter's Hill

and surrounded by open pasture, they added dramatically to the extraordinary beauty of the landscape.

Both World's End and Planter's Hill, the southern drumlin, continued to be used for agriculture and at one time supported a prize herd of Jersey cattle. After World War II, the property was suggested as a site for the United Nations and even a nuclear power plant. But in the middle of the 1960s, its owners, Mr. and Mrs. William H. C. Walker of Hingham (Mrs. Walker was the granddughter of John R. Brewer who purchased the property in 1855), growing older, decided to put the land up for sale.

The immediate threat to the property was single-lot, residential development. It was the Walkers' hope, however, that funds could be raised to purchase and preserve World's End forever as a part of the metropolitan park system. Located only 14 miles from downtown Boston, it looked out at the skyline of the city and offered an island of natural beauty — a haven of peace and tranquillity — unrivaled anywhere in the region.

Public agencies wholeheartedly supported the concept of preservation, but had urged that the property be used to construct a golf course. Local residents were wiser. With the knowledge that intensive recreation areas were plentiful, their dream was to keep World's End as it was for all time. Their choice of custodian was The Trustees of Reservations.

Probably the most passionate supporter of the proposal to preserve World's End was Charles E. Mason, Jr., a former Chairman of the Standing Committee who was later to serve as President. Mason had grown up next to the property and knew it well both as a farm and as a place where fox hunting had existed up to and even after World War II, when Hingham had become an attractive, but intensively-developed, suburban community.

Laurence M. Channing, a former Chairman and President of The Trustees himself, recalls his introduction to World's End one autumn day. "Monk [as Mason was affectionately known] asked me to drive to Hingham," he recalled with a chuckle, but not before he picked up five live chickens and tucked them into the trunk of the car. 'What are those for?,' I asked somewhat incredulously. 'You'll see,' he replied. While we drove, he told me the story of World's End and when we got there we let the chickens out with the hope that the foxes would find them for lunch and be assured that we wanted them to remain a part of the property forever. Where else, as close to the city, could you find such an incredible rural setting with such a wonderful history?"

By early 1967, with Abbott aboard as Director to run the campaign, things were beginning to move. Studies established that the asking price of $650,000 for the property's 250 acres was fair and the terms of the purchase were agreed upon as follows: The Trustees would pay $200,000 down; $200,000 would be raised in Hingham and neighboring communities prior to the year end;

Charles E. Mason, Jr., Chairman of the Standing Committee from 1958 to 1965, Vice President from 1965 to 1970, and President from 1971 to 1976

the remaining $250,000 would be sought as donations in a wider public campaign.

The use of State or Federal funds, then more available for land conservation projects, was rejected. Neither The Trustees nor the community wanted to be subject to the possibility of government restrictions. And besides, local leaders were certain that the full sum could be raised from the private sector. The major question was who was going to play the lead role and here again fortune smiled on The Trustees as Samuel Wakeman, a neighbor of World's End, agreed to become Chairman of the campaign.

As a long-time resident of Hingham and for many years general manager of Bethlehem Steel's shipyard in nearby Quincy, Sam Wakeman, just retired, was widely known and much respected in the area. World's End had a special meaning for him, and he was determined to see that it was preserved as open space. In October 1967, a committee of 15 local residents pledged to raise $200,000 before January 1. An office was established at Town Hall. A separate campaign, led by Corporate Trustees Edward B. Long and David E. Place, got underway in neighboring Cohasset. Appeals were made by mail, by phone and, most important, in person.

Besides committee members themselves, key members of the Standing Committee, such as Monk Mason and Laurence Channing, President Charles R. Strickland and Chairman Augustus P. Loring, as well as the Director, attended as many as three evening meetings a week on the South Shore at which the goals and objectives of the campaign were discussed with members of the community. The response was extraordinary. People signed up immediately following a presentation or dropped off checks at the campaign office at Town Hall. A carpenter from Weymouth walked in with $50 in $10 bills. Others provided checks and pledges. Children produced handfuls of coins. Many pledged their weekly allowances.

The publisher of Quincy's daily newspaper, *The Patriot Ledger*, contributed space for advertisements seeking donations for World's End. And every day, as the mail arrived at General Headquarters of The Trustees of Reservations in Milton, scores of contributions, large and small, pushed the total closer to the goal.

By January, thanks in large measure to the energies, enthusiasm and organizational abilities of Sam Wakeman, who seemed to be everywhere at once, the first phase of the campaign was complete: $200,000 had been raised primarily in Hingham and Cohasset.

The second, a wider campaign headed by Monk Mason, was no less successful. A warm, teddybear of a man who had legions of friends everywhere, Mason was invincible. One donor wrote excitedly: "I have set aside 1,000 bushels of corn presently stored

Laurence M. Channing, Chairman of the Standing Committee from 1965 to 1967, President from 1960 to 1964 and General Counsel of The Trustees of Reservations for more than a decade

on my farm in Illinois to meet my 1968 pledge to The Trustees of Reservations!"

Newspaper stories, an editorial in *The Boston Globe* and television interviews — one with the Director of The Trustees on the top of Planter's Hill — spread the word around the region. It seemed as if everyone everywhere, from individuals to foundations, wanted to help preserve World's End and the money continued to come in. None of it was in amounts larger than $20,000 and there were only a few of those.

The campaign truly touched the area's grass roots. Although The Trustees' long-term commitment was to pay $25,000 a year for 10 years for phase three, the funds were raised in less than five. In all, the purchase and preservation of World's End was as exciting an episode as the organization had ever experienced.

What made the campaign such a success? Monk Mason's originally persuasive proposal that The Trustees should become involved; the leadership of Sam Wakeman; and, in the community, the wisdom and cooperation of veteran Selectman Mason T. Foley, who had long been an advocate of the idea.

The hard work of the fundraising committee both in Hingham and in Cohasset was successful in meeting the early challenge. The fact that the property had been open for public use for some years thanks to the generosity of its owners, the Walker-Brewer family, meant that people knew first hand what it offered the community as open space.

And finally, there was the extraordinary profile and character of World's End itself. Magnificently it rose from the surrounding waters — each drumlin more than 100 feet high — its rural landscape in majestic contrast to the heavily developed communities around it: Hingham, Hull and Nantasket. It seemed unthinkable to the constituency of men and women from every walk of life who looked out at it from their homes and who had enjoyed visiting it both by land and water, that it should ever be developed and destroyed.

At the conclusion of the campaign, the records showed that more than 1,800 residents of the area had contributed funds to make the preservation of World's End a reality. In recognition, in 1968, at a special luncheon at the property attended by more than 200, The Trustees of Reservations presented its Conservation Award to the People of Hingham and the South Shore. For Sam Wakeman, there was a special award which expressed the community's gratitude for all he had helped accomplish.

Today, World's End is host to thousands of delighted visitors annually. And thanks to a careful management program designed to preserve not only the beauty of its landscape but to protect its wildlife as well, if you're there on a warm spring evening, you may still see a red fox and its kit "run to ground" on the outer reaches of Planter's Hill.

17

Wasque: Vineyard Residents Act to Save a Precious Point

While the campaign to preserve World's End was in full swing on the South Shore of Boston, another was in progress miles away on the outer reaches of Chappaquiddick Island, Martha's Vineyard.

For there, also in the fall of 1967, local residents — some summer, some year-round — had banded together to preserve Wasque Point, some 200 acres of moorland, dune and ocean beach, bordering Muskeget Channel and Nantucket Sound. At the northerly end of the island was Cape Poge Wildlife Refuge, some 498 acres of barrier beach and headland, given to The Trustees in 1959.

The land at Wasque Point was up for sale. Like World's End, it, too, had been subdivided at the end of the nineteenth century as had so much of the southern shoreline of Massachusetts, into a checkerboard recreational commmunity of 10,000-square-foot lots. The development was to be known as "Chappaquiddick-by-the-Sea."

Only a handful of houses had been built on the northern boundary of the property, but the possibilities were awesome to consider. For the Vineyard was on the edge of a building boom which was to last for 20 years, and the threat of the construction of scores of summer homes was immediate. The price agreed upon for the 200 acres of land at Wasque Point was $210,000. The goal of the campaign: $250,000, which included $40,000 as endowment.

By December 1967, more than $120,000 had been raised in gifts and pledges, the property had been purchased and acquired by a specially established trust, and plans were made to transfer it over time to The Trustees of Reservations. As protection against a possibility that the campaign might fail to reach its goal, the project committee divided the property at Wasque into five parcels. Each was to be given to The Trustees as contributions were raised to meet its purchase. If, in the later stages of the campaign, funds fell short of the goal, the last remaining parcel, for example, could be withheld and, if necessary, sold to raise the the cash needed.

Although wisely prudent in its approach, as it turned out, the committee needn't have worried. As campaign leader, Mrs. Seth Wakeman (no relation to Sam) declared with a smile in October 1968, "I don't think we'll have any trouble raising what we want."

At that date, more than $159,000 was already in hand and in one year the job was done. Some 850 people contributed to make the project a success.

Except for activities at General Headquarters of The Trustees in Milton, which included the production of solicitation materials and the management of the cash as it came in, and the fundraising efforts of the indefatigable Monk Mason, a summer resident of the Vineyard for many years, the campaign to preserve Wasque, by design, was kept local.

Contributors and even committee members were on the island for only a few short weeks and otherwise were to be found in nearby New York, New Jersey, or as far away as Florida or California. Solicitations were, in large part, made by mail and by telephone, but little coaxing was needed. For wherever their legal residence might have been, the Vineyard was what counted most and the response was overwhelming.

Leadership for the project was provided by Oliver D. Filley, Jr., and Mary Wakeman. Filley, who commuted regularly to the island from New Jersey during the campaign, was a second-generation summer resident of Chappaquiddick and Chairman of the Local Committee for Cape Poge Wildlife Refuge. (Cape Poge had been given to The Trustees by his father and a lifetime friend and college classmate, Charles S. Bird, a former Chairman of the Standing Committee.)

Mrs. Seth Wakeman, leader of the campaign to preserve Wasque Point, Chappaquiddick, and winner of The Trustees of Reservations' Conservation Award in 1970

Fundraising headquarters was located at Mrs. Wakeman's house in Edgartown. There, as Secretary and Treasurer, she orchestrated the details of the campaign, soliciting donors, collecting contributions, writing thank-you notes and delivering news reports to the *Vineyard Gazette*. She was generous herself, to be sure, but more than anything else, it was her energy, enthusiasm and organizational abilities which kept things going and insured the project's completion. A former resident of the midwest, she declared: "I come from a long line of farmers who loved the land [and who were] taught to take care of it."

The donor of Mytoi, Chappaquiddick, a delightfully intimate informal garden, planted with azaleas, rhododendrons, Hanoki cyprus, holly, daffodils and flowering dogwood, she also made possible the preservation of Little Neck, a rookery for snowy egret and other migratory sea and shore birds which is now a part of Cape Poge Wildlife Refuge.

Widely honored for all her efforts on behalf of the Vineyard and its environment, she received The Trustees of Reservations Conservation Award in 1970. The ceremony, which included a clambake, took place at Wasque Point which, on that warm August day, was wrapped in the soft folds of a summer fog.

Mary Wakeman died in 1984, as old as the century itself but forever young at heart. Today, the Wakeman Conservation Center at Cranberry Acres, Vineyard Haven, commemorates her wonderfully productive life. But perhaps the best memorial — and the one that everyone who loved her knows she would cherish most

— are the hundreds of wild acres of Vineyard land which will always stay that way because of her devotion to the cause.

18

The Bear's Den: a Legend from the Past

Grais Poole Burrage was a native of the town of New Salem, Massachusetts (named for its larger sister on the North Shore), which was settled in 1737. For many years she served the community as its Treasurer and Tax Collector. Always interested in history, Mrs. Burrage was also Treasurer of the Swift River Valley Historical Society, and in 1925, intrigued by a celebrated local legend, she purchased a property which had long been known as "the Bear's Den."

Just 3.4 acres of land, it is charming in its intimacy. As Standing Committee member Fletcher Steele wrote after a visit: "One descends an old path, turns toward a mass of rock through which one squeezes; turns a corner and is met by a sudden view. All that would be asked of romantic scenery lies before one — sharp crags and a tumbling river; caves, ancient forest trees twisting from the heart of the rocks themselves. All the more attractive for being in miniature." Included also are the sluiceway and rock foundations of an ancient grist mill.

But it is a "romance" from the past which captures the imagination and gives the Bear's Den its air of mystery and intrigue. Written by John C. Crane, the story appeared in the *Orange Enterprise and Journal* in February 1899. "In that wild and romantic region at North New Salem known as the Bear's Den," Crane wrote, "is the scene of a beautiful Indian legend which has touched the hearts of many who have listened to its unfolding.

"It was during King Philip's war, some time before the fight at Turner's Falls, that an Indian appeared at the Bear's Den encampment leading a little white [girl] of some five summers. None but her captor knew from whence she came or whose home was broken by her absence. A council of the Indians was held and at last it was determined, because of the supplication of the maiden, Naowa, that the child should live and be adopted by the band.

"The little one soon became reconciled to her new surroundings and was the pet of the Indian village. She was clothed in the dress of that people and among her playthings [were] a tiny bow and arrows. In and out of the wigwams she went, welcomed on every hand.

"The days passed on. Tidings came that Deerfield was in ruins and that Turner [Captain Turner who died in a battle with the Indians near Greenfield in 1676] with many of his gallant men lay cold in death at the falls which [now] bear his name. One night the camp was in a state of excitement. . . and no wonder for word went around that it was the renowned Mt. Hope chieftain, King Philip [who had arrived]. Never in the annals of Indian life was there such a commotion. A thousand men were not many miles away, awaiting the pleasure of their master, prepared for bloody work among the white settlers.

"The mission of Philip was to add numbers to his band and send messengers from here still further onward for the same purpose. As twilight fell on the day of his arrival, there was a gathering of people on the sloping land about the Bear's Den. Philip, the chief speaker, recounted in fiery eloquence the success he and his followers had at Deerfield. Bitter was his denunciation of the white invaders. He prophesied their utter extinction.

"As the torches flared and lighted the scene, the Indians became wild with excitement. Just then the little white prisoner passed, toddling in front of the swarthy orator. Philip cast upon her a withering look and inquired whence she came. He was told the story and, as his brow grew darker than usual with rage, he exclaimed, 'The child must die. Let none of the hated palefaces live!' His words cut to the quick of the heart of Naowa, the adopted Indian mother, and determination lighted her features. The child passed the gathering and on the outskirts was met by her who had, indeed, been a mother to her.

Bear's Den, a hemlock-shaded grotto with a series of sparkling waterfalls on the Middle Branch of the Swift River in North New Salem

"The pow-wow went on far into the night. When before the close, Philip inquired if his sentence of death for the white child had been carried into effect, no one knew. The litle girl was nowhere to be found. The wigwam of Naowa revealed no trace of the child, and the Indian maiden disclaimed all knowledge of her whereabouts.

"A week passed. Philip had left for other scenes and many of the braves had gone with him on his mission of ruin and death. Joy seemed to have fled from the village as the feet of the little white maiden (rechristened Mysota) no longer pattered about. None could tell of her but Naowa and she was silent.

"One morning, a little over a week after Philip had left, a hunter named Manate, in passing up the brook running by the den, saw a big black bear at the entrance. It was but the work of a moment until, with a bullet through his heart, the beast lay stretched at the opening. Securing his booty, Manate caried it to his teepee and again passed up the brook.

"As he glanced at the perpendicular face of the ledge, some 20 feet up at an opening, he saw the face of another bear peering out. A second shot followed and all was still within. Crawling through the hole at the base, and following up a winding passage, what was his surprise to find there not only the body of [the] other bear, but the living form of the little white girl, Mysota, safe and secure from all harm.

"Naowa had kept her own council and saved from the wrath of Philip somebody's darling. It was never known whose child this was, but for long years she found a home with Manate and Naowa."

Despite its dramatic detail, Crane's story of the Bear's Den appears to have little basis in fact, but in the town of New Salem, it has been passed down from generation to generation. And, if you visit the property today, you can still see clearly the dark entrances of the two caves above the brook.

Fascinated with the legend and with the intimate charm of the Bear's Den itself, Mrs. Burrage continued the tradition of allowing public access to the area. She also constantly refused lucrative offers for the property, fearing it would be exploited and developed, and its natural beauty destroyed forever.

It was her lifelong wish to have the Bear's Den remain as it had throughout the centuries, a magic and mystical place to be enjoyed by all. In 1969, following her death a year earlier, her will most generously decreed that it become a property of The Trustees of Reservations.

19

The Norris Reservation: Scenery and Shipbuilding on the North River

Mrs. Eleanor Norris, whose generosity made possible the preservation of the Albert F. Norris Reservation. The property was given in memory of her husband.

In Norwell, where the North River turns east to meet Massachusetts Bay and the Atlantic, American holly and oak, tupelo and red cedar trees crowd the edge of the marsh and a grove of tall white pine stands out against the sky.

Stretching for more than one-half mile on the west bank of the river are some 100 acres of land collected over time by Albert and Eleanor Norris. Second Herring Brook flows across the property, and grouse and pheasant, mallard and black duck, teal, great blue heron, red-tailed hawk, great horned owl, osprey, mink and an occasional red fox inhabit the area. The North River itself, still largely undeveloped, was selected as the first Scenic River in the Commonwealth to be protected by regulatory action.

Albert Norris was born in 1891 in Worcester. A graduate of Clark University, and a Navy flier in World War I, he became a teacher and a member of the faculty, first at St. Alban's School in Washington, and later at schools on Long Island, in Worcester and in Hingham. At one time he served as principal of Provincetown High School. He had an interest, too, in an iron foundry in Dorchester which he established in 1912 and operated for nearly half a century until he retired in 1961.

A man of many talents, he played both the trumpet and the cello with the Harvard Musical Association and it was this love of music and of the land in Norwell which he and Eleanor Norris shared together. A music teacher herself, she says "it was while teaching in Hingham in the early 1920s that he discovered land on the North River and began piecing it together, acre by acre, trying to hold onto it and hoping that some day it would be preserved as a reservation." In 1970, Albert Norris's dream came true as Mrs. Norris, then widowed, gave the property to The Trustees of Reservations.

During their married life, the couple lived at the foundry in Dorchester during the week and on weekends would journey to Norwell. There they worked on the land, clearing brush and cutting trails. The property included the site of an early sawmill on Second Herring Brook built in 1690.

A succession of families owned the mill through the years and local histories indicate that it was used to produce the lumber for the last vessel to be built on the North River, the *Helen M. Foster*. Later, the mill turned out quantities of boards for box factories nearby. The dam, which provided water power for the mill, is still in existence, although much improved.

The silence of the North River today, broken only by the soft swish of water moving with the tide, the cry of sea and shorebirds and the occasional splash of a paddle or an oar, is in sharp contrast to its early years. As historian and author Samuel Eliot Morison writes in his *Maritime History of Massachusetts, 1783-1860*, during the first part of the nineteenth century, the air was filled with the sound of busy shipwrights and building yards were scattered all along the river's edge. Nearby and easy to harvest were the stands of white oak and pine which made their operation possible.

"The Boston fleet," Morison explains, "second only to New York's, was largely procured from the Maine coast, the Merrimack, and the North River. That narrow, tidal stream, dividing the towns of Marshfield and Pembroke from Scituate, Norwell and Hanover, was, like the Merrimack, a cradle of New England shipbuilding.

"The North River attained the height of its activity in the Federalist days. Thirty vessels were completed here in 1801, and an average of 23 a year, from 1799 to 1804. Looking downstream from the Hanover bridge, 11 shipyards were in view, filled with vessels in various stages of construction. Every morning at daybreak, the shipwrights might be seen crossing the pastures or walking along the sedgy river bank to their work for a dollar a day, dawn to dusk.

One of a series of bronze markers along the river bank which commemorates the shipbuilding history of the North River

"When the sun rose above the Marshfield hills, like a great red ball through the river mist, there began the cheery clatter of wooden shipbuilding — clean, musical sounds of steel on wood, iron on anvil, creak of tackle and rattle of sheave; with much geeing and hawing as ox teams brought in loads of fragrant oak, pine and hackmatack, and a snatch of a chanty as a large timber is hoisted into place. At eleven o'clock, and again at four, came the foreman's welcome shout of 'Grog O!' For it took rum to build ships in those days; a quart to a ton, by rough allowance; and more to launch her properly.

"Standing on this same Hanover bridge today, it is hard to believe what the records show to be true, that within a few hundred yards, where there seems hardly water enough for a good-sized motor boat, were built for New York merchants in 1810-11 the ships *Mount Vernon* and *Mohawk*, respectively 352 and 407 tons burthen. Father down, near the *Columbia's* birthplace, even greater vessels were launched — poking their sterns into the opposite bank, and having to be dug out."

Morison continues: "Getting them down this narrow, tortuous river, full of rocks and shoals, was a ticklish business, entrusted to a special breed of North River pilots. Crews of men followed the vessels on both banks, with long ropes attached to each bow and quarter, hauling or checking as the pilot, enthroned between the knightheads, commanded, 'Haul her over to Ma'shfield!' or 'Haul her over to Sit-u-wate!'

"Motive power was provided by kedging, heaving up to an anchor dropped ahead by the pilot's boat. Fourteen tides were sometimes required to get a vessel to sea, as the mocking river sauntered for miles behind the barrier beach and dribbled out over a bar that taxed all Yankee ingenuity to surmount. When shipbuilding had ceased, a new outlet opened at the nearest point to the ocean.

"The North River builders," Morison adds, "did much work for 'foreign' (i.e., non-Massachusetts) order, and for the whalemen. Their vessels seem to have lacked even a local reputation for speed. Very few paintings of them have survived. One of the ship *Minerva*, 223 tons, built by Joshua Magoun at Pembroke in 1808 for Ezra Weston and others of Duxbury, shows a vessel built in the best style of the day; gray-blue topsides and bulwarks, with bright waist, quarter-galleries, beautiful quick work on the bows, and a finely proportioned sail plan."

It was a grand era of great accomplishment. Today, the river is quiet, but the activities of nearly two centuries ago are celebrated by a series of heavy bronze markers on the site of each of the major yards which tell the story of their life and times.

The North River is still a high priority for preservation, and The Trustees of Reservations, with other environmental agencies and organizations, continues to be aware of opportunities to protect the golden beauty of its marshes and the woodlands along its shores.

The quiet, tidal waters of the North River flow past the Norris Reservation, some 101 acres, in Norwell.

In 1980, Miss Mildred Hastings gave The Trustees a conservation restriction protecting some 90 acres of land at The Hollow, her historic farm in Norwell. The property also includes an island in the marsh, wooded upland, a brook and a small pond, as well as significant frontage on the North River.

20

At Nantucket: A Magnificent Coastal Landscape Remains Forever Wild

At 2:30 p.m. on Monday, December 30, 1974, in the offices of attorney Robert F. Mooney on Federal Street, Nantucket, deeds were signed by Mrs. J. Allen Backus and her son-in-law, Robert W. Sziklas, transferring title to 810 acres of land at Coskata and Coatue to The Trustees of Reservations. Present also for the occasion (celebrated with a bottle of champagne), were Molly Sziklas, Mrs. Backus's daughter, and Director Gordon Abbott, Jr.

The Backus family's gift, extraordinary in its generosity, preserves one of Nantucket's most dramatic landscapes. Included are some six miles of ocean beach and sand dunes north of Wauwinet; a tidal pond, salt marsh and cedar thicket at Coskata; as well as the northern portion of Coatue, the barrier beach which forms the western side of Nantucket Harbor. The new reservation was christened Coskata-Coatue Wildlife Refuge. Its establishment had taken four and one-half years to complete.

Shortly afterwards, Professor and Mrs. Christoph K. Lohmann added 186 acres to the refuge with a gift of the northern portion of Coskata and the Galls, a narrow strip of beach connecting Great Point to the remainder of the island.

Like the rest of Nantucket, Coskata-Coatue Wildlife Refuge is a part of the outwash plain created as the great glacial ice sheet melted away thousands of years ago. A dynamic ecosystem, it is today a resting and feeding area for shore and sea birds of every description: loon, grebe and gannet; black crowned night heron and snowy egret; Canada geese and black duck; least and common tern; piping plover; willets; yellowlegs; oyster catcher; and, in winter, snowy owl, eiders, goldeneyes and mergansers.

White-tailed deer, huge blacktail jack rabbit and cottontails inhabit the dunes. (Introduced to Nantucket from Kansas in 1925 by the Harrier Hunt Club, the jack rabbits were the Hunt's substitute for red fox. Small mammals such as fox, skunks or raccoons are not endemic to the island, all but eliminating major predators for nesting birdlife.)

Just offshore, bluefish, bass and flounder abound, while sheltered beaches are home to softshell clams, quahogs, mussels and crab.

With the wind and sea, the sand is constantly in motion. Great Point itself migrates westward annually as it has for centuries. No better testimonial to this is the loss of Great Point light which was finally destroyed by an early spring northeaster in March 1984. Orginally constructed in 1819, far from the edge of the sea, the light was a beacon for mariners and a landmark for island residents. As the decades passed, however, erosion took its toll, until the ocean, at high tides, surrounded the base of the stone tower. Then, in one night, it was gone.

Summer houses, built of driftwood, have also been swallowed up by the sea as the land moved relentlessly westward. The Galls, too, were breached during a winter storm some years ago, but thanks to prevailing currents which carry the sand northward, the area closed in again within a few weeks.

The light at Great Point has since been replaced by a new tower, all but a replica of the old, funded by Congress with legislation introduced by Massachusetts Senator Edward F. Kennedy. The $2 million structure sits on a concrete caisson, or man-made island, 45 feet in diameter, designed to protect it from the fiercest storms, but the power of the sea is awesome and history is on its side.

Much earlier, in 1896, ocean waves, driven by hurricane force winds, broke through just north of Wauwinet at a location since known as the Haul-Over. There, fishermen were able to pull their boats across a narrow strip of sand from the Head of the Harbor to reach the sea beyond, avoiding the long trip around Great Point. For some years after the storm, they could simply row through the inlet, but it, too, closed up again.

A series of vessels, driven ashore during the last century, led to the establishment in 1883 of Coskata Life-Saving Station. Manned year-round by a full-time crew who would launch their boat through the pounding surf, the station was involved in a number of daring rescues.

The settlement at Wauwinet, south of the refuge, has been popular with visitors since 1876, when the Backus family established the Wauwinet House Inn. Its shore dinners attracted travelers from far and wide, and in Nantucket they would board the steamers *Island Bell* and *Coskata*, and later the catboat *Lillian*, for the voyage to the Head of the Harbor. In its heyday, the *Lillian* was making two trips a day to transport visitors. Luggage, for those who wished to stay longer, usually went overland in what could be a dusty, three-hour ride by horse-drawn wagon.

Born in Somerville, Massachusetts, in 1897, Harriett Withers Backus spent her summers as a child in the Annapolis Valley of

Nova Scotia. The first time she saw Nantucket was in the early
1920s. By then a registered nurse, she came to the island to work
at the Cottage Hospital. There she met and, in 1925, married J.
Allen Backus. Allen, who lived at Wauwinet with his parents, was
Treasurer of the Town of Nantucket and of the County as well.

As a native, he loved the island and through the years collected property at Coskata and Coatue, using the area primarily
for hunting, fishing and picnicking with friends and family.
Following his death, for more than a decade, Harriett operated the
Wauwinet House herself. Through the years, it had built up a
loyal following of regular summer visitors, many of whom were
families who could boast of celebrating their second or third
generation at the Wauwinet House Inn.

*Harriet Backus, donor of
Coskata-Coatue Wildlife
Refuge, in her early thirties*

Molly, who had grown up on the island, married Bob Sziklas,
who taught science, first at Nantucket High School, and later at
Noble & Greenough School in Dedham. They had met while Bob
was in college, working one summer at the Wauwinet House.

In 1969, with an eye to the future, Harriett began to think
about the possibility of preserving the land at Coskata and
Coatue. She loved the area as Allen had and knew that it was
widely used and much appreciated by both townspeople and
summer folk for the wild beauty of its landscape. It was a magnet
for fishermen, and for many, who spent their summers on the
island, the season was not complete without a trip to Coskata and
Great Point.

Politics had infected the Nantucket school system in the 1960s,
and Harriett was determined that if the property was to be
protected for conservation purposes, it should be held by an
organization free of local influence, preferably from "off island."
After careful consideration and research, she began discussions
with The Trustees of Reservations.

At first, she proposed to sell the land and, as newcomers to
the island, The Trustees turned to the Nantucket Conservation
Foundation for advice. Headed by Roy E. Larsen, founder and
Chairman of Time Incorporated and a summer resident of the
island for many years, the Conservation Foundation had done a
superb job acquiring and preserving inland and coastal properties
from one end of the island to the other. But, however accomplished, it was still local and thus did not fit Harriett Backus's
criteria.

Thankfully, from the very beginning, the two organizations
developed a warm and cooperative relationship. What was
important to both was that the Backus land be preserved. To raise
the funds needed to purchase the property, The Trustees of
Reservations would need the assistance of the Nantucket Conservation Foundation and, with Roy Larsen at the helm, it was
gladly offered.

Augustus P. Loring, Chairman of the Standing Committee from 1969 to 1975, Vice President from 1977 to 1980, and Treasurer from 1954 to 1961, in 1968, 1981 and 1982

Theodore Chase, Chairman of the Standing Committee from 1975 to 1981 and Chairman of The Trustees of Reservations' first Capital Program

A special team was set up to direct the project. Its members were Augustus P. Loring, then Chairman of The Trustees of Reservations; Theodore Chase, a veteran member of the Standing Committee who was to become Chairman himself in 1976; and Director Gordon Abbott, Jr.

No better people could have been chosen than Loring and Chase. Gus Loring was a Boston Trustee who was to be active with The Trustees of Reservations for three decades. Bright and decisive in the ways of business and a director of numerous corporations, he was an officer and board member with more than a score of civic organizations and charitable institutions. Among them were the Boston Athenaeum, the Peabody Marine Museum of Salem (of which he was President), Harvard and Boston Universities (which he served as an Overseer and Trustee), the Boston Lying-in Hospital, and the Masonic Education and Charity Trust.

He ran his meetings at The Trustees of Reservations with dispatch and a ready wit, and little escaped his keen eye. Indeed, during World War II, when he served at sea as an officer in the U.S. Coast Guard, his initials "A.P." were said by shipmates to have stood for "Armor Piercing." But besides all these worldly accomplishments, he was a collector of rare books and a man of incredible warmth and great good humor who loved life and who cared about those around him. He died in 1986 at the age of 71.

Ted Chase, an attorney, had been a long-time partner of Palmer & Dodge and was a leading figure on the Boston scene as well. Also active in business and civic affairs, his interests, too, were broad and ranged from education — he was a Harvard Overseer as well as Chairman of the Massachusetts Board of Regional Community Colleges — to the history of early America. He served on the Council of the Massachusetts Historical Society and as President of the Association for Gravestone Studies and the New England Genealogical Society. He was also the author of a number of articles which appeared in scholarly publications.

During his term as Chairman of the Standing Committee, his ability to summarize the issues and to clarify the questions, especially after lengthy discussions of complicated matters by the board, was legendary. There are many who said he should have been a judge. A delightfully charming human being as well, he and Loring were a powerful team at The Trustees of Reservations during a memorable era.

During the next few months, Abbott shuttled back and forth between New York and Boston, discussing tactics with the Chairman of the Board at the headquarters of Time Incorporated at Rockefeller Plaza. For despite Roy Larsen's immense responsibilities and worldly position, there were few things that he would rather talk about than Nantucket and how to preserve the magic that makes it unique.

Indeed, Abbott remembers well luncheons for two in the Chairman's private dining room, warm and personable conversations, and at the end, cigars so strong that he was barely able to reach the street and catch a cab to LaGuardia.

Meanwhile, work on the title to the property at Coskata and Coatue continued at Rackemann, Sawyer & Brewster in Boston (Charles Rackemann who served as both Chairman and President of The Trustees of Reservations in the 1930s was a founder of the firm), as did discussions with the Lohmanns, who were interested ultimately in preserving all of their land at Great Point as a part of the Refuge.

Pam Lohmann, born a Fezandie, had spent summers at Great Point as a child in a driftwood house that her father, a professor of engineering at Rutgers University, had constructed in the late 1930s. Both she and her husband, Chris, a professor at the University of Illinois, loved the property and wanted their lands to be a part of its preservation. The westward migration of Great Point took its toll on the Fezandie house as well and it, too, has toppled over the dunes to be swallowed up by the sea.

Conversations also were held with representatives of the U.S. Fish & Wildlife Service, owners of Nantucket National Wildlife Refuge, some 12 acres at the tip of Great Point. It was agreed that The Trustees of Reservations would act as agent for the Fish & Wildlife Service, managing the Federal refuge as it did its own.

Finally, both The Trustees of Reservations and the Nantucket Conservation Foundation had agreed upon their roles and the

Summer surf rolls ashore at Great Point, Nantucket. The light, its stone tower orginally built in 1819, fell victim to a northeast storm in 1984. A working replica has since been erected on the site.

campaign for funds was ready to begin. But Mrs. Backus had been having other thoughts.

"I just don't see how I can ask for money from my friends," she told Abbott. "I've talked with my lawyer and I've decided to give you the land." From that moment on progress towards preservation of the property moved swiftly.

Earlier, Abbott had been asked to address the Nantucket Conservation Foundation at its Annual Meeting. With an eye on the acquisition of Coskata and Coatue, he chose as a topic the management and continuing protection of conservation lands which at Nantucket was an urgent need.

In June of that summer, he had spent a Sunday with friends and family at First Point at the south end of Coatue. The area was crowded with people, young and old, engaged in a dizzying variety of activities. Some were sailing Sunfish. Some were swimming. Others were surf-casting. Four-wheel drive vehicles weaved their way through the beach grass and low dunes. Dogs were barking. And in the midst of it all, nesting least and common terns were frantically trying to protect their territories and their young.

It was a chaotic scene, but it set the stage for what has been a hugely successful management partnership between the Nantucket Conservation Foundation and The Trustees of Reservations.

Together the properties involved total more than 1,350 acres. They include Coatue Wildlife Refuge, 350 acres, Nantucket Conservation Foundation; Coskata-Coatue Wildlife Refuge, 988 acres, The Trustees; and the Federal refuge at Great Point.

A full-time Refuge Manager was appointed by The Trustees of Reservations (today the position is held by Dick Bellevue, a long-time resident of Nantucket, who retired as a Captain with the Massachusetts State Police), and, with Jim Lentowski, veteran Executive Secretary of the Nantucket Conservation Foundation, rules and regulations were drawn up to protect the resources of the entire area.

Today, two uniformed summer rangers, stationed at an attractive gatehouse at Wauwinet, greet visitors and provide them with information about the properties. Only four-wheeled drive vehicles are allowed on the beaches and they are restricted to certain areas. A permit, which may be purchased by the day or by the season, is required for vehicular access.

As for the terns, a program modeled on those at Cape Poge and Wasque and at Crane Beach, was soon initiated. It includes a full-time tern warden during the summer months; the physical protection of nesting areas; research related to the birds' population and survival; and a project aimed at educating every visitor about the habits and activities of colonial nesting birds. Users today have a new respect for the area and its fragile resources.

Richard J. Bellevue, Refuge Manager, Coskata-Coatue Wildlife Refuge, Nantucket

Her dream of preservation accomplished, Harriett Backus died in 1979, much admired and beloved as a person and for all she did for the island that she had adopted more than half a century earlier.

21

Crane Wildlife Refuge: an Island Kingdom

The Brown Cottage, a substantial wood-shingled dwelling located at the foot of Castle Hill, is another landmark of the Crane Reservation.

Named for its former owners — farmers until John Brown made money as a contractor in Chicago — it was, until his death in 1962, the summer residence of Cornelius Crane and his attractive and talented wife, the former Miné Sawahara of Kure, Japan. It was Crane's wish that he be buried at his beloved Hog Island, but instead of the simple ceremony planned, drama intervened.

No sooner had his body been lowered into the open grave, than out of nowhere appeared a helicopter carrying his adopted daughter, Kathleen Crane Cedarquist of New York City. In her hand she held a court order to halt the burial until she could experience "the simple decency of seeing her father for the last time."

Funeral-goers at the top of the hill were aghast as Mrs. Cedarquist claimed that she had been denied permission to view the body before the burial. It was a startling moment in an otherwise peaceful scene.

The years roll by, however, and today on the windswept hilltop at Hog Island, a simple granite monument marks the grave not only of Cornelius, but of his wife Miné, who died in May, 1991.

Seventeen years earlier, in 1974, thanks to Mrs. Crane's great generosity, Hog Island, Long Island, Round Island, Deans Island and Dilley Island, some 650 acres in all, including surrounding salt marsh, were presented to The Trustees of Reservations to be preserved forever as the Cornelius and Miné S. Crane Wildlife Refuge.

The gift was frankly a surprise to The Trustees, who had expected to receive the property by bequest. At the time, there was no endowment, but it was unthinkable that an island kingdom of such haunting beauty, so rich with history and replete with wildlife of every description, could be refused, and the Standing Committee agreed to accept it. There are no regrets.

Hog Island was once a part of Castle Hill Farm, granted to

John Winthrop, Jr., in 1637. The island's first resident was Thomas Choate who, in 1725, cleared a portion of the land to raise sheep and to build a two-story farm house, which still stands today.

Eighty members of the Choate family were born at Hog Island including, in 1799, Rufus Choate, lawyer, orator, Congressman, and U.S. Senator. Others included members of the Governor's Council, representatives to Massachusetts' Great and General Court, ministers, military officers and one judge of the Court of Common Pleas. Thomas Choate himself was a member of the General Court for four years.

In 1855, Rufus, then a celebrated barrister, wrote to the New York law firm of Butler, Evans & Southmayd, recommending for employment, his second cousin, a promising young attorney named Joseph Hodges Choate, who, of course later became not only one of the nation's most astute legal minds, but a distinguished diplomat as well, serving as U. S. Ambassador to the Court of St. James's in the last days of Queen Victoria. (It was his daughter Mabel, whose interest in preservation and in the history of Stockbridge, her summer residence, made it possible for The Trustees of Reservations to acquire The Mission House as well as Naumkeag, which her father and mother had built in 1886, with all the splendor of its gardens and grounds.)

It is said that Hog Island was named for its razor-back profile, but in 1887, the residents of Essex decided that it should be changed to "Choate" and it was "so entered by order of the Selectmen, upon the town records." Both names are used today, but nautical charts still refer to the island as Hog.

The Choate House, built in 1725, overlooks the vast tidal estuaries of the Essex and Castle Neck Rivers. More than 80 members of the Choate family were born in the homestead at Hog Island, Essex.

For more than a century, the only way to reach the islands was by boat at high water (a ferry ran regularly) and by stone and gravel road (the stones were laid on the creek bottom) at low. But in 1886, a wood bridge was built from Choate Island to Dean's Island. Planked with white pine and supported with spruce pilings, it finally gave way to strong currents and winter ice.

Before the bridge was built, crossings on the old stone road could be exciting, and one Essex resident writes that as a child she remembers her father telling her one night to hold her feet up to keep them dry as the rising tide lapped at the wood slats which formed the bottom of the wagon, and the horses struggled to reach dry land on the other side.

During the nineteenth century, the island was divided into three farms: the Choate Farm, the Burnham Farm, and the Marshall Farm. Hay was a primary crop and was not only used to feed island dairy cattle, but was also shipped to Boston to provide fodder for the thousands of draft animals used in the city to draw carriages, carts and wagons.

In the 1880s, a number of summer cottages were constructed and leased to friends and relatives of island residents. Years later, one man commuted daily during the warm months from Hog Island to Boston, keeping his flivver on the mainland. With the bridge now gone, he would cross the waterway using a canoe, a wheelbarrow and a pair of rubber boots. At high water, he would put the boots and the wheelbarrow in the canoe and paddle it to the other side. At low water, he would pull on the boots, put the canoe in the wheelbarrow and, pushing it ahead, wade his way home on the remains of the old stone road at the bottom of the creek.

Richard T. Crane, Jr., purchased Hog Island — the largest in the cluster of five islands southwest of Castle Neck — in 1916. With the assistance of landscape architect Arthur A. Shurtleff, he removed the summer cottages and began a careful restoration of the landscape. For its visual effect, he replaced the mixed forest on the island with a plantation of Northern white spruce. Now mature, the dark green conifers contrast dramatically with surrounding hardwoods as well as with the soft, golden hues of the marshes.

The Choate House, an historic centerpiece, was first restored in 1919. Additional work took place in 1975. Today the house remains, by design, unfurnished so that visitors may imagine for themselves the activities of daily life which took place within its walls over nearly two centuries.

Cornelius and Miné Crane continued the older generation's interest in the islands. They constructed a comfortable summer cottage for themselves which serves today as a Visitor Center. The Cranes returned to it often after voyages to the Baltic and Caribbean seas aboard *Oshidori*, their 58-foot auxiliary ketch.

Mrs. Miné S. Crane, generous donor of the Cornelius and Miné S. Crane Wildlife Refuge

After her husband's death, Mrs. Crane continued to use the property until she gave it to The Trustees of Reservations. Through the years, however, her interest in it and its preservation never waned. She would often return to Crane Wildlife Refuge for Field Days with the Friends of Hog Island, and upon her own death, a provision in her will established a wonderfully welcome endowment in the amount of $2 million.

Her great interests were music and the arts, and she was as talented as she was charming. An accomplished pianist, she studied with such celebrities as Anya Dorfmann and Miklos Schwab. Her love of music also led to the establishment of the Mrs. Cornelius Crane Scholarship at the Juilliard School of Music in New York City, which provides financial aid for advanced students of the violin, cello and piano. A painter of note as well, she specialized in oils; her work includes primitives of life in Maine towns (she had a summer house at Dark Harbor, Islesboro) as well as in other New England communities. Her abilities also led her to begin a new business venture in the world of fashion, creating many of the original fabric designs herself for "Tsuru," her own dress salon, featuring hand-painted silks.

In keeping with her own and Cornelius Crane's fascination with the South Seas, where they had cruised extensively together, Mrs. Crane was also a principal benefactor of the California Institute of Tropical Disease.

Today, under the watchful eye of Refuge Manager Walter A. Prisby, the islands of Crane Wildlife Refuge, once the summer home of the Agawam Indians and still splendid in their isolation from the busy world around them, continue as a habitat for a wide variety of mammals as well as a myriad of sea and shore birds.

And the happy ghosts of centuries past who still inhabit the Choate House are able to look out on the landscape around them and see it little changed in the past two centuries.

22

Doane's Falls: a Gentle Persistence

As early as 1929, the report of the Committee on the Needs and Uses of Open Spaces had recommended that "immediate action" be taken to protect the scenic beauty of a spectacular series of waterfalls known as Doane's Falls.

Located on Lawrence Brook in Royalston in the northwest corner of Worcester County near the New Hampshire border, the falls were described as early as 1841 by Professor Edward Hitchcock in his *Geology of Massachusetts.*

"In a short distance," Hitchcock wrote, "the water descends in several successive leaps, as much as 200 feet between the high walls of gneiss and granite." A trail follows the brook as it descends the falls and the area is shaded with pine and hemlock. Farther down, Lawrence Brook joins Tully Brook above Tully Dam in an area set aside for flood control by the U.S. Army Corps of Engineers.

Despite the area's proximity to Royalston and Athol, there are still remarkably few signs of human settlement. And the view from Jacob Hill, north of the falls looking west over Long Pond, is of ridges of wild forest land as far as the eye can see. There, The Trustees of Reservations owns some 53 acres just west of Spirit Falls as a part of its program to protect additional properties in what is still a large area of outstanding open space. (Jacob's Hill Reservation today also includes 82 acres at nearby Little Pond, now becoming a classic northern bog.)

Named for Amos Doane, who built a mill which overlooked the area — "a large and rambling building three stories tall" — Doane's Falls today provides dramatic scenery for hundreds of visitors annually as well as thrills and pleasure for local youngsters who, despite the dangers, dive into the deep pools below the falls and swim to shore, as they have for generations.

Never utilized, Doane's Mill was finally dismantled board by board, although in the nineteenth century many mills for the manufacture of wool and cotton thrived in the area. There are still mill stones in the vicinity of the Falls today.

But it was not until 1959 that The Trustees of Reservations was able to acquire 12 acres of land bordering Lawrence Brook. Doane's Falls, though nearby, was not included. It was, however, a first step.

With a family homestead in Petersham, a few miles east of Royalston, John M. Woolsey, Jr., knew and loved the still rural sections of central Massachusetts, the country towns that had changed little through the years, and the features of the landscape that would be of interest to The Trustees of Reservations.

Elected to the Standing Committee in 1950 — he later served as Chairman of the organization (1967-1969) and as President (1977-1980) — he was a graduate of Yale and Yale Law School and brought a welcome diversity to balance the Harvard tradition. Bright and very able, he was tenacious when it came to seeking out and preserving special places, especially in Worcester County. Hardly a property acquired within the Central Management Region has failed to bear his stamp, and Doane's Falls was no exception.

For many years, Woolsey continued corresponding with representatives of the Bragg Trust (Edward R. Bragg once owned

*John M. Woolsey, Jr.,
Chairman of the Standing
Committee from 1967 to 1969
and President of The Trustees
of Reservations from 1977 to
1980*

the Falls) as well as with others who had indicated an interest in
the site, but without success. One difficulty was reaching agreement on a value for the property. What was a series of waterfalls
worth? The Trustees commissioned an appraiser to find out.

Meanwhile, one day in 1974, Woolsey was contacted by a
long-time resident of Princeton and Fitchburg whose family roots
reached far back into the history of Royalston. His name was
Richard Bullock.

Descended from Moulton Bullock, who had settled in the
town prior to the Revolution, and Alexander H. Bullock, a
Royalston native who had served as Governor of the Commonwealth from 1866 to 1868, Richard Bullock was interested in
making a substantial contribution to help preserve Doane's Falls.

"My father, Brigham Bullock," he explained, "was a
Royalston boy. He began [his working career] as paymaster on the
Vermont-Massachusetts railroad, the Fitchburg branch of the
Boston & Maine. He married my mother late in life. He was 57.
She was 24. My father died when I was 13 in 1906. My mother
then married Benjamin Poore who became a major general in the
U.S. Army. He died in 1940. He was a wonderful man.

"My own father became Treasurer of the Home Savings Bank
and then President of the Fitchburg National Bank. When I was a
youngster we used to spend summers in Royalston, and, of
course, we always swam at the Falls. We sold our house there in
1922. I want to do something," he said, "to help preserve the Falls
in memory of my father, my mother and General Poore."

Discussions with representatives of the owners of the Falls
began again, with Woolsey leading the negotiations. Finally, in

*At Doane's Falls, Royalston,
benefactor Richard Bullock, left,
meets with Standing
Committee members Mrs.
Frances Forbes and Paul
Brooks. At right, Mrs. Brooks.*

March 1975, agreement was reached. And shortly thereafter, deeds were recorded which transferred ownership of some 18 acres of land — which this time included the Falls themselves — from Frances C. Bragg and Annabelle H. Bragg to The Trustees of Reservations.

The successful conclusion of the project was due first, to the patient and persistent efforts of John Woolsey, but also, it must be emphasized, to the conviction on the part of the Bragg family — especially Mr. and Mrs. David Ashenden and Mrs. Robert Ebaugh, daughter of Edward Bragg — that, if at all possible, Doane's Falls should be preserved in perpetuity.

It had been 46 years since the property had been mentioned in the Report of the Committee on the Needs and Uses of Open Spaces, and 16 years since The Trustees of Reservations had acquired its first parcel of land on Lawrence Brook, proving, once again, that when the cause is just, persistence, on the part of all involved, is a critical ingredient on the road to success.

23

Long Point: from Gun Club to Wildlife Refuge

A part of the outwash plain of the great glacier which once covered all New England, Long Point Wildlife Refuge preserves some 580 acres of land on the south shore of Martha's Vineyard. The property, located in the town of West Tisbury, includes a portion of the eastern shore of Tisbury Great Pond; the eastern shore of Middle Point Cove; all land around Long Cove; and nearly one-half mile of South Beach where the surf rolls in from the Atlantic Ocean.

Secluded fresh water and salt water ponds, as well as salt marshes, sandy beaches and open ocean, combine to produce excellent habitat for waterfowl and shorebirds during migration. Inland from the beach, openings and edges along the coves, and the oak-pine woodland provide habitat as well for many varieties of upland wildlife.

In the nineteenth century, the land was used for grazing sheep and, until 1889, it was the site as well of Scrubby Neck School House. The small, one-room school building with its blackboard still in place may be seen by visitors today. But it is as the former Tisbury Pond Club that the property is best known.

Established in 1912, the Tisbury Pond Club was one of a number of gunning clubs on the island of Martha's Vineyard. Another, the Watcha Club, was located only a mile or so to the east. These were the days when field sports were enormously popular, game was plentiful, and Boston and New York businessmen journeyed to the Vineyard to enjoy the thrill of the hunt itself, and the pleasure of dining upon the game they shot.

There were no daily limits on birds. Live decoys were often used (indeed, the Club had its own flock of tame geese which were always in its yard). Market gunners were still in existence. Wild celery was planted in the ponds. And shorebirds — yellow legs and golden plover — yet to be protected, were killed in large numbers.

The first club house at Tisbury Pond was much like the building today, a farm house, shingled with white cedar, with a veranda on two sides. Duck blinds were constructed in the marsh and, at the end of the day, hunters would meet back at the house for cocktails and a game dinner.

Bedtime was early, for the next day could mean sitting in a cold blind for up to four hours, often in the rain or sleet with decoys and a dog, waiting for redheads, blue bills, black duck and Canada geese to appear. And in those days, there were birds everywhere.

The club's log, for example, reports on Tuesday, December 17, 1912: "Lots of geese, 200-300 in pond; 400-500 pond fowl; 200-300 blacks. . . Shot 13 blacks and 3 bluebills. . . ."And on Monday, November l, 1915: "Back at blind. Large bunches of redheads flew across the Point about 8:30 and again at ll a.m., probably thousands. Birds flew well up the point and low, [lighting] in Tisbury Pond."

Relaxing on the porch of the Tisbury Pond Club in 1913. The former gunning club, which borders Tisbury Great Pond on the south shore of Martha's Vineyard, is now Long Point Wildlife Refuge.

Even as late as 1920, flocks were impressive: "About 4:45," the log continues, "geese began to come from the east in fours and tens and twenties and kept coming until eight o'clock and went into Long Cove, the Pond and Middle Cove. Nothing like it at this time of year has ever been seen. The noise of fighting ganders and crying goslings is tremendous at times. Can only guess at the numbers, but there must be more than fifty in Middle Cove [alone]. . . ."

Winters were different then, as well the log indicates on the day before Christmas in 1912. "Cold and calm. Eight degress above [zero]. All on point early. Few birds flying. . . ice six inches thick on Long Cove. . . . Pump froze in the cottage within four feet of the cook fire. . . ."

Humor and good fellowship were also an important part of the experience at the Tisbury Pond Club. One wag penned a special grace "to be said by the assembled members, and their guests, prior to the evening repast on each day of the week except Saturday." (Shooting was forbidden on Sunday.) It went as follows: "Oh Lord, from errors' ways defend us, Lest we mistake Thy Will for luck; Give us, at dawn, a flight stupendous; Don't send us coot, but geese and duck."

A label pasted into the club's first logbook also shows how at least a few members beat the cold of early mornings in December. It reads: "Tisbury Pond Club Breakfast Port." And again, verse written by a grateful member commemorates the potion: "A po'm I could write, Were I in good form, of Proverbial Port that is good in a storm. But Club members agree, when at breakfast together, T.P.C. Port is good in any old weather."

Members stayed to shoot from two days to a week and then, laden with game for friends and family back home, they departed on the steamer for the mainland. Total birds shot for the year varied from 19 in 1914 to 339 in 1920. Banded birds were always reported to the Bureau of Biological Survey.

By 1932, competition was fierce between members of the Tisbury Pond Club and the nearby Watcha Club for the birds coming into the ponds during fall migration. At one point, the caretaker of the Tisbury Pond Club is said to have crawled to the edge of the marsh at Watcha Pond, lit a cigar, and blown smoke at a flock of geese to scare them away. It was meant to be all in fun, but it ended up in court. At issue was the ownership, use and occupancy of Home Point and a portion of the western shore of Watcha Pond, both of which offered opportunities for "valuable shooting and gunning."

An arbitrator appointed by the judge, with the agreement of both parties, determined the common boundary once and for all and, in a unique move, ordered that for 20 years, a "no man's land" or restricted area, be established between the two clubs where shooting by members of either was prohibited. The rivalry quieted down.

By the late 1930s, the Tisbury Pond Club had three owners, all Bostonians: Frederick N. Blodgett, who was to become a senior vice president at the then First National Bank of Boston; attorney Carl J. Gilbert, a partner of Ropes & Gray who, after World War II, served as President of the Gillette Corporation; and William B. Rogers, President of Fabreeka Products Company of Milton, whose father had been an early member of the club.

Blodgett was a crack shot who loved to hunt upland game as well as water fowl. At age 88, he still shoots today (1991), following woodcock from Nova Scotia to New England and seeking quail in Georgia and Florida. "In the old days in West Tisbury," he said, "we had everything. . . black ducks, geese and blue bills. There were also lots steamers [clams] in the pond which was opened to the sea every year. My, were they good!"

But by the late 1940s, Blodgett recalls, the old building was in sad shape and "we built a new club house. My wife," he added proudly, "drew the plans." As tradition would have it, they were much like the original. One major change, however, was the addition of an electric generator located in the school house which allowed the club to retire its kerosene lamps.

By the '70s, the owners, growing older, looked for a way to preserve the property which had given them and others so much pleasure for so many years. "We loved the place so much, we didn't want to see it sold," Blodgett said, "and we trusted you people [The Trustees] to do the right thing with it."

At first, a one-tenth unidivided ownership was transferred to The Trustees of Reservations each year. But in 1979, the Tisbury Pond Club became a full-fledged property of The Trustees and everyone agreed that, considering its past, it should now become a permanent refuge for wildlife.

Today, sadly, there are nowhere near the numbers of birds there used to be at the beginning of the century. But in the fall, the ponds at Long Point Wildlife Refuge are still used as a resting and feeding place for thousands of migrating water fowl on their way south.

24

Appleton Farms: Nine Generations of New England Agriculture

More than 970 acres of fields and woodland in Ipswich and Hamilton, Appleton Farms is the oldest working farm in the United States owned by a single family. It was first acquired in 1638 by Samuel Appleton as a grant from the Town of Ipswich during the reign of Charles I of England. Francis Randall Appleton, Jr., who represented the ninth generation to operate the farm, died at age 89 in 1974. Today, the property is owned by his widow, Joan E. Appleton, who supervises it with extraordinary energy and skill.

With its distinguished history and magnificent landscape, Appleton Farms will ultimately be offered to The Trustees of Reservations to be preserved in perpetuity.

In 1970, thanks to the generosity of Colonel and Mrs. Appleton, The Trustees began to receive gifts of land in Hamilton. Today, they are a part of Appleton Farms Grass Rides Reservation, some 228 acres of woodland, forest plantations and wetland with more than five miles of trails for walking and cross-country skiing.

The Rides, with their six converging grass avenues and Round Point (the center of the star), reflect the equestrian tradition at Appleton Farms. Dedicated at a Hunt Breakfast and meet of the Myopia Hounds on Columbus Day, 1912, they were conceived and created by Francis Randall Appleton, Sr. They include, as a memorial to his son Charles Lanier Appleton, who died in 1921, the C.L.A. Mile, marked with its own marble quarter posts.

A granite pinnacle from Gore Hall, which until 1913 served Harvard College as its library, stands at Round Point. The Gothic Revival building was named for Christopher Gore (Harvard, 1776), who became Governor of the Commonwealth in 1809 and built Gore Place in Waltham, preserved today by the Gore Place Society.

As Chairman of the Overseers' Committee to Visit the Library, Francis Appleton, Sr., (Harvard, 1875) was given four of the building's 20 pinnacles when the structure was razed. A second was erected at Appleton Farms in his memory by his widow in 1929. Two others, placed on Pigeon Hill and in Monument Field, in 1975, honor Francis Randall Appleton, Jr., and his mother, Fanny Egleston Lanier Appleton. Two identical pinnacles guard the doorway to Widener Library, which was constructed on the site of Gore Hall, and, coincidentally, named for Harry Widener, a classmate of Frank Appleton, Jr.'s (Harvard, 1907), who was lost on the liner *Titanic* when she struck an iceberg and sank on her maiden voyage across the Atlantic in 1912.

Samuel Appleton was 50 years old in 1635 when, with his wife and five children, he arrived in Ipswich, then, according to one historian, "the most remote and isolated settlement in Massachusetts Bay." He had followed his friend John Winthrop, Jr., who, like his father before him, was a leader of The Bay Colony. (The Trustees of Reservations' present Director, Frederic Winthrop, Jr., is a direct descendant.)

Members of the Massachusetts Bay Company had voted as early as 1633 to "hasten the planting of Agawam [the Indian name for Ipswich], one of the most commodious places in the country for cattle and tillage." Today, more than three and one-half centuries later, the fields and pastures of Appleton Farms are still in active agriculture.

As the *Ipswich News-Chronicle* declared at the farm's tercentenary in 1938, "Here. . . one family has molded the landscape without any feeling of violation, having accomplished what no landscape architect ever could, that is, a synthesis of the two Englands. Appleton Farms is now, as it always has been, not another summer estate, but. . . a place where the earth brings forth her increase. The ample acres, now a thousand in number, are no mere barren pride of conspicuous wealth, but a three century-old living farm, a nexus of the best in the agrarian tradition."

Early ledgers show that from 1789 to 1862, the farm produced beef, pork, mutton, lamb, veal, wool, cow hides, sheep skins, butter and cheese for local families. Crops such corn, rye, apples,

Colonel Francis Randall Appleton, Jr. and Silver Prince, *and Mrs. Appleton and* Juno, *in the Great Pasture at Appleton Farms, 1970*

pears, beans, flaxseed, walnut wood, timber and cord wood were traded, and hay was sold to neighbors.

The farm's dairy herd began to win prizes as early as 1865, and after the Civil War and the development of pasteurization, milk production began in earnest. Appleton Farms' blue-ribbon Jersey cattle soon won national recognition. Fields were improved and new barns constructed, and, again, milk production soared.

By 1929, Frank Appleton, Jr., who had served in the Army as a lieutenant-colonel during World War I and was among those who had established the American Legion, had begun to assemble Appleton Farms' famous herd of Guernsey cattle. As a recent history of the property declares, "golden Guernsey milk filled the buckets at Appleton Farms for nearly 50 years."

By 1934, the Great Pasture, some 135 acres, had been cleared and was producing summer feed. In 1950, there were 170 head of dairy and beef cattle, 130 sheep, 950 turkeys and 35 pigs. The flock of White Holland turkeys were an innovation for the time and were sold dressed to the New York City market.

For nearly 20 years now, Joan Appleton has continued to oversee the farm property. For 15 of those years, she operated Appleton Farms herself with its prize-winning Guernseys. In the face of economic realities, the herd was sold in 1977. Then in 1979, Mrs. Appleton engaged, as general manager, James S. Geiger, a graduate of the University of Wisconsin who grew up on a family farm near Madison. Geiger has served with great distinction. Given the state of agriculture in New England, it has not been easy. But the success of the property is a wonderful testimonial to tenacity and imagination.

Appleton Farms has been able not only to survive but to prosper with a combination of diversification and resourcefulness. In 1973, it began to develop a herd of Beefalo cattle which today is thriving. Geiger turned a new herd of Holstein and Jerseys into a brood cattle operation. And in recent years he has begun to explore new areas which could be marketed directly, such as livestock genetics and the production of agricultural compost to utilize better the waste products of farm and food industries.

In 1988, the property celebrated its 350th anniversary with a gala occasion. That same year the enterprise of Appleton Farms was incorporated and passed to James and Caroline Geiger, who had done so much to make it viable. To Joan Appleton and the Geiger family in their respective capacities as owner and stewards of the land and business, Appleton Farms is much more than a tract of landscape and an economic unit. It is, as they say, "a public trust to be treated with care and maintained for posterity" with untold possibilities for public education in agriculture and ecology. Indeed, the future does looks bright.

In August, 1920, at the dedication of a tablet in the Great Pasture memorializing his ancestor Samuel Appleton, Francis

Appleton, Sr., concluded his remarks with some lines written by
Alexander Pope (1688-1744) when the poet was 12 years old.
"When I was a boy," Appleton said, "my father taught me to
recite these verses." They seem to speak for every generation at
Appleton Farms.

> *Happy the man whose wish and care*
> *A few paternal acres bound;*
> *Content to breathe his native air*
> *In his own ground;*
> *Whose herds with milk, whose fields with bread,*
> *Whose flocks supply him with attire,*
> *Whose trees in summer yield him shade,*
> *In winter, fire.*

25

Monument Mountain: a Landmark Under Siege

In 1899, Miss Helen C. Butler gave to The Trustees of Reservations
some 260 acres of land on Monument Mountain "in fulfillment of
a wish of the late Rosalie Butler [her sister], that it might be
preserved forever for the enjoyment of the public."

A landmark of South Berkshire County, Monument Mountain
takes its name from the legend of an Indian maiden, disappointed
in love, who hurled herself from the mountain top, and the stone
cairn, or monument, which marks her grave. The story is immor-
talized in a poem by William Cullen Bryant.

Revered throughout history, Monument Mountain was also
the site of a celebrated picnic on a summer day in 1850. It was
attended by, among others, authors Nathaniel Hawthorne,
Herman Melville, David Dudley Field, and Oliver Wendell
Holmes, as well as by publisher James T. Field, who was visiting
Hawthorne at the time.

Reported Field (according to an account some years later):
"We all assembled in a shady spot, and one of the party then read
us Bryant's beautiful poem commemorating Monument Mountain. Then we lunched among the rocks, and somebody proposed
Bryant's health, and 'long life to the dear old poet.' This was the
most popular toast of the day, and it took, I remember, a considerable quantity of Heidsieck to do it justice." As in those days,
hundreds climb Monument Mountain annually today to admire
its views of the surrounding landscape.

Miss Butler's gift included the summit of the mountain at
Squaw Peak and its steep eastern face. It did not, however,

include the western slope, which overlooks the Housatonic River and the town of Great Barrington.

For more than 100 years, the western side of the mountain, in private hands, remained undisturbed. That is until 1984. "One day," Stanley I. Piatczyc reports (Piatczyc is Supervisor of The Trustees of Reservations' Western Management Region), "I got a call from a surveyor who said 'Stan, do you know that there is a proposal to build 210 condominium units on a plateau of land on Monument Mountain overlooking Great Barrington?'

"I was shocked," said Piatczyc, "and could hardly believe it, but a visit to the site put me straight. There were the test holes for percolation. It was true!"

When the news broke that night with a story in *The Berkshire Eagle*, the community was up in arms. What the developer proposed was an intense complex of condominiums, townhouses and single residences, sited in clusters and located on some 160 acres of land overlooking the valley below. The project would have destroyed the visual qualities and resource values of a wide area.

As Director Gordon Abbott, Jr., declared: "After exhaustive study of the preliminary plans for the development as well as other information provided by the developers and their consultants, we have concluded that the proposed project would introduce into a magnificent wild and scenic landscape, totally incompatible and inappropriate urban elements, such as a swimming pool and bath house, tennis courts and roadways and parking lots for what could be as many as 400 vehicles," as well as more than 200 living units.

The ridge line of Monument Mountain in the late 19th century as viewed from Great Barrington. Early photo shows the west side of the mountain, which was proposed for development in 1984 and later successfully preserved as a part of the reservation.

Others agreed. Attorney Jim McElroy, a member of the Western Regional Committee of The Trustees of Reservations, summed up local sentiment. "Monument Mountain," he said, "is one of the first things you see when you come into the Great Barrington area. It's a very sensitive and very beautiful property.

"I think a lot of people suddenly realized that what they had taken for granted for so many years was now in jeopardy. And to even think about looking up at the mountain and rather than seeing just a beautiful landscape with trees and birds, they would actually be seeing buildings and rooftops, was just too scary a proposition to handle."

Shortly thereafter, Housatonic resident Stephen Root, who farmed land bordering the proposed development, called Piatczyc to report that he had been offered $500,000 for a parcel of his land which could provide vital access to the development site.

"As an individual," McElroy explained, "he [Root] didn't feel there was much he could do to prevent [all] this from happening, but after talking with Stan he realized he had a very stong ally in The Trustees of Reservations. Stephen then began to see a way to preserve the land he loved, and, rather than selling to the developer for $500,000, which is an incredible sum of money to anybody, and particularly to him, he agreed to sell it to The Trustees for $10,000."

Meanwhile, faced with mounting opposition throughout the community as well as from the Planning Board and the Conservation Commission, the developer withdrew his proposal. Shortly afterwards, voters at Great Barrington's Town Meeting approved a one-year moratorium on multi-family dwellings to provide time to review the community's zoning by-laws. The margin to "save Great Barrington," as one voter put it, was 349 to 5.

The Trustees of Reservations had been busy as well. A special committee had been appointed to deal with the project. Committee members included Jim McElroy, Rush Taggart of Stockbridge, Chairman of the Local Committee for The Mission House; Syd Smithers of Windsor, an attorney in Pittsfield, Chairman of the Western Regional Committee and a member of the Standing Committee, and Stan Piatczyc.

Their goal was to complete a purchase of the 164-acre parcel and to preserve it as open space as a part of Monument Mountain Reservation. Following negotiations, The Trustees of Reservations was able to satisfy a first mortgage on the property for $15,000 held by an earlier owner. It then purchased a second mortage held by the Lee National Bank for $12,000. "That put us in a position," as Jim McElroy explained, "where the developer had to deal with The Trustees directly."

Following negotiations, agreement was finally reached and using the Revolving Loan Fund, The Trustees of Reservations was able to purchase the land. "Then," McElroy added, "we had to find out how we were going to get the money" to pay the fund back. The goal was $70,000 and a campaign to raise it was set in motion.

"One Saturday," Stan Piatczyc explained, "we met at the Youth Center in Great Barrington. There were Boy Scouts, people who lived at the base of the mountain and people who lived elsewhere throughout the region, all licking stamps and sealing envelopes which contained the appeal for funds."

Individual donors were also contacted and within three months, thanks to the generosity of scores of contributors, including local businesses and banks, and even the real estate agency which was to market the condominium project, the money was in hand.

McElroy put the effort into perspective for many of those involved. "I'm not against development," he said. "I'm a lawyer. I represent a lot of real estate developers. But I think there's a happy medium between development where none of the environment is taken into consideration and the fanatical conservationists who don't want any development."

The hero, of course, of the battle to save the western slope of Monument Mountain is Stephen Root, who could have grown rich in the process but chose another way instead.

"I like living here," he said, "but I didn't want to live here if that [development] was there. I was proud of telling friends 'I own half-way up that mountain.' I like working in the woods. I guess I was brought up that way. It's a part of me. I'm glad that Monument Mountain is going to stay the way it is, and I feel pretty good I was able to help."

It goes to show that one person can, indeed, make a difference between victory and defeat.

26

Cherry Hill: Home of an Eminent American Family

In 1865, Dr. Samuel Cabot of Boston, a former colonel in the Sanitary Corps of the Army of the Potomac, bought land in Canton which some day he hoped to build upon.

Dr. Cabot (1815-1885) was a member of the medical staff of the Massachusetts General Hospital. A man of many interests and talents, he also served as Curator of Ornithology at Boston's Museum of Natural History. Prior to the Civil War, he had been Director of the Stevens-Catherwood Expedition to Yucatan. He was a leader in the early campaigns for women's suffrage. And as a staunch abolitionist, he made his house in the city a resting place on the Underground Railway.

But it was left to his son, Arthur Tracy Cabot, also a doctor of medicine, to fulfill his dream of a building a house in the expanding suburbs south of Boston. Born in 1852, Arthur Cabot was a surgeon and, like his father, practiced at Massachusetts General Hospital. He served as President of the Massachusetts Medical Society and, for more than a decade, he was a member of the Harvard Corporation and a Trustee of the Museum of Fine Arts.

The years passed quickly, and in 1902 the Cabots decided to construct a country home on the land in Canton. As architect, the couple chose Charles Platt, who had already made a name for himself around the nation. Unlike many of his contemporaries — whose lavish work, much of it in the European fashion, was begining to embellish the countryside — Platt was a man of exquisite taste and a master of understatement.

Originally interested in landscape architecture (in 1894, he and his brother had produced a book entitled *Italian Gardens*), Platt was an artist of some ability and combined his talents to design buildings, as one critic has said, which were remarkable for their "fitness and restraint."

"His houses," the critic continued, "which begin by fitting their sites, have invariably a quiet and distinguished way of looking as though he had conceived them with the invention that goes into the making of a good picture or statue."

In 1902, architect Charles Platt designed this handsome house at Cherry Hill, Canton, for Dr. and Mrs. Arthur T. Cabot of Boston. His niece, Mrs. Eleanor Cabot Bradley, bequeathed the house and its surrounding 84 acres to The Trustees in 1991.

For Cherry Hill in Canton, which overlooks a series of woodland ridges to the west across the Neponset River valley, and to
the north commands a magnificent view of Great Blue Hill, Platt
chose the friendly formality of a Georgian mansion of red brick.
The access drive is perfectly proportioned. The walled garden at
the back of the house, a few steps down from its broad, bluestone
terrace, is elegant in its simplicity.

The interior of the house is both decorative and utilitarian, for
Platt "had a flair " for doing the right thing. Painted and panelled
walls, cornices and doorways, even light fixtures, "are kept
beautifully in hand." Indeed, as a critic explains, "he has a way of
making a well-appointed room beautiful without causing you to
notice any specific thing in it. . . . You [feel] at home, very comfortable, and with a sense of refined charm about you." In sum, Platt's
work was a wonderful mix of tradition and originality.

By 1912, Arthur Cabot had died, but Mrs. Cabot lived on in
the house until her death in 1944. The next year, the property was
purchased from the estate by Mr. and Mrs. Ralph Bradley of
Boston. Mrs. Bradley, Mrs. Arthur Cabot's niece, was the former
Eleanor Cabot, daughter of Godfrey L. Cabot, younger brother of
Arthur, founder of the Cabot Corporation, and then patriarch of
the Cabot clan.

The Bradleys continued to maintain 242 Beacon Street as their
primary residence, but commuted to Canton on weekends to
work around the place and make it their own. Mr. Bradley,
himself a Vice President and Treasurer of the Cabot Corporation,
had distinguished careers not only in business, but in public
service as well. He served in World War I as a major with the U.S.
Army in England. And during World War II, he was appointed
head of Civil Defense for Greater Boston by then Governor
Leverett Saltonstall.

Interested in horticulture and garden design, Mrs. Bradley
attended the Cambridge School of Architecture and Landscape
Architecture, now a part of Harvard University, and for two
decades was an active member of the Visiting Committee for the
Arnold Arboretum.

During World War II, she was busy as chairman of the USO's
recreation centers for service men and women and helped found
the Pan-American Society of Massachusetts, whose purpose was
to meet the needs of Latin-American dignitaries, intellectuals and
students during the war years. A great philanthropist, she supported many Boston charities and made possible the construction
of the Ralph and Eleanor Bradley Building at the Museum School
of the Boston Museum of Fine Arts.

In 1961, following Godfrey Cabot's death in Boston at age 101,
the Bradleys moved full-time to Cherry Hill in Canton. The place
with its gardens, pool, and more than 90 acres of field and wood-

land served as a center for gatherings of family and friends. Fresh cream, milk and eggs were provided by farm animals and the greenhouse was filled with flowers.

There was a walled cutting garden as well, and a sunken camellia house where delicate white and pink petals lay scattered on the ground. In the forest, woodland dells, surrounded by naturalized ornamental plantings such as dogwood and Japanese holly, were there to surprise and delight visitors. A number of small ponds add to the diversity of the property, which also includes the site of a Colonial tavern built in 1740 but moved later to make way for Route 128.

By hand and with tractor and truck, the Bradleys improved the property themselves, pulling stumps and clearing pastures, for both loved to work the land. Ralph Bradley died in 1970, but Mrs. Bradley lived on at the farm in Canton, which she loved dearly, until her own death at age 96 in 1990. At one point, she had hoped that one of her children might take over the property and live there. But with lives of their own to lead, that was not to be. "If none of them want it," she told Director Gordon Abbott, Jr., in 1968, "then I want to preserve it. I like The Trustees because they are people of taste and distinction."

In early 1991, Cherry Hill, with a generous endowment, became a property of The Trustees of Reservations. Today, as the Eleanor Cabot Bradley Reservation, it serves as Headquarters for the Southeast Management Region. Within easy driving distance of the city for visitors, it also adds additional open space to the extensive holdings in the area of the Metropolitan District Commission. These include Blue Hills Reservation and Ponkapog Golf Course. Blue Hills, of course, was an original property of the Metropolitan Park Commission founded in 1893 by Charles Eliot and The Trustees of Reservations.

"The Bradley Reservation," says Director Fred Winthrop, "is a distinguished property, not only because of its landscape and its architecture, but because of its association with an eminent and extraordinary American family."

As with every acquistion, a planning process has begun which will provide for passive recreational opportunities for the public, while still preserving the property's natural, scenic and historic values, as well as the elegance of another era.

27

Coolidge Point: 'a Wild Promontory Surrounded by the Ocean'

In 1871, Thomas Jefferson Coolidge of Boston, great-grandson of the third President of the United States, purchased for $12,000 the old Goldsmith Farm in Manchester on Millett's Neck, a point of land just east of Kettle Cove.

Following in the tradition of Richard Henry Dana (father of the author of the classic *Two Years Before the Mast*), who in 1845 became Manchester's first summer resident, Coolidge and his wife, the former Hetty Sullivan Appleton, built, in 1873, "a country house," as he wrote in his autobiography, "on a wild promontory surrounded by the ocean." Of simple wood clapboard, the three-story structure looked westward over Kettle Cove into the setting sun.

In his long and accomplished life, Coolidge was not only a hugely successful financier and merchant, but served his country and his community in many ways. Schooled in England, Switzerland and Germany, he graduated from Harvard in 1850 at the age of 19. He was raised and educated as an aristocrat with ideas that were occasionally more European than American. "I believed myself," he wrote in later years, "to belong to a superior class, and that the principle that the ignorant and the poor should have the

White marble columns enclose the porch of the great summer house at Coolidge Point, Manchester, built in 1902 for Thomas Jefferson Coolidge, Jr. Designed by the celebrated New York architectural firm of McKim, Mead & White, the structure was known locally as the "Marble Palace."

same right to make laws and govern as the educated and the refined was an absurdity."

At the invitation of his father-in-law, he entered the milling industry and became an officer and director of such firms as Lawrence Manufacturing Company and New Hampshire's Amoskeag Mills. Active in banking as well, he was a director of the Merchants National Bank of Boston and one of the original founders of the Old Colony Trust Company.

He also devoted himself to public service and was an early member of the Metropolitan Park Commission, established at the urging of Charles Eliot and The Trustees of Reservations. Manchester can thank him for the gift of its town library, a handsome stone building of cut Ashlar granite (designed by architect Charles Follen McKim), and Harvard University for its Jefferson Physical Laboratory.

In 1889, he was appointed a member of the Pan-American Congress and three years later, following in the footsteps of his revered great-grandfather, he was named Minister to France by President Benjamin Harrison. He also served his state as a member of the Massachusetts Taxation Commission and his nation again as a member of a Joint High Commission with Canada which examined the question of the Alaskan boundary, the state of the fisheries, and the status of armaments upon the Great Lakes. He died in 1920 in his ninetieth year, predeceased by his only son.

For his own summer place on the point, Thomas Jefferson Coolidge, Jr., who became President of the Old Colony Trust Company, chose a house of dimensions very different from his father's. As architects he engaged the celebrated firm of McKim, Mead & White, which designed in 1902 what became known locally as the "Marble Palace." Of brick and white marble, its two wings and Roman columns reflected the Classic Revival style made famous, appropriately, by Thomas Jefferson. As *The Boston Transcript* declared at the time: "No house on the North Shore is more solid or substantial in appearance than is that nearing finish at this time for Thomas Jefferson Coolidge, Jr., of Manchester."

With its gracious porches and finely-manicured grass terrace overlooking Great Egg Rock and the waters of Massachusetts Bay, the Marble Palace was a monument to comfort in the gilded age of great summer houses. It was also host to a number of dignitaries during its 58 years. They included President and Mrs. Woodrow Wilson, who were given the house for a week in 1918. Colonel Edward M. House, the President's aide and confidant, regularly vacationed nearby in Magnolia. The Crown Prince and Princess of Norway were also guests in the mid-1930s. A grand luncheon and lawn party celebrated their stay.

The accomplishments of the senior Coolidge's son and grandsons were no less distinguished than his own. Thomas

Financier and diplomat Thomas Jefferson Coolidge, who purchased the old Goldsmith Farm on Millet's Neck in 1871. Photo taken in early 1900s. Mr. Coolidge died in 1920 in his ninetieth year.

Thomas Jefferson Coolidge, Jr., President of the Old Colony Trust Company. It was he who built the "Marble Palace" at Coolidge Point. Photo taken in 1908, shortly before his death in 1912.

Jefferson Coolidge III, who graduated from Harvard in 1915, following in his father's footsteps, was also a highly successful banker and financier. Chairman of the Old Colony Trust Company and of the United Fruit Company during its most productive years, he was active as a director of many banking institutions including the First National Bank of Boston, where he served as a senior officer as well. He was also appointed Undersecretary of the Treasury by President Franklin D. Roosevelt during his first term.

Through the decades, successive Coolidge families have all spent their summers (in later years they were there year-round) at what soon became known as Coolidge Point. As if to mark a change in eras, the Marble Palace was torn down in 1958 shortly before the death of T.J. Coolidge III. A far simpler, single-story, brick house (designed by New York architect Page Cross) was then constructed and lived in for many years by his widow, the former Katherine H. Kuhn of California. (It, too, was razed after Mrs. Coolidge's death.)

Subdivision of the orginal 116-acre property was begun shortly after its purchase, as, in the 1870s, Mr. Coolidge sold off lots to friends and acquaintances. Among those who lived at Coolidge Point were financier Robert Treat Paine II, once Commodore of the Eastern Yacht Club, who, in good weather, moored his 80-foot schooner and 110-foot motor yacht just off Coolidge Point. The *Blue Dolphin*, a 100-foot schooner owned by Amory Coolidge, younger brother of T. Jefferson Coolidge III, was also often kept nearby in Gloucester.

Mrs. Thomas Jefferson Coolidge, Jr. (the former Clara Amory), who lived on at Coolidge Point after her husband's death and kept the property together for succeeding generations

On the steps of the Marble Palace in 1917, from left, William A. Coolidge, Amory Coolidge, John Linzee Coolidge and Thomas Jefferson Coolidge, III

Other residents included noted landscape artist Ernest W. Longfellow; attorney Reginald Foster, also a director of United Fruit and the First National Bank of Boston; and later, Edward L. Bigelow, President of Boston's State Street Bank; Alan Cunningham (who married Robert Treat Paine's daughter Ruth), President of The Boston Gas Company; and physician George W. Thorn, distinguished Hersey Professor of the Theory and Practice of Physics at what was then Boston's Peter Bent Brigham Hospital. According to those who lived there, Coolidge Point was a small community of congenial friends, but it was also one where a family's privacy was honored and respected.

It was not until the mid-1970s that thoughts turned to the possibility of preserving all or a portion of the property. William A. Coolidge, now head of the family, called Chairman Augustus P. Loring, Chairman of the Standing Committee of The Trustees of Reservations, and Loring and Director Gordon Abbott, Jr., visited Coolidge Point.

Both were immensely impressed with the area and its diversity: a small pond and brook, a section of sand beach facing Magnolia Cove, a ridge of high granite ledges to the north, and, of course, the rocky point itself with Kettle Island to the east, Boston's growing skyline to the west, Egg Rock just off shore, and the sweep of Massachusetts Bay.

But ownership of the land was in many hands. Mrs. Coolidge herself was still alive and her three children — Kitty (Dr. Catherine Coolidge Lastavica, an authority on Lyme disease, and now an Assistant Professor at Tufts University's School of Medicine); Jeff (T. Jefferson Coolidge IV, President, Coolidge Investment Corp.) and Linzee (J. Linzee Coolidge, owner and manager of real estate properties in Boston) — were understandably not yet ready to make a decision about the future. Putting a meaningful parcel together to make preservation work would have to wait.

Dr. Catherine Coolidge Lastavica, who, with her brothers, made possible the preservation of Coolidge Point

By 1984, Mrs. Coolidge had died and Dr. Lastavica had purchased 19.1 acres, the so-called Clarke Pond parcel (the Rev. James Freeman Clarke, an early owner, had a house nearby) from her brother Jeff to be able to maintain the option of conservation. She and her Uncle Bill (William A. Coolidge) had previously donated Bungalow Hill, 16.2 acres of woodland which included the high granite ledges, to Essex County Greenbelt Association, a regional conservation organization with headquarters nearby in Essex.

Earlier, Abbott, also had met with Coolidge Point summer residents Mr. and Mrs. Middleton G. C. Train, who were anxious to preserve their property, some five acres of land overlooking Magnolia Harbor, with a conservation restriction. It, too, at Abbott's suggestion, was given to Essex County Greenbelt.

As time passed, however, it became clearer just how the property as a whole might be protected. And in 1989, Dr.

Lastavica explained, "I called [Director] Fred Winthrop at The Trustees of Reservations. Actually," she added, "it was Fred's father, a cousin of the family's, who first suggested to my Uncle Bill the idea of conservation back in the 1970s."

Working with Dr. Lastavica and her advisors, staff members of The Trustees, led by Deputy Director for Land Conservation Wesley T. Ward, put together a plan to protect a total of 57.8 acres of land at Coolidge Point.

In December, 1990, Dr. Lastavica donated 14.1 acres to The Trustees of Reservations. The parcel included most of Clarke Pond and its shoreline, woodland carriage paths, and 375-feet of Magnolia Beach, all adjacent to the land at Bungalow Hill. Then, at the end of 1991, The Trustees of Reservations acquired an additional 22.5 acres of magnificent shorefront land known as the Ocean Lawn, former site of the Marble Palace. Dr. Lastavica gave her 50 percent interest in the property. The remaining interest was acquired with a grant from a charitable trust established by William A. Coolidge in 1954.

For herself and her husband John, a founder and Treasurer of the Gloucester Bank and Trust Company, Dr. Lastavica retained lifetime rights of occupancy and use of 6.9 acres of land adjacent to the Ocean Lawn. The parcel includes a handsome, shingle-style stable located off Coolidge Drive; a wood barn; a caretaker's cottage faced earlier with brick to match the Marble Palace; and greenhouses and related structures — all part of the original estate.

Finally, to simplify management activities at Coolidge Point, Essex County Greenbelt Association agreed to transfer ownership of its 16.2-acre parcel at Bungalow Hill to The Trustees of Reservations. In return, The Trustees voted to give Essex County Greenbelt a conservation restriction which guarantees that the open, natural and scenic condition of at least 60 acres of Coolidge land will be preserved forever.

An initial endowment of $673,000 for what is now the Coolidge Reservation has already been received. Additional gifts are expected to increase the amount in the years ahead. Work to complete a Master Plan for the management of the property is underway. Initial plans call for the Clarke Pond area to be open to the public seven days a week from dawn to dusk. A major challenge will be to balance public and private use of the Point.

"The generosity of the Coolidge family in conserving this landscape for the enjoyment of the public has been extraordinary," said Director Fred Winthrop, Jr. "In an increasingly urban environment, a property of this caliber dedicated to conservation use is a remarkable treasure.

"We also greatly appreciate the support and encouragement of Essex County Greenbelt," he added. "A cooperative effort of this sort, between two land trusts, speaks to the future of the land conservation movement."

There have been Coolidges on the point now for 121 years. "It is no longer [wild] country," as Thomas Jefferson Coolidge, Sr., wrote in 1902, ". . . houses having sprung up around us." But the Coolidge land itself still retains the magnificent views and vistas as well as the myriad of natural features which gave it its charm in the early years.

They will remain always for the use and enjoyment of generations yet to come, thanks to the generosity and thoughtfulness of the Coolidge family and, most especially, to Catherine Coolidge Lastavica, whose interest and initiative made possible their preservation.

Conservation Restrictions

1

A New Way to Protect Open Space

There were only a handful of people present at a special meeting
of the corporation held at General Headquarters in Milton on that
April afternoon in 1971, but proxies numbering 115 easily created
a quorum.

The matter at hand was a much-discussed and long-heralded
amendment to the charter of The Trustees of Reservations which
would permit it to accept conservation restrictions or easements,
a practice authorized by Act of the State Legislature. The motion
was approved unanimously and the organization entered a new
era in land conservation.

A conservation easement or restriction, as they are called in
Massachusetts, is a legal agreement between the owner of a
property and a non-profit organization, which restricts the use of
a defined area of land without affecting the ownership thereof.
Conservation restrictions are designed to maintain a parcel of
land in its "natural, scenic, and open condition" by transferring
the rights to develop it to a land trust, a municipal Conservation
Commission, or to a state or federal resource agency. The law
also provides for preservation restrictions designed to protect a
structure, feature or site "historically significant for its architecture, archaeology or associations."

The most significant characteristic of a conservation restriction is that the land affected remains private property. No rights
are provided for public access unless, of course, specific permission is granted by the owner. Conservation restrictions allow
landowners to enjoy their properties as they choose on the
condition, of course, that their use is consistent with the terms of
the restriction. They may continue to live on it, or use it for

"agricultural, farming or forest" purposes, provided it is kept in its "natural, scenic and open condition."

Properties protected with conservation or preservation restrictions may be sold or leased. Their disposition may also be directed by will. The restriction runs with the land or building and will always be binding upon lessees, grantees, heirs, or assigns — indeed, upon any other future owner.

Restrictions are recorded at the Registry of Deeds and it is the responsibility of the charitable organization or public agency which holds the restriction to see that its provisions are enforced. This involves periodic inspections of the property by the holder of the restriction and, in the case of a violation, possible legal action.

Restrictions that are given in perpetuity and meet Internal Revenue Service criteria, entitle a donor to a Federal income tax deduction. The appraised value of the restriction may also be deducted from the donor's estate, thus perhaps significantly reducing estate taxes.

Many early conservation restrictions negotiated by The Trustees and other organizations allowed landowners to reserve the right to build a specified number of houses within the restricted area, subject, of course, to the terms and purposes of the restriction. Such arrangements came to be called "floating house lots" because their exact location would not be established until some time in the future when the owner of the land and the holder of the restriction could agree upon a site.

In 1981, this practice was challenged by assessors in the Town of Medfield (see chapter 8). One important result of the initially unfavorable decisions in the case was to focus attention on the need for more care and specificity in locating structures, especially residences, within a restricted area.

Two approaches to the matter are now commonly employed, depending upon the particular characteristics being considered, the wishes of the donor, and the purposes of the restriction. One is to exclude from the restriction any lots which may be built upon in the future. The other is to establish defined "building envelopes" within the restricited area. Because these "envelopes" are controlled by the approval process and standards written into the restriction itself, any development, construction or reconstruction within a "building envelope" is subject to the holder's review and approval.

Conservation restrictions offer a number of unique features. For landowners, they can provide a flexible way to help keep a property in family ownership by reducing its value for estate tax purposes. And, as the owner retains title to the restricted land, it need not be open to the public. If it is to qualify for tax advantages, however, the restricted land must offer significant public benefits. It can protect a scenic vista along a public roadway, for example, a major wetland, prime agricultural soils, or an important wildlife habitat.

Communities often prefer conservation restrictions to gifts in fee as a way to preserve open space. Restricted land may still be taxed as private property although, theoretically, at a reduced rate. It is difficult, however, to predict how local real estate assessors will act. Cities and towns vary widely in how they appraise land restricted for conservation purposes, although the law does require that the parcel be assessed separately.

Finally, land trusts also find conservation restrictions useful as another way to protect a property's scenic and environmental values where public access is not needed. The cost of maintaining and enforcing restrictions is usually far less than managing a parcel of land which is open for public use and enjoyment. It has often been pointed out, however, that the majority of restricted properties at present are still in the hands of the original donor. Ownership by another individual, perhaps less interested in the environment, may raise the costs of enforcement in the future.

Today, conservation easements or restrictions are used by hundreds of land trusts throughout the United States. They are not, however, a recent invention. As early as 1930, they were employed to protect streams and scenic roads in the nation's capital as well as vistas along the Blue Ridge Parkway in Virginia and North Carolina, a property of the National Park Service.

In Massachusetts, the Conservation Restriction Act (Chapter 184, SS 31, 32 and 33) was authorized by the Legislature as early as 1969. Its requirements, which call for the approval of the Board of Selectmen in the community where the restriction is located, as well as the signature of the Secretary of the Commonwealth's Executive Office of Environmental Affairs, have often been cited as a model for the country as a whole because of their oversight provisions.

2

River Corridors: a Natural for Restrictions

Work had already begun to acquire The Trustees of Reservations' first conservation restriction before the special meeting of the corporation had taken place in April 1971.

More than half a year earlier, Standing Committee members Theodore Chase and Thomas B. Williams, and the Director, had met with Mrs. Muriel Lewis, her son George and her brother Richard Saltonstall to discuss the preservation of some two miles of frontage on the Charles River in Sherborn. A part of their properties bordered Rocky Narrows and all of it was within the project area of The Trustees' just-launched Charles River Protection Program. George Lewis, Sr., had served as the Chairman of the Local Committee for Rocky Narrows Reservation and the Lewis family had been generously interested in the preservation of the river and its environs for many years.

In Ipswich, too, discussions had begun with a score or more landowners along Argilla Road about using conservation restrictions to protect salt marsh along the Castle Neck River, a tidal estuary which borders Crane Memorial Reservation and the islands of Crane Wildlife Refuge.

The project was to be a part of the ongoing Ipswich-Essex Salt Marsh Protection Program initiated earlier at the urging of Ipswich resident and Advisory Council member Charles W. Eliot II. Designed to be a comprehensive and cooperative neighborhood effort, the program to protect the river was coordinated and administered locally by volunteers John C. Vincent, Jr., an attorney whose advice proved to be invaluable in the process, and architect Charles S. Shurcliff, Jr., a resident of Argilla Road, who met personally with each landowner.

By the end of 1971, it was clear that conservation restrictions were going to play a major role in The Trustees of Reservations' land conservation efforts. The Standing Committee wisely proposed that a "contingency fund" be established to enable the organization to meet legal expenses which might be involved in defense of easement agreements. It was to be called the Conserva-

Members of the study team for the Upper Charles River Protection Program confer at Harvard's Graduate School of Design. From left, Ellis N. Allen, Chairman, Local Committee for Rocky Woods Reservation; Project Chief Garlund S. Okerlund, Department of Landscape Architecture, Harvard School of Design; GSD Associate Professor Peter L. Hornbeck and Project Chairman Thomas B. Williams, both members of the Standing Committee; David P. DeSmit, Project staff; and Professor Charles W. Eliot II, a member of the Advisory Council.

tion Restriction Fund and it was to set a precedent followed today by land trusts throughout the country.

It was agreed unanimously by the board that "contributions should be sought to accompany restrictions which may be accepted, to provide funds for their administration, maintenance and enforcement should the need arise."

All contributions were to become a part of a pooled reserve fund, the income and principal of which could both be used in case of a legal challenge. Standing Committee Chairman Augustus P. Loring initiated the fund with a contribution of $200. Thanks to many other generous gifts along the way, the Conservation Restriction Fund today totals more than $300,000. Considering the possible costs associated with litigation, and the organization's growing number of conservation restrictions (which topped 100 in 1991), gifts to the Fund continue to be sought whenever a restriction is acquired.

The Lewis restriction, which preserved wetland and upland along the Charles River, was recorded in December 1972. Some 81 acres in all, it was The Trustees of Reservations' first conservation restriction. With Broadmoor Wildlife Sanctuary nearby, the Saltonstall restriction was given to Massachusetts Audubon Society.

Today, nearly 20 years later, The Trustees of Reservations holds 16 conservation restrictions (located in eight different riverside communities) protecting a total of 663 acres of wetland and upland along the upper Charles River and two of its tributaries, Bogastow Brook and Trout Brook. Many hundreds of additional acres within the river corridor, of course, are preserved by properties held in fee, such as Noon Hill, the Shattuck Reservation, and Charles River Peninsula.

By 1974, 14 landowners along Argilla Road in Ipswich had preserved a total of 247 acres of upland and salt marsh bordering the Castle Neck River, again using conservation restrictions.

The concept was beginning to catch on with landowners throughout the Commonwealth. In the next few years, The Trustees of Reservations received gifts of conservation restrictions protecting Prospect Hill, Chilmark, the Vineyard's highest hilltop, as well some 75 acres of woodland and ocean frontage on the island's north shore. Another important restriction protected 63 acres of agricultural land in Medfield bordering Hartford Street and Rocky Woods.

3

Hunnewell Pinetum and Seven Gates Farm

In 1975, The Trustees of Reservations also accepted restrictions protecting some nine acres of land in Wellesely, site of "a remarkable collection of evergreens." The "Pinetum," much respected and admired by the Arnold Arboretum (which itself was unable to accept the restriction), was created in 1867 by Hollis H. Hunnewell whose aim was "to plant in it every conifer, native and foreign, that will be found sufficiently hardy to thrive in our New England climate." More than a century of experimentation with their growth and culture has resulted in the production of scores of new evergreens which are grown widely throughout the region today.

Because of the temporal nature and obvious fragility of any horticultural collection, The Trustees of Reservations prudently reserved the right to transfer the Hunnewell restriction to an organization of similar purposes, perhaps local, should that be necessary as time passes.

Meanwhile, discussions had begun as well with the president and shareholders of Seven Gates Farm, Chilmark, Martha's Vineyard, about the possibility of using conservation restrictions to protect areas of land at the property which were held in common. Originally purchased and planned at the end of the last century by Harvard geologist Nathaniel Shaler, Seven Gates includes more than 1,500 acres. Some 476 acres are allocated as house sites; the remainder are owned in common by the corporation's stockholders.

The common land is extraordinary in its beauty and diversity. It includes a mile and one-half of sand beach and rocky shore on Vineyard Sound, three freshwater ponds, as well as open fields and woodland. Topography and soil conditions have encouraged the growth of sizable trees for the Vineyard, and there is an impressive forest of beech. Scenic cart roads and trails wind their way through the property. And the views everywhere are much the same today as they were a century ago.

Seven Gates is also a uniquely-planned community. Professor Shaler insisted that no one house be visible from another. The result is that buildings are sited in remarkable harmony with the natural environment that surrounds them.

In December, 1975, following review of a number of drafts, a conservation restriction protecting 1,126 acres of common land at Seven Gates was accepted by the Standing Committee.

Of interest among its usual provisions preserving the natural qualities of the environment, were the following: a) that "not more than 10 additional residences. . . shall, without the consent of [The

Trustees of Reservations] or their successors, be erected on the Restricted Property." And b) that "all the foregoing restrictions shall automatically terminate with respect to any property taken by eminent domain or affected by any governmental action for which the owners would be entitled to compensation had these restrictions not been imposed, upon the effective date of such taking or action."

This so-called "snap-back" provision was designed to maintain the full and fair market value of the property in case of condemnation by a government agency, local, state or Federal. It was hoped that this would discourage eminent domain by preventing the land from being taken at its restricted value or, as one landowner put it, "on the cheap."

The conservation restriction at Seven Gates Farm preserves a major portion of the north shore of Martha's Vineyard and every member of the Standing Committee agreed with Charles W. Schmidt, President of Seven Gates, who told *The Vineyard Gazette* "It's a great feeling among those who love the land to be able to preserve some of the most beautiful. . . in the world."

Schmidt, who with former Seven Gates President Richard D. Leahy, led the campaign to protect the common land, also initiated the second phase of the preservation project, the protection of individual house lots, also with conservation restrictions. By 1979, landowners had given The Trustees restrictions maintaining the open and scenic condition of five lots totalling 128.5 acres.

East of Seven Gates, a restriction very generously given to The Trustees of Reservations in 1975 by Dr. and Mrs. Robert Gantz protects 75 acres of their magnificent property with frontage on Vineyard Sound.

4

Nashawena Island: Vision and Generosity at Work

As land values rose, shareholders of properties held in trust, such as those at Seven Gates Farm, were justifiably concerned about the properties they held in common and their ultimate effect on their estate taxes. Could they continue to afford to pass these shares through from generation to generation? One of the ways the value of the land could be reduced was to give away the development rights using conservation restrictions.

In early 1976, the managing trustee of another major property contacted The Trustees of Reservations. He was Stephen H.

Forbes of Nashawena, one of the dramatically beautiful Elizabeth Islands which separate Vineyard Sound from Buzzard's Bay.

There was, of course, mixed with tax considerations, a genuine concern as well about the future of these magnificent properties themselves. In view of rising costs, would coming generations be able to preserve their open landscapes, or would they be forced to subdivide and sell off sections to help pay real estate taxes and other operating expenses? It seemed to the present generation of managers that now was the time to act. Discussions began immediately on a draft restriction for Nashawena.

One of the largest of the Elizabeth Islands (others of major size are Naushon, Pasque and Cuttyhunk), Nashawena totals some 1,900 acres. Primarily grassy moorland, the island is home to more than 300 sheep as well as wildlife of every description. Its landscape is wild and rolling. The open downs and high, sand cliffs are spectacular. And the views in every direction are extraordinary. Indeed, the *Massachusetts Landscape Inventory* lists Nashawena as "Class A — Distinctive," its highest category.

There are several freshwater ponds on the island as well, resting and feeding areas for waterfowl, and about five major structures. These include a two-family, white clapboard farm house, built prior to 1800 and located just up from the harbor; a large barn which can shelter the cows and horses with an attached sheep shed; a spring house; toolhouse; grain shed and two hen houses.

Further to the west are two other houses which are occupied at various times and seasons by members of the Forbes family and

Representatives of The Trustees of Reservations visit Nashawena each year to inspect the property's conservation restriction. With Director Fred Winthrop, far right, are, standing, Joannah Harris and Advisory Council member Nancy Claflin. On this occasion, Nashawena's welcoming committee included Amelia Forbes, seated, and Elliot Forbes, left foreground.

their guests. In a small burying ground, southwest of the farm-house, there is a headstone dated 1736 and marked with the name of "Sarah Roon."

By design and by desire, life on the island is simple, as Stephen Forbes writes, in part, in this delightful memorandum dated 1976: "The two staff members and their wives [who run the farm and care for the structures] live the year round on the island. [Winters] are very quiet except for emergencies such as stranded vessels or accidents. The wives sew or knit or crochet or bird watch [and help] the men haul or cut fuel which is now wood, feed the animals, mend fences, do some repairs, keep up the paths, pump out the 'Islander' (a 40-foot, heavy-hulled power boat used to service the island), and [do] other necessary chores.

"In the summer, the island often hums with activity. Usually, the Edward Forbes' descendants come down for periods ranging from 10 days to seven or eight weeks. . . the Waldo Forbes' descendants come less [often]. Guests are frequent and partake of the island life which is rather varied. Riding, swimming, occasional fishing, occasional sailing or rowing, watching the farm animals (cows, hens, ducks and geese), cooking, washing dishes, singing, painting, [doing] odd repairs, reading, writing, photography, the list is endless. A very healthy outdoor life." Twice each year also, vast numbers of people gather to take part in a drive to collect and corral the sheep for shearing.

There are also, Stephen Forbes adds, "two vegetable gardens, one of pretty fair size. We grow corn, potatoes, squash, asparagus, peas, carrots, spinach, cabbage, celery, lettuce, onions, beets, and other truck garden products, including melons." Two tractors and a tilling machine, a mower and a manure spreader, help make work easier.

A Visting Committee from The Trustees of Reservations (Standing Committee members Theodore Chase; Peter L. Hornbeck; Robert Livermore, Jr.; Edo Potter; Thomas B. Williams and Director Gordon Abbott, Jr.) inspected the island with Mr. and Mrs. Forbes in May of 1976. By July, the Standing Committee had accepted the gift of a restriction and President Charles E. Mason, Jr., had signed the document for The Trustees of Reservations. It limits the construction of additional dwellings to 15, with no more than six to be built in any 20-year period. It also includes the so-called "snap-back" provision (today considered unnecessary), which first appeared in the conservation restriction for Seven Gates Farm, in case of a taking by eminent domain. And contributions were pledged over the years to the Conservation Restriction Fund.

In 1976, the 1,900-acre island of Nashawena was the largest land area in the Commonwealth to be protected with a conservation restriction. To preserve such a unique and historic landscape was an extraordinary accomplishment, made possible, of course, by the vision and generosity of the Trustees of the Nashawena Trust. To Managing Trustee Stephen Forbes, who steered the restriction to a safe harbor, The Trustees of Reservations, on behalf of the public at large, expressed a lasting gratitude.

5

For Bothways Farm, Flexibility Was the Answer

Bothways Farm is the southern gateway to the Town of Essex, which today still mixes an historic riverfront where fishing vessels were constructed as early as the mid-seventeenth century, with the charm and beauty of an agricultural landscape.

Some 98 acres of land, Bothways Farm is bisected by Southern Avenue, which connects Essex and Manchester. Its barn, outbuildings and cottages, painted a cheerful yellow with white trim; its fields marked with gray stone walls and dotted with grazing sheep; and its willow pond where ducks and geese splash and play, are appreciated by thousands who pass it yearly. And all is maintained in mint condition by its owner, Mrs. Frederick C. Bartlett of Beverly.

For years, the property had been on every land trust's list for preservation. This was Mrs. Bartlett's desire as well, but by 1975, no satisfactory plan had been produced. There were those who proposed that it become a demonstration farm where the public could learn about agriculture and the ways of raising domestic farm animals. This, of course, would have called for an endowment of major proportions. There were others who urged that it be given as open space to Essex to be used as a town park.

The Trustees of Reservations, however, suggested a conservation restriction. Its flexibility would allow Mrs. Bartlett's heirs to sell the property upon her death and even subdivide it, making use of each of the outlying cottages, if the zoning by-law then permitted it, as separately-owned dwellings. The remainder of the property could not be built upon, thus ensuring that Bothways Farm would retain its open and scenic condition in perpetuity, its lovely landscape looking always much the same as it does today. With the restriction, the farm would also continue as private property, still providing valuable real estate taxes to the community.

Mrs. Bartlett and her advisors were delighted with the idea (as, indeed, was the Town of Essex), and in November 1976, the

Standing Committee accepted her gift with the understanding also that a contribution would be made to the Conservation Restriction Fund.

One condition of the restriction was that it permit the construction of a single, primary dwelling north of the barn which could serve a future owner as the main house. No such structure then existed.

Although there was some apprehension that seeking an additional gift to the Conservation Restriction Fund might be asking too much of an already generous donor, it did not turn out that way. Indeed, The Trustees' experience shows that landowners in general seem to understand and appreciate that the existence of the fund shows that the organization means business and will defend the terms of their restrictions against all comers. It is, in effect, seen as welcome insurance for the future.

Some years later, with a symbolic 100 friends and family members, Mrs. Bartlett, bright and spry as ever, celebrated her centennial birthday with an elegant luncheon on a sunny, summer day in the spruce grove at Bothways Farm. Perhaps the best birthday present of all was the knowledge that the farm she loved so much would be preserved as open space forever.

6

Tuckernuck Island: a Race with Time

The island of Tuckernuck lies west of Nantucket, some three miles from Madaket Harbor. Approximately two miles long and one mile wide, it totals some 980 acres. Together with Cape Cod, Martha's Vineyard and Nantucket, Tuckernuck (and its neighbor Muskegat) mark the southeastern edge of the Laurentide Ice Sheet which covered much of North America until 15,000 years ago.

The island's first settlers were Indians. "Tookernook" is Algonquin for "loaf of bread," which may have been how the island was shaped in earlier days. The first Europeans, fishermen and farmers, arrived in the late seventeenth or early eighteenth century and by 1829 there were 30 houses on the island.

Since its beginning, life at Tuckernuck has been shaped by the always-changing natural world around it, and this has been its magic. Its size, isolation and lack of twentieth century services; the small number of now seasonal residents; and its delicate and dynamic ecosystems, make it a unique resource.

The simplicity of its essentially eighteenth century community is still intact. It is a place where summer fogs are quiet and comforting; where storms are always exciting and where dawns and sunsets can be unsurpassed in beauty.

Its hilly morain, flat and expansive moors and low, sandy ocean shoreline, make it an ideal model for studying and monitoring coastal processes. It is important archaeologically because of its early Indian settlements. It supports a varied collection of flora and fauna and is a favorite spot for shore and surf fishing.

Above all, it is a place where people can be individuals, private unto themselves, but without the need for fences to protect their privacy. None of these alone make Tuckernuck unique, but taken together they create the spirit of the island, still a place, so rare today, where man lives quietly in harmony with nature.

Landowners at Tuckernuck, many of whom represent a fourth generation or more, have a special feeling for the island's wild beauty and remoteness, and a fierce pride in the simplicity and strength-giving qualities of its way of life. Yet in 1977, the island was caught in the whirlpool of a rapidly changing world. Pressures from every side menaced its tranquility and threatened ultimately to destroy the fragile beauty of its landscape.

There were at the time 26 houses on the island. Under the existing zoning by-law for the Town of Nantucket, an additional 726 standing structures, including 363 dwelling units and 363 accessory buildings, could be built if landowners exercised their rights and maximized the development of their properties. Although this was obviously unlikely, the potential was still there and a building boom was underway on both the Vineyard and Nantucket. One thing was certain: changes would take place at Tuckernuck in the years ahead.

To their great credit, property owners, young and old, were already searching for a way to deal with the pressures that were sure to come. On their own they had completed an extensive inventory entitled *Studies in the Ecology and Social History of Tuckernuck Island* to support a proposed change in zoning for Nantucket's out-islands. They had also begun conversations with The Trustees of Reservations about how to protect the island's precious resources in the years ahead.

Some months of discussion followed. There were meetings at General Headquarters in Milton with Henry A. La Farge, president of the Tuckernuck Landowners Association, and later in New York City with additional property owners. It seemed both to members of a special Steering Committee (La Farge, Scott Bartlett, William T. Howard, Mrs. Stanley Smith, Mrs. John Walker and Frederick R.H. Witherby) and to The Trustees of Reservations that a series of conservation restrictions would provide the best protection in the shortest time.

Wrote La Farge: "We estimate that 50 percent of the landowners will be interested in a restriction." There were 47 in all, but many of those already committed were owners of larger parcels which had special environmental significance.

Of major interest also was the fact that the Tax Reform Act of 1976, just approved by Congress, provided for the deductibility for Federal income tax purposes of gifts to a charitable corporation of conservation restrictions of not less that 30 years' duration, if the gift or transfer was made prior to June 14, 1977. Congress, in effect, had created a window of opportunity of one year's duration, during which a limited-life restriction would receive tax benefits. After June 14, to qualify for deductibility, all restrictions would have to be perpetual.

For landowners at Tuckernuck, a 30-year restriction had considerable appeal. First of all, the rush to record before June 14 left too little time to persuade each landowner to join the conservation program. This meant that some would reduce the value of their properties significantly, perhaps increasing the value of a neighbor's who ultimately intended to develop. That seemed hardly fair.

Second, a scattered pattern of restrictions simply wouldn't provide the level of protection the island deserved. What was needed was a comprehensive program agreed to by every landowner. But it would involve completion of the inventory of the island's natural resources, the development of plans for the use of specific land areas including open space, the identification of future building sites, and an agreement on rights of way and access points for boats, the only practical way to reach the island in both good and bad weather. (A primitive landing strip for small aircraft did exist.)

A series of 30-year restrictions could provide time for this more comprehensive program of protection at least to be initiated and, if possible, completed. That was what sold the proposal to The Trustees of Reservations — that plus the fact that a number of the restrictions already proposed would protect significant portions of the island's two tidal ponds as well as major sections of its ocean shoreline. But June 14 was fast approaching.

In mid-April, at the River House in New York City, 13 Tuckernuck landowners (there were 20 at the meeting), whose properties totaled some 426 acres, told the Director they were sincerely interested in a program of 30-year conservation restrictions. A visiting committee of The Trustees of Reservations was organized immediately and arranged to meet on the island on May 20 and 21. With the deadline less than a month away, the race with time was on.

It was clear to visiting committee members Ann Brewer, Laurence Channing, Peter Hornbeck, Edo Potter and Director Gordon Abbott, Jr., that it was better at this point to concentrate on protecting key environmental areas of the island and to ask owners of unconnected, smaller parcels of land inland, many of whom were willing to restrict their properties, to become a part of the proposed longer-range process of preservation.

Back in Boston, with now less than two weeks before the deadline for recording, the number of conservation restrictions in hand had dwindled to six. But they still preserved a total of 297 acres of land — some 30 percent of the island — all of it with pond or shore frontage. The Standing Committee had given the visiting committee authority to act and it agreed to accept the six restrictions.

Abbott and Tuckernuck Steering Committee members Mr. and Mrs. Frederick R. Witherby, who represented the grantors, flew to Nantucket on June 8 to present the restrictions to members of the Board of Selectmen for their approval. Duplicate copies had been delivered to Nantucket's Town Counsel in Wellesley, Massachusetts, and with his agreement reported by phone, the Chairman of the Board of Selectmen signed the documents the following day. They were then flown to Boston where Abbott picked them up by hand. A day later, on June 10, he met with Evelyn Murphy, the Commonwealth's Secretary for Environmental Affairs, who expressed her enthusiasm for the program to preserve Tuckernuck and added her signature to the restrictions.

Additional legal and administrative details (which included dealing with an estate) were finally completed at 2:30 p.m. on Monday, June 13. A chartered aircraft delivered the completed instruments to Nantucket. There they were met by Robert J. Marks, then Manager of The Trustees of Reservations' Coskata-Coatue Wildlife Refuge. Marks drove to the Registry of Deeds and recorded the documents at 3:40 p.m., 20 minutes before closing. The June 14 deadline had been met.

Today, nine permanent conservation restrictions, some of them formerly of 30-years' duration, are held locally by the Nantucket Land Council. The Trustees of Reservations holds one permanent restriction and four which will cease to exist after the year 2007. Work is underway to convert these to permanent status as well. Two properties are also protected with deed restrictions of 30 years' duration.

The job of preserving the open landscape of the island, however, is far from complete. And with growth and change still very much a threat to its special way of life, discussions continue about how to preserve the magic that is so much a part of Tuckernuck.

7

'For All Who Find Renewal in the Spirit of Nature'

There is little doubt that golf courses protect important areas of open space in their communities. Their landscapes are often scenic. Their vegetation, which varies in texture from smooth fairways and greens to rough grasses, shrubs and woodlands, is a fine habitat for song birds and small mammals. If there is a water hole, its pond can attract wildfowl as well as aquatic animals and fish. And a sizable number of golf courses throughout the country are also open for public use.

That is why in 1978, when discussions began with Mr. and Mrs. James N. Stavros about the possibility of using a conservation restriction to preserve Cape Ann Golf Course in Essex, The Trustees of Reservations expressed immediate interest.

There were, however, other reasons as well. The property, a landmark on the North Shore which the public had enjoyed for many years, bordered a marshland parcel of Crane Wildlife Refuge and had considerable frontage on scenic Route 133 which still provides passers-by with turn-of-the-century views of a primarily agricultural landscape.

At White's Hill, Essex, Mrs. Mary Stavros, whose generosity made possible the James N. and Mary F. Stavros Reservation.

For the Stavroses, the gift of a conservation restriction meant the surrender of a considerable sum of money which could have been theirs had the land been subdivided for development and sold to the highest bidder. That it was not, and instead placed in trust for the benefit of future generations, is a testimonial to their remarkable generosity and concern for the needs and aspirations of all mankind.

Mrs. Stavros, a graduate of Radcliffe College, had been a teacher in the Gloucester School System. James Stavros was born in Lagadia, Greece, a mountain town in the Peloponnesus, in 1892. At age 16, he left home and emigrated to the United States, settling in Gloucester. A veteran of World War I, he began his work as a factory hand. Later, despite difficulties with the English language, he graduated from Boston University and Suffolk Law School. He was associated with Cape Ann Golf Course for more than 50 years and was owner of the property from 1947 until his death in 1981.

Thanks to his generosity in his lifetime, and to the generosity of Mary Stavros in the years that followed, more than 173 acres of their land have been preserved, much of it with conservation restrictions.

The restriction protecting Cape Ann Golf Course has been used as a model by other communities around the country which recognize the value and stability of knowing that significant areas of open space within their boundaries are protected in perpetuity.

White's Hill (which borders Cape Ann Golf Course) with its magnificent views of Ipswich Bay, Castle Neck, salt marsh and the tidal estuary of the Essex River, was sold by Mrs. Stavros to The Trustees of Reservations in 1988 for a fraction of its market value. Funds to meet its purchase price were raised from public subscription, and it is now a full-fledged reservation. The Trustees also holds an agricultural preservation restriction on some 70 acres of Stavros land west of Route 133.

At the dedication of White's Hill, Mrs. Stavros explained with gentle eloquence why she had chosen to preserve the property as open space and, indeed, why all her gifts of land had meant so much to her.

"This morning," she said, "I have two thoughts. The American Indian's closeness to the land as well as his idea of the spirit of a place. I believe that special places have special roles. It is very painful to me when they are ignored — when a marsh is destroyed for a shopping mall, a tract of woodland is demolished for a supermarket, or the rocky contours of a hillside are blemished by unsightly and inappropriate buildings. I, therefore, feel great gratitude that you, The Trustees of Reservations, have helped me save my lovely land from ruthless and insensitive exploitation."

She paused and spoke again. "My second thought. Shortly a stone will be placed here with the inscription: 'This land is a memorial to James Nickis Stavros; for the enjoyment of all who find renewal in the of spirit in Nature.'

"In this cluttered and complex life, we all need space — vistas of beauty, solitude, relaxation, recreation for assessing values, renewing courage, receiving inspiration. I believe the role of this place to be the enrichment of life for all who come here or pass by; and I hope they will appreciate this beauty as my husband did. So shall we all share in something good."

Little more that day needed to be said.

8

The Parkinson Case: a Clarification from the Highest Court

Thanks to the generosity of Mrs. Ellen T. Parkinson, The Trustees of Reservations in 1980 was able to preserve some 82.6 acres of pine and oak woodland and field bordering Hartford Street in Medfield. Located at the entrance to the town, the property also includes two brooks and a small pond. It is not far from Rocky Woods Reservation. The restriction prohibits the construction of any building other than "one single family residence with the usual appurtenant outbuildings and structures." One, which Mrs. Parkinson inhabited, already existed. To build another it would have to be torn down.

Medfield's Board of Selectmen, aware that the gift would help maintain the charm and character of the community itself by preserving a precious piece of open space on its very threshhold, was elated. Indeed, its members made a personal pilgrimage to Mrs. Parkinson to tell her so. But the Assessors, unfortunately, disagreed.

They declined to recognize the restriction as valid and enforceable, despite that fact that it had been approved and signed by their own Selectmen and by the Secretary of the Executive Office of Environmental Affairs. Their reasons are best explained by a court document: "It was the policy of the board," it declared, "'to assess land properly subject to a conservation easement or restriction at no more than 25 [percent] of full and fair cash value.' (The law provides that any land subject to a conservation restriction shall be assessed as a separate parcel of real estate.)

"Nonetheless, when the Board assessed [Mrs.] Parkinson's real estate in fiscal 1982 and 1983 at $317,300 and $346,700, respectively, it refused to discount the value of her property. [It] claimed that the conservation easement was invalid because it purported to apply not only to the land, but to [Mrs.] Parkinson's residence and outbuildings.

"The easement [was] invalid," the document declared, "not because it is prohibited by statute, but because its terms are so vague that it precludes any meaningful identification of the servient [restricted] estate. While no particular words are necessary for the grant of an easement, the instrument must identify with reasonable certainty the easement created and the dominant and servient tenements."

The contention was that the boundary between the restricted land which could be appraised for less than full and fair market value, and the land upon which the house stood was unclear, and thus a separate appraisal of the restricted land was impossible.

Mrs. Parkinson, assured that there were many other restrictions like her own which had been accepted as valid, properly paid her taxes in full for two years while filing for abatement with the Appellate Tax Board. The appeal was denied and Mrs. Parkinson sought redress from the state's Supreme Judicial Court.

Initially, the SJC upheld the decision of the Appellate Tax Board. The enviromental community was in shock. There were scores of conservation restrictions like Mrs. Parkinson's which had been recorded over the past decade, restrictions which the Commonwealth itself had been a part of as a signatory.

Eleven conservation organizations besides The Trustees of Reservations filed for a rehearing of the matter before the Supreme Court and collectively submitted an amicus brief. They were joined in their efforts by the Attorney General of Massachusetts who emphasized the importance of the case "to the cause of environmental conservation." Faced with new information, the SJC declared it was willing to reconsider its decision and in May 1986, much to the relief of conservationists everywhere, it reversed itself and found for the plaintiff.

"We conclude," the justices wrote in a landmark decision, "that the board [Appellate Tax Board] erred in affirming the assessors' denial of real estate tax abatements on the taxpayer's property. The taxpayer's conservation restriction is valid because it meets all the requirements for a valid conservation restriction under G.L. c.184, SS 31 (the Conservation Restriction Act). Because the conservation restriction was approved by the Medfield selectmen and the Secretary of Environmental Affairs, it is enforceable by the express terms of G.L. c. 184, SS 32.

"Although the restriction," they continued, "permits one single-family residence with appurtenant outbuildings and structures, such use of restricted land is not prohibited by the statutes. The statutory requirement is that the land be kept 'predominantly' in its natural, scenic or open condition; and, significantly, the statute forbids that a conservation restriction may 'forbid or *limit*' building construction (emphasis added). G.L. c. 184, SS 31. The board was in error in so far as it concluded that G.L. c. 184, SS 31, does not authorize a conservation restriction on dwelling and appurtenant buildings."

The justices held also that although the law did, indeed, stipulate that restricted and unrestricted portions of land be assessed separately, the instrument in Mrs. Parkinson's case subjects all her property to the terms of the conservation restriction.

The question that remains then, the court said, is what is "the fair cash value of the taxpayer's land as encumbered by the restriction?" Previous decisions had upheld the concept that a "restriction on the use of property may reduce its value below that which would be appropriate in the absence of such restrictions."

Earlier, too, Mrs. Parkinson's real estate appraiser, appearing as a witness before the Appellate Tax Board, had testified that the property as restricted, including buildings, was worth $212,500. In making the determination, he explained, he had calculated that the occupation of the single-family residence and outbuildings, expressly permitted by the easement, required the use of about seven acres of land. He valued the house and this "hypothetical" seven-acre parcel at $175,000. He then valued the remainder of the land, encumbered by the restriction, at $500 an acre.

Medfield assessors did not dispute the $212,500 valuation, if the conservation restriction was presumed to be valid. The justices, therefore, declared that "the taxpayer has thus sustained her burden of proving overvaluation in the amount of $104,800 and $134,200 for the years 1982 and 1983, respectively." The case was remanded to Appellate Tax Board to take appropriate action. It was a victory for Mrs. Parkinson and for environmentalists everywhere.

Are there lessons to be learned from the Parkinson experience? "Most definitely," says Wesley Ward, The Trustees of Reservations' Deputy Director for Land Conservation. "First, we've begun to watch these challenges to restrictions more carefully, sharing information with other conservation organizations and with the Department of Food and Agriculture which holds numerous APRs (agricultural preservation restrictions).

"Second, we have mostly abandoned the idea of 'floating house lots' as in the Parkinson restriction, and are now defining specific 'building envelopes' where future residential construction may take place. This may be done," Ward explains, "with a survey or with boundary descriptions. Two or three possible building envelopes, for example, may be marked on a plan agreed to by the land owner before the restriction is accepted by The Trustees of Reservations."

The goal, of course, is to make the sites of future buildings as specific and unambiguous as possible while the restriction is being negotiated to prevent confusion, misunderstandings or disagreements later on. To cope with this in the early days of the conservation restriction program, The Trustees suggested successfully that restrictions state, for example, that three additional houses may be constructed in the future, but "only with the approval of The Trustees of Reservations, such approval not to be unreasonably withheld." Again, this phraseology, although it provided some control over siting, was no substitute for prescribing specific locations which all parties to the restriction agree will not jeopardize the "scenic, open and natural condition" of the landscape.

Finally, the Parkinson case demonstrated the vital importance of the Conservation Restriction Fund which, although significant contributions were made by other conservation organizations, was used to pay the lion's share of legal expenses.

9

Old Deerfield: an Historic Agricultural Landscape

By 1988, changes in Federal tax laws and rising property values had taken their toll. Gifts of major parcels of land and the endowments needed to accompany them had slowed to a trickle. And The Trustees of Reservations, wrote Director Fred Winthrop, Jr., had begun "to concentrate less on fee acquisition and more on conservation restrictions" to accomplish its mission.

Since 1972, the organization had acquired 70 conservation restrictions preserving more than 6,656 acres of land. It was equal to 37 percent of the land the organization held in fee title. It included, during the mid-1980s, four additional restrictions in Needham, increasing land protected by restrictions along the upper Charles River to 356 acres; a restriction protecting some 46 acres of shorefront in Mattapoisett; a restriction on the north shore of Goose Pond in Lee, protecting 112 acres of woodland; and a restriction in Salisbury, Connecticut (held by The Trustees' affiliate, the Massachusetts Farm and Conservation Lands Trust), which provides protection for some 433 acres of well-managed, white pine and mixed hardwood forest, bordering Bartholomew's Cobble.

Among the restrictions also was one which preserved some 240 acres — and one of the last barrier beaches in Massachusetts — at Great Island, Yarmouth, Cape Cod. The area also includes some 20 acres of upland and 14 acres of headland surrounding an historic lighthouse at Point Gammon as well as Pine Island, a smaller island of some 22 acres north of Great Island in Lewis Bay.

Of considerable significance also was a restriction which today protects the scenic beauty and agricultural values of some 71 acres of land in Deerfield. Site of one of the nation's most exquisite collections of museum houses, Deerfield today bears a remarkable resemblance to the Colonial village it was in the early eighteenth century. Ravaged by French and Indian raiders during the winter of 1704, most of the town was burned and 49 residents, including children, were killed. One hundred and eleven were taken captive and forced to march to Montreal.

By 1735, thanks to a treaty with the Indians, Deerfield residents could once again harvest their crops without fear. The town was rebuilt and soon became one of the largest and wealthiest in the region. A series of elegant houses were constructed. Many today, such as the Ashley House built for 35 pounds in 1733 for the town's Tory minister, and the Asa Stebbins House with its French wallpapers, Chinese porcelain and Federal-period furniture, are preserved by Historic Deerfield Incorporated.

But as much as the houses are a part of protecting the historic charm and character of the community, so is the prime-quality, highly-productive farm land which surrounds it. "The soils have been cultivated for 300 years by the settlers of Deerfield and before that by Native Americans," says Peter Spang, Curator of Historic Deerfield and a member of the Standing Committee of The Trustees of Reservations. But condominium developers also saw the benefits of building in Deerfield. Of special interest was the open agricultural land, well drained and ideal for construction purposes.

Aware of the threat of development and anxious to protect their property, William and Julie Hester, owners of some 71 acres of farm land south of Main Street, asked the Department of Food & Agriculture about the possibility of selling their development rights to the Commonwealth. The Department appraised the land but the Hesters felt the figure was too low to accept. Historic Deerfield asked The Trustees of Reservations to help negotiate the sale. At the urging of The Trustees, the Department reviewed its appraisal, agreeing that land values had risen significantly since it was initially completed.

The Hesters kindly said they would await the outcome of the process. It was also suggested by The Trustees that Historic Deerfield itself consider contributing 10 percent of the cost of the proposed agricultural preservation restriction.

A new appraisal put the value at $187,000 and this time the Hesters agreed to sell. In return for Historic Deerfield's contribution, The Trustees of Reservations also succeeded in getting the landowner to strengthen the restriction with a scenic easement to provide additional protection for the property which lies within Old Deerfield's Historic District.

That same year, as a part of The Trustees' continuing program to protect the outstanding agricultural landscapes of both Deerfield and its neighbor, the town of Sunderland, the Massachusetts Farm and Conservation Lands Trust purchased 8.5 acres of crop land in Sunderland and preserved it with an agricultural preservation restriction sold to the Department of Food & Agriculture. The restricted land was then bought by a farmer who wanted it to raise potatoes and vegetables.

A year earlier, retired Sunderland potato farmer Clarence F. Clark generously gave The Trustees of Reservations a restriction which today preserves some 80 acres of his land, much of which borders the Connecticut River. The property includes some 70 acres in active agriculture.

10

Scenic Roads: an Important Part of America's Past

Just west of New Marlborough, Monterey Road turns north towards the town of Monterey. Its unpaved surface is lined with stone walls built by settlers more than a century and a half ago. On either side then were fields and woodlots as well as the occasional two-story, wood clapboard farm houses with their barns and corn cribs, spring houses and wood sheds, chicken houses and carriage sheds, which were so much a part of the New England landscape.

Today, the fields have all but disappeared, taken over by a succession of white pine and hardwood, but the road itself, narrow and unpaved, is much the same as it must have been in earlier days. More than two miles in length, it is free of power lines and development of any sort and the surrounding forest with its marshes, streams, steep slopes and bankings, is habitat for a variety of wildlife.

A road of any sort promises the traveler adventure and excitement, and so it was for The Trustees of Reservations. In 1988, Philadelphia's Natural Lands Trust called to ask if The Trustees would accept a conservation restriction protecting some 197 acres of land along Monterey Road. Aware of the importance of preserving fast-disappearing scenic and historic roadways

Scenic Monterey Road, a significant portion of which is now protected with conservation restrictions, recalls earlier days in western Massachusetts when road surfaces were unpaved and horses and wagons were used for transportation.

throughout the Commonwealth, the organization responded positively and discussions began.

The owner, Miss Margaret Phillips, proposed the following imaginative scenario: she would first donate a conservation restriction to The Trustees of Reservations to protect the property's scenic, open and natural condition in perpetuity. Second, she would give fee title to the restricted property to Springside School in Philadephia which, in turn, would sell the land to a private buyer, using the proceeds for its educational purposes.

An agreement had been reached earlier with a buyer who wished to reserve the right to construct his own as well as three other houses on the property as a part of his pledge to purchase the land for $250,000. All that was left was to negotiate the site of the building envelopes so that they would be in keeping with the purposes of the restriction.

It was also agreed that there would be a trail, open to the public, for walking and horseback riding; that in keeping with the traditions of the land, commercial agriculture and forestry would be encouraged; and that The Trustees of Reservations would receive $10,000 as a contribution to the Conservation Restriction Fund.

The buyer reported it was his intent to enlarge the existing hayfields and to inhabit the property during his retirement. Power lines for new construction would be installed out of sight of the road.

"One of the attractions of this parcel," explained Wesley Ward, Deputy Director for Land Conservation for The Trustees of Reservations, "is that it could be the first piece of the puzzle. With two land trusts now in the area in New Marlborough and Monterey, we have a significant opportunity, working with them, to protect a substantial amount of additional land along scenic Monterey Road."

Preservation of the land is also in keeping with environmental policies and objectives established by the Berkshire Regional Planning Commission.

11

The Brick Yard: Industrial Archaeology and Open Space

In 1973, the Vineyard Open Land Foundation, established to "promote the preservation of the natural beauty and rural character of Martha's Vineyard," issued a detailed report which looked at the visual characteristics of the island and discussed steps which might be taken to protect areas of unique interest and importance.

Entitled *Looking at the Vineyard*, the study compiled a list of "Special Places" about which, it said, Vineyarders hold strong feelings "because of their historic value, their scenic beauty or personal associations" which may have been experienced by a number of generations. One of these "special places," located in Chilmark, is known as "The Brick Yard."

"The ruins of this early Island industry," the report explains, "is a notable landmark of the North Shore when seen from passing boats. The tall chimney still stands, flanked by a great sand cliff and rolling hills, and backed by Roaring Brook Swamp. No other man-made structure is within sight. The outlet of the brook makes a good fishing ground nearby."

The brickyard, which, in its active days, was known as the Chilmark Brick and Tile Works, was operated by Nathaniel Harris

The Brick Yard at Roaring Brook, Chilmark, Martha's Vineyard, from an old post card. During its heyday, as many as a dozen schooners could be seen waiting off the dock for bricks to be brought aboard and shipped to the mainland.

from 1863 until the late 1880s. The property today is owned by
Harris's granddaughter, Flora Harris Epstein, who lives nearby.

Bounded on the east by Roaring Brook, the area, some 37
acres in all, includes a sand and cobble beach, wetland, maritime
shrub thicket, a riparian shrub community and mixed hardwood
forest. Of particular historic interest, however, are the ruins and
archaeological remains of a brick manufactory, an industry
reportedly dating back to 1642 on this specific site. What made it
so attractive to early industry was the availability of water power,
rich clay deposits located at nearby Menemsha Hills, and its
coastal location, which enabled bricks to be off-loaded to schooners, lighters and other vessels anchored just off shore.

The ruins visible today date back to the mid-nineteenth
century and Nathaniel Harris's Brick and Tile Works. Included is
the brick chimney, water wheel and wheel pit, as well as the
remains of the foundations of brick buildings used for administrative, manufacturing and residential purposes.

The great hurricane of 1938 destroyed a sea wall which had
protected the area for decades, and the ensuing flood waters
destroyed most of the buildings. Photographs in 1900 show the
structures intact. Twenty years later there was some decay, but
after 1938 the only prominent feature was the brick chimney.
Today, it is in poor condition and continues to disintegrate.

The Trustees of Reservations had been interested in the site
for more than two decades. As early as 1966, it had begun to
acquire annually from Nathaniel L. Harris and his sister Catherine
P. Harris gifts of undivided interests in what was to become
Menemsha Hills Reservation. Some 149 acres in all, Menemsha
Hills includes a dramatic marine escarpment or sand cliff, more
than 150 feet high overlooking Vineyard Sound.

In 1973, the Trustees of Prospect Hill Realty Trust gave The
Trustees of Reservation a conservation restriction protecting 8.3
acres of land, including the summit of Prospect Hill which, at 308
feet above sea level, is the highest hilltop on the Vineyard. But the
brickyard, although in good hands, remained unprotected. There
was, however, always hope for the future.

By December 1990, the moment had arrived and Mrs. Epstein
generously agreed to give The Trustees of Reservations a conservation restriction which protects in perpetuity some 37 acres of
her land, including the historic brickyard. The restriction contains
special provisions for archaeological site protection as well as the
right to stabilize or restore the existing ruins. It also allows The
Trustees selected public access and the right to lead occasional
tours of the property to interpret its history, both natural and
cultural.

As part of the agreement as well, Mrs. Epstein graciously
contributed two percent of the appraised value of the property to

the Conservation Restriction Fund. Today, the "two percent rule" is standard policy for donors of conservation restrictions.

Thus it was that another of the Vineyard's "special places" was preserved for generations to come.

12

Three Generations Act to Become 'Caretakers for the Future'

When the railroad came to Berkshire County in the 1840s, it by-passed the towns of Monterey and New Marlborough. But isolation from commerce soon became a blessing in disguise. For some decades later, their quiet hills and small farms began to attract a new economy — summer people — who sought to escape the noise and confusion of the city.

New Marborough was first settled in 1739 by Benjamin Wheeler, who had come to the wilderness of western Massachusetts from the Town of Marlborough in Middlesex County, just west of Boston, now on Route 495. During the stagecoach era, the village was a way station between Hartford and Albany and included a number of taverns and many handsome houses, some of which still exist today.

Monterey, named to commemorate one of the great battles of General Zachary Taylor, was once the home of a number of small industries, including a paper mill. Taylor, a national hero, later became President of the United States. Monterey, too, like New Marlborough, became popular as a summer resort, and today the shores of Lake Garfield and Lake Buell are ringed with seasonal homes.

The countryside surrounding both communities was, until recent years, agricultural land — a charming mosaic of fields and forest, farm houses and barns. Today, however, only a few farms remain and most of the pastures have succeeded to woodland.

Among the summer-dwellers of the late 1920s was the Reverend Wilbur K. Thomas, who purchased the old Hyde Farm, some 120 acres of land in Monterey. Thomas hoped to establish a collective community with utopian ideals. "We first went there as kids," Andrew J. W. Scheffey explains. "It was a summer camp where we could live a rustic life. Wilbur Thomas, a remarkable man, was a friend of my mother's. A resident of Philadelphia, as we were, he was the administrator of the Carl Schurz Memorial Foundation which had been established by my grandfather to promote German-American understanding."

Scheffey, a former professor at the University of Massachusetts-Amherst's Department of Landscape Architecture and Regional Planning, is an environmental policy specialist, and in the 1970s was a member of the Standing Committee of The Trustees of Reservations.

With their children in the Berkshires, Dr. Lewis C. Scheffey and his wife, Anna (a gynecologist, Dr. Scheffey was Professor of Gynecology and Obstetrics at Jefferson Medical College), fell in love with the area themselves, and in 1938, purchased one acre of land at Hyde Farm. That winter they built a small cabin, without electricity, which in the ensuing years provided much pleasure for the whole family.

Three years later, in 1941, now unequivocally devoted to the charm and character of south Berkshire County, they were able to acquire an adjoining parcel of some 250 acres, part of a hunting preserve owned by the New Marlborough Association, and, as Andrew Scheffey says, "we became landowners in our own right."

By 1956, the Rev. Thomas had died, and, with Mrs. Scheffey's sister Hildegard Thu Plehn and her husband, Dr. and Mrs. Scheffey and their five children purchased from Mrs. Thomas all of Hyde Farm. With it came a fine early nineteenth century wood frame house with seven bedrooms, three fireplaces and a field stone foundation together with barn and outbuildings. "My aunt and her family," Andy Scheffey adds, "also built an A-frame house on a lovely site nearby above an open field." There were now three houses on the property.

When in 1965 the Clark Farm, some 200 acres, which also bordered the property, was advertised for sale, it was decided to acquire it, too, to preserve the integrity of the area as a whole. The Scheffey-Plehn families now owned a total of some 550 acres of land located both in New Marlborough and Monterey.

It is today primarily forest. Its landscape includes a diversity of wildlife habitats — streams, ponds and steep slopes as well as small areas of field. Views of the surrounding hills and ridges are outstanding. The New Marlborough-Monterey Road, a scenic roadway which pre-dates the Civil War, also passes through the property. Little development is visible along its entire five-mile length.

By the 1970s, the land and buildings were held in three trusts reflecting the proportionate ownership of the Scheffey and Plehn families, which now, with children and grandchildren, total 25 persons. Highly popular with family members, the property is used regularly.

Late in the same decade, one member of the family, deciding to relocate to south Berkshire County, inquired about the possibility of using a portion of the land to construct a permanent residence. The proposal stirred a powerful response. Different members of the family voiced strongly-held positions both pro and con. Yet collectively, they reflected deeply-rooted, emotional ties to the property and the traditional values it represented. At issue, of course, was the larger question: what was to happen to the land in the years ahead? And how could it best accomodate the desires of every family member?

In 1977, the entire family, young and old, met together to discuss the future. Moderated by a skilled and gentle attorney, the meeting explored new patterns of organization and a decision-making process. It was also agreed to engage landscape architect and planner Walter Cudnohufsky, founder and Director of the Conway School of Landscape Design, to further identify and examine the issues involved.

Impressed with the landscape, Cudnohufsky wrote that it is "primitive, tranquil, quiet, secluded, elevated, contained, modest, overgrown and ragged. . . a remote woodland farm." Indeed, he added, "the overall physiological balm which R.F.F. [Ravine Falls Farm] provides," is that it offers a feeling of permanence and stability. It may allow some of the members to function more successfully in everyday life knowing that R.F.F. is there, not only as a memory but as a reality."

Looking at the needs of the family in the years ahead, he raised three basic questions: first, he asked, is it possible to locate three or four additional buildings at Ravine Falls Farm without damaging the character of the site or the image of it held by family members? Second, are there good reasons to use the property and to participate in its maintenance? And third, are there some key facets of the character and image of the property which may presently be taken for granted?

Cudnohufsky also suggested a process be devised to discuss and eventually determine future directions. "You need," he said, "supported group leadership to help establish policy decisions and a work and management program for the farm buildings, meadows and woodlands."

He listed 10 considerations which he felt should be a part of the planning process: 1. There were many more people now involved, some young, some reaching retirement age. 2. Taxes and maintenance costs were rising. 3. Much of the land was underused or not used at all. 4. There were proposals from individuals to use the property more actively. 5. The rights, privileges and obligations of each family member must be de-fined. 6. A policy should to be established to guide future deci-sions. 7. Social congestion and privacy issues should be ad-dressed. 8. Questions of permanent occupancy and/or temporary occupancy needed answering. 9. Management decisions, includ-ing the possibility of forestry activities, should be discussed.

10. Maintainance of the property's structures — its houses, barn and dam — should be arranged for in the years ahead.

Although there was an extraordinary unanimity about preserving the natural character and environmental qualities of the property, there was some disagreement about the number of houses that might be permitted in the future which could accomodate family members without jeopardizing the values that everyone felt were important.

A decade passed and the lives of family members matured. Ideas for the property continued to be discussed and when disagreements arose, as they must in every family, it was Mrs. Scheffey, Sr., beloved and admired by all, who was able to hold young and old together.

Upon her death in 1987, her five children became the senior members of the family and it was decided to move ahead again. With professional assistance from the Kantor Family Institute in Cambridge, a process was developed for dealing with the "big question." Although options had been discussed and conservation was still the highest priority, formal agreement was now needed to take the necessary steps.

First, a plan was developed in conjunction with The Trustees of Reservations which protected 545 acres of the property with conservation restrictions to be held also, as appropriate, by two local land trusts: the New Marlborough Land Preservation Trust and the Monterey Preservation Land Trust.

Excluded from the restricted area were the three existing home sites and up to seven reserved building envelopes upon which additional structures might be placed in the future. Second, the three existing trusts were abolished and replaced by a new trust which will own the entire property and its dwellings. All members of the family above the age of 21 will be eligible to participate in the new trust.

The three dwellings, previously owned by individual families and family members, were each designated Individual Dwelling Groups (IDG). Any member of the family may join one or more IDG, and each IDG will be responsible for its own operating costs, rules of conduct and general upkeep. A newly-formed Board of Trustees will assess all members annually to cover the costs of maintenance, taxes and insurance. The Board will also be responsible for policies regarding use of the land for forestry, recreation and limited agriculture, and for overseeing the provisions of the conservation restrictions held by The Trustees of Reservations and the two local land trusts.

Early in the process, senior members of the two families contributed to the establishment of a Preservation Planning Fund, which has been used to generate final plans and surveys for the restrictions as well as for the reserved building sites, to carry out soil testing and site analysis, to secure legal assistance and advice, and to prepare all required documents.

The process was orchestrated by an Interim Executive Committee, working with a number of sub-committees. In the fall of 1988, Walden Associates of Concord, Massachusetts, prepared the preliminary discussion report, which included planning and development options. The final evaluation and appraisal was completed in the fall of 1991. Gifts of the restrictions were made at the end of the year.

Director Fred Winthrop expressed the gratitude of The Trustees of Reservations. "This is an extraordinary property," he said, "hundreds of acres of forest, fields, streams and marsh, in one of the most scenic parts of the Berkshires. Its preservation is a real tribute to this family's conservation ethic."

"We grew up knowing and loving this place," Lewis C. Scheffey explains. "It is one of the few places on earth that really hasn't changed in our lifetimes. Now it has a good chance of surviving so future generations can understand how this part of New England looked in the early days.

"Our grandfather and our parents began a family tradition of respect for and appreciation of the land. There are now three generations who agree that we are all caretakers for the future."

Just to the south of the Scheffey and Plehn land is another 200 acres also protected with a conservation restriction given to The Trustees of Reservations in 1988 by Margaret E. Phillips. The property includes a portion of Harmon Brook and one mile of frontage on scenic New Marlborough-Monterey Road. Sandisfield State Forest is nearby as well.

13

Moraine Farm: an Olmsted Landscape Overlooking Wenham Lake

Like his Harvard classmate, Henry P. Walcott, who served as Chairman of the Standing Committee of The Trustees of Reservations for 23 years (1903-1926), John C. Phillips was interested in nature and the out-of-doors. But unlike Walcott, a physician who specialized in public health and recreation, Phillips's passion was agriculture.

His early years were filled with travel and adventure. Following graduation from college in 1858, he served as shipping agent in Boston and in Calcutta, finally establishing his own firm in New York. There, Phillips did business with Cuba. Later, he moved his offices to Boston, where he dealt primarily with China and the Philippines.

But it was through the good fortune of gifts and inheritance, not success in business, that John Phillips became a wealthy man. According to a memoir written by his college roommate, the Reverend Edward G. Porter, William Phillips, John's fourth cousin, who never married, "took a fancy to him during a voyage together at sea," and offered him $50,000 plus another $50,000 "should he decide to marry." In 1873, William Phillips died, leaving John, now heir to his estate, "a large fortune in trust."

The following year in London, John married Anna Tucker of Boston. Returning to the United States, the couple built a handsome town house in the Back Bay at the corner of Berkeley and Marlborough Streets. Some years later, in 1879, with John's interest in farming, they purchased 275 acres of land on the shores of Wenham Lake in North Beverly; they called the estate Moraine Farm. (Actually, the property was misnamed. It includes glacial eskers, but no moraines.)

For advice about what to do next, Phillips called upon Charles Sprague Sargent, founding Director of the Arnold Arboretum and an early member of the Standing Committee of The Trustees of Reservations. To develop the property, Sargent suggested that Phillips engage the celebrated landscape architect, Frederick Law Olmsted, whose offices were in nearby Brookline.

According to Charles E. Beveridge, editor of the Olmsted Papers at American University in Washington, what resulted was a masterpiece in landscape design. It combined a country seat with active agriculture and an experimental forest. It was also, as Beveridge explains, the "forerunner of two extensive estates" that Olmsted planned "for members of the Vanderbilt family in the early 1890s — Biltmore in Asheville, North Carolina, and Shelburne Farms in Shelburne, Vermont.

"If Biltmore is, indeed," Beveridge writes, "the 'cradle of American forestry', as [both] the National Park Service and the U.S. Forest Service now [deem] it to be, then, in an important sense, Moraine Farm is the cradle of the cradle and deserves. . . recognition on that basis alone. . . ."

Most of Olmsted's ideas for the property are still in place today and will be in perpetuity, thanks to the thoughtful generosity of its present owners, Mr. and Mrs. George Batchelder, who in 1992 gave to The Trustees of Reservations and to Essex County Greenbelt Association an intricate and innovative conservation and preservation restriction protecting the environmental values and historic character of the centerpiece 175 acres of Moraine Farm.

Planning for the development of the property began in earnest in May of 1880. An inspection of the landscape and an analysis of its soils revealed that about 40 acres were economically suited to tillage. What Olmsted urged be done with the remainder showed his genius for creating designs which adapted inventive development ideas to the limitations as well as the opportunities provided by the natural qualities of the site.

As Charles Sargent explained in an article which appeared in *Garden and Forest* in March 1892, "Mr. Olmsted's idea was to convert the whole estate, with the exception of the arable land in the northwest, into more or less open forest, in the midst of which the manor house should stand like a forest lodge in an oasis of kept grounds, confined to its immediate neighborhood and encircled by the boundaries of the terrace. . . ."

The "lodge" itself, with its outbuildings, was to be designed by the notable Boston architectural firm of Peabody & Stearns, but it was quite clear from the beginning which professional would take the lead. "I send you two suggestions for the treatment of your house site on Wenham Lake," wrote Olmsted in a letter to John Phillips in May 1880. "As the charm of the situation lies wholly in the look down upon and over the lake, whatever increases the down-looking and over-looking effect adds to its value. . . the second is that. . . the more you avoid the common-place [look] of the villa or suburban cottage, and the more bold, rustic and weather proof. . . you make the immediate artworks of the house, the better."

Olmsted proposed the house "be set high, as near to the lake as it conveniently can be" and that it be "supported by a terrace, boldly projected, following natural lines, 'country-made' and highly picturesque in its outlines and material. . . mainly field stones, laid with a large but variable batter and with many crannies. . . ."

Peabody & Stearns did their job well. The main dwelling with its three stories and five distinctive brick and stone chimneys was a pleasing mix of shingle and half-timber with numerous gables. Its siting was just as Olmsted had specified. As a visitor approached the house, there was no "suspicion of the broad extended views" to the east and south. The lake was visible only from inside the house itself, and the view was made more exciting by the height of the stone terrace, a concept which Charles Beveridge reports was used later at Biltmore.

Just south of the house, Olmsted called for the construction of a "pavilion," a small octagonal structure of stone and wood, "not a mere shelter, but a more useful room, large enough for a coffee, reading or a ladies' room with windows and shutters. . . strongly but rudely and forest fashion built into the wild hillside. . . ."

In keeping with his concept of creating separate spaces for separate functions — or "outdoor apartments," as he called them — Olmsted originally called for a "wild garden" planted with

ferns and perennials to be placed nearby at a level below the
terrace so that it would be invisible on the approach to the house.
Indeed, as Olmsted wrote to John Phillips, "if the gardener shows
himself outside the walls, 'off with his head!'"

All this, of course, was in keeping with the primary goal of
creating and maintaining an open forest landscape which would
dominate the property without "landscape gardening or group-
ings or displays of foliage" which were commonly employed in so
many of the great summer estates then being developed along the
North Shore.

Today, more than a century later, as Beveridge notes, the
character of the landscape at Moraine Farm still reflects the
fundamental principles of Olmsted's design. The drive, the
carriage roads, the pavilion, the entrance lodge, the barn, the farm
house, the shed, the chicken coop (now a comfortable cottage),
and even the main house itself, which has been extensively
remodeled through the years, are still in place. To be sure,
Olmsted was forced to give way to Mrs. Phillips's insistence that
an "old-fashioned flower garden" be included, but it remained
hidden from view below.

An active benefactor and trustee of many charitable institutions, John Phillips died in 1885 at age 46, leaving a young widow
and four children. The oldest, John Charles (who was nine at the
time), became widely known and much respected for his knowledge of world wildlife, as well as a valued member of the Standing Committee of The Trustees of Reservations and winner of its

*Aerial view of Moraine Farm
in 1929 looking east towards
Wenham Lake shows
serpentine roadways leading to
the original residence designed
Peabody & Stearns, Olmsted's
indoor and outdoor spaces
south of the house, and the
surrounding woodlands of
hemlock, Norway spruce,
sugar maple, red and white
oak, and native red cedar*

first Conservation Award. (His son Arthur served for six years as Secretary of The Trustees, and his grandson today continues the tradition as the Commonwealth's Commissioner of Fisheries & Wildlife.) Mrs. Phillips continued to live at Moraine Farm for six months each year until her death in 1925. Her son William, although often away as a career diplomat, build his own house on the property at some distance from his mother's. He called it Highover and it was home until his death in 1968. Phillips began his diplomatic service in London in 1903 as private secretary to Joseph Hodges Choate, whose summer place in Stockbridge, Naumkeag, was bequeathed to The Trustees of Reservations by his daughter Mabel. Choate was then U.S. Ambassador to the Court of St. James's.

Phillips also served as Second Secretary at the U.S. Legation in Peking. First Secretary at the time was John Gardner Coolidge, who with his wife Helen owned Ashdale Farm in North Andover. It later became the Stevens Coolidge Place, which The Trustees acquired in 1962. With a distinguished diplomatic record that included service as the U.S. Ambassador to Canada, Holland, Belgium and Italy, Phillips climaxed his career as Undersecretary of State.

In 1928, a major portion of the Phillips's property, including the main house, the gate house and the carriage roads, was purchased by George and Katherine Batchelder of Boston. A graduate of Harvard with the class of 1919, Batchelder was president of Batchelder & Whittemore Coal Company and later, following service in the Navy, during World War II, business manager of the Blood Protein Laboratory at Massachusetts General Hospital. His wife, an able and enthusiastic horticulturist, was a president of the North Shore Garden Club and a major figure in the Garden Club of America.

With the Batchelders in residence, the main house underwent a series of renovations designed to simplify it for a less formal, postwar way of life. But with a keen interest in the heritage of the property, they continued to maintain the landscape in the Olmsted tradition. By 1977, both George and Katherine Batchelder had died, and the remainder of the Phillips property, bordering Moraine Farm to the north, had been purchased for development. A few years earlier, Highover, which had been abandoned, was destroyed by fire.

Moraine Farm itself had been inherited by George Batchelder III and his wife, Mimi. Then residents of California, both decided to move back to Beverly. Batchelder had been a professor of biology at San Francisco State University and, at Moraine Farm, his Pollen Research Associates soon was collecting data for allergists around the nation. Mimi, a trained conservator specializing in works on paper, was asked to join the staff of the Northeast Document Conservation Center in North Andover. Together they

Rows of summer squash and hay are now planted in the 18-acre field near the barn designed by Peabody & Stearns and built in 1907.

began to rejuvenate the practice of forestry and agriculture at Moraine Farm.

George was appointed a member of the Conservation Commission in Beverly and, by happenstance, soon found himself involved in efforts to acquire the neighboring Phillips land to protect it from development and to preserve it as open space. Six single residence lots had been planned close to the shore of Wenham Lake, a regional water supply. The remainder of the land was to be used for the construction of as many as 75 single housing units or condominiums.

Finally, the City of Beverly prevailed. In 1987, in a joint effort with the Town of Wenham and with a grant of $900,000 from the Executive Office of Environmental Affairs Self-Help Program for Massachusetts communities, $1.2 million was appropriated to purchase the property. (George, careful to avoid a conflict of interest, separated himself from much of the process.)

Today, the city-owned John C. Phillips Nature Preserve totals 85 acres. It provides valuable open space for passive recreation and protects a critical portion of the watershed of Wenham Lake within the city limits, as well as much of the original Olmsted carriage road from Moraine Farm.

The Batchelders, meanwhile, as early as 1982, had begun discussions with The Trustees of Reservations about options which might be available to preserve major portions of their own property. A visit by Charles Beveridge, as well as by representatives of the Massachusetts Association of Olmsted Parks and the Massachusetts Historical Commission, had confirmed its historic and architectural significance.

Happily, the couple had also been joined by their son Terry, a graduate of Oregon State University with an advanced degree in animal nutrition from Cornell, and his wife Erica, who were with them for four years. With the enthusiastic support of their parents, the two added sheep to the agricultural mix at Moraine Farm, which now included firewood chips, Christmas trees, a young plantation of sugar-maples, nursery plants, hay and commercial vegetables. And all this in conjunction with the continued maintenance of the Olmsted landscape.

Hay, chopped for silage to feed a local herd of dairy cows, is raised today on the 10-acre field south of the approach road at Moraine Farm. With its sinuous edges and islands of trees, the landscape still reflects the characteristics of its original design.

One of the preservation programs studied by both the Batchelders and by The Trustees (land conservation specialists Davis Cherington and Wesley T. Ward were most closely involved) proposed that a portion of the property become an active open space reservation. It was suggested, first, that a predetermined number of acres at Moraine Farm be given to The Trustees of Reservations. The Department of Environmental Management was then to agree to purchase its development rights. The funds received from this transaction were to be reserved by The Trustees as a perpetual endowment for the area's management and protection.

"But," George Batchelder explained, "we had trouble rationalizing the intensity of public use which would have followed. We have seen other Olmsted parks where the impact of visitation had been enormous. Moraine Farm wasn't meant to be a park and we knew that if it became one, the details of the design would suffer."

The Batchelders wanted to continue the traditions of agricultural use as well as the original emphasis on managing forest lands. And, of course, implicitly, they wanted to preserve the features and the character of the Olmsted landscape and the significant architectural qualities of both the main house and other selected structures.

The final result was a unique agreement which combined both conservation and preservation objectives in a restriction designed to keep the property in private hands but to protect its public values. The instrument is held jointly by The Trustees of Reservations and by Essex County Greenbelt Association. Because Moraine Farm is such a historic and cultural treasure the restriction generously provides for two specially conducted tours of the property each year. Residents of the surrounding neighborhood are always welcome to walk the land, and there is an open invitation to anyone involved in academic research in the fields of forestry and agriculture.

The restriction, which totals 45 pages, was drafted, with legal assistance, by Charles Wyman, Land Protection Specialist at The Trustees of Reservations. It preserves 176 acres of open space, as well as the "materials and configuration of the main house" designed by Peabody & Stearns; "the rustic structure of the terrace; the pavilion; the wild garden with its brownstone stairways and grotto;" the shed; the farm barn (while allowing for its adaptive re-use); the hen house cottage; the gate house; the property's stone walls; the walks and carriage roads; the "well-drained field"; and the Olmsted pasture. Most important, the restriction protects the concept of "outdoor rooms" so ingeniously proposed by Frederick Law Olmsted. To provide flexibility for present and future owners, a right is retained to build on six lots carefully sited so as not to disturb the integrity of the property as a whole.

"Moraine Farm," Wyman explains, "represents the first time in Massachusetts that a combined conservation and preservation restriction has been used to preserve an historic landscape. It also provides a model which we hope may be useful elsewhere."

Today, as they have since 1977, George and Mimi Batchelder still continue the original purposes of Moraine Farm. The "well-drained field" is leased to local farmers and is still one of the most productive in Essex County. The Christmas tree business (they raise Colorado Blue Spruce, Douglas Fir and Scotch Pine) is thriving and if you visit the property before the holidays, you can enjoy a cup of hot chocolate in the great barn and inspect decorated wreaths, homemade herbs and preserves, locally raised honey, as well as seasoned firewood, all charmingly arranged and available for purchase.

"Here in America," wrote Charles Sargent a century ago about Moraine Farm, "carefully prepared schemes for the improvement of country estates generally die with the person who makes them and his efforts and expenditure are too often lost, but a better fate has attended the Phillips Place, which fortunately has passed into sympathetic hands, and is administered with intelligence, energy and steadiness of purpose, and with the determination to develop and perfect the well-considered plans of the original owner."

He could have been writing today about the stewardship of George and Mimi Batchelder. Their thoughtful appreciation of the past and their generous concern for the future mean that the extraordinary qualities and characteristics of the landscape and structures of Moraine Farm will be protected in perpetuity.

Mimi and George Batchelder, whose generous gift of a conservation restriction for Moraine Farm, Beverly, uniquely combines both historic preservation and environmental conservation to protect an Olmsted landscape

5

The Massachusetts
Farm and Conservation
Lands Trust

1

New Ideas to Meet Changing Needs in Land Conservation

By 1972, as predicted earlier, The Trustees of Reservations had, indeed, received most of its 53 properties as gifts. But there were indications that the world was changing.

Land values were increasing. There was a continuing uncertainty about the direction of Federal tax laws. The number of great estates with their spectacular landscapes was shrinking. And it was clear that in the future gifts of properties would not come as easily as they had in earlier days. Neither would the endowments which were so necessary to support them. It seemed to a few, at least, that other alternatives were needed.

There was another dimension, as well, which was of special interest to Director Gordon Abbott, Jr. It was the changing role of open space conservation within rural or exurban communities. Heretofore, planning surveys had identified and recommended for preservation isolated, specific sites — a gorge, a headland, a mountaintop, a streamside — each admittedly important for its own scenic, natural and environmental values. But it was Abbott's belief that these areas should not be considered as seemingly separate portions of the landscape, but as parts of a comprehensive plan for the preservation of the traditional character of a community as a whole.

There was no doubt that open space played a major role in maintaining and protecting the scenic and environmental values not only of individual towns but of regional landscapes as well. There was little disagreement also that growth and development would and should continue to meet the needs of an evolving society. How to mix the two then was the key to what would happen both to communities and to the countryside in the years ahead.

It was clear that existing building patterns — both residential and commercial — were doing more to destroy the landscape than to protect it. Large-lot zoning ordinances and commercial regulations actually mandated the loss of open space by spreading development across the countryside. Hundreds of farms, forests and prime wildlife habitats had already disappeared. Scenic views, beloved for generations, had been destroyed. And water supplies — lakes, rivers, streams and wetlands — had been threatened or, worse still, polluted.

How could The Trustees continue its traditional role of acquiring and opening to the public "beautiful and historic places," and, at the same time, obtain the flexibility it would need to meet the challenges and opportunities that lay ahead?

The answer was not long in coming. Abbott, who had devoted more than a year of study and discussion to the matter, proposed the establishment of a new affiliate of The Trustees of Reservations. It was to be called The Land Conservation Trust (TLCT). Supported by a Revolving Loan Fund, TLCT was designed to make use of innovative and imaginative techniques to protect open space, and to act quickly when land which should be preserved for public purposes was threatened with development.

The Revolving Fund could make emergency loans to acquire carefully selected properties, loans that would be repaid within 24 months by one or more of the following techniques: fundraising by a project committee appointed to oversee the acquisition of the threatened property; sale of all or a portion of the property to another appropriate conservation organization or government resource agency; or — most exciting for its potential — limited, sensitive development of a portion of a property to finance preservation of the remaining, more environmentally significant land.

This way TLCT could not only protect valuable open space, but could also contribute to the community in another way as well by providing for the construction of well-designed, well-sited residential housing units whose value was both economic and social. It was the best of both worlds: land conservation and high quality development, a mix which it was hoped could help retain the charm and character of a community's landscape.

In 1972, these were revolutionary ideas. To be sure, revolving loan funds were in existence, but for the most part, they were used solely to purchase conservation lands. But the concept of a conservative and well-respected environmental organization like The Trustees of Reservations buying and selling properties and engaging in the development process, was different, indeed. That was why an affiliate was necessary, Abbott explained.

The Trustees of Reservations itself must continue to be perceived as the fiduciary it is for the reservations it acquires, without so much of a hint that it would do anything but protect them in perpetuity. It would continue to seek and preserve properties of outstanding scenic, historic and environmental value. Its affiliate would do the buying and selling and engage in limited development.

As it happened, the timing was perfect. Thanks primarily to the efforts of then Standing Committee Chairman Augustus P. Loring, the organization received a grant in the amount of $100,000 from the Spaulding-Potter Charitable Trusts, and The Land Conservation Trust was born. A tax-exempt charity in its own right, it derived its standing from its association with The Trustees of Reservations. Its goals, of course, were the same as its parent's, but, thanks to its charter, drafted by Boston attorney Kingsbury Browne, a specialist in conservation law, it could act in different ways.

In its early years, TLCT and its Revolving Loan Fund helped a number of organizations purchase and preserve key parcels of conservation land. They included the Museum of the American-China Trade in Milton, the Richard Sever Hale Reservation in Dover, and Brewster's much-respected Cape Cod Museum of Natural History. Loans were made usually at a rate of one percent less than prime. Funds were raised by each of the organizations by public subscription. Loans were repaid promptly, replenishing the revolving fund, and readying it to do its good work elsewhere.

Thanks to a generous gift, TLCT also acquired some 4.5 acres of open field bordering Weir Hill in North Andover. Two houses, part of a larger subdivision plan, had already been partially constructed on the property before conservation interests could act. TLCT was able to arrange to have the houses removed and the site restored to its natural, open and scenic condition. After careful planning, a single building lot was identified and ultimately sold to a local developer. The proceeds were added to the Revolving Loan Fund. Today, the remainder of the land, which for some years produced a crop of hay annually, is an important part of Weir Hill Reservation and continues the agricultural character of a special portion of the community. It also preserves historic open space opposite the birthplace of Samuel Osgood, the first Postmaster-General of the U.S. The house, still standing, was built around 1740.

Some 65 acres of field and forest land in Ashley Falls as well as 60 acres of woodland and salt marsh on the North River in Marshfield were also given to The Land Conservation Trust. Again, following extensive planning, both parcels were subdivided. A limited number of building lots were identified which protected the rural character of the land as well as the important river frontage in Marshfield. Each parcel was later sold, and again, the proceeds added to the Revolving Loan Fund. By 1978, the potential of TLCT was considered so exciting that it became the subject of a study conducted by students at the Harvard Business School as a part of a course in real property management.

But with Abbott attempting to administer both The Trustees of Reservations and its new affiliate, it was obvious that The Land Conservation Trust was not accomplishing all it could. Help was needed and it came the following year as Davis Cherington joined the staff as full-time Executive Director of TLCT and Deputy Director for Land Conservation for The Trustees of Reservations.

Cherington, a graduate of Boston University and Yale's School of Forestry and the Environment, was a former Field Representative for The Nature Conservancy in Vermont with previous experience in commercial real estate. He brought with him also a new and timely concern — the disappearance of agricultural land and its impact on the traditional character of the New England landscape.

In Massachusetts alone, the loss of productive farmlands was staggering. Statistics showed that in 1940 35,000 farms covered 2 million acres of land. By 1975 only 4,700 farms remained, covering just 630,000 acres. Throughout the decades, scores of communities had changed from rural to suburban as fields, forests and pastures were subdivided and developed, and the trend was continung with an alarming velocity.

Davis Cherington, Deputy Director for Land Conservation for The Trustees of Reservations and Executive Director of its affiliate, the Massachusetts Farm and Conservation Lands Trust

A year or two earlier, the Commonwealth had learned the cost of importing its foodstuffs during a transportation strike and the concept of retaining its farmland began to grow in popularity and importance. In response to a statewide referendum, legislators approved the Farmland Assessment Act, which permitted land to be valued for real estate tax purposes according to its use, not for its development potential. In 1977, the General Court took an additional step to preserve productive farm lands with the Agricultural Preservation Restriction Act, which provided for the purchase of development rights to protect high quality agricultural soils.

Many farmers, however, who sought to sell their properties wanted, and often needed, immediate action. The idea of first selling development rights seemed, to many, too complicated. And here, it was decided, was where The Trustees of Reservations' new affiliate could be most useful.

2

The Massachusetts Farm and Conservation Lands Trust

By 1980, following a formal, four-month planning study, The Land Conservation Trust had become the Massachusetts Farm and Conservation Lands Trust (MFCLT) to reflect its new interests and directions. Cherington was on his way.

Its charter was all but identical to its older sister's, TLCT. Only its name had been changed. Again, it was an organization above all designed to move quickly and to provide flexibility. It had (and has today) its own Board of Trustees appointed by the Standing Committee. They were initially Standing Committee members Robert Livermore, Jr., and Thomas L. P. O'Donnell, as well as Walter Robbins, an attorney with extensive real estate experience. Livermore, as a former President of Hunneman & Company, was a real estate professional with a lifetime of interest and involvement in land conservation and resource protection. O'Donnell, also an attorney, was Managing Partner of Ropes & Gray and a former Chairman of the Standing Committee. Later, they were joined by Standing Committee and Advisory Committee members Albert M. Creighton, Jr., who for many years has served as the spirit of The Trustees' land conservation programs, Thomas A. Ellsworth and Herbert M. Temple III.

The staff at MFCLT was small and highly skilled. By this time, it also included Wesley T. Ward. A graduate of Marlboro College in Vermont, Ward had received a Master's Degree in Landscape Architecture from the University of Massachusetts at Amherst and had worked in Vermont as an open space planner for the Windham Regional Commission. Offices for MFCLT, separate from those at General Headquarters in Milton, were located in Beverly at Long Hill. Abbott, by choice and by design, served the Trust in an advisory capacity to increase its separation from The Trustees of Reservations.

The Massachusetts Farm and Conservation Lands Trust was now prepared to purchase farmlands using the Revolving Loan Fund, which by this point had increased in value to some $200,000. Equally important, Cherington had also arranged for bank lines of credit of up to a million dollars. MFCLT could now hold properties in its own name, ultimately placing the ownership of agricultural preservation restrictions with the Commonwealth.

The individual farms, whose values had been proportionately reduced with the sale of their development rights, could then be purchased by qualified buyers at prices which would permit their continued operation as economically viable agricultural units.

Thomas L. P. O'Donnell, Chairman of the Standing Committee from 1975 to 1976; Vice President from 1985 to 1989; Chairman of the Land Conservation Committee; original member of the Board of Trustees of the Massachusetts Farm and Conservation Lands Trust; and member of the Standing Committee and of the Advisory Council for more than two decades

It its first few months, Cherington reported, "MFCLT contracted to purchase three very different farms: a beef and sweet corn operation of 106 acres in Chilmark, Martha's Vineyard; a market garden of 97 acres in Bellingham; and 120 acres of pasture land bordering the Bryant Homestead in Cummington. Before the end of the year, the Trust will acquire title to these properties and the Commonwealth will immediately purchase restrictions from the Trust using funds allocated by the Agricultural Preservation Act.

Wesley T. Ward, Deputy Director for Land Conservation and Director of the Land Conservation Center

"The restrictions," he continued, "represent a significant portion of the farms' $750,000 value. The land itself will then be sold to established farmers in each area at the restricted value so that the Trust will completely recover its investment." In its first year and a half, MFCLT preserved nine parcels of farmland totalling nearly 1,000 acres.

Key to its success was its relationship with the Massachusetts Department of Food & Agriculture. Legislation simply did not authorize the Commonwealth to purchase farmland outright or to control the disposition of land once it was restricted. "The Trust is able to act more quickly and in ways not always possible by the Commonwealth," said Commissioner Frederic Winthrop, Jr. "We could not have preserved these three farms without the Trust's help."

It was a classic example of a much-discussed and long-heralded concept — the public-private partnership — which worked successfully for the benefit of the people of Massachusetts for a half dozen years. Winthrop, who served with distinction as Commissioner of Food & Agriculture for two Governors, one a Democrat, the other a Republican, became Director of The Trustees of Reservations following Abbott's retirement in 1984.

By 1981, MFCLT had become a model throughout the nation for organizations interested in farmland preservation. Included in its projects was the preservation of a 148-acre parcel in Holliston. Some 70 acres of the property had been rented for growing hay, corn and squash. The remainder included wetland and productive timberland. An independent appraiser for the Commonwealth had declared: "there is no question that rapid development would take place if the land was available." But, working with the Department of Food & Agriculture, MFCLT was able to purchase and preserve the property instead.

On the same day, it conveyed an agricultural preservation restriction to the Commonwealth which paid $210,000 of the purchase price, and to the Town of Holliston (the restriction was jointly held), which contributed $10,000. MFCLT then sold the restricted property to a market gardener for $70,000. The difference between the purchase price and the proceeds of $290,000 was used to pay for legal, engineering and overhead costs incurred by MFCLT.

By early spring, the town of Sudbury, concerned about growing development pressures and the loss of agricultural land, authorized its Conservation Commission to contribute $500 per acre towards the purchase of agricultural preservation restrictions on six parcels of farmland in North Sudbury.

The land was being leased by five non-farm landowners to dairy, produce and nursery farmers. Each parcel was highly suitable for residential development. At the request of the Town and the Department of Food & Agriculture, MFCLT negotiated purchase of five of the six parcels. Acquisition of the sixth, owned by the Farmers Home Administration, needed the approval of Town Meeting. In exchange for the Conservation Commission's contribution to the project, MFCLT also created Perpetual Trail Easements to allow appropriate public access to the restricted parcels.

3

Limited Development and Farmland Preservation

Two of the six parcels in Sudbury included land suitable for residential development but unsuitable for agriculture. Again, at the request of the town and the Department of Food & Agriculture, MFCLT agreed to explore the feasibility of a combined limited development and open space conservation plan for some 80.5 acres known as the Barton Farm.

Although the owner, now on in years, had stopped farming in the 1960s, the land remained intact and areas of better soil had been leased to local farmers. The property also included a complex of historic barns which through the years had become a much-beloved symbol of the community's rural traditions. Voters at Town Meeting quickly moved to appropriate $110,000 to aid the preservation effort in exchange for conveyance to the Town of 15 acres of conservation land, which included a small pond, a brook with bordering wetlands, and a grove of maples near the barns.

Working with professional land planners, MFCLT identified a total of 19.2 acres which could accomodate 12 residential lots without conflicting with agricultural or conservation use of the remaining land. In addition, a 2.7-acre lot was created to include the barns. It would be sold at a "discount" with a preservation restriction (held by MFCLT and recorded at the Registry of Deeds as a part of the title) requiring the buyer to restore the historic barn buildings to prescribed standards.

Encouraged by favorable public reaction to the plan, MFCLT concluded negotiations with the owner and a local builder-developer. In October, MFCLT signed a purchase agreement for $537,500, and sales agreements with the builder-developer, the Town and the Commonwealth. The closing took place in February, 1982.

The Barton Farm project was a victory for the effectiveness of thoughtful land use planning. It was on a small scale to be sure, but it resulted in top-quality soils being protected for agricultural use; in a brook and surrounding wetlands being preserved for conservation; and in the construction of an appropriate number of well-designed, well-sited residential housing units. The character of the landscape is still agricultural and the old barns, which for so many years were an important community landmark, will be preserved in perpetuity.

The project also proved that limited development, in the right place and with the right economic conditions, was a feasible method of assisting the preservation of open land and an alternative to purchasing a property in its entirety with public or privately-contributed funds, and retaining it to insure its preservation.

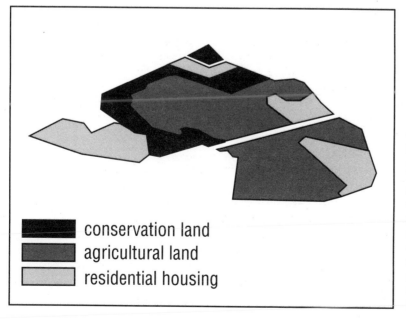

conservation land
agricultural land
residential housing

Barton Farm, Sudbury, a project of the Massachsetts Farm and Conservation Lands Trust. One portion of the 80-acre property is preserved for conservation; another is permanently restricted for agriculture. Three parcels are carefully planned for residential housing. Both siting and architecture match the best traditions of the New England landscape.

4

MFCLT: More Magic with the Landscape

By the end of its fourth year, MFCLT had purchased, restricted and resold 16 parcels of agricultural land totaling 1,517 acres, with an appraised market value of $4,158,000. The per-acre price of restricted farm land had averaged $550, a great aid to communities seeking to keep productive land in agricultural use.

The Agricultural Preservation Restriction (APR) Program had been such a success that the Legislature authorized bonding another $20 million (to make a total commitment of $40 million) to purchase "development rights" from owners of prime agricultural land. The following year it added another $5 million, making the program the most active of its kind in the nation.

Gifts and grants had helped support the Massachusetts Farm and Conservation Lands Trust in its early years, but it was determined not to become dependent upon the generosity of foundations for its general operating expenses. Indeed, it moved as quickly as it could toward eventual self-sufficiency, when it would rely primarily on project fees and income from the Revolving Loan Fund for support. The real key to its success would be an increase in the Revolving Fund, which served MFCLT both as its "endowment" and as a source of "front-end" money to cover options, purchase deposits, and to meet project expenses.

Fresh snow covers corn fields in winter at the Bryant Homestead in Cummington. A significant amount of land around the Homestead, a National Historic Landmark, is protected with agricultural preservation restrictions arranged for by the Massachusetts Farm and Conservation Lands Trust.

Meanwhile, of course, many of the Commonwealth's great estates, which often included agricultural land, were also threatened by subdivision and development. Property values were rising dramatically in the mid-1980s and with them real estate taxes. Families were concerned as well about the long-term implications of the estate tax, which, as land values increased, cast a somber shadow on the future.

But MFCLT was there to help, as it did in a number of specific cases, working with landowners to identify their options for the future. Again, limited development of a portion of a property could provide housing for children or grandchildren as well as income which might make it possible to preserve significant areas of open space, retaining the original character of the place both for descendants and for the community as a whole. Again, the key ingredients were first-class legal advice — usually from MFCLT's General Counsel, attorney Daniel A. Taylor — careful financial analysis, and imaginative land use planning.

Meanwhile also, thanks to a number of welcome grants and income from the sale of so-called "trade lands" given to MFCLT specifically to be restricted and sold for limited development, the Revolving Loan Fund increased to more than $700,000. Its resources were further strengthened in 1984 with the establishment of the Gordon Abbott, Jr., Land Preservation Fund, which honored the retiring Director. By the end of its first year, the Abbott Fund totaled more than $107,000.

With expanding financial resources and a growing confidence in its abilities that came with experience, MFCLT was able to work more of its magic on the landscape. Adding to its list of projects, it preserved some 98 acres in Worthington. Included were 47 acres of prime tillable soils and an historic farmhouse built in 1790.

Following purchase of the property, MFCLT protected the house and 14 acres of land around it with a preservation restriction which it conveyed to the Worthington Historical Commission. It then sold the restricted house and acreage to a family which used it to establish an attractive bed and breakfast operation. An APR on the 47 acres of farmland was sold to the Commonwealth, and the land itself to a dairy farmer who planned to raise corn silage and alfalfa hay. An abuttor bought the remaining 37 acres of undevelopable woodland.

5

Powisset Farm: a Mix of Public and Private Initiatives

In 1985, in what was to be its most ambitious financial commitment, the Massachusetts Farm and Conservation Lands Trust purchased Powisset Farm in Dover for $2.4 million. Some 187 acres, the farm had been the property of Miss Amelia Peabody, who had died a year earlier.

Miss Peabody was a lady of many interests and talents. A sculptress whose works were exhibited at the New York World's Fair as well as at the Whitney Museum, the Boston Athenaeum and numerous galleries, her subjects ranged in size and composition from commemorative medals to statues larger than life. She specialized in the sculpture of small animals. Many of her pieces are still displayed at headquarters of the Massachusetts Audubon Society in Lincoln.

An outstanding sportswoman in her younger days, she also bred and raised race horses. Always a devoted environmentalist, for more than two decades she served as a Vice President of The Trustees of Reservations and as a member of its Standing Committee and Advisory Council. And as a philanthropist, she aided scores of charities and causes throughout New England.

Her love of landscape came from a lifetime of association with the out-of-doors. "I knew," she said, "that the Marblehead of my childhood was a beautiful and precious place and that Boston itself was surrounded by beautiful vistas that should be preserved if possible." In keeping with her wish, she left to The Trustees of Reservations by bequest and with endowment, 542 acres of her land in Dover which is today, in her memory, Noanet Woodlands Reservation.

Bordering Noanet Woodlands to the south, Powisset Farm in its heyday was known throughout the country for its prize Hereford cattle and Yorkshire pigs. The land included 98 acres of prime agricultural soils, as well as pasture, forest and wetlands at the headwaters of Noanet Brook.

"In buying Powisset Farm," said Director Frederic Winthrop, Jr., at the time, "we have three main objectives. We hope to protect high quality soils for agricultural production, reduce the amount of development that would otherwise take place adjacent to Noanet Woodlands, and increase the amount of protected open space between Noanet Woodlands and Rocky Woods Reservation in neighboring Medfield. Eventually, we hope to link the two reservations with a trail system for walking, horseback riding and cross-country skiing." Such a greenway had long been eyed by residents of the area and by The Trustees of Reservations.

MFCLT's plan for the future of Powisset Farm once again called for a mix of public and private involvement. Thirty-three acres of the property were to be purchased by the Town of Dover as conservation land. Following a presentation to a packed Town Meeting by MFCLT Associate Director Wesley Ward, voters unanimously agreed to appropriate $250,000 for the purpose. The action was followed by a standing ovation. Such was the popularity of the proposal.

Some 103 acres of the farm were to be protected in perpetuity with agricultural preservation restrictions. They were to be purchased by the Commonwealth's Department of Food & Agriculture, assisted by the Dover Conservation Commission which had raised $50,000 for the purpose. The farmstead, farm buildings and protected agricultural land were to be leased to a working farmer with MFCLT still holding title to insure the quality of farm operations.

Bridle trails along the southern boundary of the farm were also to be protected and open to visitors. And finally, 33 acres, not essential for agriculture, were to be developed for eight units of single-family, residential housing. Four existing houses were to be sold as well. Each building lot and house was sold subject to deed restrictions.

As Davis Cherington, MFCLT's Executive Director, explained, "The high purchase price made some development necessary to enable us to recoup our investment, but we controlled that development carefully through deed restrictions and good site planning."

Visitors gather to inspect the barn at Powisset Farm, Dover, during an Open House shortly after the property was purchased by the Massachusetts Farm and Conservation Lands Trust.

To purchase the property, MFCLT borrowed $400,000 from its Revolving Loan Fund. To this was added the $250,000 appropriated by the Town of Dover for conservation land, and $350,000 provided by the town and the Massachusetts Department of Food & Agriculture to purchase an Agricultural Preservation Restriction. The remainder was acquired using MFCLT's bank line of credit. Miss Peabody's executors used the proceeds from the sale of Powisset Farm to help fund two charitable foundations established in her name.

Following successful completion of the project, Fred Winthrop was deservedly elated. "This is a perfect example of the kind of bold and creative approach," he said, "that must be taken to protect open space in today's booming real estate market."

With all the details involved, each limited development project has its unsung hero. Clearly, Powissett Farm's was Stephen E. Bassett, Supervisor of the Medfield Management Unit. As on-site manager, Bassett served as liaison with state and town officials; coordinated the activities of survey teams, well-drilling contractors and clean-up crews; and provided vital, ongoing security for farm buildings.

Meanwhile, thanks to the generosity of Mr. and Mrs. Philip S. Weld of Gloucester, MFCLT accepted a gift of some 100 acres of land in Essex, sold a single building lot at one corner of the property to raise funds to endow the remainder, and, at the donors' request, conveyed both the land and its endowment to Essex County Greenbelt Association with appropriate restrictive covenants.

(Former owner and Publisher of Essex County Newspapers, Phil Weld was for many years a member of the corporation of The Trustees of Reservations. Also a world-renowned sailor, Weld, at age 65, won the celebrated OSTAR — Observer Single-handed Trans-Atlantic Race — in his trimaran *Moxie* in 1980.)

As it is empowered to hold lands outside of Massachusetts, MFCLT also acquired as a gift a conservation restriction protecting more than 433 acres in Salisbury, Connecticut, bordering Bartholomew's Cobble. And in Bellingham, Massachusetts, as a part of The Trustees of Reservations' Charles River Protection Program, it arranged for the purchase and conveyance of an important ll.7 acre parcel fronting the river to the Bellingham Conservation Commission. Additional protection for the property was provided for with a conservation restriction given to the Metacomet Land Trust.

Money for the initial acquisition came from the Charles River Corridor Land Acquisition Fund, established by a one-time court settlement for damages resulting from a developer's violation in Waltham of the state's Wetlands Protection Act. The Corridor Fund is administered jointly by the Charles River Watershed Association and The Trustees of Reservations. A cooperative project from beginning to end, it was typical of what is increasingly happening in land conservation activities today.

Other lands were acquired as well, primarily as gifts, but with the real estate market cooling off in the late 1980s, activities at MFCLT slowed considerably. The Commonwealth, too, was running out of APR funds and there was little hope for future bond issues as the economy of Massachusetts began its steep downward slide. Indeed, in 1987, the State Legislature authorized a $500 million bond issue for parks and recreation. Some $250 million was to be for land acquisition, but because of the cost of servicing the debt, two successive administrations have kept a tight rein on expenditures for open space.

6

Back to the Future: the New Land Conservation Center

Today, MFCLT continues to offer its flexibility to The Trustees of Reservations' new Land Conservation Center, administered by Wesley Ward, Deputy Director for Land Conservation. Thanks to new funding and a renewed focus on open space preservation, Ward is assisted by two Land Protection Specialists, Charles Wyman and Valerie Talmage. Wyman, former conservation agent for the Town of Lexington, works out of General Headquarters in Beverly, while Talmage is responsible for land conservation actitivies in Central Massachusetts and in the Charles River Valley.

The Center has increased emphasis also on the acquisition of conservation restrictions."They represent," as Fred Winthrop explains, "the most promising and cost-effective opportunity for expansion of our land protection efforts."

To ensure that a first-class program of monitoring and enforcing restrictions exists, The Trustees is also strengthening its relationship with local land trusts. For example, in Duxbury, the Rural and Historical Society is a co-holder of a preservation restriction on the historic Captain Daniel Bradford property, and in Bolton, The Trustees and the Conservation Commission jointly hold a conservation restriction protecting some 152 acres of land on Rattlesnake Hill.

The Land Conservation Center has also expanded and accelerated the organization's traditional relationship with private landowners. A video entitled *Land in Trust: Conservation Options for Private Landowners* was produced in cooperation with the Society for the Protection of New Hampshire Forests and the Land Planning and Management Foundation, a regional, three-state non-profit established to initiate innovative techniques in land conservation, including limited development.

A booklet which contains more detailed information about gifts of land, conservation restrictions, and accompanying tax advantages supplements the film. Workshops for groups of landowners have been held as well, at times in cooperation with local land trusts.

"The long-term success of our land conservation efforts," Winthrop continues, "will depend upon our ability to make landowners and their advisors aware of financially sound alternatives to subdivision and development of properties that are of environmental importance to the Commonwealth."

The Land Conservation Center also functions as a service

organization for local land trusts statewide, organizing conferences and providing training sessions and technical assistance for
land trust staff and volunteers. In Massachusetts now there are
more than 100 local and regional land trusts — a remarkable
constituency for the conservation of open space. Working with
this group, The Trustees is able to multiply by many times its own
capacity, experience and abilities.

The program of the Land Conservation Center also includes a
new dimension — archaeological research and preservation —
which the organization has only flirted with in the past. From the
Dinosaur Footprints in Holyoke and Barthomew's Cobble, to the
islands of Crane Wildlife Refuge, properties of The Trustees of
Reservations offer the most extraordinary opportunities for the
scientific study and interpretation of material evidence of human
life and culture through the ages.

As indicated earlier, the organization has also refined its
programmatic goals and criteria in the field of land conservation.
The acquisition of "in-holdings" still leads the list of priorities.
Farmland preservation has been melded into a more general
category which includes "lands of exceptional scenic, ecological,
recreational, historic or archaeological importance."

Finally, "geographic priorities" for land conservation have
been established in keeping with The Trustees' goals and objectives as well as with the strength of its physical presence. They
include coastal properties in Manchester, Essex and Ipswich; the
corridor of the upper Charles River; the towns of Cohasset and

*Staff members of the Land
Conservation Center. Land
Conservation Specialists
Charles Wyman and Valerie
Talmage discuss a project with
Director Wes Ward.*

Hingham; coastal and agricultural lands in Westport and South Dartmouth (where the organization holds conservation restrictions); the landscape of Martha's Vineyard; land in rural Worcester County; lands in historic Deerfield and Sutherland; agricultural landscapes in the hill towns of Cummington and Worthington; agricultural lands in South Williamstown; and the rural landscape of South Berkshire County including especially the towns of Monterey, New Marlborough, Sheffield and Tyringham.

In cooperation with the Executive Office of Environmental Affairs, the Appalachian Mountain Club and other organizations, the Land Conservation Center is developing a program to protect major "greenways," or environmental and open space corridors, throughout the Commonwealth.

As for limited development, which was so widely heralded intially as a succesful technique to preserve conservation lands, much has been learned. First, it became obvious that a significant subsidy was usually needed to underwrite the cost of reducing the number of developable lots if the land was purchased at full and fair market value. This could be, as it was in so many cases with MFCLT, the state's purchase of development rights protecting a portion of the land to be retained for agriculture. It could be — during an up-market — the increase in the value of the land between the time of its purchase and the sale of its residential lots. Or it could be in an initial bargain sale of the property made by a generous owner to the land trust planning the limited development project.

Second, it soon became clear that becoming involved in even environmentally sensitive development activities can be uncomfortable for those who take a pure approach to open space preservation.

Finally, experience showed that there were no firm ground rules. Each project has its own special characteristics and identity. But if conditions are right, as MFCLT proved conclusively time after time, limited development can be a highly effective way to preserve desirable portions of the landscape.

The point was, and still is today, to have an organization in place with the skills and flexibility to deal with every conservation option available.

Caring for
the Collection

1

Early Management: Local Committees and a Field Secretary

As early as 1904, management, or the continuing protection of the special qualities of each reservation, was becoming a growing concern of The Trustees of Reservations.

Even then, properties were scattered throughout the state from nearby Stoneham to Falmouth on the Cape and as far away as Great Barrington. Gypsy moths especially and the blight that so sadly killed the region's American chestnut trees were among the most common problems. "Rust" was endangering the health and longevity of pines at Virginia Woods.

Public use was increasing as well. It was not unusual, it was reported in 1905, "to see as many as 20 canoes on a pleasant Sunday pass [through Rocky Narrows] and up through Medfield Meadows beyond." And hardly a year went by that the carriage road to the summit of Monument Mountain didn't need to be resurfaced with stone and gravel.

Wisely, provisions had been made shortly after the organization was founded for the appointment of Local Committees, whose responsibility it was to provide supervision for properties in their immediate vicinity. Composed entirely of volunteers who had an affection for the site and an interest in its future welfare and preservation, Local Committees soon came to play an indispensable role in the management structure. Indeed, their worth was such that the idea was adopted as well by The National Trust in England.

As they do today, most members of Local Committees lived no more than a few miles from their reservation. This meant that they could easily provide immediate physical assistance to deal with such activities as trail maintenance, storm and insect damage and the effects of vandalism. No less important — as taxpayers in the community — they were a political constituency, which gave them an important standing with local government and enabled them to communicate effectively with public officials. Obviously, for an organization whose governing board had its roots firmly planted in Boston, Local Committees were, and are, the eyes and ears — in many ways, the heart and soul — of The Trustees of Reservations in outlying communities.

By 1924, however, administrative pressures on the Standing Committee had increased markedly. Its responsibilities now included eight properties totaling more than 740 acres of land. The automobile was making it possible for a rapidly growing number of people to visit the countryside. It was difficult and time-consuming to communicate with Local Committee members living in cities and towns from Sherborn in the east, to Sheffield in the west. There was a feeling of a loss of control, not only of the details of physical management, but of operating costs as well.

"The time has come," the Standing Committee declared, "when changes should be made in the methods of administration." A new proposal called for the appointment of a Field Secretary who would "visit reservations as needed; supervise the expenditure of monies; direct custodians; and confer and consult with Local Committees."

"Such a position," the board continued, "would require the services of a young, active man with some knowledge of forestry and landscape work." At age 25, just out of Harvard's Graduate School of Landscape Architecture, Charles William Eliot II, nephew of the organization's founder, fit the bill perfectly. The job was part time (its first year it paid $360) and, equally important, Charles could double in brass as Secretary of the corporation, for John Woodbury, who had served in the office quietly and effectively since 1894, was about to retire.

The appointment of a Field Secretary in no way implied a criticism of Local Committees. Their role was still indispensable. But their activities did need coordination and the new position not only improved the organization's control over what was happening at its properties, it also gave Local Committee members better access to the Standing Committee so that their needs could be more effectively met. There is no indication that the appointment engendered anything but praise.

Eliot served as Field Secretary for two years, from 1924 to 1926. Three years later, Laurence Fletcher joined The Trustees as its Executive Secretary and first full-time employee. (Bradford Williams, also a landscape architect and author of the Massachusetts Landscape Survey, served as Field Secretary, again part time, from 1934 to 1938, primarily as an aide to Fletcher. He later became a member of the Standing Committee.)

2

Master Plans: a Systematic Approach

It was not until 1942, however, that The Trustees of Reservations began to establish a systematic management program for its then 22 properties. It was first proposed by Standing Committee member Fletcher Steele. As a landscape architect, Steele served as Chairman of the Reservations Committee which acted as liaison between each Local Committee and the governing board.

During the summer of that wartime year, "I went over to the newly-acquired Elliott Reservation (in Phillipston)," he reported, "with Miss Olive Simes of the Local Committee. (Miss Simes was also a donor of the property.) It had just been appointed and was ready to go ahead but had no definite instructions.

"Sprout growth," Steele explained, "was coming up every-where, hurting the laurel, swallowing open glades and obscuring vistas. Miss Simes remarked that the place had been more beautiful some years ago, shortly after the cattle had been turned out. She was modest about the scope of the Local Committee work and supposed that Nature was to be allowed to go its own way.

"I took the liberty (as a member of the governing board)," he continued, "of making a policy, saying: 'You remember how this place looked at its best. Why not put it back as it was then and keep it that way? Cut out all interfering scrub. Let in the same amount of light that it formerly had. Clear the vales and openings in the woods. Encourage big trees and remove the young stuff that is getting in their way. Borrow some cattle for a week or two if that would help.' Miss Simes allowed that this was a definite, tangible policy which they could work by, and they did, all summer."

A later visit to Concord and The Old Manse raised many of the same kind of questions. What should be done about about "some neglected planting next to the house? Should the property as a whole be brought back to its original aspect — as it looked when the Battle [at the North Bridge] was fought? Or as it was when Concord was the cultural center of the country? Or as it was when taken over by The Trustees?"

It was clear, as Steele said, "that without a program, it was impossible to advise." Each of these experiences and others marked the beginnings of a study by the Reservations Committee of management needs and policies at every property of The Trustees of Reservations. It was a program that continued until Steele left the board. Because of professional demands elsewhere, however, only a handful of properties were able to benefit from his wisdom and experience.

By 1969, with new administrative leadership, the program was reinitiated to provide what were called "Master Plans" for each reservation — a blueprint for their future management and preservation. The approach was more sophisticated. It was designed to identify and inventory the property's resources, both natural and cultural; to establish preservation policies; and to provide procedures which would enable Local Committees and, by this time, members of the professional field staff, to implement management policies day by day.

One of the major roles of a Master Plan is to balance the protection of a property's resources — the very reason it was preserved — with a rapidly growing demand for public use. As the prophet of continuing preservation, Steele was without peer. As early as 1947 he wrote, "our reservartions have been described as museum holdings. And it is clearly stated in our charter that we are obligated to preserve them. To do this we are empowered to maintain 'suitable regulations.'

"Until recently it has seemed important to inveigle people into our empty acres on any pretext in order to justify our existence. . . . We became somewhat confused about our major purpose which is to encourage study and appreciation of our collection of valuable natural and historic objects. We let it get mixed up with public recreation. Recreation is good. It must be provided for. But it is not the object for which our museum was established. . . ."

As time passed and the organization grew, it became clear that reservations could support activities of varying intensity according to their character and environments. What was appropriate at one was forbidden at another because of its impact on the property's natural systems or historic fabric. This was what the process of master planning helped determine in a rational and scientific way.

But Steele's early concepts of management had great validity. To this day, The Trustees discourages "picnic tables next to public roads. Shops for selling ginger pop and chewing gum. And any resemblance to public parks, amusement grounds or general recreation areas."

Rather than cater to generic "groups," the organization welcomes "individuals" to its properties with the hope that its policies provide a rewarding experience for each and every person. Its goal, even today, as Steele explained so well, is to "increase the worth of living through development of love of the earth and thankful appreciation of all our historic inheritance."

The model for future Master Plans was completed at the Richard T. Crane, Jr., Memorial Reservation in 1970 by a team from the Department of Landscape Architecture at Harvard University's Graduate School of Design. The idea arose in 1968.

Landscape architect Peter L. Hornbeck, member of the Standing Committee and the Advisory Council

Herring gull stands watch at Cape Poge Wildlife Refuge, Chappaquiddick Island, Martha's Vineyard.

Fertilizing culms of beach grass planted at Crane Beach and Castle Neck, Ipswich, to halt erosion and stabilze sand dunes

An agreement, arrived at in 1952 when The Trustees of Reservations acquired Crane Beach, gave the Town of Ipswich a percentage of the revenue received from parking receipts. Not surprisingly, through the years, there were a few town officials who saw this as an endless cornucopia of cash for the community.

One even suggested to the then recently-appointed Director Gordon Abbott, Jr., that The Trustees consider running a road further down Castle Neck and creating a second parking facility for 1,500 or more vehicles which could double existing revenues. It was at this moment that Abbott realized the desperate need for a Master Plan to define and proclaim the Reservation's environmental values and to propose regulations to protect them.

Director of the project was Peter L. Hornbeck, Assistant Professor at the Graduate School of Design, who was later to become a much-valued member of the Standing Committee. The study itself included the formal landscape at Castle Hill with its Great House and surrounding buildings, but focused primarily on the delicate natural resources of Crane Beach and Castle Neck, which were visited by nearly one-half million people annually.

As a result of the Master Plan, a unique and pioneering program was initiated which involved the restoration, stabilization and continuing protection of the sand dune environment. It aimed first at providing information for visitors about the fragility of a barrier beach, its sand dunes and neighboring salt marsh and their related wildlife resources. It included an interpretive program with panel boards, special books and pamphlets, a self-guided nature trail and a lecture series illustrated with color slides entitled "This Fragile Shore."

Volunteers and staff members planted more than 6,000 culms of American beach grass and 200 salt spray rose plants to anchor the constantly moving sand. Snow fences were erected to help prevailing wind action create new dunes and stabilize old. The parking facility was redesigned and new patterns of pedestrian circulation developed to lessen human impact on the beach environment. A full-time ranger was hired and a special annual effort was launched to protect nesting least and common terns. The dune restoration program at Castle Neck was an unqualified success. Wisely, it has been continued through the years.

Fire had just destroyed the refreshment stand at Crane Beach and a handsome new structure, which also housed beach administration offices, was built of fluted concrete block which harmonized with the natural world around it.

Most important, the Master Plan for the Crane Reservation, approved as policy by both the Local Committee and the Standing Committee, established new standards of professional management. With few changes, it still functions today, providing policies which preserve the beach area and maintain its extraordinary scenic and environmental values for the enjoyment and appreciation of every visitor.

The process of master planning continues to be the cornerstone of effective and responsible property management. Today, comprehensive management and preservation plans are being completed for a growing number of properties of The Trustees of Reservations. A wealth of information has been gathered, not only about natural features, but about architecture and archaeology, gardens and garden design, as well as the remarkable collections of furniture, china and glass, and the decorative arts which are characteristic of so many of The Trustees' historic houses.

In 1982, members of the Local Committee for The Old Manse (including especially Martha Hamilton and Judy Keyes, who was later to join the Standing Committee), working with Regional Supervisor Thomas S. Foster, initiated a study which led to the development of a model "collections management policy." A first for the organization, it guided much of the critical restoration work which took place at The Manse in 1983 and 1984 (funded, in part, by a grant of $10,000 received from the Massachusetts Historical Commission) and set an example which was duplicated at properties elsewhere.

Judy Keyes, member of the Standing Committee and Chairman of The Trustees of Reservations' Centennial Committee

Today, Master Plans continue to guide management decisions and to help maintain the delicate balance between public access and use and The Trustees of Reservations' responsibility to protect and preserve its properties for the benefit and pleasure of generations yet to come.

3

Rocky Woods: a Winter Wonderland

Because of the number of visitors they welcome annually and the complexity of the programs they offer, few of the properties of The Trustees of Reservations have historically required or received as much management attention as Rocky Woods in Medfield and Crane Beach and Castle Hill in Ipswich.

Rocky Woods, today some 491 acres of forest land which includes three sizable ponds, was given to The Trustees in 1942 by Dr. Joel E. Goldthwait of Boston, a major figure in the world of orthopaedic medicine. A graduate of Massachusetts Agricultural College (now the University of Massachusetts at Amherst) where he majored in botany, and Harvard Medical School (1890) at the age of 24, Dr. Goldthwait was destined early for a career filled with "firsts."

As a young surgeon, he established the first clinic for handicapped adults at Carney Hospital in Boston. A few years later, in 1899, he organized the first outpatient department at Massachusetts General Hospital and, in 1909, its first orthopaedic ward, serving as chief of each. In 1914, following a particular interest in arthritis, he was also largely responsible for the establishment of the Robert Breck Brigham Hospital for Chronic Illness.

During World War I, as director of the of the Division of Orthopaedic Surgery for the American Expeditionary Forces, he pioneered the development of modern orthopaedic techniques, including diagnosis, surgical innovations, and physical therapy and rehabilitation. The author of more than 100 books and publications, he was fascinated with body mechanics and posture, and with steps that could be taken to avoid surgery whenever possible.

Widely respected and much honored both in this country and abroad, he was active throughout his long life. As a paper written for the American Orthopaedic Association states, "he practiced the good posture he preached." He "was extremely tall, erect, always well groomed and most imposing looking. He had a magnetic personality and rapidly inspired the confidence of his patients" and all who worked with him. A towering figure in American medicine, Dr. Goldthwait continued some office practice right up to the day he died in January 1961 at age 94.

Deeply interested in the out-of-doors and in the healthful benefits of outdoor recreation, Dr. Goldthwait assembled some 300 acres in Medfield which, in the early years of World War II, he offered to The Trustees of Reservations. In those "uncertain times," he chose not to accompany his gift with endowment which, he added, would follow later. He did, however, propose that he give The Trustees $1,000 a year for maintenance purposes.

With the organization then skating on thin financial ice, the idea of acquiring a sizable amount of land without endowment did not sit well with a number of influential Standing Committee members. But Chairman Charles S. Bird's recommendation that the property be accepted finally prevailed, as did Dr. Goldthwait's promise. Not only did he faithfully contribute operating funds annually for the next 19 years until his death, but significant amounts also to improve the property including money to construct a number of buildings. Finally, his will established an endowment in the amount of $180,000 for Rocky Woods Reservation.

The interests of its donor and of the members of its Local Committee; the character of the property itself with its woodland trails already used for hiking and horseback riding; its three ponds (originally created for fire protection purposes); its hills and its easy access from the surrounding towns of Dover,

Sherborn, Westwood and Millis — all combined to make active recreation a major feature of Rocky Woods. Winter sports led the way and in 1946, nearby Cedar Hill with its steep face, was purchased and added to the Reservation to provide opportunities for downhill skiing. Slopes and trails were constructed and two rope tows installed.

There was an equal demand for ice skating, and Chickering Pond, the largest of the three, was selected as a logical site for development. A portion of the shoreline was graded and a comfortable lodge, designed by local architect Nathaniel Saltonstall, was constructed to provide heat and shelter for both skaters and skiers.

Dr. Joel E. Goldthwait, celebrated orthopaedic surgeon and donor of Rocky Woods Reservation, Medfield

The ice was cleared of snow using plows mounted on small tractors and a war-surplus Jeep. A generator provided lights for nighttime skating and the cheerful sounds of waltzes and alpine music could be heard emanating from loudspeakers. With its newly expanded parking facility, which accomodated as many as 100 cars, Rocky Woods by1950 had become an immensely popular "winter resort." Throughout the history of the natural ice program, as many as 70 skating days have been recorded in a single season.

Families flocked to the area each weekend. To help meet the cost of operating winter programs, the Rocky Woods Club was established in the late 1950s. Members could join for $1, families for $2, youngsters for 50 cents. During the spring, summer and fall, many winter visitors returned to enjoy picnics beside the pond, to walk the trails, and to climb a newly-installed observation tower. Used during World War II for spotting airplanes, it too was purchased as surplus and moved to the Reservation. Later, a dock was installed and rowing skiffs and paddle boats were made available for public use. For several years, the pond was stocked with trout.

But although recreation was the hallmark of Rocky Woods, resource management was not forgotten. Forest improvement programs were begun with the assistance of professionals and continued through the years. And to awaken public interest in the natural environment of the area, interpretive booklets were published: the *Geology of Rocky Woods Reservation* produced by Hervey Woodburn Shimer, Professor Emeritus of Paleontology at Massachusetts Institute of Technology (1951) and *Hemlock Knoll Nature Trail* produced by The Trustees of Reservations' Deputy Director for Environmental Services, Garret F. VanWart (1981).

With public use increasing markedly, management of the property became a major responsibility and, in 1955, the officers of the Rocky Woods Club combined with members of the existing Local Committee to form a new committee with Mario Pederzini as Executive Chairman. Moreover, Mario was to become a profes-

Mario Pederzini,
Superintendent of Rocky
Woods for more than 30 years,
and a pioneer in the operation
of natural ice skating areas

sional employee serving as Superintendent of Rocky Woods
Reservation, with a salary of $2,000 per year and a house on the
property to provide for its security.

Considering the demands of its programs, especially ice
skating, the contributions of the members of the Local Committee
at Rocky Woods were unique. All volunteers, they pitched in
seemingly day and night during the winter season. They helped
to scrape and flood the ice. Cleared it in case of snow. Manned the
refreshment stand, which later offered grilled hot dogs and
hamburgers as well as ice cream and soft drinks. Cut and split
wood to feed the fires and stoves which kept the hut warm.
Supervised parking, which on busy days was a major task. And
helped maintain picnic tables and fireplaces during the summer
season. There was also the annual Winter Carnival with skaters in
costume and special performances which lasted a full day.

Many of the children of Local Committee members as well as
other youngsters in the neighborhood grew up helping at Rocky
Woods, always under the watchful eye of Mario Pederzini. Mario,
whose service at Rocky Woods, both part time and later full time,
spanned more than three decades, taught by example and by
direction the values of hard work and the thrill of accomplishing a
job well done.

Youngsters were given responsibility and respect, and many
later reported that their experiences at Rocky Woods had played a
major role in the development of their character and maturity.
One of these was Steven Bassett, who served as Superintendent of

Families flocked to Rocky
Woods during the cold winter
months to skate on the smooth
ice surface at Chickering Pond
and later to warm themselves
in the pond-side shelter.

Rocky Woods himself, as well as of other properties in the Charles River Valley Management Unit, for more than a decade.

Because of an appreciation of the skills, attention to detail and high standards of quality with which the staff at Rocky Woods maintained its own sizable collection of vehicles, equipment and machinery, the property was chosen in 1969 to become Maintenance Headquarters of The Trustees of Reservations. No little factor in the choice was the existence there of staff member Robert E. Kreger, whose remarkable abilities as a machinist and mechanic, as well as carpenter and joiner, soon led to his appointment as Equipment Supervisor for the organization.

Stephen E. Bassett, Superintendent, Medfield Management Unit

A new shop building was constructed with design skills contributed by architect and Standing Committee member Daniel C. Coolidge. Through the years, Coolidge also designed the Arthur D. Budd Visitor Center at Notchview and the Victorian Gate House at World's End, as well as contributing countless hours of professional advice and consultation for projects needing architectural assistance from restoration and repairs at The Old Manse, Naumkeag, and The Mission House, to a redesign of the interior at the Pierce House, 224 Adams Street, Milton, which for more than 25 years served as General Headquarters.

As the years passed, however, it became increasingly difficult to get volunteers to contribute the time needed to help plow, flood and scrape the ice at Chickering Pond. Expenses grew and revenues fell as a string of warmer winters arrived.

In 1983, after extensive analysis of the issues provided by Regional Supervisor Thomas S. Foster, and much discussion and deliberation by committee members at every level of responsibility, it was reluctantly agreed to give up the formal ice skating program at Rocky Woods. It was an agonizingly difficult decision, but the only one that made sense. Neither the property nor The Trustees itself could continue to afford to subsidize one program at the expense of others more closely related to the mission of the organization as a whole.

With the development of major downhill ski areas to the north, cross-country skiing took over at the property and became a popular winter sport, but it could never rival the excitement and satisfaction offered to all ages in the community by natural ice skating. And those who remembered past years, when black ice covered the pond and cheerful crowds skated to the sounds of alpine music, shed a sad tear of nostalgia.

Today, despite the accelerated construction of housing in the area during the 1980s, Hartford Street, where visitors enter Rocky Woods, is still bordered by forest land. In large part, this is due to the existence of Fork Factory Brook Reservation (62 acres) which now includes Longacre Farm, (63 acres). Both are located south of Rocky Woods itself.

Fork Factory Brook, which protects the century-old site of a former pitchfork factory, was given to The Trustees of Reservations in 1966 by Pliney Jewell, Jr., and his sister, Mrs. Barrett Williams, in memory of their parents, Mr. and Mrs. Pliney Jewell. Longacre Farm, for many years in active agriculture, was protected first with a conservation restriction contributed by Dr. Goldthwait's son, Joel A. Goldthwait, who lived on the property. After his death, fee title to the restricted land was given to The Trustees of Reservations.

4

Castle Hill: Escaping the Heat of Chicago

Richard Teller Crane, Jr., was 35 years old in 1909 when he and his wife Florence arrived in Ipswich in search of a summer place to escape the heat of Chicago.

Vice President of the Crane Company at the time, the nation's leading manufacturer of plumbing supplies, he was told that property at Castle Hill was for sale. Owned by the Estate of John Burnham Brown, it included land where John Winthrop, Jr., had settled in 1638. Crane saw it one day and bought it the next. The original parcel, which features the hilltop with its spectacular views of Ipswich Bay, totaled some 800 acres. Its selling price was $125,000.

Shortly after purchasing the property, Crane engaged the architectural firm of Shepley, Rutan & Coolidge to design and construct at the top of Castle Hill an Italianate villa of stucco with a red tile roof. To create an appropriate landscape, he called on the firm of Olmsted Brothers, which produced the Italian Garden in place today.

He also continued to acquire abutting properties until, in 1918, he owned more than 3,500 acres. About a third of the area was salt marsh, sand dunes and beach, the major portion of which is known as Castle Neck. The remainder included not only Castle Hill and Steep Hill but Choate or Hog Island, Woodbury's Landing, Wigwam Hill, Claverly Hill, and a sizable farm bordering Labor-in-Vain Creek which was turned into a private, nine-hole golf course.

In 1921, convinced that the Italian villa was unsuited to the windswept site, Mr. and Mrs. Crane ordered that it be razed. In its place was built the present 59-room structure known as the Great House. Designed by Chicago architect David Adler, its Holland brick and stone exterior mirrors the Great Houses of England during the reign of the Stuarts. Adler also designed with a meticulous eye for detail, the gate house and garages. The huge barn and tenant's house he allowed to remain.

Inside the Great House, the details were equally elegant. Included were Abram Poole paintings in the circular hall; ornamental wood carvings by seventeenth-century English craftsman Grinling Gibbons; and bedroom panelling which was originally believed to have been part of the London residence of William Hogarth, eighteenth-century English satirist, although this is in doubt today. And there was, of course, in keeping with the Crane Company's interests, a collection of 10 luxurious bathrooms, embellished with painted glass panels, soft-hued Italian marble and sterling silver fixtures.

Landscape architect and long-time member of the Standing Committee Sidney N. Shurcliff

The exterior landscaping was magnificent as well. It featured a grand allée, one-half mile in length, stretching from the terrace of the house to the sea. Lined with statuary and bordered originally by poplar and later by spruce, its design was first begun by Olmsted Brothers and subsequently extended by landscape architect Arthur A. Shurtleff.

On a clear day, the Isles of Shoals, which span the ocean border between New Hampshire and Maine, are visible some 18 miles away. Shurtleff (who later changed his name to Shurcliff) was a favorite of the Crane family, and designed and directed as well the construction of the driveways, the rose garden, the vegetable garden, and other landscape features which exist today. He was later joined in practice by his son Sidney, also a landscape architect, who later became a much-valued member of the Stand-

Houses and barns of the Woodbury Farm on the south side of Castle Neck in the late 19th century. Family members engaged in fishing, dug clams as bait for tub trawlers, raised apples and cut salt hay.

ing Committee of The Trustees of Reservations and, as a life-long
Ipswich resident and neighbor of the property on Argilla Road,
served as a key member of the first group of volunteers to operate
the beach and later as Chairman of the Local Committee for the
Crane Reservation.

Indeed, friendships along Argilla Road which included the
Eliots, the Cranes, the Crocketts and the Shurcliffs, had much to
do with building the trust which led to the Crane family's gift of
Crane Beach and Castle Hill to The Trustees of Reservations.

Unlike many major industrialists of his time, Richard Crane
continued his father's concern for the happiness and well-being of
the corporation's more than 20,000 employees worldwide. He
established the Crane Veteran League and distributed among his
workers some $12 million in Crane Company stock, much of it
from his own private fortune. His efforts to create a partnership
between management and labor were recognized by Hobart
College which presented him in 1931, six months before his death,
with an honorary degree.

A legendary philanthropist, he supported causes throughout
the country. For 22 years, until his death in November 1931,
Ipswich played a very special role in his life. He developed an
affection for the community which was returned in kind. He was
interested particularly in the work of the YMCA and the Historical Society. And, following a tragic auto accident in which he was
driving and a Yale classmate, Benjamin Stickney Cable, was
killed, he had constructed a community hospital and named it as
a memorial for his friend. It was said at the time that if Cable had
been able to receive medical attention earlier he might have
survived. But by the end of 1931, Richard Crane himself was gone
and a grand era had ended.

5

Crane Beach Becomes a Public Reservation

In the early 1930s, Castle Neck had already begun to attract an
increasing number of beachgoers. As many as a thousand people
could be seen on hot summer weekends, their cars parked along
both sides of Argilla Road. As the number of visitors grew, so did
the concerns of the Crane family, about how to provide management for what was fast becoming a major recreational resource.

By 1935 a special committee of local residents had been
appointed to help with its administration. And by 1939 a more
formal Ipswich Beach Association was established. Simple bath-

house facilities were constructed and an entrance fee of 25 cents was charged.

The Trustees of Reservations' interest in acquiring the beach began as early as 1943. There had been conversations with Mrs. Crane and with her children, Cornelius Crane and his sister Florence Crane Belloselsky, ultimate heirs to the property. It was the family's hope that not only Crane Beach but Castle Hill would eventually become part of a public reservation. Income from beach receipts, some $7,500 a year during World War II, could be used to help meet management expenses. But there was one major hitch: title to the property was in question.

The Town of Ipswich claimed historic rights to the beach. Others disagreed. It was proposed that the Land Court settle the matter. Meanwhile, conversations with Cornelius Crane and with counsel for the Crane family, Lothrop Withington, who was to play a major role in determining the terms of gift, continued. The Trustees of Reservations was ably represented by Vice President Henry M. Channing.

Henry Channing was a man of many interests and abilities. A widely-respected attorney himself and head of his own small firm, he was a charming, thoughtful and articulate facilitator. He was also a great sportsman: a crack shot with both rifle and shotgun and an avid bird hunter, a freshwater fisherman, an excellent tennis player, and later in his life, an equally committed horseback rider.

Firm-minded and principled, he was a tower of strength for The Trustees. Devoted to its work, he gave countless hours of his

Attorney Henry M. Channing, Vice President of The Trustees of Reservations from 1938 to 1950

Visitors enjoy the sands of Crane Beach and the calm waters of Ipswich Bay on a quiet summer morning in the early 1960s.

time to help steer its projects in the right direction. Certainly, such was the case with the Crane Reservation, of which he saw the value in the very beginning.

Basically, it was proposed that The Trustees acquire the beach and most of Castle Neck with a parcel reserved for Cornelius Crane at Wigwam Hill, and for Florence Belloselsky at Steep Hill, just east of the allée. The beach, it was stipulated, must always be open to residents of the Town of Ipswich (access for the general public was a second consideration), while Mrs. Crane would retain ownership of Castle Hill, although that, too, it was planned, would ultimately be preserved.

By 1945 negotiations and discussions had ended. The necessary deeds of gift had been signed and, in March, 943 acres of land at Castle Neck became the Richard T. Crane, Jr., Memorial Reservation, a property of The Trustees of Reservations. With Crane Beach, the organization had become engaged in earnest in the business of outdoor recreation.

By the end of the year also, World War II had ended and peace had come to Europe and the Far East. With gasoline rationing now a thing of the past, the number of visitors at properties of The Trustees of Reservations soared. In 1945 The Old Manse reported 5,543, a 30 percent rise over the year before. Two thousand people found their way to Misery Islands by boat now that the Coast Guard's wartime watch had disappeared. And in the following year, 1946, Crane Beach welcomed more than 140,000 visitors, who arrived in more than 35,000 cars.

Management of the beach was still in the hands of the Local Committee. The Superintendent reported that receipts for the 1947 season from all sources totaled $35,530. The charge was 75 cents per vehicle for parking.

6

Castle Hill Is Preserved and a Title Agreement Reached

By 1949, Mrs. Crane had died, and in November the Standing Committee, following the unanimous recommendation of the Reservations Committee, accepted the devise of Castle Hill and Cedar Neck as well as an additional mile of beach, some 300 acres in all.

Included were the Great House and its surrounding buildings as well as its gardens and other landscape features. However, there was no endowment. It had been generally agreed by both parties that income from the beach would pay for the maintenance of the structures at Castle Hill. There was a caveat, however, which let The Trustees off the hook financially should this not be the case. In the letter of agreement signed by both Cornelius Crane and Florence Belosselsky, it was clearly stated that acceptance of the gift "does not require that The Trustees of Reservations maintain or preserve any buildings now on the property. . . if it was found unwise or uneconomical. . . . "

The immediate question then was what to do with the Great House. Its grandeur was embellished by a remarkable collection of English and early American furniture; paintings, including a number of notable portraits of eighteenth century English nobility; and an impressive assemblage of decorative arts both from the Georgian and Stuart periods of England, as well as from the Orient.

It was hoped that the furniture and other personal property would remain in place at least long enough to allow the house to be opened to the public. But that was not to be. Portions were removed from time to time by the family and in the spring of 1950, Parke-Bernet Galleries of New York was called in to auction off the remainder.

The house was stripped bare. More than 350 pieces were sold in the first day. They netted a total of $46,872.50. In the three days of the auction, a fabulous collection of furniture, china, glass, fabrics and the decorative arts sold for far less than they had cost when orginally purchased in 1925. In retrospect, it was a tragic

East terrace of the Great House at Castle Hill. From it, there is a dramatic view down the Grande Allée and out across Ipswich Bay of the Isles of Shoals some 20 miles away.

mistake. Funds might have been raised locally to keep them at Castle Hill.

The statuary along the allée was saved. It was sold for $30 but on the condition that it be removed in two days. Fortunately, the requirement could not be met.

Meanwhile, in mid-1951, negotiations began again with the Town of Ipswich over the title to the beach. Every effort was made to keep the issue out of court, which would have been costly to all, but matters were soon deadlocked and talks broke off. It took a special effort by Ipswich resident Albert C. Burrage, Jr., to bring the parties together again.

Burrage, who had friends on both sides and whose only interest was in resolving the issues, asked representatives — without their lawyers — to meet at his house on Heartbreak Road. From that moment on, a solution was in sight. Maurice M. Osborn, also an Ipswich resident, who later became Chairman of the Standing Committee, represented The Trustees in subcommittee conversations with the Town Manager where the real work was done to come up with an acceptable compromise.

By the time of Town Meeting in March 1952, agreement had been reached. The title issue was bypassed in favor of a series of arrangements which provided certain parcels for the Crane family; which gave to The Trustees land at Steep Hill including the allée; which kept the entire property from commercial use for a period of 500 years; which called upon The Trustees to manage the beach area; and which provided that the Town be given annually seven and one-half percent of the gross income from beach receipts.

It was also agreed that the Town should have its own parking area, which would be reserved exclusively for Ipswich residents (as well as the right to park up to 200 cars on crowded days at the parking facility of The Trustees of Reservations), and that visitors would adhere to a series of specifically listed rules and regulations. Finally, it was agreed that funds received by the Town "shall be applied primarily to the rebuilding and maintenance of Argilla Road," although this portion of the agreement was not binding.

As Lawrence Fletcher wrote, following the Selectmens' approval of the proposals, the room was "all smiles and everything but the National Anthem. [There were] many handshakes and goodbyes."

The scene was now set for The Trustees of Reservations to undertake what was to become its most demanding management responsibility.

7

A Model for Recreation Management

The Crane Reservation now totaled 1,293 acres. Three times the size of Rocky Woods, it presented major challenges in preservation.

Its landscape characteristics varied widely from upland — both field and woodland — to ocean beach, salt marsh and sand dunes. Included were structures of major proportions and architectural significance, as well as outbuildings of every size and description, drives and roadways, a series of formal gardens, lawns and statuary, terraces and courtyards, all located within an easy, 45-minute drive of Boston, one of the nation's largest metropolitan areas.

The obligations of The Trustees of Reservations involved the protection of the natural values of a fragile barrier beach ecosystem, the maintenance of stone, wood, stucco and brick structures in a harsh, seaside environment where wind velocities could reach hurricane force and where temperatures could range from well below zero to more than 90 degrees Fahrenheit. Coupled with this was an annual influx of visitors, which in recent decades has neared a half million people per year, a parking facility for 1,500 vehicles, and a management system complicated by interests in the area held by the Town of Ipswich, The Trustees of Reservations and, later, the Castle Hill Foundation.

What has made management work successfully through the years has been the involvement of a collection of remarkable people, both volunteers and professionals. Ultimately, despite often conflicting ideas, it was their interest and commitment to the outstanding values of the property itself which helped logic lead the way. They have included through the years Ipswich residents Charles Bird, Charles Cobb, David Crockett, Charles Eliot, Dr. Robert Goodale, George Mathey, Sheila Mathey, Dorothy Monnelly, Arthur Phillips, David Scudder, Sidney Shurcliff, Norton Sloan, Jack Vincent, Hope Wigglesworth and Frederic Winthrop, Sr. All were members of the Local Committee.

But it was the good judgment and leadership of the professional staff which enabled the property to function successfully from day to day. Although it increased to a total of more than 150 men and women who worked different hours during the summer months, full-time staff members totaled no more than five.

Two of the area's superindendents were retired Army officers of senior rank, J. Perry Smith and Charles E. Coates, Jr. Other veteran employees through the years have included Superintendent Michael Gormley; Chief Ranger Harry Mears;

George Mathey, architect, long-time member of the Standing Committee, and Vice President of the Castle Hill Foundation, played a major role in the restoration of Castle Hill.

Sheila Mathey, Chairman of the Local Committee for the Richard T. Crane, Jr., Memorial Reservation

Charles C. Coates, Jr., retired Army officer and superintendent of the Richard T. Crane, Jr. Memorial Reservation from 1968 to 1978

Refreshment Stand Manager Bill Cruikshank (whose service of more than 30 years sets a record at The Trustees of Reservations); Maintenance Supervisor Ed Paquin; Beach Managers Charles Pickard, Walter Dembrowski and Roland Hinckley; Chief of Security Robert Chambers; and Head Lifeguard Kenneth Spellman. The area's present superintendent, Peter Pinciaro, started while in high school as a volunteer at Crane Wildlife Refuge.

Most important, for more than 16 years, Northeast Regional Supervisor Wayne N. Mitton has provided a cool head and a steady hand which has enabled The Trustees of Reservations' most-visited property to function successfully, to protect its resources, and to serve the public with distinction.

Mitton, no stranger to the busy world of Crane Beach, served as superintendent himself and, with his family, lived for a while in a cottage on the property. As a resource and recreation manager, he has seen it all. And despite the need at times to make difficult and unpopular decisions, he has won the respect and admiration not only of his staff, but of the community as a whole.

In 1968, following completion of the Master Plan, it was decided that the Reservation should be presented to the public as a conservation area, whereas before the emphasis had been on recreation. Panel boards, a self-guiding nature trail and interpretive booklets at the entrance to Castle Neck described the environmental features of the property.

The uniform for security officers and the Chief Ranger was changed from standard, blue police issue to handsome, dark green trousers, a khaki shirt and a straw campaign hat. Signage was improved and modernized. The difference in appearance was striking. (Indeed, the Ipswich Police Department was so taken by the changes that, shortly afterwards, it, too, redesigned its uniform to include a campaign-style hat.)

The number of beachgoers increased annually for decades until recently, when fear of Lyme disease (deer ticks have been a major problem in wooded areas of the reservation but not at the beach) and publicity given to the dangers of exposure to the sun have taken their toll. As expenses increased, parking fees grew from 25 cents per car in the late 1940s to $10 a car on summer weekends today.

At the height of its use in 1983, a record 89,547 vehicles visited Crane Beach, yielding a gross income, including sales of refreshments, of $597,380. Because of an increase in fees, income in 1985 reached a top of $606,294, but the number of vehicles slid to 79,600.

Through the years, however, despite increasing revenues, the beach has done little more than break even. The costs of inflation; of the sizable payroll which must be maintained to provide necessary services; of managing and protecting the beach and beach parking area (which often must be restored after the effects of winter storms); of maintaining the vast and complicated landscape at Castle Hill; of the Town's share of gross revenues from the beach; of the replacement of such essential pieces of equipment as pickup trucks, the work horses of the reservation; and of the repair and improvement of existing buildings, have kept up with increases in operating income.

But although its management is complicated, Crane's has prided itself on being the model others try to copy. And, from all reports, it has succeeded. A national magazine once listed it as one of the best beaches in the country. Visitors regularly produce many more compliments than complaints. And the organization receives letters from around the world praising the property and the quality of the recreational experience it offers.

No story of Crane Beach or any other property with significant management demands would be complete without mention of Nathan W. Bates. A resident of Cohasset and a former high school mathematics teacher, Bates was hired in 1949 to assist Executive Secretary Lawrence Fletcher. He had been Chairman of the Local Committee for Whitney Woods and, with Fletcher involved in recruiting new members, his lecture series and land acquisition, Bates was appointed Coordinator of Reservations. His responsibilities included the management and protection of The Trustees' then 25 properties, a total of more than 4,150 acres.

Coordinator of Reservations Nathan W. Bates, a valued staff member of The Trustees of Reservations from 1949 to 1976

A graduate of Northeastern University, Bates was a civil engineer by training and his talents proved invaluable. There were plans to compile and maintain, deeds to file, boundaries to mark, woodlands and fields to care for, and community officials to relate to. Bates was good at all of these things and, in his quiet way, immensely effective. A member of the Cohasset Planning Board and of its School Committee for many years, he understood local government and knew how it worked.

In later years, as the organization grew, he traveled around the state from property to property in a three-quarter ton, four-wheel drive, pickup truck with two other Cohasset residents, Herbert and Russell Marsh. The three of them combined to create a wonderful collection of country skills and abilities which enabled them to solve most every problem on the spot, whether it involved plumbing at Naumkeag, tree removal at Monument Mountain, or designing and building a steel farm gate to keep unauthorized vehicles off a woodland roadway at Chesterfield Gorge.

The original design for Bates' steel gate, incidentally, was copied extensively (with the approval of The Trustees) by the Metropolitan District Commission, by the State Department of Environmental Management, and by the U.S. Army Corps of Engineers. It may be seen throughout their properties today.

Both Bates and the Marsh brothers could weld steel or work in wood, use a transit to survey property lines and produce plans, operate tractors and trucks, chain saws and chippers, prune shrubbery, and plant perennials. No task was too formidable to tackle, and in good New England fashion, their budget was as lean and spare as the up-country farmers whose practices they followed.

As the organization grew in size and complexity, however, more sophisticated skills were needed. But for 26 years, until his retirement in 1976, Nate Bates played a unique and invaluable role in the activities of The Trustees of Reservations.

8

A Near Taking: Other Eyes on the Prize

While the Town, the Crane family, and The Trustees of Reservations worked out an effective management program for one of the most magnificent ocean beaches in the northeast, there were other eyes on the property as well.

In the mid-1930s, the Works Progress Administration (WPA), a federal agency, proposed a coastal highway which would have straddled not only Crane Beach but Plum Island and the Town of Salisbury. And in 1946, the United Nations, seeking a site for its headquarters, also looked at Castle Hill. But it was the Commonwealth of Massachusetts that turned out to be the most dangerous ogre of all.

In 1949, Governor Paul A. Dever filed a bill which would have allowed the State to acquire recreation areas — including beaches and historic sites — and to develop at or near them, to help provide revenue, restaurants, cafeterias, refreshment stands, gift shops, liquor stores, and amusement parks. The news took Ipswich by storm and citizens of the community reacted with indignation. Headlines in the *Ipswich Chronicle* shouted: "HERE IS BILL UPON WHICH BOSTON HEARING WILL BE BASED; PACKED WITH WILD, CRAZY THINKING; *Authority Empowered to Run Beer Joints by Thousands; Could Ruin All Our Beaches.*"

A five-page letter signed by members of the Local Committee for the Crane Reservation, and mailed to every Ipswich resident, warned that Crane Beach, "one of the most beautiful natural beaches in the nation," would become another "Jones Beach" with "dance floors, restaurants, bath houses and roller-skating rinks."

A fleet of buses coordinated by David C. Crockett of Argilla Road, secretary of the Citizens' Committee for the Development of Recreation Areas (Crockett was shortly to become a member of the Standing Committee), and the spirited Albert Burrage were hired to take residents to the legislative hearing at the State House. The efforts paid off. Crane was soon dropped from the list of beaches proposed for state acquisition.

Indeed, two years later when a new administration issued a revised plan for beach acquisition, Commissioner of Conservation Arthur T. Lyman, when asked how a state-owned beach would be operated, replied: "we'd run it like Crane's." The Trustees and the Town of Ipswich had reason to be proud of their accomplishments.

Lyman's comments also indicate the cordial and effective relationship that existed between The Trustees of Reservations and the administrators and staff of the Massachusetts Department of Natural Resources. It is a relationship which continues today with the Executive Office of Environmental Affairs, the Department of Environmental Management, the Division of Fisheries & Wildlife, the Department of Food & Agriculture, and, indeed, with all resource agencies including the Metropolitan District Commission. In fact, it is an early example of a partnership of public and private interests which through the years has accomplished much in the way of open space preservation. Lyman himself served briefly as Executive Director of The Trustees after Lawrence Fletcher retired in 1956. His successor as Commissioner of Natural Resources, Francis W. Sargent, continued the department's close cooperation with The Trustees, also serving as an active member of the Standing Committee in the early 1960s until he assumed elected office and ultimately became Governor of the Commonwealth.

Governor Francis W. Sargent, a former member of the Standing Committee and, at one time, Massachusetts Commissioner of Fisheries & Wildlife

9

The Sound of Music

Meanwhile, the question of how best to present and protect the Great House at Castle Hill loomed larger and larger. Without furniture, the use of it as a museum, Henry Channing's hoped-for solution, was out of the question. After considerable research and discussion, the best solution seemed to be to turn the place into an art center.

Accordingly, with Mrs. Channing's advice and assistance, Harold F. Lindergreen, former Director of the Vesper George School of Art, was engaged to establish an art school at Castle

Hill. Arrangements for the school were provided for by a special committee. Its chairman was Standing Committee member Bradford Williams of Westwood, a landscape architect who, 17 years earlier, had completed the first landscape survey of Massachusetts.

There were administrative difficulties immediately between activities at the Great House and those at Crane Beach. They were very different in character and objective and, quite naturally, questions arose about who was in charge of what. The matter was settled in January 1951 with the establishment of the Castle Hill Foundation, a charitable corporation in its own right that was devoted to the arts.

The Foundation was to run all events that took place at Castle Hill. It had its own board of directors (to be sure, a few were also members of the Standing Committee of The Trustees of Reservations) and its own administrative staff. It was soon agreed that a series of concerts should be presented each summer in the out-of-doors. A tradition had begun which was to win wide recognition and acclaim in the world of music, and was to continue, in varying forms, until the present day.

As the concert program was to be created and directed by the Board of Governors of the newly-formed organization, the initial choice of board members was of vital importance. The first President of the Castle Hill Foundation was Mrs. Albert C. Burrage. Bradford Williams served as Secretary-Treasurer. Other members of the board were North Shore residents William Phillips, then U.S. Ambassador to Italy; Congressman and former

Picnicking on the grass of the Grande Allée, a concert crowd in the early 1960s makes itself comfortable before an evening performance begins.

Mayor of Cambridge Richard M. Russell; Wallace T. Goodrich of Manchester, then President of the New England Conservatory of Music; and David C. Crockett, a native of Ipswich and son of one of the first Boston physicians who had purchased homes on Argilla Road in the late nineteenth century.

As director of the music company, the group engaged Samuel L. M. Barlow of New York, a composer, producer and summer resident of Gloucester, whose knowledge and enthusiasm buoyed everyone's spirits and, more pragmatically, helped raised the needed funds.

However successful artistically, culture was a risky business financially as the years ahead were to prove, and The Trustees made it quite clear from the beginning that the Foundation was to be responsible for the musical presentations on the Hill. With imaginative leadership and an impressive commitment of volunteer time, the Foundation's programs were a huge and lasting success, winning national acclaim for more than two decades.

Among the first performers was the celebrated José Greco and his troupe of Spanish dancers. He was followed by such stars as soprano Leontyne Price, who was yet to celebrate her debut at New York's Metropolitan Opera; violinist Isaac Stern; pianist Claudio Arrau, and flutist Jean Pierre Rampal.

Jazz evenings featured such greats as Louis Armstrong, Duke Ellington and Ahmad Jamal. When the folk era arrived in the 1960s, Castle Hill hosted the Kingston Trio, Arlo Guthrie, and, at a record presentation attended by more than 10,000 people, Joan Baez and the Weavers.

Concerts were held either in the Italian Garden or at the pool area on the allée depending upon the numbers of people attending. On warm summer evenings before the programs began, guests brought picnic suppers, spread their white tablecloths on the lawns, and sat overlooking the sea. As concerts began, a hush of anticipation would fall on the audience to be broken only by the occasional slap at a mosquito.

Among those who reviewed the concerts during the early 1960s was author John Updike, a resident of Ipswich, later to win two Pulitzer Prizes. Updike's reviews appeared in the weekly *Ipswich Chronicle*, over the pseudonymous initials "H.H."

But in the 1970s, the cost of talent for major stars caught up with and soon surpassed ticket revenues. The weather, which was always a gamble, was another major factor, making it difficult to count on a predictable level of gate receipts throughout the season. And with a heavy heart, the Foundation finally drew the curtain upon an extraordinary era.

What was needed now was a simpler program format which had a special niche of its own in the world of the arts. The board found it in Early Music. A smaller number of performers, and the change from an all but weekly reliance on big-name stars, reduced the Foundation's financial exposure significantly, although balancing income and expense was always a delicate matter.

The professional competence of musicians and other performers at these smaller concerts remained high and, in their own way, they also won wide acclaim, especially those under the direction of resident music master Tom Kelly.

The Executive Director of the Foundation, William J. Conner, greatly expanded the concert schedule and extended the publicity world-wide. Indeed, the production of Peter Seller's "Cosi fan tutti" at Castle Hill was reviewed with great favor by newspapers in London and here with equal enthusiasm by *The New Yorker* magazine. The Castle Hill Festival Series, an eclectic mix of musical and theatrical performances, continues today, appealing to audiences of all ages.

10

The Impresario of Argilla Road

For more than 40 years, the Great House has served the public in many ways. First, of course, as an art school, and later, for two years, as the summer home of the New England Conservatory of Music.

For decades also, it has offered itself with great success as a site for weddings, banquets, dances, business conferences, seminars and civic gatherings. It is for these events, as well as for its concerts, that Castle Hill is best known today.

Its reputation for excellence both in the arts and entertainment has been, in a large measure, due to the interest and commitment of the Board of Governors of the Castle Hill Foundation. Each year, they have been responsible for the final determination of the music program; for raising funds to meet the predictable, annual shortfall in revenue; and, indeed, for serving as volunteers, helping to present and coordinate each event.

The men and women of the small professional staff, who through the years have administered the Foundation, deserve a special salute of their own. For it has been their insistence on quality and their attention to service that have helped increase the pleasure and enjoyment of hundreds of thousands of visitors throughout more than four decades.

It is perhaps fair to say, however, that no one member of the Board of Governors has played a more important role with Castle Hill than David C. Crockett of Ipswich. A member of the Standing

Committee for many years and later President of The Trustees of Reservations, Crockett devoted much of his spare time for nearly two decades to making sure that the summer arts and music series at Castle Hill was a success. A man of great intellect, energy, humor and charm, Crockett could organize calm out of chaos, an ability often needed at Castle Hill.

A professional fundraiser without peer, he joined the Massachusetts General Hospital after distinguished wartime service with the Office of Strategic Services. His ability to acquire charitable gifts and grants was legendary. He knew everyone and everyone knew him. Always in great demand, the records show that at the end of his professional career, he served as a volunteer with 17 different charities in scores of capacities from committee member to, most often, President or Chairman. Many were connected with the arts, others with medicine and still others with education. But it was to the Castle Hill Foundation that he gave more than most could dream of.

Throughout the legendary decades of the late 1950s, '60s and early 1970s, when concerts were held each Friday and Saturday night during the summer season, Crockett was on stage as President of the Castle Hill Foundation, welcoming a crowd of thousands and introducing each performance. As always, with public presentations, not everything went smoothly. "Once," he recalls, "Arlo Guthrie's plane was delayed for two hours. I kept everyone there telling stories and finally, in desperation, leading them in song until he arrived. The audience stayed until 2 a.m.!"

For Crockett, it was a labor of love. And without him there would have been no concert series. All but single-handedly during those years, he booked the entertainment; organized, with his committees, parking and traffic flow for what were always sizable audiences; and personally hosted the evening. He also raised most of the money needed and looked after the Great House as if it were his own.

It was he, with the assistance of the noted sculptress, Mrs. Kay Lane Weems of Manchester; Charles S. Bird, long-time Chairman of the Standing Committee; Mr. and Mrs. Ellery Sedgwick of Beverly; Francis Randall Appleton, Jr., of nearby Appleton Farms; and Philip S. Weld, newspaper publisher and later world sailor, of Gloucester, who furnished the property after the auction had stripped much of it bare in 1956. Huge, leather-backed books were purchased by the yard in Ireland to fill the library and the committee struggled to find donations of furniture of a size and scale necessary to fit each room throughout the house.

Crockett and Mrs. Charlotte Terry, the Foundation's longest-serving General Manager, retired together in 1975. He became President Emeritus and passed on his administrative responsibilities and title to David C. Scudder who, in more difficult financial

David C. Crockett, veteran officer of The Trustees of Reservations and legendary president of the Castle Hill Foundation

times, provided the leadership needed to take the Foundation into a new era. Scudder's knowledge of music, finance and fundraising made him a worthy successor to his legendary neighbor on Argilla Road.

Repair and restoration of the interior of the Great House has continued as well and has reached new heights thanks to the efforts of former Standing Committee member Frances Colburn, Ipswich artist Katrina Hart, and Carroll Cabot, author also of a recently-completed history of Castle Hill and the Crane family published in booklet form by The Trustees of Reservations. The improvements have made it possible now to welcome scores of fascinated visitors who tour the now fully-furnished rooms of the Great House and gaze in wonder at the opulence of an earlier era.

Today, to clarify responsibilities and to simplify management procedures, The Trustees of Reservations has assumed direction of all activities at Castle Hill. Music programs, still presented each summer, are coordinated by Betsy Hathaway, Manager of Public Programs. And the Great House continues to be enjoyed by thousands each year for weddings and other functions, activities directed by Private Events Coordinator Mary Ellen Colligan.

And over all, there is now a committee of some 50 volunteers for all of the Crane properties. Its Executive Committee, which reports directly to the Standing Committee, is led by Norton Q. Sloan, a Vice President of The Trustees of Reservations. Sloan, also Chairman of an earlier Long-range Planning Committee for Castle Hill (and the author of its report), is credited with playing the major role in bringing The Trustees and the Castle Hill Foundation together. He was assisted by Standing Committee members Preston H. Saunders (then Chairman), David W. Scudder (former Foundation President), Peter E. Madsen, Herbert W. Vaughan (recently Chairman), and William Shields, a Corporate Trustee.

As always in these cases, charm, tact, and reason are needed to reach amicable conclusions. Sloan and his team were able to provide them all to make the transition a success.

A former Treasurer of The Trustees of Reservations, Ipswich resident Norton Q. Sloan is the present Chairman of the Standing Committee, the organization's governing board.

11

The Great House Acquires a New Legitimacy

Maintaining the Great House and its surrounding landscape structures — the latter so essential to the drama and integrity of its site — has been a major challenge since its acquisition. And as maintenance costs escalated in the early 1970s, the debate about whether the Great House was worth preserving began again.

The alternative, provided for in its fire insurance policy, was to tear the structure to the ground, fill in its gigantic cellar hole, and create a terrace from which visitors could admire views of Castle Neck and the ocean shore. But pressure from Ipswich residents and others, including those board members who had a lifetime association with the Crane family, prevailed and the struggle to raise funds for repairs continued.

The cause was given another boost with the publication by the Art Institute of Chicago of *David Adler, The Architect and His Work*. The book extolled the Great House as Adler's "masterpiece at Castle Hill." Knowledge of the property bred enthusiasm, and the house was soon listed on the National Register of Historic Places. A party was held to celebrate the opening of an exhibition of Adler drawings of the structure on loan from the Art Institute, and Secretary of State Paul M. Guzzie, Chairman of the Massachusetts Historical Commission, was present to provide an official blessing.

In the early 1970s, preservation grants made possible the restoration of the so-called swimming pool area, an essential part of the allée. (The pool was filled with earth as a safety measure by Mrs. Crane shortly after a drowning accident in Hamilton.) And, thanks to the CETA program, The Trustees was able to hire a full-time mason to reconstruct and restore deteriorating exterior brick and stone work.

Countless hours of consultation and advice — all voluteered — were also provided by architect George Mathey of Ipswich and landscape architects Peter Hornbeck and Sidney Shurcliff, all members of the Standing Committee. But, with its age and exposure, efforts to maintain particularly the Great House seemed to have no end.

In 1984, an independent engineering study summarized the magnitude of maintenance needs at Castle Hill, indicated their priorities and divided them into projects. Today, many of these have been completed. More, however, remains to be done and the Great House and selected structures at Castle Hill are to be beneficiaries of The Trustees of Reservations' current capital fund raising program.

One goal will be to raise an endowment fund for the property which, ironically, The Trustees was unable to acquire when it accepted it, now more than 40 years ago. Happily, thanks to the continuing efforts of Director Fred Winthrop, Jr., the goal has been realized and a portion of the Crane fortune has returned to Ipswich.

At her death in 1991, Mrs. Miné S. Crane most generously bequeathed the sum of $3 million to The Trustees of Reservations. Her will stipulates that $1 million be used to endow the landscape and structures at Castle Hill, and that $2 million be used to support the Cornelius and Miné S. Crane Wildlife Refuge at Hog Island across the Castle Neck River.

12

Deer: the Quandary of Overpopulation

As a part of an analysis of the quality and character of the natural landscape at Castle Neck, it was discovered in 1980 that the area's herd of white-tailed deer had increased significantly.

Wildlife biologists indicated that the carrying capacity of the 2,100 acres which comprise the Crane Reservation and Crane Wildlife Refuge, was about 62 deer. A count, however, estimated that there were nearer 350 to 400 animals trying to survive on the properties.

Vegetation, which served as a critical anchor to stabilize drifting dunes, was heavily overbrowsed. There was evidence of starvation among members of the herd. Then, too, deer serve as hosts to a tick which carries the dreaded Lyme disease, and there were few residents of Argilla Road who had not been afflicted by it. It was clear that large numbers of deer were a menace not only to themselves, but to public health and, equally important, could, by destroying vegetation, jeopardize the natural stability — and even existence — of a delicate and fragile barrier beach ecosystem.

In cooperation with the State's Department of Public Health and its Division of Fisheries & Wildlife, a carefully controlled, highly organized hunt was proposed in 1983 to cull the herd. (Hunters had to have passed a specific examination which tested their proficiency and only a certain number were assigned the task.) Although the community, which had to live with Lyme disease, was in favor of the hunt, the same could not be said for others, especially those devoted to animal rights.

For months, the arguments raged in major newspapers of the metropolitan region, on nightly television, and on radio talk shows. It seemed as if people everywhere could think of little else than the proposal to reduce the herd. Critics and supporters were equally vocal. Finally, the day before the hunt was to occur, a small group of animal rights activists announced they would appear to stand between the hunters and the deer. That was enough for The Trustees. In consultation with Standing Committee Chairman Preston H. Saunders and Regional Supervisor Wayne N. Mitton, who was in charge at the scene, Director Gordon Abbott, Jr., called off the hunt to avoid possible danger to human life.

Countless hours had gone into the project. Indeed, nothing that The Trustees of Reservations had been engaged in during recent years brought the organization more into the public eye or consumed as much staff and volunteer time as the program to manage white-tailed deer.

Research continued, this time directed by Dr. Aaron Moen, Professor of Wildlife Ecology at Cornell University and a well-known and much-respected deer biologist. Dr. Moen's report confirmed earlier findings of the Commonwealth's Division of Fisheries & Wildlife that the deer population both at the Crane Reservation and at Crane Wildlife Refuge had far outgrown available food resources.

There was new evidence of starvation and the destruction of vegetation. Fear of Lyme disease continued to grow as well, as researchers from Harvard University's School of Public Health confirmed a growing number of deer ticks, carriers of the insidious illness. Throughout what was now fast becoming a two-year controversy, the position of The Trustees of Reservations remained simple and consistent. It maintained that the three problems of starvation, habitat reduction and the threat to public health had been established, and that to deal with them, the herd must be reduced in the most practical and humane way available. Each member of the organization's advisory group, carefully selected to represent every segment of the controversy, including animal rights, agreed that the problems existed. Arguments arose only over how to address them.

Finally, at the end of 1984, The Trustees and the Division of Fisheries & Wildlife, which must by law approve any comprehensive solution, reached agreement. It included, in early 1985, the use of a marksman, to be followed by a limited public hunt in the fall to accomplish a carefully monitored and phased reduction of the herd.

Every year since 1985 a hunt has taken place, supervised and administered by The Trustees of Reservations with the approval of the Division of Fisheries & Wildlife. Participants are still tested and certified for their knowledge of wildlife behavior and use of firearms.

The herd has been reduced to an estimated 60 deer. Necropsies performed by biologists for The Trustees of Reservations on each deer harvested have shown that as the number of deer have decreased, the health of the remaining animals has improved markedly. As the habitat recovered, its carrying capacity expanded as well, and staff ecologists, who monitor vegetation, report that the number and diversity of other species have also shown significant growth.

As for Lyme disease, The Trustees of Reservations has worked closely with researchers from the School of Public Health at Harvard and with specialists at Tufts University since its appearance in the region. Out of this relationship has come the discovery of a pesticide called *Damminex*. It is available in tubes containing cotton treated with the substance which must be placed around tick-infested areas. White-footed mice, which serve as a primary host for the tick (deer are a secondary host), take the cotton to their nests. The result has been the virtual elimination of ticks in spots where *Damminex* has been employed.

In 1985, to assist The Trustees of Reservations with its program of scientific wildlife management, the organization appointed as Staff Ecologist Robert D. Deblinger. Named Associate Director for Natural Science in 1988, Deblinger received his doctorate from the Department of Fisheries and Wildlife Biology at Colorado State University. His dissertation dealt with the ecology and social behavior of the pronghorn antelope in Wyoming's Red Desert with special reference to the impacts of energy development.

While at The Trustees of Reservations, Deblinger has written extensively about the management of white-tailed deer, and, with Crane Reservation biologist David W. Rimmer, about the organization's efforts to protect colonial nesting birds, particularly least terns and piping plovers. He has also been trained professionally in the use of Geographic Information Systems. In 1991, Colorado State University honored him with the presentation of its Professional Achievement Award.

It took an exhausting two years to obtain universal acceptance of The Trustees' deer management program at its properties in Ipswich and Essex. Twice, the organization was forced to defend itself in court and once before the State Legislature. "In each instance," Director Fred Winthrop, Jr. reported, "our arguments carried the day."

The man on the hot seat throughout the ordeal was Wayne Mitton, who early in 1984 had been appointed not only chief of the wildlife management project, but sole spokesman for it as well. Mitton's calm and courteous manner under continual fire, his knowledge and understanding of every detail, and his commitment to the project itself, deserve special recognition.

Although dependent upon public support for its existence, The Trustees of Reservations never wavered in its convictions throughout the conflict. Its courage and its strength came from the belief that what it was doing was right. Happily, today, there are few who disagree.

13

Barrier Beaches: Protecting a Fragile and Dynamic Resource

Of all of the ecosystems preserved by The Trustees of Reservations, few are as dynamic as those which include a barrier beach, sand dunes, salt marsh and a tidal estuary.

Since its first involvement with the Province Lands at Cape Cod in the late nineteenth century, the organization has taken a special interest in the management and protection of its barrier beaches. They include today, Crane Beach and Castle Neck, Ipswich; Cape Poge Wildlife Refuge and Wasque Reservation, Chappaquiddick Island, Martha's Vineyard; and Coskata-Coatue Wildlife Refuge, Nantucket. In all, they total more than 2,400 acres.

Because of their natural tendency to move with wind and wave, barrier beaches, with their sand dunes and salt marsh, are able to absorb the punishing force of winter storms and protect the salt ponds and estuaries behind them, a critical habitat for fin and shell fish.

But this delicate environment, particularly during the summer months, is increasingly subject to pressure from visitors. Pedestrian traffic and sports fishermen, using four-wheel drive vehicles to reach isolated areas of the beach to surf cast for bluefish and striped bass, unknowingly trample or crush delicate culms of beach grass which anchor sand dunes, so essential to the existence of the entire ecosystem

Boats deliver scores of swimmers, picnickers, and sun bathers to spots also chosen as nesting areas by sea and shore birds, many species of which are fighting for survival. Piping plovers, for example, often lay their eggs in vehicle tracks and well-meaning drivers, following the "road" down the beach, run over just-hatched chicks which, with nature's coloring, blend almost perfectly with the sand around them.

To resolve this conflict between man and nature, The Trustees of Reservations established a Barrier Beach Ecology Program. By the late 1960s, permits were required for oversand vehicles. Indeed, the Vineyard's Oversand Vehicle sticker, with its map of Chappaquiddick Island, became such a status symbol for beach vehicles that it was featured as a requirement for "proper" Vineyard residents in *The Yuppie Handbook*.

Through the years also, The Trustees' shorebird monitoring and protection programs, which focus attention especially on least and common terns and piping plovers, have become a model for other environmental agencies and organizations.

The protection of nesting least and common terns has been a major commitment of The Trustees of Reservations as it manages its coastal ecosystems.

Other elements of the Barrier Beach Ecology Program have included beachgrass transplantation, dune fencing techniques, elevated pedestrian walkways, vehicle ramps, appropriate signage, and, most important, interpretive and educational materials such as booklets and panel boards, all designed to inform visitors about the workings of a barrier beach ecosystem, its wildlife, and how they can help preserve them.

One key to the success of an intensive management program such as this is the active participation of local Standing Committee and Advisory Council members. For example, on the Vineyard, former Standing Committee member Edith "Edo" Potter, owner of Pimpney Mouse Farm, Chappaquiddick, who served as a member and later as Chairman of the Edgartown Board of Selectmen, provided invaluable liaison with Local Committees and day-to-day support for the professional staff. Much the same could be said for Nancy Claflin at Nantucket, a great naturalist herself, who took a special interest in the program to protect colonial nesting birds at Coskata-Coatue Wildlife Refuge.

In recent years as well, scientific support and direction has come from the work of Robert Deblinger, Associate Director for Natural Science, and Staff Biologist David Rimmer, whose joint research studies and subsequent publications have been invaluable.

But perhaps the most important role in protecting the delicate resources of The Trustees of Reservations' barrier beaches is played by those who manage the properties themselves — the refuge managers, superintendents, and rangers for the organization's shorebird nesting programs. Their continuing presence at the sites and their ability to interact with visitors is crucial to the success of any management program.

The Trustees has been blessed with some remarkable professionals who care for its barrier beaches, but few who knew him would disagree that Foster Silva was unique. Superintendent of Cape Poge Wildlife Refuge and Wasque Reservation for more than a decade, Foster was born at Chappaquiddick Island and his knowledge of nature came from living with it for a lifetime.

He knew the weather. Where birds were nesting. How to scallop and dig razor clams. Where deer sought sanctuary. And where bluefish and stripers could be caught. His formal education ended with high school, but his learning continued at what, with a twinkle, he called "Katama University" (Katama is the bay just west of Chappaquiddick). In this school of experience and association, he learned far more about his subjects than many who have received advanced degrees.

A trip down the beach with Foster in his familiar green truck with its Trustees of Reservations shield was a treat sought and enjoyed by scores of people each year. For he saw things in nature

Edo Potter, chairman of the Regional Committee for Martha's Vineyard

Nancy Claflin, chairman of the Local Committee for Nantucket's Coskata-Coatue Wildlife Refuge

that others didn't see. It was special to be with Foster for another reason, as well. For he was, in the best best country fashion, a philosopher. He loved people of all ages and he was much beloved himself in return.

He was a man of many talents: a photographer of birds of all-but-professional ability; a hunter; a fisherman; a building contractor; a farmer; a member of the Edgartown Fire Department with the rank of Captain; a member of the town's Board of Appeals and a fundraiser without peer.

As a youth at Chappaquddick, he received a medal for bravery from the Massachusetts Humane Society for rescuing a drowning person. During World War II, he served in the Army Air Force and was wounded in combat. For many years he owned and operated the *On Time*, the ferry that runs between Edgartown and Chappaquiddick. At one time in his life, seeking warmer climes, he and his wife Dodie moved to California where he found himself master of the ferry that runs between Newport Beach and Balboa Island. But the pull of the Vineyard was too strong and he soon returned to Chappaquiddick.

With Foster, in 1970, The Trustees of Reservations was able to bring to Martha's Vineyard and Chappaquiddick the island's first formal management program for conservation lands. It is still widely admired today. Sadly, in 1981, Foster died, suddenly and unexpectedly. But the legend he created lives on. Somehow, the outer beach at Cape Poge and the point at Wasque will never be the same without him.

Foster B. Silva, Superintendent of the Martha's Vineyard Management Region, 1970 to 1980

14

Gardens: a Universal Appeal to the Heart and Mind

"He who plants a garden," states an old Chinese proverb, "plants happiness."

Certainly no one of The Trustees' benefactors enjoyed her gardens more than Miss Mabel Choate. Her letters to landscape architect Fletcher Steele, who was so responsible for extending and developing her ideas for the gardens at Naumkeag and The Mission House, are filled with intimate details.

Captivated with Steele's suggestion of a period herb and flower garden which would reflect the Colonial era of The Mission House in its new setting, she wrote enthusiastically, "the idea of Pot-Pourri and Tisanes seem to me the most practical [but] as soon as you get into distilling and cooking things, it is much more difficult. . . if we could [only] make lavender grow with any profusion as it does in England!"

During the restoration of The Mission House in the 1930s, Steele, who, was as widely respected for his knowledge of plant materials as for his imaginative garden designs, called for a pattern "copied from a pre-Colonial Herbal [garden] by Sir John Hill (1716-1775; author of *British Herbal*).

"The beds," Steele explained, "are shaped like capital T's fitted together, each made up of small squares measuring two feet on a side. . . Herbs don't mind a good deal of heat and drought and do better if the soil is not too good. If you have a little compost to put in, so much the better. But I doubt if fertilizer would help them much." The herb garden at the Mission House was an instant and continuing success.

Later, during a much-needed renovation of the garden in 1972, Mrs. G. Douglas Krumbhaar, who as Chairman of the Garden Committee had lovingly maintained it from day to day, and design consultant Peter Hornbeck, an Associate Professor in the Department of Landscape Architecture at Harvard University and a member of the Standing Committee, decided to consider other period plant materials. For historic reasons as well as horticultural, they chose to add a Colonial orchard. Species included such early apples as the Roxbury Russet, which originated in Roxbury, Massachusetts, in 1649; the Sops of Wine, of English origin; the Duchess of Oldenburg, of Russian extraction; and the Baldwin Woodpecker, which originated in Wilmington, near Lowell, in 1740.

But Miss Choate was most involved with the gardens at Naumkeag. Her interest in things horticultural came naturally from her father, who, although a distinguished barrister and diplomat of international reputation, liked nothing more than digging in his garden. Indeed, his granddaughter, Helen Choate Platt, recalls finding him on his knees one summer's day in the midst of a flower bed.

Parasols protect the petals of tree peonies from falling rain at Sedgwick Gardens.

"The gardens at Naumkeag," she writes, "were very different in those days; not monuments to landscape architecture as they are now, but great beds of flowers which we were sometimes allowed to pick. [There was] Grandpa transplanting something. His hands were covered with dirt. 'Oh, Grandpa,' we said, 'just look at your fingernails, they are absolutely black!' 'I sometimes wear them this way,' he smiled mischievously, 'in mourning for my first wife.'" And then Mrs. Platt added somewhat wistfully, "our own grandmother, Grandpa's one and only wife, to whom he was devoted, was not good with children. We found her cold and remote and we had nothing to say to each other. Often we yearned for that mythical 'first wife' of Grandpa's and wished she had been with us."

Preserving gardens presents a special set of problems. Landscape gardens such as many of those now at Naumkeag — the Afternoon Garden with its Venetian pilings, black mirror pool and small fountains; the Chinese Garden with its Moon Gate, tile-roofed temple, and nine magic Ginkgo trees; the rose garden with its serpentine pathways of marble chips; and the topiary garden with its white marble stairs and and gravel pathways which lead past dark, green ovals of arbor-vitae — derive their character from their design. Given sufficient funds, technical knowledge, labor and, of course, an understanding of the original design concept and an appreciation for its subtleties, they can be maintained with relative ease.

But it is the personal gardens such as those at Long Hill or at the Stevens-Coolidge Place, whose poetic charm has come from the special interests, tastes and sensibilities of an individual, which present the greatest challenge. For these are characteristics which spring from the soul and are not easy to institutionalize.

The gardens at Long Hill, now General Headquarters of The Trustees of Reservations, surround an elegant reproduction of a Charleston, South Carolina, house of the early 1800s. With its comfortable porches and high ceilings, it was constructed in 1918 as a summer home for Ellery Sedgwick, Editor and Publisher of Boston's famous literary magazine, *The Atlantic Monthly*, from 1909 to 1938.

Its interior woodwork — mantles, cornices, dados and doorways — came from the Isaac Ball house in Charleston, built in 1802, and were rescued shortly before the structure was to be

Discussing plant materials at The Mission House garden in Stockbridge in the early 1970s are, from left, Mrs. G. Douglas Krumbhaar, Chairman of the Garden Committee; Superintendent Stanley I. Piatczyc; Mrs. Erastus Corning II, Chairman; and J. D. Hatch, member of the Local Committee for Naumkeag.

converted to a railroad workers' dormitory. Bricks used in the building came from an early mill in Ipswich. The property also includes a nineteenth century farmhouse.

The gardens were orginally created by Mrs. Mabel Cabot Sedgwick, author, in 1907, of *The Garden Month by Month,* a book delightful to read and still wonderfully informative. Using native materials, Mrs. Sedgwick combined pasture cedars with weeping Japanese cherries. Mountain laurel was planted along the drive and garden paths, as was a large collection of bulbs, snowdrops, scillas and chinodoxas. An extensive cutting garden provided flowers for the house, and, even then, gardens and grounds were open to everyone by invitation.

After the death of Mabel Sedgwick, the gardens at Long Hill were further developed and extended by the second Mrs. Sedgwick, the former Marjorie Russell of England, a distinguished gardener in her own right and a propagator of rare plants.

Working with the Arnold Arboretum and, once again, with landscape architect Fletcher Steele, she added exhibitions of flowering trees and shrubs, many of them rare; an enlarged display of a greater variety of spring bulbs; collections of azaleas, Japanese maples, and rhododendrons; a luxuriance of tree peonies, many grown from seed; as well as lotus pools, sink gardens, and trees and shrubs dramatically sited to provide spectacular autumn foliage.

A walk with Mrs. Sedgwick around the gardens was a special treat and every interested visitor was welcome. She would begin always at the front circle and move counter-clockwise, pointing

Watercolor by Charleston artist Alfred Tutty shows Ellery and Marjorie Sedgwick relaxing in the gardens at Long Hill. With visitors to the property, Mrs. Sedgwick "would begin at the front circle and walk clockwise around the house. She was always glad to answer questions and eager to make her guests feel that they, too, could grow everything they saw at Long Hill."

with her cane at examples of this species and that, describing in charming detail where they came from and how they survived and prospered.

On rainy days, the tree peonies had their own parasols or umbrellas to protect their petals. And each seemingly random spray had an intentional place in the patterns, textures and colors of the gardens. She would point out which were the work of birds and which she had added herself. Both were intertwined so perfectly that the whole seemed solely the magical work of nature alone. Such was her genius.

To try to duplicate so personal a touch after Mrs. Sedgwick's death in 1979, The Trustees turned to the Sedgwick family and to Mrs. Sedgwick's friends for advice and guidance. Most helpful were her stepchildren Henrietta Sedgwick Bond and her brothers, Ellery and Cabot, donors of the property, as well as members of the North Shore Garden Club who had worked with Mrs. Sedgwick, loved her, and appreciated her wonderful ways with growing things. Mary Ann Streeter was the first Chairman of the Sedgwick Gardens Committee. Others whose advice has proved invaluable through the years, have been Katherine Hull and Margo Parrot, both award-winning gardeners themselves, whose knowledge of plants and plant materials is unsurpassed.

In the early days, too, shortly after The Trustees acquired the property, Isador Smith, a great horticulturist, author of three histories of early American gardens, and a friend of Mrs. Sedgwick, helped to set the course for the future of Sedgwick Gardens. At Long Hill today, there is a guide to a walking tour of the gardens, a horticultural library, a lecture series well attended by plant lovers throughout the region, and a now-celebrated Mother's Day sale of plants and plant materials which raises as much as $14,000 annually to benefit the gardens.

None of these accomplishments, of course, would have been possible without the energies and imagination of veteran Superintendent and Horticulturalist Larry J. Simpson, who has been at Long Hill since 1980.

Other garden properties of The Trustees of Reservations include the Stevens-Coolidge Place, where Mrs. Coolidge's prize-winning rose garden is being restored by members of the Local Committee and Superintendent Robert Murray; Castle Hill, where a major capital program seeks funds to restore and endow the Great House and its surrounding gardens — most especially, the Italian Garden, designed by landscape architect Arthur Shurtleff; and the Bradley Reservation, Canton, acquired in 1991, where plans are being made to maintain Mrs. Eleanor Cabot Bradley's formal gardens and woodland wildflowers, which are an essential part of the property's personality and charm.

There are also those reservations which preserve special horticultural features, such as Elliott Laurel in Phillipston, with its outstanding collection of mountain laurel; Medfield Rhododendrons in Medfield, which protects one of the few stands of native rhododendron remaining in the Commonwealth; and Lowell Holly, Mashpee, whose more than 300 trees of native American holly are enjoyed by scores of visitors annually.

Finally, there are the wild gardens. The most famous, of course, is Bartholomew's Cobble, a National Natural Landmark. Here, management consists of maintaining that gentle ecological balance which allows a fascinating diversity of plant materials to exist. For the Local Committee and for members of the professional staff, it is a mixture of art and science.

But whether wild or formal, gardens offer the spirit and the mind a special experience. As Walter Prichard Eaton, Yale University Professor and Chairman of the Local Committee for Bartholomew's Cobble, once wrote in *Wild Gardens of New England*, "Greece made no inventions to speak of, but it made designs, and those designs, with the spirit behind them, the passion for beauty and perfection, conquered the ancient world, and conquered the world anew almost two thousand years later. Indeed, they have dominion over us still.

"What kind of other conquests do we want or should we strive for? Of trade, of machinery? They are nothing but the multiplication of troubles, the accelerated complexity of mere existence. But the sweet bays of lawn in the folds of the cobble, the spirit that thrills to them, the power that puts them in paint on canvas, the passion for beauty, the conquest through art of the baser instincts of man, the union of nations in a common enjoyment of gardens and flowers — these are what matter and endure."

15

The Household Staff: Essential to Life at the Great Estates

It was impossible, of course, for the original owners to maintain properties of the magnitude and complexity of Naumkeag, Castle Hill, and the Stevens-Coolidge Place without the assistance of a household staff. Its size was determined by the intricacies of the place itself, by the financial resources available, and, of course, by the demands of the owner which could vary from the simple to the prodigious.

For example, to meet the needs of the property outside, there had to be a caretaker, a series of gardeners, perhaps one or two herdsmen, a coachman and a stable boy in the early days, and later, with the arrival of the automobile, a chauffeur. Inside, the list could be endless: a cook, one or two kitchenmaids and several parlormaids to clean and wait on table. In larger households, there was often a lady's maid and perhaps a footman, and, certainly, a butler.

Members of the household staff were provided with room and board, and where they lived and what they did is very much a part of the story of these estates and how they were able to function successfully from day to day. Indeed, The Trustees of Reservations pays special attention in its interpretive programs and guided tours (as does The National Trust in England) to the working areas of the household as well as to the grounds and gardens — the kitchen, the pantry, the servants' wing, the potting shed, the greenhouse, the barn, the milk shed and other outbuildings, and the cottages on the estate that housed the caretaker and his staff.

Among the most elaborate properties of The Trustees is Naumkeag. Helen Choate Platt, who spent a part of many summers there with her grandparents and later with her aunt, Miss Mabel Choate, describes what life was like both "upstairs and downstairs" in those gilded years.

"The chief charm of Naumkeag," she wrote, "other than Aunt Mabel herself, was its atmosphere of Friendly Comfort. This wasn't Newporty, Butlery Comfort, but something created by Aunt Mabel's servants, all of whom had been there for at least 15 years, and all of whom were members of the family. Chief among them were Margaret, the waitress, and Rose, the parlormaid. Margaret was a great, handsome, red-faced Grenadier. Rose was a tiny Irish saint. Margaret appeared to run things with quite a lot of bluster, but it was really tiny, humorous Rose who made everything go.

"Just in passing, we all remember Margaret's martinis which were incredibly potent. Two of these made us all very merry. We afterwards found out why. She would mix the gin and vermouth, unshaken, undiluted, and left in the refrigerator, icy cold. They were dynamite!"

Earlier, as a child, Mrs. Platt recalled "we had to behave under the disapproving eye of Osborne, the rather effeminate English butler, who hated our visits. And we had to behave, eating the wonderful food provided by Ellen, the dear Swedish cook, who years later married Osborne. There were servants all over the place and they formed sort of a bridge between children and grown-ups which I still think was valuable. I particularly remember Johanna, Granny's lady's maid. We would be allowed to watch her dress Granny's hair, a ritual of twirling irons and poking in extra pieces and locks never grown by Granny."

Finally, there could be the humiliation of being treated too kindly — and too royally — by a well-meaning member of the household staff. "One summer," Mrs. Platt continued, "our youngest, maybe six (at the time), was sent up to a day-camp in Lee, carrying a picnic lunch. Next session, to our surprise, Geoff absolutely refused to go. He screamed and howled and kicked and we had to give in. Years later, I found out why. It was the picnic lunch. All the other boys had a peanut butter sandwich stuffed in their pockets. The lunch Rose had put up for young Geoff consisted of broiled chicken, stuffed eggs, hot house toma-toes and peaches and a piece of chocolate cake. Mortification!"

But for adults, it was a different story. The luxuries of life at Naumkeag, made possible to a great extent by a devoted staff, were moments to be savored forever. "In the evening," Mrs. Platt concluded, "we would drag the reclining chairs to the very edge of the west terrace and watch the sun go down (with one of Margaret's bombshells in hand). Then we would go in to a heavenly dinner, the simplest and the best: tiny vegetables, fresh from the garden, and butter and cream from the farm. Oh, Friendly Comfort!"

Changes in society after World War II, meant the beginning of the end of domestic service as the world once knew it. It also meant the end of the great estates and an era not to be seen again.

16

Island Management: Crossing the Waters

As a part of its collection of outstanding landscapes, The Trustees of Reservations owns a series of small islands: Great Misery and Little Misery, 84 acres in all, located in Salem Bay two miles west of Manchester's inner harbor; Crowninshield Island, five acres, located in Dolliber Cove, Marblehead, some 300 yards offshore; and the five islands of Crane Wildlife Refuge: Hog or Choate, Long, Round, Dean and Dilley, a total of some 500 acres of upland and salt marsh, located in the vast tidal estuary of the Essex and Castle Neck Rivers. (Crane Wildlife Refuge actually includes nearly 700 acres of land; 200 acres, however, is located on the mainland at Castle Neck.)

Each is a special jewel, but each also presents a unique administrative challenge. First, islands can be reached only by boat. Second, because of this, what can be delivered to them or removed from them, is limited. And third, because of their relative isolation and the skills needed to manage them, it takes a special breed of men and women to provide the services needed.

The Trustees has been fortunate in finding just the right people. When Gordon Abbott, Jr., took over as Director in early 1967, Misery Islands were visited by a crew from Headquarters just once a year. Enjoyed by thousands during the summer months, the islands were covered with accumulated litter. Field succession was rapidly destroying open areas. And unauthorized camping created problems related to public health. Each year as well, at least one picnic fire would burn out of control, destroying sizable areas of shrubbery. It was obvious that a continuing, professional management program was urgently needed.

In the spring of 1969, David A. Ryan of Manchester was appointed Superintendent of Misery Islands Reservation, establishing a relationship that lasted successfully for 23 summers. Ryan, at the time, was a teacher at Pingree School in Hamilton, and chairman of the Science Department. Shortly thereafter he joined the faculty at Manchester High School where he remains today. A biologist and ecologist, he had also served as director of a wildlife sanctuary in New Hampshire.

Misery Islands management program got underway in May. Ryan and one helper, a high school student, equipped with a 13-foot, outboard-powered Boston Whaler, a lawn mower and gardening tools, tackled the islands' trash problem first, carrying scores of bags — primarily cans and bottles — back to the mainland. On top of this massive long-term clean up, was the need to keep up with current use. For example, 17 huge plastic bags of fresh litter were removed after one July 4 weekend. Camping was also prohibited, gently at first as many families had spent weekends at the property for decades. But it was obvious to all that for hygienic reasons, the islands should be for day use only.

Through the years, Ryan, assisted each summer by one and later two high school youngsters, worked wonders with the landscape. Portions of the field land, grown over with weed trees, were cleared, restoring views and vistas. The freshwater pond at Misery Cove was reclaimed, encouraging its use by migratory waterfowl. Brush was removed from around the ruins of the old Casino, adding interest to an already historic site. And a network of trails was established which led visitors around the islands. Most important, work on a master plan was initiated for the property's future use and preservation.

Once the islands were cleared of trash, it was decided to close the dump which had existed for years at Great Misery, and to institute a "carry-on, carry-off" program which would ask visitors to take picnic litter with them as they returned to their boats. Instructional signs were erected and dispensers with small plastic bags for the convenience of picnickers were attached.

Would it work? Staff members were more than apprehensive. But work it did, primarily because Dave Ryan and his crew had

Superintendent David A. Ryan is at the wheel as Charity *heads for Misery Islands Reservation, Salem Bay.*

created a new respect for the islands. Regular visitors, and there were many, felt a special affection for the property and policed other users. Indeed, when a thoughtless sailor started a brush fire with his flare gun, boat owners rushed ashore with buckets and fire extinguishers to quell the blaze. By the time Ryan arrived, the fire was out and he was surrounded by smiling faces proudly telling of their exploits. In fact the program was such a success that it became a model for the management of island parks throughout the region. The dispensers, too, were soon done away with, for it was discovered that their most popular use was for water wings. Children would inflate two of the plastic bags, tie them together, and use them as floats while swimming.

With expansion of the management program, came the need for a larger boat and The Trustees purchased a 16-foot Amesbury skiff. A rise and fall of nine and one-half feet of tide also meant that the service launch needed to be anchored out, otherwise it would ground at low water. Equipment was transferred to a dinghy and rowed ashore, leaving the larger craft afloat. The dinghy, known by the crew as "Big Ugly" because of its weight, often had to be pulled the length of the beach at Misery Cove to reach the water, a back-breaking task.

By 1981, the program had outgrown the Amesbury skiff. A special effort by General Headquarters had added new capital to the property's endowment and the Friends of Misery Islands were then raising as much as $8,500 a year for operating purposes. Members of the Local Committee and the administration decided that the time had come to acquire a new launch, large enough to

Charity *enroute to Misery Islands (background) with Regional Supervisor Wayne Mitton and volunteers from Pingree School aboard. Superintendent Lucia Corwin is at the wheel.*

carry what now could be as many as four lawn mowers, and rugged enough to beach and land the equipment easily and then back off, leaving only one member of the crew to row ashore in a light skiff.

A special campaign was launched to raise funds for the new craft, designed by naval architect Philip Bolger of Gloucester. Twenty-six feet overall, she was to be built of aluminum by Winninghoff Boats, Rowley. Committee members for the project were Standing Committee member Ann W. Brewer, Chairman of the Friends of Misery Islands, Local Committee member Eleanor B. Crocker and, of course, Ryan, Abbott and Regional Supervisor Wayne N. Mitton.

The new service launch, funded entirely with grants and gifts, was completed in May 1981 and appropriately christened *Charity*. Powered by outboard, she proudly bears the letters LCLM on her bow, standing, in the best tradition of the Navy's amphibious forces, for "Landing Craft Lawn Mower."

Thanks to the kindness of Manchester Marine Corporation, the local shipyard, where *Charity* is moored, tools and equipment are stored on yard property nearby in a vandal-proof steel locker. *Charity* still services the islands today, but after more than two decades as the Superintendent of both Misery Islands and Crowninshield Island and the skipper of three successive service craft, Dave Ryan has retired and a new generation has taken over.

Some four and one-half miles west of Manchester, Crowninshield Island has had its own management teams composed of reliable youngsters of high school age who love the island, live nearby, and know their way about in boats. For more than a decade and a half, they included the sons and daughters of two Marblehead families: Jim and Lisa Wetherald, and later, Jimmy and Mary Beth Magee. Their parents, the James T. Wetheralds and the Carl V. Magees, were members of the Local Committee, and were there to provide advice and assistance when needed.

Supplies such as plastic trash bags were delivered by the crew from Misery Islands. Using their own skiffs, the youngsters kept the property immaculate, depositing trash at the Town Landing on the mainland nearby where it could be picked up for disposal. High school students continue to manage the island today supervised by Regional Headquarters in Ipswich.

With its five islands and some 200 acres on the mainland at Castle Neck — a total of nearly 700 acres of upland, salt marsh and beach — Crane Wildlife Refuge is administered full-time by Refuge Manager Walter A. Prisby. A former U.S. Navy Chief Petty Officer, Prisby was hired initially by Mrs. Miné S. Crane in 1963. Thankfully, when the property was given to The Trustees of Reservations in 1974, he stayed on.

In the 1960s, the islands were serviced with a 26-foot motor launch driven by a 100-horsepower Gray Lugger. During the summer months, cushioned seats, a canvas top and curtains were added to make the short trip to the islands more comfortable for Mrs. Crane, who often entertained guests at the cottage at Hog Island.

When The Trustees took over, the launch was sold and a 17-foot Amesbury skiff with a 35-horsepower outboard was used for transport purposes. This was replaced in recent years by a rugged, 19-foot, Maine-built fiberglass boat which, with its turn of speed, can also be used by Ranger Walter R. Swan for security patrols throughout the estuary.

Should a piece of heavy equipment, such as the islands' truck or tractor, need major repairs, it can be carried the third-of-a-mile to the mainland by the property's 15 by 30-foot barge constructed especially for the purpose. The barge, propelled by outboard skiff tied alongside, is also used to ferry building supplies, fertilizer and other materials, and serves as a float at the mainland service area, which includes a shop and a barn where the running boats are stored. "Although the barge can hold up to 12 tons," Prisby recalls, "one year we nearly lost a big truck on the way over. It was loaded with shingles and lumber to be used to repair the barn. We thought we'd figured it correctly, but we had about two inches of freeboard. I held my breath, but we made it safely."

In winter, the channel between the mainland and the islands can ice up and Prisby uses a 12-foot aluminum dinghy to commute to work. If there is snow, he will often ski from the landing to the barn at Long Island where a wood stove heats the shop and he can overhaul equipment to be used during warmer weather. In the old days, he remembers, when the channel was frozen, "I used to push the skiff across ahead of me and if the ice broke, I would jump aboard. But winters today aren't what they used to be."

For Prisby, working alone much of the time off season (he's equipped with a hand-held, short-wave radio for safety purposes), there are also structures to maintain: the Choate House, built between 1725 and 1740; the cottage, constructed by Mr. and Mrs. Crane, which now includes the property's Visitor Center; and, of course, the barn, which itself is of significant historic value.

For more than a decade during the summer months, Ranger and Wildlife Technician Elizabeth Ann Rizzotti and her husband spent weekends at the cottage for security purposes and to continue research on migratory song birds and waterfowl and, in cooperation with the Massachusetts Division of Fisheries & Wildlife, on the island's herd of white-tailed deer. It was here, Prisby says, that "we discovered that the deer tick had been brought to the area by birds." Today, thousands of visitors are drawn to the island properties of The Trustees of Reservations each year to enjoy their isolation and to experience the peace and tranquility that comes from being just offshore away from the bustle of the mainland. It's this feeling, too, that makes them such special places to work for the men and women who maintain them.

17

Building a Professional Staff and a New System of Management

Since its beginnings, The Trustees of Reservations has been blessed with a full-time, paid staff whose quality is second to none. At every level, its hallmarks have been a total commitment to the cause of environmental conservation; an impressive loyalty to the organization itself; adherence to the highest standards of personal and professional performance; and a cheerful and mature presence which has, happily, made the organization an exciting and rewarding place to work. It is no exaggeration to say that together, The Trustees of Reservations' employees pride themselves upon being "a happy band of warriors."

Few are cut from the same cloth. Through the years, some, such as veteran Superintendents Mario Pederzini of Rocky Woods and Warren Drew of Notchview, employed by the original owners of their properties, have agreed, upon acquisition, to join The Trustees, much to the satisfaction and delight of the Standing Committee and the Administration. Others, both men and women, have come to the organization after graduation from school or college, release from military service, or work in related fields.

Until the mid-1960s, less than a dozen full-time field employees were needed to manage the then 44 properties. But following the addition of World's End in 1967, acquisitions began to accelerate. It was obvious to Director Gordon Abbott, Jr., that additional personnel and a reorganization of management systems were needed.

Instead of each property operating on its own, Abbott established a series of management regions — Northeast, Southeast, Central, Western, Martha's Vineyard and Nantucket — and within them, Management Units, which clustered smaller properties with larger ones whose staff and equipment could care for the unit as a whole. Each management region was headed by a Regional Supervisor; each management unit, by a Superintendent. The system is still in effect today.

Wayne N. Mitton, Supervisor, Northeast Management Region

For example, headquarters of the Western Management Region are located in Stockbridge with offices at The Mission House. The Region includes:

a) the *Stockbridge Management Unit*, which operates out of Naumkeag and provides management services for Bartholomew's Cobble and the Ashley House in Sheffield; Goose Pond Reservation, McLennan Reservation and Tyringham Cobble, all in Tyringham; Monument Mountain in Great Barrington; and Naumkeag and The Mission House in Stockbridge

b) the *Windsor Management Unit*, which operates out of Notchview and provides management services for Bear Swamp and Chapelbrook in Ashfield; the Bryant Homestead in Cummington; Chesterfield Gorge in West Chesterfield; Glendale Falls in Middlefield; Petticoat Hill in Williamsburg; and Dinosaur Footprints in Holyoke

c) the *Williamstown Management Unit* which, at present, includes only Field Farm.

Each of the properties lies within reasonable driving distance from Unit headquarters allowing easy transport of personnel and equipment. The responsibility for overseeing and inspecting conservation restrictions rests with each Regional Supervisor.

The goal was to make the delivery of services more efficient and effective by decentralizing many of the activities of management and by allocating responsibility to the regions. Earlier, services had been provided by a crew from General Headquarters in Milton which could, in the case of Berkshire County, consume some two and one-half hours each way for transportation alone.

Stanley I. Piatczyc, Superintendent of the Western Management Region, congratulates Joshua Burch, Assistant Superintendent, Stockbridge Management Unit, 1991 Employee of the Year.

Needless to say, what was accomplished in the field increased markedly.

Indeed, the Standing Committee was so impressed with the results that Abbott proposed that a portion of the governance of the organization itself be decentralized as well to relieve the Standing Committee of a growing number of decisions which related more to the details of administration than to policy. A new system of Regional Committees, which report directly to the Standing Committee, followed. Each is chaired by a member of the governing board who lives within the region. Thus it is that major issues of policy are still decided in Boston, while others can quite properly be dealt with in the field.

As the number of properties grew in the early 1970s, and as visitation and the complexities of management increased as well, Abbott set about to build a professional staff that would be unrivaled anywhere for its excellence. As a nucleus, he chose three graduates of the University of Massachusetts at Amherst who, as senior managers of field resources and personnel, were to provide an ideal personal model for others to emulate, and who were to set the course and tone of the organization's property management practices and procedures for the years ahead. They were Stanley I. Piatczyc, Wayne N. Mitton and Thomas S. Foster.

Each was a specialist in resource management, knowledgable in the fields of arboriculture, forestry, park administration and environmental design. All were family men, in their early or mid-thirties, and veterans of military service. Besides their abilities in the management of natural resources, each could list skills in other areas as well: carpentry, masonry, plumbing, electric wiring, and auto and engine mechanics.

But, most important, all demonstrated outstanding leadership characteristics which enabled them to inspire employees, work creatively with volunteers, relate effectively to visitors as well as to public officials, and win the confidence and affection of the governing board.

Later, they were joined by Richard O'Brien, now Supervisor of the Central Management Region, and Christopher P. Kennedy, who is responsible for properties at Martha's Vineyard and Nantucket. O'Brien, also a graduate of the University of Massachusetts, holds a Masters Degree in Forestry from West Virginia University. Kennedy, a former Assistant Commissioner for Administration with the Massachusetts Department of Fisheries & Wildlife, received his Masters from Suffolk University in Public Administration.

Today, these five men serve as the senior field managers of The Trustees of Reservations and the quality of their own staffs is a reflection of their continuing good judgment and professional capabilities.

Thomas S. Foster, Supervisor, Southeast Management Region

Christopher Kennedy, Supervisor, Islands Management Region

Richard O'Brien, Supervisor, Central Management Region

No activity of The Trustees of Reservations would be possible without the support of an equally competent and impressive collection of staff members at General Headquarters. Abbott's table of organization called for a Deputy Director to serve as second in command as well as three departments heads: a Deputy Director for Land Conservation, a Deputy Director for Development and a Deputy Director for Environmental Services. The Controller reported directly to the Deputy Director.

In 1979, with a capital program on the horizon which would demand a large percentage of the Director's time, William S. Clendaniel, an attorney and former legal counsel for the Massachusetts Coastal Zone Management Program, was appointed Deputy Director in charge of administration and finance. A Rhodes Scholar, Clendaniel was a graduate of Williams College and Harvard Law School and had served as a deck officer in the Navy during the conflict in Vietnam. He was with The Trustees of Reservations for seven years, and was appointed Acting Director in 1984.

His strengths were many. His cool head and steady hand kept budget matters under control. He expanded and systematized bookkeeping and accounting operations and directed activities which led to the acquisition of the organization's first computer. His continued emphasis on the quality of management standards inspired members of the field staff throughout the Commonwealth.

As a senior part of the administrative team at General Headquarters, his wisdom and good judgment helped to steer The

William C. Clendaniel, Deputy Director from 1979 to 1984, and Acting Director from 1984 to 1985

Field managers meet at the Harvard Forest in the mid-1970s. From left, kneeling: Walter A. Prisby, Thomas S. Foster. Standing: Ernest M. Gould, Jr., Harvard Forest; C. Charles Tacito, Warren A. Drew, Robert A. Kreger, Stanley I. Piatzcyc, Garret F. VanWart, Wayne N. Mitton, Stephen E. Bassett and Foster B. Silva.

Trustees towards many accomplishments, including decentralization and the transfer of additional authority to the management regions. Today, Clendaniel is president of Mount Auburn Cemetery in Cambridge and Watertown. Founded in 1831, it is celebrated for its horticulture and as the first rural cemetery in America.

Clendaniel was succeeded as Deputy Director by Davis Cherington, who returned to The Trustees after a year as President of the Land Planning and Management Foundation. Today, Cherington is in Washington as Vice President for Adminstration at the American Farmlands Trust.

The management staff at General Headquarters presently includes Fred Winthrop, of course, Director; John Coleman, Deputy Director for Finance and Administration; Richard Howe, Deputy Director for Property Management; Lisa McFadden, Deputy Director for Public Information; Ann Powell, Deputy Director for Development; and Wesley T. Ward, Deputy Director for Land Conservation.

There are other Headquarters specialists in the fields of membership and development, administration, accounting, publications and land conservation, whose contributions from day to day are vital to the organization's health and stability.

The same, of course, must be said for field employees, some of whom — full time or part time — have been with The Trustees of Reservations for one or more decades:

Richard Bellevue, Refuge Manager, Coskata-Coatue Wildlife Refuge; Joshua Birch, Assistant Superintendent, Stockbridge Management Unit; Robert Chambers, Chief of Security, Coskata-Coatue Wildlife Refuge; William H. Cruikshank, Refreshment Stand Manager, Coskata-Coatue Wildlife Refuge; Roland A. Hinckley, Beach Manager; Coskata-Coatue Wildlife Refuge; Marcel LaJeauness, Maintenance, Andover-North Andover Management Unit; Stephen E. McMahon, Superintendent, Crane Memorial Reservation; Harry L. Mears, Ranger, Coskata-Coatue Wildlife Refuge; Robert Murray, Superintendent, Andover-North Andover Management Unit; Edwin F. Paquin, Maintenance Supervisor, Coskata-Coatue Wildlife Refuge; Peter Pinciaro, Superintendent, Coskata-Coatue Wildlife Refuge; Walter A. Prisby, Refuge Manager, Crane Wildlife Refuge; David A. Ryan, Superintendent, Misery Island and Crowninshield Island; Larry J. Simpson, Superintendent and Chief Horticulturalist, Long Hill; Kenneth Spellman, Head Life Guard, Crane Memorial Reservation; Walter R. Swan, Ranger, Crane Wildlife Refuge; and Albert H. Yalenezian, Superintendent, South Shore Management Unit.

Thanks to a constant and careful emphasis on communications, not only between members of the professional staff but between the staff and members of volunteer committees, The

Trustees of Reservations, with some 60 full-time employees and more than double that number of active volunteer committee members, has managed to avoid the polarizing effects of institutional politics.

This, combined with effective planning, which defines the organization's goals and objectives for the short and long term, has enabled both volunteers and staff members to function together, quite literally, as a "family," motivated and stimulated by the good works they are engaged in. Despite the organization's growth, which admittedly makes it difficult, every effort is made to continue management policies and practices which encourage and maintain this kind of institutional philosophy. So far, thanks to the quality and character of the men and women involved, it has worked with remarkable success.

7

Interpretive Programs

1

Interpretation: from Understanding Comes Affection and Respect

Perceptive as always to the needs of the moment, it was Fletcher Steele who, in 1947, proposed expanding the interpretive programs of The Trustees of Reservations.

With World War II ended and prosperity returning, Americans everywhere were discovering the out-of-doors. A year earlier, more than 200,000 people had visited Crane Beach in Ipswich, a new record. Other reservations were reporting comparable increases as well. And the organization was discussing, with some concern, how it could best accommodate this new demand while at the same time protecting the very things that visitors came to enjoy — the beauty of a landscape, the environment of a fragile natural area, or the splendor of an historic house.

The ultimate answer, of course, was to be decided property by property, using the planning process to identify the special qualities and characteristics of each reservation and to then determine what kind of management policies could best protect them. The result, formalized in 1967, was called a "Master Plan."

Increasingly, a vital part of every Master Plan during the 1960s and '70s was an emphasis on interpretation. For it was universally agreed that if visitors could understand the significance of a property — why it is being preserved — they would be more likely to respect it and to act in ways that would help protect it in the years to come. It was hoped they would enjoy it more as well.

As Steele declared in an earlier pronouncement: "We must provide more interpretations and descriptions of our reservations [and] we must build up a library of reports to satisfy the many legitimate demands of curiosity concerning the geology, flora, fauna, history and all other aspects of our lands."

By the late 1940s a start had already been made. At Bartholomew's Cobble, Warden S. Waldo Bailey and geologist Professor Herbert J. Arnold, a former member of the faculty at Columbia University, had produced a natural history of the property. It included a brief account of its geology as well as a list of plant species noted by the late C.A. Weatherby, Senior Curator of the Gray Herbarium at Harvard. Scholarly, informative and still wonderfully readable, it set a style for others to follow.

With its extraordinary collection of flora and fauna, the Cobble was a natural for interpretation. After Waldo Bailey's death in 1963, it was decided by members of the Local Committee, with the blessing of the Standing Committee, that a small natural history museum should be established at the Cobble in memory of the Warden who had served it so devotedly for 16 years.

Today, the Bailey Trailside Museum is enjoyed by more than 9,000 visitors annually. Its exhibits reflect the remarkable natural diversity of the Cobble and even include, for archaeologists, an impressive collection of Indian arrowheads and stone tools found on the property itself.

At about the same time, Hervey Woodburn Shimer, Professor Emeritus of Paleontology at Massachusetts Institute of Technology, also authored a booklet which described the geological history of Rocky Woods Reservation in Medfield. A brief geological history of the Charles W. Ward Reservation was written by

Illustrated, interpretive panels of weather-resistant, imbedded fiberglass tell the story of programs to protect sand dunes and sea and shorebirds at Crane Beach, Ipswich. They are viewed by an estimated one-half million visitors annually.

George E. Zink, Head of the Science Department at nearby Brooks School in North Andover. And in Concord, historian Allen French provided copy for what later became a booklet entitled *Hawthorne at The Old Manse*, a charming story of the celebrated author's three years at the Manse with his wife Sophia which gave rise to his own legendary work, *Mosses from an Old Manse* published in 1842.

As interpretive material, each of these booklets, illustrated with drawings and photographs and published in a handy six-by-nine-inch size, added immeasurably to the pleasure and understanding of every visitor. And there were more to come.

2

Self-Guided Trails and a Series of Informative Booklets

In the 1960s, Director Gordon Abbott, Jr., made expansion of the organization's interpretive programs a major management objective. Self-guided trails were established at the Crane Reservation to explain the fragile ecology of a barrier beach; at Bartholomew's Cobble, to enable visitors to tour the property on their own if the Warden-Naturalist was busy elsewhere; and at the Ward Reservation, where a boardwalk leads to the heart of a typical northern bog.

Other trails were created at Rocky Woods, where visitors can explore the special features of a woodland environment; and at Notchview Reservation, where a demonstration forest is designed to help private owners of forest lands establish a program of scientific management. Illustrated booklets, which explain dozens of points of interest along the way, are available for each self-guided trail.

A new signing system, which made use of new graphics and new materials, was developed for the organization as a whole. The seal of The Trustees of Reservations with its distinctive white pine, was redesigned and improved without losing its historic character. At many of the larger reservations, attractive panel boards were installed at the entrance, welcoming visitors and describing features of the property.

Rules and regulations were established for each reservation which, when posted, told visitors first a bit about the area and its special characteristics before listing prohibited activities which were obviously inconsistent with their preservation.

A series of illustrated folders, which included a map of the property, directions to it from major roadways, a description of features and its programs, as well as its hours of operation and admission fees, were produced for many larger reservations. And an attractive, pocket-size, 64-page guide to all the properties of The Trustees of Reservations was published and made available for every member.

Meanwhile, Abbott was busy encouraging the production of other booklets as well. Author and columnist for the *The Berkshire Eagle*, Morgan G. Bulkeley (who was also Chairman of the Local Committee for Bartholomew's Cobble), wrote an engaging history of Naumkeag. Bulkeley and Warden-Naturalist Howard T. Bain produced a booklet on the birds of Bartholomew's Cobble. Freelance writer Gerard Chapman, long an admirer of the Bryant Homestead, provided a manuscript which later became a booklet entitled *William Cullen Bryant, The Cummington Years*.

Local Committee member Arthur C. Chase, a teacher and administrator at Berkshire School, wrote *The Ashleys — A Pioneer Berkshire Family*, which tells the story of the Colonel John Ashley House and the legendary events which took place there. Research material was provided by Gerard Chapman.

On the Vineyard, educator W. Gray Mattern, then chief executive of the European Council of International Schools and a member of the Local Committee, wrote an illustrated natural history of Cape Poge Wildlife Refuge and Wasque Reservation. He was assisted by wildlife biologist Susan B. Whiting.

A number of distinguished professional authors have contributed their talents to produce booklets which tell the story of properties of The Trustees of Reservations and the families associated with them throughout their history.

In North Andover, the celebrated historian, author and Director of the Boston Athenaeum, Walter M. Whitehill, produced a manuscript which told in a wonderfully personal way the story of the Stevens-Coolidge Place. Whitehill, whose wife Jane was a niece of Mrs. Helen Stevens Coolidge, was a near neighbor of the property and a distinguished member of its Local Committee.

In Concord, Standing Committee member Paul Brooks, former Editor-in-Chief at the publishing firm of Houghton Mifflin and author of numerous books and articles about the environment, wrote an elegant and delightfully readable history entitled *The Old Manse and the People Who Lived There*. It was illustrated with color photographs of the Manse and its gardens which appeared in *Antiques* magazine. And at Long Hill, horticulturist and author Isador Smith produced a 28-page *Guide to Sedgwick Gardens*. She was assisted by Pattie Hall.

With Abbott's encouragement also, Willard Brewer Walker, a Professor of Anthropology at Wesleyan University, collaborated with his father to write *A History of World's End* which tells the remarkable story of the property and its people. Professor Walker's great-grandfather, John R. Brewer, purchased what was to become World's End Farm in 1855. His father, Willard H.C. Walker, managed the property for many years, and, with Mrs. Walker, his mother, was responsible for steering it towards preservation.

Writer and editor Paul Brooks, a member of the Standing Committee, chairman of the Friends of The Old Manse and author of a history of the property

Because of the costs of printing and the difficulties of finding writers who have both the necessary time and skill, many histories still remain unpublished. But it is hoped that some day funds will be found to complete the collection, for every property has its own fascinating story which can add so much to its understanding and enjoyment.

Other elements of The Trustees of Reservations' interpretive programs included, for many years, an annual lecture series at Naumkeag which featured such topics as the architecture of the Gilded Age of Berkshire County; the area's authors — Bryant, Melville and Edith Wharton; and, in keeping with the character of the property itself, the decorative arts, and gardens and garden design. There was also, for some years, a program at the Stevens-Coolidge Place (in cooperation with the Merrimack Valley Textile Museum and the North Andover Historical Society) which was designed to teach elementary school students about the social, industrial, and agricultural history of their community.

Certainly one of the most successful events of its kind is the Annual Fall Field Trip. Initiated during the 1970s, it continues today. Enormously popular, it is designed to provide opportunities for members of the governing board and others to visit properties throughout The Trustees' realm. Couples are welcome, and every participant pays his or her own way.

Usually of three days' duration, Fall Field Trips are scheduled in each of The Trustees of Reservations' five management regions. This, of course, means the excitement and fun of transportation by bus and by plane, by boat (large and small), by horse and cart, by tractor, and by four-wheel drive vehicles, all depending upon the location and terrain.

Luncheons are in the field. Dinners were (and on occasion still are) hosted by local residents, some of whom are members of Local Committees, the Standing Committee or the Advisory Council.

Visits to specific properties offer Field Trip participants a chance to learn first-hand not only about the special characteristics of an area, but about the challenges faced by both professional staff and volunteers as they attempt to implement management programs from day to day. Representatives of local land trusts, State and Federal resource officers, and town officials are often invited to meet with Field Trip participants. The discussions which take place invariably increase understanding of each others' roles and responsibilities.

Still a major fixture of The Trustees of Reservations' calendar, the annual Fall Field Trip has proved its worth time and again. Nowhere is this better demonstrated than at meetings in Boston, where experience in the field can add immeasurably to the quality of discussions and the decisions which must be made by members of the governing board.

Umbrellas serve as sails as committee members John and Katharine Plimpton canoe the upper Charles River during a Fall Field Trip.

3

'Walks and Talks:' Education and Entertainment

Perhaps the best example of the imagination and diversity offered by the interpretive programs of The Trustees of Reservations today is found in its Calendar of Events. It appears in each issue of the organization's newsletter, which is mailed to every member. A mix of education and entertainment, the Calendar offers activities for all ages which range from piano recitals at Castle Hill, a dinner dance at Naumkeag and a Victorian Christmas celebration at The Old Manse, to nature walks at the Norris Reservation, a photo exhibit of gardens designed by Fletcher Steele at Long Hill, and ski touring by moonlight at Notchview Reservation in Windsor.

Under the direction of Fred Winthrop, activities at each of the properties have been accelerated to introduce visitors to their particular qualities and characteristics, and to recruit new members to support the cause. The results have been wonderfully successful.

During the celebration of the organization's Centennial, a series of "Discovery Days" at selected properties were attended by literally thousands of visitors. At North Common Meadow in Petersham, for example, the day began at seven a.m. with a bird and wildflower walk. Later, there were carriage rides around the town and fiddle music on the Green. A storyteller spun yarns of what life was like in the community a century ago. Nature walks took place at nearby Brooks Woodland Preserve. A chorus sang madrigals, native Americans of the Nipmuck Tribe described their own rich heritage, and, in the evening, there was a concert of classical, traditional and contemporary music presented by members of the First Parish Unitarian Church.

Fred Winthrop also welcomed Discovery Day guests to the Meadow and celebrated The Trustees of Reservations' first century with a birthday cake and the ceremonial planting of a centennial sugar maple. It was a joyous and festive scene repeated around the Commonwealth.

On other occasions, there are activities of a more practical bent as well, as volunteers gather to cut brush to maintain a vista at Pegan Hill, Dover, or to improve trails at Notchview in Windsor.

Continuing programs include wildlife biologist David Rimmer's "walks and talks" at the Crane Reservation in Ipswich — one, for elementary school groups, another for college students concentrating in the field of natural resources. Rimmer's responsibilities also include management of the area's herd of white-tailed deer and administering the property's long-term efforts to provide protection for nesting shorebirds.

Indeed, The Trustees of Reservations' shorebirds protection programs at each of its barrier beaches have led to major efforts to inform visitors about the shoreline environment and the nesting habits of piping plovers and least and common terns. A model program was established in Nantucket by then Warden-Naturalist Nan Jenks-Jay which involved well-organized newspaper publicity, special handouts, meetings with youth and adult groups, and one-to-one conversations at the property itself.

In recent years, a series of distinguished experts in the field of horticulture have presented an annual program of up to nine hugely-popular lectures at Long Hill. And at the Stevens-Coolidge Place, visitors were fascinated with an exhibition of unique photographs of early twentieth-century China collected by John Gardner Coolidge, who served there as an American diplomat. They now also enjoy an annual Garden Symposium initiated by members of the Local Committee and the property's professional staff.

Even The Trustees of Reservations' standard *Guide to Properties* has been enlarged to measure now six by nine inches, and rewritten to provide significantly more information about each reservation. The new guide now encompasses some 112 pages and highlights 16 properties with 500-word descriptions, while others have been expanded to 150 words each. Illustrations, of course, are included.

Although difficult to measure, it is generally agreed by both staff and volunteers, that, through the years, The Trustees of Reservations' interpretive programs have helped increase understanding, not only of the properties, but, equally important, of the mission and make-up of the organization itself. That has been a major goal of the present administration.

Although most of The Trustees of Reservations' interpretive programs today are appropriately created and directed within each management region, much credit for their initial development must go to Garret F. VanWart who joined the Trustees as Deputy Director in 1969. A graduate of the University of Maine with a Bachelor of Science degree in wildlife management, VanWart had extensive experience in interpretation and education as Director of the Trailside Museum, located in the heart of the Blue Hills Reservation in Milton. In 1979, in keeping with his interests and abilities, he was áppointed Deputy Director for Environmental Services.

A naturalist of impressive ability, he had a warm and wonderful enthusiasm for his work with The Trustees which captivated audiences on field trips throughout the state. His knowledge of wildflowers, of trees and shrubs, and of animals and birds was immense. Like the good teacher he was, he knew how to

Garret F. VanWart, Deputy Director for Environmental Services

weave them all together. He was equally at home in an upland or
seaside environment and accompanying him on a walk through
the countryside was a special treat.

He designed, marked in the field, and helped construct, all of
the existing self-guided trails and, with Abbott, wrote many of
their associated booklets. He created "This Fragile Shore," the
interpretive program at Crane Beach and Castle Neck which
included not only an interpretive trail, but instructive panel
boards, and a slide presentation for local schools and community
organizations. He initiated and administered the programs to
protect nesting shorebirds which continue so successfuly today at
Castle Neck, Wasque and Cape Poge, and at Coskata-Coatue
Wildlife Refuge.

VanWart directed the program, begun in 1968, to produce
resource inventories and detailed Master Plans for the management and protection of every property of The Trustees of Reservations. He was particularly involved with World's End, Hingham:
Chapelbrook, Ashfield; Long Point Wildlife Refuge, West
Tisbury; Crane Wildlife Refuge, Ipswich and Essex; Notchview
Reservation, Windsor (where he designed and created a demonstration forest); and Halibut Point, Rockport, where he helped
create a cooperative management program with the State's
Department of Environmental Management which now owns
land nearby. (Present-day Halibut Point State Park came into
being primarily because of the long-term efforts of the Town of
Rockport and The Trustees of Reservations.)

Above all, VanWart was a passionate and persuasive spokesman for the protection of the natural features of every property of
The Trustees of Reservations, large or small. For nearly a decade
after leaving The Trustees, he served as Director of Reservations
for the Metropolitan District Commission, which began its life as
the Metropolitan Park Commission, established by The Trustees
and others, a century ago. He continues his good work today as
Executive Director of the Natural Resources Trust of Easton,
Massachusetts.

4

For Distinguished Service: the Conservation Award

In 1934, seeking not only to honor outstanding accomplishments
in the field of conservation, but, it must be admitted, greater
recognition for The Trustees of Reservations, Executive Director

Laurence Fletcher proposed the establishment of an annual Conservation Award. A handsome eight-inch silver salver with appropriate engraving, it was to be presented each year at the Annual Meeting. The idea won the immediate approval of members of the Standing Committee and that year the first recipient of the award was one of their own, Dr. John C. Phillips of Ipswich, a nationally known figure in the world of environmental conservation.

Although trained in medicine and the commanding officer of a U.S. Army Field Hospital in World War I, Dr. Phillips practiced professionally for only a few years. Then, fascinated with the science of wildlife and blessed with the means to be able to enjoy its study, he traveled widely and adventurously throughout the world, combining his love of hunting and the out-of-doors with a passion for collecting.

The recipient of most of his generosity was the Museum of Comparative Zoology at Harvard, which in 1929 received a collection of heads and horns representing more than 250 species including a number of world records.

A member of the faculty of the Peabody Museum of Cambridge, he also served as Research Curator of Birds at the Museum of Comparative Zoology. His four-volume *Natural History of the Ducks*, has been called "the best monograph of its kind which has been done by any American naturalist." He was the author as well of a delightful collection of essays on field sports and camping entitled the *Sportsman's Scrapbook*, and co-author with Thomas B. Cabot, a former President of the Appalachian Mountain Club, of *White Water and Smooth*, the first New England guide for canoeists published by the AMC. Cabot himself, long an active proponent of open space preservation, received The Trustees' Conservation Award in 1974.

It was the preservation of wildlife habitat which interested Dr. Phillips most, and as Cabot writes of his friend, he "devoted his active mind, abundant energy and independent means to the cause of conservation." He was a founder and later Chairman of the Massachusetts Conservation Council and President of the Massachusetts Fish and Game Association. As a member of the Standing Committee of The Trustees of Reservations, his initiative and generosity established two reservations: Halibut Point in Rockport and Pine and Hemlock Knoll in Wenham. He was equally supportive of other properties, especially Misery Islands in Salem Bay. He also made possible the existence of several state-owned wildlife refuges, including East Sandwich Game Farm Refuge in Sandwich; Watatic Mountain Wildlife Reservation in Ashby; and Edward Howe Forbush Wildlife Reservation in Hancock.

Dr. Phillips died unexpectedly at age 62, too early in life, but as he might have wished — hunting for woodcock in the field. His youngest son Arthur, followed him as a member of the Standing Commitee, serving as Secretary of The Trustees of Reservations from 1956 to 1966.

Despite all of his accomplishments, Arthur recalls, "father was very shy. When he first won the Conservation Award, he pretended he was sick and Mother had to [attend the luncheon and] accept it for him."

Arthur Phillips also recalled how his father had acquired the inheritance which enabled him to devote his life to pursuits which greatly enlarged public understanding of wildlife and ornithology. William Phillips, an early ancestor, he explained, made a substantial fortune in the clipper trade in Salem. He took a shine "to my grandfather and promised him $5 million if he got married. He did and had five children one of whom was father. That was what made it all possible!"

The presentation to Dr. Phillips set high standards for The Trustees of Reservations' Conservation Award. He was followed by an illustrious list of other recipients until the award was retired in 1980. They included Robert Moses, New York's visionary park planner; Fairfield Osborn, President of the New York Zoological Society and author of the landmark publication *Our Plundered Planet*; Benton McKaye, father of the Appalachian Trail; U.S. Senator Leverett Saltonstall, who originated legislation to create Massachusetts' Cape Cod National Seashore and Minuteman National Park; and Francis W. Sargent, a former member of the Standing Committee, who went on to win national acclaim for his work as Director of the Outdoor Recreation Review Commission

1972 Conservation Award winner Morgan G. Bulkeley, second from right, with author Hal Borland (holding plaque designating Bartholomew's Cobble a National Natural Landmark); Paul G. Favour, (left), Special Assistant to the Regional Director, National Park Service; and Charles E. Mason, Jr., (right), President of The Trustees of Reservations

which completed the first study of outdoor recreation needs throughout the country. Sargent, former Massachusetts Commissioner of Fisheries & Wildlife, known affectionately as the "Fish Commish," also served his state as Lieutenant-Governor and then as Governor from 1972 to 1976.

Later recipients of The Trustees of Reservations' Conservation Award were, by design, more local — people throughout the Commonwealth whose good works had helped in a major way to preserve open space. They included Donald B. Miller, Publisher of *The Berkshire Eagle*; Mrs. Horatio Rogers, who led an imaginative effort to protect the historic character of the Town of North Andover; John W. Pierce, founder of Essex County Greenbelt Association; and Janet Wilder Dakin, who established the Kestrel (Land) Trust in Amherst.

In its early days, the Conservation Award was presented at Annual Meetings of the corporation, which usually took place over luncheon at the old Copley-Plaza Hotel in Boston. During the 1960s, however, the Award became an event in itself. A simple, seated luncheon (usually chowder, corn bread, a salad and apple pie) was served under a tent at one of the organization's properties.

These "moveable feasts" were enormously popular, attracting as many as 300 guests. Besides the Conservation Award ceremony, there was usually a featured speaker. But rising expenses took their toll and rather than charge its members what luncheons actually cost, the organization chose, at least temporarily, to end what had been a delightful tradition.

As the years passed, the Conservation Award, much to everyone's pleasure, was revived and presented again, this time at the Annual Meeting. With it, there were awards also for Volunteer of the Year and for Employee of the Year, initiated by Director Frederic Winthrop, Jr.

In its 100th anniversary year, Winthrop and The Trustees of Reservations established a new award. Named for the organization's much-heralded founder, the Charles Eliot Conservation Award was presented to two recipients at The Trustees' Gala Birthday Party in June 1991 at Castle Hill. First honored was Patrick F. Noonan, former President of The Nature Conservancy, founder and President of the American Farmlands Trust and founder and President of The Conservation Fund. Second was a member of The Trustees' own family, Gordon Abbott, Jr., founder of the Center for Rural Massachusetts at the University of Massachusetts, Amherst, a founder of the Land Trust Alliance, and Director of The Trustees of Reservations for more than 17 years.

The Charles Eliot Conservation Award will be presented in the future as occasion warrants.

Dealing with the Unexpected

1

A Robbery at The Old Manse

Despite the best efforts of the Standing Committee and the Administration to prepare management plans and policies which deal with the unexpected, surprises do occur. Thankfully, even over a century, they have been few and far between.

Take the story of the young security officer at Crane Beach in the mid-1950s who, surrounded by a group of angry and threatening young people (the reason for the incident is lost to history), drew his revolver (security officers were Special Police in those days and could carry sidearms) and fired into the air, presumably to scare off his would-be assailants. The bullet, as bullets do, reached the apex of its trajectory and started downward. With only its own weight propelling it now, it struck a woman sunbather on the arm farther down the beach. "It felt like a bee sting," she reported.

Fortunately, the consequence was only a bruise. But the incident caused sweeping changes in management procedures. Only a few ranking security officers and rangers who stand watch at the beach at night carry sidearms today, and those who do are professionally and regularly trained by police instructors and licensed by the Commonwealth.

Then there was the robbery at The Old Manse in Concord. On a warm September night in 1968, thieves parked their truck nearby, silenced the alarm system, climbed up on the roof, and entered the house through a dormer window. With the Manse set back from the road in the shadow of surrounding trees, it was impossible to see what was going on, and there was plenty of time to take what they wanted.

The next morning the break was discovered by Chairman of the Local Committee Charles L. Ward, who visited the house daily. His first call was to the Concord Police Department. His next, to the Director of The Trustees of Reservations. Abbott immediately set off to visit the scene. What had been stolen were antiques of considerable financial value, but, more important, of irreplaceable historic interest and significance. Missing, for example, was a mahogany block-front chest of drawers with original brasses made about 1760. It had been the property of the Reverend William Emerson, the original owner of the Manse, who served as Chaplain to Washington's Army during the Revolution. Gone, too, was a three-cornered chair used by Emerson while he wrote his Sunday sermons, as well as some 25 other pieces of furniture, each obviously carefully selected for its value. It was clear the thieves knew just what they were doing.

Two police inspectors, W. Robert Nutter and Salvatore C. Silvio, were assigned to the case and, with a tenacity created by a desire to restore the integrity of a famous local landmark as well as by inherent professional zeal, they scoured auctions and antique shops throughout New England. Luckily, thanks to the earlier wisdom of the Local Committee, they were equipped with copies of photographs which had been taken of the pieces only weeks before during a reappraisal for insurance purposes.

A few days later, in a small town in Western Massachusetts, their efforts paid off. Showed the photographs, an antique dealer said he had seen some of the furniture and he immediately called two other dealers who were able to help as well. From that moment on, things began to fall into place. The block-front chest

The parlor at The Old Manse is in keeping with Phoebe Emerson's desire, expressed to her husband William when he built the house in 1769, to have "small boxes of rooms." On the left side of the mantle is the stuffed Great Horned Owl which, Sophia Hawthorne observed, had eyes that seemed to follow her about.

of drawers, for example, was discovered only hours before it was to be loaded on a truck bound for Ohio.

By tracing the sales from shop to shop with the assistance of antique store owners, most of whom were anxious to cooperate, police inspectors were able to collect most of the furniture stolen from the Old Manse. Emerson's three-cornered chair had been sold three times in two states before it was discovered.

Finally, some weeks after the robbery, Concord Police Chief William J. Costello called General Headquarters of The Trustees in Milton. "I have a surprise for you," he said to the Director. "Can you come straight here to the Police Station in Concord?"

Abbott was in his car in a minute. When he arrived he was led to a small cell block, and there, locked safely behind bars, were all but two or three of the pieces that had been taken. Beside them stood the two inspectors, smiling broadly. It was a first-class example of a police work and in gratitude the Standing Committee approved a generous contribution to the Pension Fund of the Concord Police Department.

Today, the alarm system at The Old Manse — this time tied directly to Police Headquarters — is technically the most sophisticated that money can buy. Other steps to increase security have been taken as well to insure that The Old Manse with all its treasures stays out of harm's way.

Alarm systems provide a high level of protection for the collections at other historic houses as well. Many, in rural communities, sound first at a security company office, manned 24 hours a day, which contacts the appropriate superintendent. The interior contents, too, of every historic house today have been itemized, described and photographed as a part of its curatorial inventory.

As for insurance, museum houses require special consideration. Buildings are insured to permit logical reconstruction after, say, a fire. But no one would suggest producing a replica of The Old Manse or The Mission House, for example, if they burned to the ground.

Furnishings are self-insured as is the practice with many small museums throughout the nation. Some pieces, such as the Reverend John Sargent's own chair at The Mission House, are unique and once lost or stolen can never be replaced no matter how much insurance is carried. If other objects are taken, however, funds may be raised to replace them with pieces of like character from the same period so that the house may continue to be shown without disturbing gaps in its collection.

2

Case of the Missing Dinosaur Tracks

In 1936, a theft of another nature occurred at Dinosaur Footprints Reservation bordering the Connecticut River in Holyoke. Discovered in 1836 by then Professor and later President Hitchcock of Amherst College, the tracks were made by some of the earliest known dinosaurs in Triassic time, 190 million years ago.

Acquired by The Trustees of Reservations in 1935, the tracks, according to a paleontologist, "were made in or about mud puddles which dried up. The mud was sun-baked so that the next rains which refilled the puddles, covered the tracks instead of washing them away. The whole mass was then buried under thousands of feet of sandstone, until it was re-exposed by the Connecticut River after the glacier receded, the action of the river, over time, carrying away layer after layer."

The reservation includes several groups of five or ten tracks each, as well as numerous single tracks. In the early nineteenth century, it was reputed to be the largest collection of dinosaur footprints in the eastern United States. Some years ago, a Yale University paleontologist presented a paper which created considerable interest in the property in professional circles. It held that the patterns of these specific tracks preserved by The Trustees were unique and showed that dinosaurs, or at least members of this species, were "gregarious" by nature.

Fearing its exploitation for commercial purposes, The Trustees agreed to purchase the site from its sympathetic owner for $4,800. Eight hundred dollars was provided to clinch the sale. The remainder was to be raised from public subscription.

The area, which borders directly on busy Route 5, has always presented management problems. These have involved primarily its use for incidental dumping of unwanted refuse. No problem, however, exceeded in severity the discovery in the mid-1930s that thieves had chiseled away layers of sandstone and actually removed and stolen some of the tracks themselves.

"What light-fingered gentry," an editorial in *The Boston Transcript* asked indignantly in December 1936, "would normally wish to go about robbing them, and having stolen such specimens, what could he do with them?" The question was never answered.

Most of the tracks remain in place today. Access to the site is still difficult, although there is a small parking facility. The tracks are used primarily by schools and colleges for instructional purposes. And so far, no "light-fingered gentry" have attempted to run off with any others.

3

The Mission House and Its Indian Bible

One of the prized possessions of The Mission House in Stockbridge was an impressive, leather-bound, two-volume Bible, dated 1739. It was presented to the Indians, and so inscribed, by the Reverend Francis Ayscough, Chaplain to the Prince of Wales. And it was used by the Reverend John Sergeant, a graduate of Yale and a young missionary, who came to "that vast wilderness called New England" to preach the Gospel of Christianity in the early years of the eighteenth century.

When the Indians migrated west following the Revolution in 1785, they took the Bible with them to Wisconsin where they settled down and established a new community. In the 1930s, when Miss Mabel Choate restored the old mission and moved it to Main Street, she sought to purchase the Bible and bring it home to Stockbridge. Once they understood that it was to be a part of a museum which would celebrate the relationship between the early Christian mission and their ancestors, tribal leaders were happy to part with the Bible, and a deal was struck. In fact, members of the tribe were present, in traditional Native American dress, at the formal dedication of the property in Stockbridge, and, according to newspaper accounts of the era, all seemed well.

Attitudes change, however, with the times, and in the early 1970s, a delegation of Indians, now residents of Munsee, Wiscon-

At the ceremony returning The Mission House Bible to the Stockbridge-Munsee Community in 1991 are, from left, Herbert W. Vaughan, Chairman of The Trustees of Reservations; Tribal Council Member Leonard E. Miller; Director Fred Winthrop; and Supervisor Stanley I. Piacvzyc.

sin, visited Stockbridge, toured The Mission House and discovered the Bible once again. Upon their return home, they wrote to ask if they could have it back. But, however feelings may have run on either side, it was not that easy. As a gift of Mabel Choate, the Bible was held in public trust by The Trustees of Reservations. Thus not only the Choate family, but the State Attorney General, representing the people of Massachusetts, were party to its protection for public purposes.

After some years of discussion and research, however, which included visits with representatives of the tribe in Wisconsin, it was determined that the Bible would be well cared for and displayed in a small museum devoted to tribal history. At that point, The Trustees agreed to return it if all parties of interest could concur.

The question was not without controversy, particularly among members of the Local and Regional Committees, who held that it was an orginal part of The Mission House museum, legally acquired, and should remain in Stockbridge.

But tribal leaders argued persuasively that there was a new interest within the community in its early history and origins (its tribal museum was an example), and the Standing Committee agreed that to give the Bible back was the right thing to do.

It was transferred officially, with court approval and under terms which provided for its protection in perpetuity, at a special ceremony at The Mission House in March 1991. Present were representatives of the Stockbridge-Munsee Indians, local officials, and Standing Committee Chairman Herbert W. Vaughan and Director Frederic Winthrop, Jr.

4

Eminent Domain: as a Red Flag to a Bull

The dictionary defines "eminent domain" as "the right of government to appropriate private property for public use, usually with compensation for the owner." Despite the prospect of compensation, however, The Trustees of Reservations has responded to threats that a municipality may exercise eminent domain proceedings to take a portion of its lands as a bull responds to the sight of a red flag.

Such a case occurred in the Town of Stockbridge in 1963. Voters there, upon the recommendation of the school building committee, selected as one of two sites for a new high school, a portion of the lower field at Naumkeag. Somehow, without the knowledge of the Administration or of the Standing Committee, the State Legislature also approved a bill authorizing the acquisition of some 20 acres of land for the purpose "by purchase or otherwise."

Members of the governing board expressed outrage with the proposal. "Naturally," Secretary Arthur H. Phillips reported at the Annual Meeting, "we are opposing this move by every means in our power, not only because of the detriment to our Naumkeag reservation, which it entails, but also in implementation of our policy opposing the misuse of park land which has been left in trust for public enjoyment." There were other sites, the organization believed, which would be equally suitable for school construction.

An appeal by The Trustees of Reservations to the Supreme Judicial Court was turned down, and the following year Stockbridge residents voted in favor of the taking. Secretary Phillips once again told the Annual Meeting: "we are currently working on legislation to make such steals of open space areas impossible in the future." But there appeared to be a more immediate way out.

The towns of Stockbridge, West Stockbridge and Great Barrington shortly agreed to establish a regional high school which would serve all three communities. A significant amount of state aid served as bait. And a year or so afterwards, voters acted to return the 20 acres of land to Naumkeag.

In North Andover, nearly a decade later (1970), an eminent domain proposal also threatened the 83-acre Stevens-Coolidge Place. Again, the land was scheduled to become the site of a new high school. But a community-wide concern for the environment and the preservation of an historic site made the outcome a happy one.

The Trustees had publicly opposed the proposal more than a year earlier and, in response to the request of a special citizens' committee, had opened the house (generally closed during the winter months) for public inspection. On a gray afternoon in mid-March, more than 600 North Andover residents took advantage of the opportunity, touring the grounds as well.

A few days later, thanks to the efforts of the Town's Conservation Commission, Director Gordon Abbott, Jr., was invited to address what turned out to be nearly 1,000 voters at Town Meeting, many of whom had to view the proceedings at the existing high school on closed circuit television. Abbott presented a comprehensive view of the proposal and discussed how it might affect the quality of life in the community in the years to come. His statement also explained much about the style, the values and the philosophy of the organization he represented.

"This has been as agonizing a period for us as we are sure it has been for you," he declared. "We are deeply sympathetic to the community's need for additional school facilities. And we are highly respectful of the hours of research and discussion which have been applied by the School Building Committee to help answer this need.

"Our concerns and responsibilities, quite naturally, embrace a different area, but one which we believe is no less important. They involve not only our fiduciary obligations to a generous and public-spirited lady (donor Helen Stevens Coolidge), but, in fact, the total environment, the quality of life here in North Andover now, and perhaps more important, in the years that lie ahead. . . .

"We believe in the development of communities to meet inevitable growth, but we plead first for planning, on a local and on a regional basis, to balance this development, weighing every factor vital to our existence.

"A balanced plan can help maintain and cherish the values which give order and stability to our lives. And it can conserve for future generations, those vital natural resources without which neither we or our children can survive.

"The Stevens-Coolidge Place, we believe, exemplifies, in an outstanding and emphatic way, this delicate and crucial balance between man and nature. In a growing suburban community, whose population is expected to rise from its present 15,100 to more than 24,800 persons in the next two decades, the Stevens-Coolidge land provides needed, natural open space within the town's most populated area.

"On either side of the 52-acre portion of the property now proposed for school development, there are, by report, 638

Part of a grant from the Massachusetts Bay Colony to John Stevens in 1645, the Stevens-Coolidge Place was known for many years as Ashdale Farm. Today, with its grounds, gardens and collections, it is preserved as an elegant example of country life in the early 20th century and an important parcel of open space.

apartment units completed or under construction. These will house, according to accepted indexes, some 2,000 persons. This open area west of Chickering Road with its trees and grasses, follows the *Open Space Plan for North Andover* completed by the community's Conservation Commission. It is a key portion of the green corridors recommended to retain the historic, rural character of the town.

"... Separating two areas of high density settlement, it also provides citizens with the visual satisfaction of nature, and its very openness offers psychological relief from crowding — relief profoundly important in our increasingly hectic urban world. This open space also answers a growing need for room for low-intensity recreation, a place for all of us and our children to walk and wonder at nature's ways.

"It has another basic function as well. Open space provides a vital sponge which soaks up rain and melting snows, prevents flooding and renews precious supplies of ground water which help sustain life. In a very real way, too, it helps dampen and absorb the noise of traffic and other sounds which are a growing problem to our health and well-being. And practical experience shows that open space makes the land around it a more valuable place to live, thus increasing tax revenues and providing for quality growth.

Off to an Easter Sunday service in 1935, Mr. and Mrs. John Gardner Coolidge walk one of Boston's brick-paved sidewalks on their way to church.

"The fields and pasture land of the Stevens-Coolidge Place are much the same today as they were in the early days of North Andover's history. East of Chickering Road, they offer a charming and pleasant change of scene which contributes so immensely to the still country feeling of the town.

"With its red barn, gray stone walls and the graciousness of the main house itself, the property also provides vital and harmonious protection for the Old (town) Center whose magnificent restoration and preservation means so much in personal pleasure and property values to each North Andover resident and homeowner....

"... Mrs. Coolidge bequeathed the present Stevens-Coolidge Place to The Trustees of Reservations in 1962. It was her wish that the property be preserved for the enjoyment of her community as an example of New England's early heritage and close relation to the land.

"Her generosity, her thoughtfulness, and her vision of the community's future needs as it grew and expanded, deserve enormous respect and consideration. This kind of philanthropy benefits every resident, not only of North Andover, but of the Commonwealth, by preserving for our fulfillment and enjoyment, natural and historic areas of interest and significance without immediate cost to the community.

"It is our hope that the willing concern for the future of our environment, so beautifuly exemplified by Mrs. Coolidge's gift, will be encouraged to continue. There may well be others of similar mind and property who are watching these events with justifiable concern.

"Public parkland today is under enormous pressure, and nowhere is this more evident than in the urban and suburban areas where it is most needed. If we are to maintain the quality of our communities, and defend the very reason we chose to live in them in the first place, we must resist this erosion. The amount of land we have is obviously limited. It grows more precious day by day. How we use it, therefore, must deserve the most careful consideration. For once its naturalness is destroyed, it can never be replaced...."

Abbott's statement was followed by applause and later by a vote. It showed 772 opposed, 154 in favor — a margin of five to one against the taking.

Happily, somewhat later, a high school was constructed on a site donated for the purpose and far better suited to its location.

The question of an eminent domain taking surfaced again in 1989, as the South Essex Sewerage District, which serves the North Shore cities of Salem and Beverly as well as Danvers, Peabody and Marblehead, selected Great Misery Island as a possible site for a long-discussed regional sewer treatment facility.

Once again, The Trustees of Reservations, led by Director Frederic Winthrop, Jr., mobilized its resources to oppose the proposal and to urge the consideration of other more suitable sites also on the list and not already dedicated as public park land.

Scores of members of The Trustees rallied at a hearing on the project in Salem. Many spoke against it. In a public appeal, more than $33,850 was raised to meet the costs of legal services needed for an environmental defense fund. Finally, after much dialogue, more than a year later, to the relief of all, Great Misery Island was removed from the list of prospective sites for a sewage treatment plant.

The Trustees of Reservations still supports efforts to site the plant, much needed to improve the quality of water both in Salem Bay and in surrounding harbors, but not at the expense of publicly-dedicated open space.

5

Mashpee River: the Ironic Consequences of a Tribal Suit

From its source at Mashpee-Wakeby Ponds, the Mashpee River, some four miles in length, runs into Poponesset Bay bordering Nantucket Sound on the south shore of Cape Cod.

Some 242 acres in all, Mashpee River Reservation preserves a major portion of the watershed of the upper reaches of the river including some three miles of river frontage. The Trustees of Reservations acquired the property in 1959, the gift of Boston attorney John W. "Mike" Farley.

Mashpee River flows through a region which is, for the most part, wooded, a quiet bower far from the busy towns and high-ways of the Cape. The principal trees are pitch pine, red maple, black oak and American holly. The forest cover comes down to the banks of the river on both sides for its first two miles, its green canopy shading the water course below.

South of Route 28, marshy areas on the sides of the river begin to hold back the forest, the stream widens, and the river corridor opens up from here to its mouth at Poponesset Bay. Here, too, the river is tidal and thus more brackish or saline. Observations show that 19 species of birds nest along the river with more than 100 varieties of bird life observed there during migration.

Mashpee River is still one of the largest and finest trout streams on the Cape, and records kept for more than 100 years show that it is an outstanding source of "salters" or sea-run brook trout. Its relatively undeveloped banks, lack of dams and other obstructions, as well as the excellent quality of its waters and natural spawning areas, make it an ideal habitat for trout.

In the upper reaches, where the river curves to form natural pools, small logs were anchored to the bank years ago to provide shelter for trout, creating what fishermen in those days called "hides." Some are still visible today.

Because of their size (larger than the average native brook trout), salters have long interested anglers as a game fish. Mike Farley, an ardent fisherman and member of the Mashpee River Trout Club, carefully noted the daily catch of trout from 1915 to 1958. His reports are also a social history of a fisherman's life on the river in simpler, less hectic times. He wrote the diary entry below on Sunday, June 9, 1929.

"Started about 7:00 in canoe, not fishing until 'Best' hide. There B [a friend] took one 1 1/4 with fly. Then did not fish until the 'Lowest' hide, where JWF [John W. Farley] took one 1 3/8 and one 1 1/4 with bait. Nothing at Lagoon, Amos, or estuary, which we fished down to Mashpee Neck. Fish seemed to have moved up with the stream.

"After lunch and a short loaf, we went up to a little below Asher's [where a ford now exists to cross the river]. B fished with a short leader, split shot and Parmacheenee. He caught 3 fair fish, 1 lb., 3/4 and 3/8. F [Farley] following with bait and only fishing a few places, but got three good fish, 1 5/8, 1 1/2, 1 1/2.

"After tea, B started at wire and finished to hide below Camp where he took one beautiful 2 1/4 lb. fish, having degenerated to using bait.

"Then dinner — cocktails, caviar, broiled trout, asparagus, toast, ale, [and] demi-tasse." Those were, indeed, the good old days.

Mashpee River no longer produces trout of the size which Mike Farley used to catch but it is still a special place, and much the same today as when Mr. Farley described it so lyrically decades ago. "It is in this more confined stretch of the stream," he wrote, "that its magic is most potent. Here the early shad bush makes a white border along the water. Later the high bush blueberries and then the wild azalea take its place. When the leaves come fully out, the stream on sunny days is a patchwork of glistening water and deep shade. Late in June or early July, the sweet pepper bush and swamp azalea brighten up the green mosses and fill the air with perfume.

"Through all this the brook runs, rather rapid, very crooked, a pool at every corner; deep, fast water under the bushes, making

Canoeist enjoys the shallow waters of the Mashpee River dappled with sunlight and deep shade on a sunny spring day.

pools under the banks and around old tree trunks, and then
straightening out again into rapids. Its bottom is a clean, yellow
sand, and except in the deeper, still pools, where it seems quite
black, this gives the stream a golden color, even on dark days,
while on bright days, it goes from flashing yellow in the sun, to
purples and oranges in the shadows.

"Often as we are fishing, especially if it be towards evening,
when the thrushes begin their bell-like calling, we meet a run of
herring that has come in with the tide. . . heron come to the stream
to feed on herring [and] we catch a glimpse of them sitting in a
tree or along the bank, and they add to the variety of the scene
and complete the feeling of remoteness. . . ."

By 1976, The Trustees of Reservations had initiated a major
program to protect the unique resources of the Mashpee River. A
partnership had been formed with the Town of Mashpee's Board
of Selectmen, Planning Board, Board of Assessors, and Conservation Commission as well as with the U.S. Soil Conservation
Service and the Massachusetts Division of Fisheries & Wildlife.
The goal was to preserve the "entire river corridor."

A special Mashpee River Preservation Committee was established and community representatives discussed the need for a
moratorium on development along the river until a plan for its
protection could be completed. Standing Committee member
Marion F. Thornton, meanwhile, a member of the committee, was
busy in the registry of deeds as a part of the planning process,
collecting information about properties within the watershed.

Of immediate interest, however, was the acquisition and
protection of some 350 acres still in private hands bordering
Mashpee River Reservation downstream and including more than
a mile of frontage on both sides of the river. Thanks to the continuing efforts of The Trustees of Reservations, the Massachusetts
Division of Fisheries & Wildlife had expressed "keen interest" in
the property.

*Standing Committee member
Marion F. Thornton*

Following discussions with the owner, who was anxious to
the see the stream protected, Division representatives reached
agreement on a less-than-market-value or "bargain sale" price for
the land of $550,000. A purchase and sales agreement was to be
prepared and signed by both parties within a few days. It was a
major step towards the protection of a remarkable resource.
Unfortunately, however, other issues were also brewing.

Before a P&S agreement could be drafted to seal the sale, the
Mashpee Wampanoag Indian Tribal Council, claiming to represent all Mashpee Indians as the "duly constituted tribal body,"
filed suit in U.S. District Court, Boston, to gain possession "of just
about all the land in Mashpee." Included were the 350 acres about
to be purchased by Fisheries & Wildlife for preservation purposes.

A news article in the *Falmouth Enterprise* on August 27, 1976,
told the rest of the story. "The Indians" it reported, "rest their

case on a U.S. Act of 1790, which confirms the right of tribes to their lands and says none of these lands can be alienated without the express consent of Congress.

"Mashpee's Indians say their land was taken from them without consent of Congress when the Commonwealth 'unilaterally' declared Mashpee to be a town in 1870. They charge that the result of this action. . . is that nearly all of the land in Mashpee is now held unlawfully by non-natives.

"The suit that was filed in Boston yesterday was authorized by the Mashpee Wampanoag Indian Tribal Council. The resolution soberly declares that the tribal government is the rightful government of Mashpee" and that it is the "intention of the Indians of Mashpee to halt 'indiscriminate development' and to preserve the land in its natural character and beauty."

Ironically, however, the suit derailed a major effort to do just that, for with the title to 350 acres of riverside land now confused by the Wampanoag's suit, the Commonwealth was forced to put its plans to purchase the property on hold.

All of those who had labored so hard to see their dream come true were in a state of shock. "It was the biggest disappointment of my professional career," says Gordon Abbott, Jr., Director of The Trustees of Reservations. Floyd Richardson, Chief of Wildlife Lands for the Massachusetts Division of Fisheries & Wildlife, wrote the owner sympathetically: "It is, indeed, [a] sad commentary, when a person like yourself with philanthropic ideals is denied the right to exercise those beliefs. . . ."

The Trustees of Reservations, meanwhile, as a landowner, became one of 123 defendents in the suit filed by the Mashpee Wampanoag Indian Tribal Council. The class action case, entitled *Mashpee Tribe vs. New Seabury Corporation et al*, also involved 135-acre Lowell Holly Reservation acquired in 1942 as a bequest of Abbott Lawrence Lowell, former President of Harvard University.

At issue in the case first was the question of whether Mashpee's Wampanoag Indians constituted a tribe and were thus able to bring action to recover the lands they claimed under the Indian Nonintercourse Act of 1790. After 5,000 pages of testimony, more than 1,000 exhibits, 52 witnesses and 37 days of legal proceedings in Federal District Court, Boston, the jury of nine men and five women delivered its verdict.

It determined that the Wampanoag Indians of Mashpee did not fulfill the legal definition of a tribe. The court, therefore, in January 1978, granted the defendants' motion to dismiss the suit.

Eight years later, in 1986, still anxious to protect the scenic and environmental values of the Mashpee River corridor, the Town of Mashpee, with the assistance of a state open space grant, purchased the same 350 acres of land mentioned above. Its cost: four and one-half million dollars.

Wesley T. Ward, Deputy Director for Land Conservation for The Trustees of Reservations, and Regional Supervisor Thomas H. Foster helped community officials organize the appeal for public funds. Later, The Trustees was delighted to support the Town of Mashpee's efforts to acquire additional land along the Mashpee River at Canaway Cove with a loan from its Revolving Fund for Land Conservation.

6

Chesterwood: Finally, a Happy Ending

Sculptor Daniel Chester French, one of the great figures of the renaissance in American art during the late nineteenth century, spent the summer months at his studio in Stockbridge. Based in Manhattan for six months of the year, he sought relief from the heat in the cool hills of Berkshire County. There he traveled with his family and there at "Chesterwood" (named for his grandfather's house in Chester, New Hampshire) he created many of his great masterpieces.

French began his meteoric rise to national prominence at the age of only 24 with his statue of "The Minute Man" in Concord. But he is probably best known for his monumental presentation of the seated figure of Abraham Lincoln at the Lincoln Memorial in Washington. His other works include the statue of John Harvard in the Yard at Cambridge; an equestrian statue of George Washington for the Place d'Iena in Paris; and the sculpture "Memory," in marble, at the Metropolitan Museum in New York City.

French, who died in 1931 at the age of 81, left Chesterwood to his daughter, Mrs. William Penn Cresson, who in 1955 gave the property to The Trustees of Reservations. Its centerpiece, of course, was the sculptor's studio.

Built in 1898 from plans by Henry Bacon, architect of the Lincoln Memorial, it was filled with plaster models of his statues, casts and a unique collection of many of his smaller pieces as well. An unusual feature of the studio building was a railroad track upon which a statue could be rolled out-of-doors to be seen under natural light.

It was the view from the property which attracted French to it in the first place — a sweeping prospect of the entire valley looking out over Monument Mountain to the far-off ridge of the Taconics. It was the best "dry view," French said, that he had ever seen.

Charles S. Bird, then Chairman of the Standing Committee, announced the acquisition of Chesterwood at the annual meeting of the corporation in 1955. Quoting Walter Prichard Eaton he declared, "This gift constitutes a memorial of great artistic interest and natural beauty which will bring visitors closer to one of the most beloved artists of all time." The gift, Bird reported, was accompanied by "an ample endowment." Sadly, however, this was not to be the case.

Peggy Cresson, a fiery and fascinating person, was very much a part of summer life and the social scene in Stockbridge. A great friend of Mabel Choate's and of other Berkshire luminaries, she began conversations about preserving Chesterwood in 1953 with Laurence Fletcher, then Secretary of The Trustees of Reservations.

She had originally suggested a gift of the property to the American Academy in Rome, but in those days when the Cold War was beginning to chill world relationships, Fletcher was fearful, like many others, that going international might establish "a hot-bed for Communists in lovely Stockbridge. " His concerns apparently changed her mind.

After much discussion and with support from major figures on the Standing Committee, it was agreed that The Trustees of Reservations would acquire the studio and 18 acres of land; that Mrs. Cresson would contribute $3,000 a year to help maintain the property; that she would sell her own cottage, "Dormouse," and move into the residence at Chesterwood retaining a life estate upon the house which, with an additional 50 acres of land, would then become a part of the Daniel Chester French Memorial Reservation. Ultimately, upon her death, her will would provide the site with a permanent endowment.

The first few years were a great success. Chesterwood welcomed some 2,500 people each season, many from Europe and the Far East. Scores of school children visited the studio as well. The barn had been adapted for use as an exhibition gallery and gate receipts totaled an average of some $1,400 a year. But the need for maintenance soon began. The barn roof was replaced at a cost of $1,045 and other repairs were identified as necessary on both the barn and on the studio.

To meet rising expenses, it was agreed to establish a new organization — the *Friends of Chesterwood* — which could appeal for contributions annually. One year, some $1,700 was raised, but the property continued to operate at a deficit. Costs were exceeding income at an increasing rate. There were the gardens to maintain as well as three sizable structures, and staff was needed throughout the season to assist visitors at the museum. And although the Standing Committee, faced with deficit budgets itself, had advanced the property $5,000, by 1956 the Local Committee announced that funds were running low and friction began to grow. Stockbridge, at times, seemed a long way from Boston.

Coordinator of Reservations Nathan W. Bates, who had attended a meeting at Chesterwood, reported that "members of the Local Committee felt that The Trustees had a duty to maintain Chesterwood." And in a letter, Peggy Cresson reminded the governing board that she "had promised to give $3,000 a year to help defray expenses as long as The Trustees maintained the property as a memorial to her father."

Bates suggested that The Trustees of Reservations' budget was for operating expenses only, with no allowance for major repairs and, at the urging of the Local Committee, it was agreed to initiate a campaign for funds to help repair and restore both the residence and the studio.

In March 1957, the Local Committee mailed 717 letters as a part of a special appeal. In August, it was reported that a total of only $375 was received from 14 subscribers. The plight of Chesterwood was desperate. Among the alternatives discussed by The Trustees was an effort to persuade Mrs. Cresson to change her will, and the possibility of "closing the studio for the balance of the year."

It was also agreed, according to the minutes of the Standing Committee, that Secretary Fletcher "inform Mrs. Cresson that The Trustees of Reservations cannot afford further deficits and that in the spring, economies must be started which will bring about a balanced budget."

By 1961, The Trustees of Reservations had transferred $10,000 from its general funds to meet the increasing needs of Chesterwood and frustrations on both sides were at an all-time high. It was obvious that Mrs. Cresson's annual contribution was not enough to meet even operating expenses and that funds for major repairs, following a failed appeal, could not be raised locally. Something had to be done.

As was often the case, Standing Committee Chairman Charles E. "Monk" Mason, ambassador plenipotentiary for The Trustees of Reservations, was asked to meet with Mrs. Cresson to discuss the future of Chesterwood. Over tea in Washington at Mrs. Cresson's winter residence, the two got nowhere. Suddenly, Mason declared in frustration, "Well, maybe we ought to give it back to you." "Maybe I ought to take it back," Mrs. Cresson replied. And that was exactly what happened.

A bill was filed (House 3821) which authorized The Trustees of Reservations to "execute and deliver a deed covering the Studio and its contents together with approximately 68 acres, to the Daniel Chester French Foundation, upon payment to The Trustees of Reservations of the deficit incurred by Chesterwood up to and including the date of delivery of said deed."

The transfer was completed in November 1962. The new foundation was obligated under the law to administer

Chesterwood for the benefit of the public substantially as it had been by The Trustees of Reservations. Peggy Cresson continued to retain a life interest in the residence and the French Foundation began a series of payments to reimburse The Trustees for its loan of $10,000.

It was too bad for everyone that the arrangement failed to work out. Essentially, both sides were to blame. From the very beginning there was a failure to address fully and completely the issues involved prior to acquisition. The result was a continuing series of expectations which were either difficult or impossible to resolve. Despite the best intent of all parties, the cost of maintaining the property, and most especially the residence, simply did not match its ability to raise income.

To make matters worse, The Trustees of Reservations had suffered a number of annual operating deficits. In 1957, the deficit totaled $17,154; in 1959, it amounted to $9,721; and in 1961, $7,778. Taking more out of principal was, understandably, out of the question.

Of course, a number of properties have been accepted without adequate endowment because their scenic, historic or environmental values have been outstanding and because it was unthinkable that they should not be preserved. Somehow, in each case, however, The Trustees of Reservations has always been able to acquire grants and contributions, both locally and elsewhere, to meet their needs. But this was not to be so with Chesterwood.

The ending, however, is a happy one. For in 1973, upon Mrs. Cresson's death, Chesterwood became a property of The National Trust for Historic Preservation. As expected, it received a bequest for endowment purposes of some $400,000. Today, this has increased to $700,000. Now also, with aggressive local management, the Friends of Chesterwood and the Daniel Chester French Society raise some $40,000 a year.

But none of this is enough to enable the property to break even. Paul W. Ivory, administrator of the site for two decades now, reports that The National Trust still contributes as much as $65,000 a year to keep Chesterwood going. "We are on our way to self-sufficiency, though," Ivory reports, as contributions increase annually.

Other properties de-accessioned by The Trustees throughout its history include Virginia Woods, now a part of the park system of the Metropolitan District Commission; Goodwill Park, owned by the Town of Falmouth as a part of its supply of drinking water; Magnolia Shore, owned by the City of Gloucester; and Pamet River, now a property of the Truro Land Trust, which itself was founded with assistance from The Trustees of Reservations. Although it is the policy of The Trustees to accept only properties which meet its standards and satisfy its purposes, and to hold them as a fiduciary, it realizes that under certain circumstances, as time passes and conditions change, another organization of similar purposes may be able to accomplish better the objectives of preservation.

9

Governance

1

By-Laws: How the Organization Works

By-laws may seem dry and dull, but they form the framework and define the boundaries within which an organization functions. Second only to the charter, do they set the course for action. They are, in effect, the rules by which the game is played.

It was, of course, Charles Eliot himself who drafted the by-laws of The Trustees of Reservations. The fact that their general format has been little changed for a century is a ready testimonial to their effectiveness.

Their genius, as former President and Chairman Laurence M. Channing once declared, lies in their essential simplicity which allows the governing board maximum flexibility. They are different from those of many other organizations in that they do not provide for participation in the governance of the charity by "members" or "contributors." Instead, the ultimate responsibility for the conduct and activities of The Trustees of Reservations is placed in the hands of "members of the corporation," who function much like stockholders. Each is elected for a term of three years. Originally 15, they now may number up to 400.

The responsibility for nominating new members of the corporation belongs to the Standing Committee. And, as the Standing Committee (or governing board) is itself elected by members of the corporation, The Trustees of Reservations is, like many charities, self-perpetuating. Thus its stability, continuing reputation and success is dependent upon its ability to attract and elect people of like conscience and commitment through the years. And, as the record clearly shows, it has done so.

The nominating process seeks not only to promote from within, reaching out for promising members of the corporation, local and regional committees and the Advisory Council, but also from without, searching for candidates who have served local land trusts or other environmental organizations with energy and distinction. Ann W. Brewer of Manchester, for example, a vice president in the early 1980s, was a former chairman of the Friends of Misery Islands Reservation, as well as a veteran of the Standing Committee and of the Advisory Council, while Boston attorney Preston H. "Sandy" Saunders, Chairman of the Standing Committee from 1982 to 1987, came to The Trustees of Reservations after a term as President of the Appalachian Mountain Club, an office to which he was re-elected in 1992.

Chairman Preston H. "Sandy" Saunders

No two members of the governing board have been more active with the Nominating Committee in recent years than the husband and wife team of Mr. and Mrs. Henry R. Guild, Jr., whose family's two-generation involvement with The Trustees of Reservations (Harry Guild's father was elected a member of the Standing Committee in 1959) and broad acquaintance with the Boston scene have helped enlist a wide number of wonderful men and women, among them, the former Chairman of the Standing Committee, Herbert W. Vaughan.

Initially, the duties of the president were conceived to be primarily ceremonial. Indeed, according to the by-laws, the only responsibility of the office is to preside at annual meetings. This may have been because it was contemplated that presidents would be major figures, chosen to add luster and credibility to a then fledgling organization, but, as such, busy people with little time to get involved in a personal way.

This appeared to be the case at least with Senator George F. Hoar, who served as president from 1891 to 1904, and with Charles William Eliot, who held the office for 21 years from 1905 to 1926, overlapping in part with his presidency of Harvard (although President Eliot is said never to have missed an Annual Meeting). With the election of George Wigglesworth in 1927, however, the organization had, for the first time, a president who could be active and helpful in many other ways as well. At the time of his election, Wigglesworth had served as treasurer for 29 years, from 1891 to 1920.

The leader of The Trustees of Reservations was, and still is, the chairman of the Standing Committee, who presides over the governing body and who, by force of intellect and personality, maintains the interest and the momentum of the board which enables it to function successfully. The chairman and the director make up the organization's top management team.

Ann W. Brewer, Vice President of The Trustees of Reservations

Fifteen chairmen have served The Trustees in its century of existence. Four have also served as president; they are: Charles S. Rackemann, chairman from 1926 to 1933; Charles E. Mason, Jr., chairman from 1958 to 1965; Laurence M. Channing, chairman from 1965 to 1967; and John M. Woolsey, Jr., chairman from 1967 to 1969.

Chairmen have been chosen from nearly every branch of the governing board. Augustus P. Loring, chairman from 1969 to 1975, had served as treasurer; Thomas L. P. O'Donnell, chairman from 1975 to 1976, was a vice president; Theodore Chase, chairman from 1975 to 1981, was chosen from the Advisory Council; Sandy Saunders had served as secretary, and chairman Herbert W. Vaughan, elected in 1988, like Saunders a distinguished Boston attorney, was a member of the Standing Committee.

The average length of service for chairmen of the Standing Committee has been just more than six years. Two men, however, each served for 23 years. They are Henry P. Walcott, Chairman from 1903 to 1926, and Charles S. Bird, Chairman from 1933 to 1956.

Election to the presidency has generally been considered a reward for faithful and meritorious service to the organization, and presidents, too, have come from other offices than chairman. Judge Robert Walcott, who followed Charles Rackemann as president and served from 1938 to 1956, was a former member of the Standing Committee. Architect William Roger Greeley, president from 1957 to 1959, had a been a vice president of the corporation. Charles R. Strickland, another architect, who served as president from 1965 to 1970, had been a member of the Standing Committee and of the Advisory Council.

Henry R. Guild, Jr., served for many years as Secretary of The Trustees before his election as President.

David C. Crockett, who was elected president in 1980, joined the Standing Committee initially in 1954 and subsequently served in every capacity available to volunteers, including more than two decades as president of the Castle Hill Foundation and as a member of the local committee for the Crane Reservation. Henry R. Guild, Jr., President from 1983 to 1989, had been secretary of The Trustees for 13 years, from 1967 to 1980. And Hall J. Peterson, who serves as president today, was a vice president when he was elected in 1990. Earlier, he had been a member of the Standing Committee and of the Central Regional Committee.

The by-laws provide the Standing Committee with all the "executive powers of the organization," charging it with the responsibility for the acquisition and management of properties, all money matters, and personnel, especially the appointment of the director. Members may be elected for two three-year terms, whereupon, if still active and interested, they may descend to the Advisory Council, step sideways to another office or after a year's hiatus, be re-elected to the Standing Committee. Augustus P. Loring, for example, a mainstay of The Trustees for more than 30 years, was considered so valuable a member of the Executive Committee that he was asked to serve as treasurer for three terms (1954 to 1961, 1968, and from 1981 to 1982) in between his election as chairman and his service on the Standing Committee and the Advisory Council.

Standing Committee member Gale R. Guild, leader of many successful Annual Appeals

Others, such as Thomas L. P. O'Donnell, who, as a busy
attorney was able to serve for only a year as Chairman, have
followed the pattern. O'Donnell, for example, has been a member
of the Standing Committee and the Advisory Council, has served
as a Vice President and as an officer and board member of the
Massachusetts Farm and Conservation Lands Trust for more than
21 years. Again, the system is flexible enough, as Channing said,
to enable the organization to retain those senior people who have
meant so much to its success, while still making essential room for
new faces, many of whom themselves will become the senior
board members of the future.

The Standing Committee now meets seven times each year;
the Executive Committee once a month, making for a well-
informed and much involved governing board, which, despite the
necessary delegation of administrative matters to what is now a
sizable professional staff, is still the major force in determining the
organization's policies and procedures.

The Advisory Council was established in 1955, to provide
broader opportunities for representation and participation. It
meets with the Standing Committee but does not have authority
to vote. A farm team for future members of the governing board,
it has also proved invaluable as a way to keep board members
who have served their terms as active and involved as ever.
Today, the Advisory Council includes as many as 52 members, far
outnumbering the Standing Committee of 20 men and women.

Meetings of the boards take place in Boston at the downtown
Harvard Club over luncheon on the third Wednesday of every

*Architect Charles R.
Strickland, President from
1965 to 1970*

*President William Roger
Greeley confers with former
officers of The Trustees of
Reservations in the late 1950s.
From left, Robert Walcott,
President Greeley, Charles S.
Bird and Francis E.
Frothingham.*

month. They are busy and cheerful affairs, rarely attended by less
than 45 people including key members of the professional staff.
The record of attendance is outstanding. Many board members,
rightfully chosen with an eye to geography as well as other
attributes, travel by car, by train and by boat each month to be
present. From Berkshire and Franklin counties, "regulars" have
included Edith B. Hibbard, J. Graham Parsons, F. Sydney Smithers
IV, Joseph P. Spang III and Rush Taggart; from Worcester: Wyatt
Garfield, Richard Prouty and Hall J. Peterson; and from Martha's
Vineyard and Nantucket, Edith W. Potter, and Nancy A. Claflin,
Flora Epstein, and Jane C. Saltonstall.

The challenge for the Chairman and the Director is to complete the business of the meeting by 2 p.m, hearing all points of
view, acting on every agenda item and providing time to present
issues of an informational nature. Continued high attendance
through the years attests to the fact that the meetings are interesting and fun, as well to the faithfulness and commitment of every
member.

Admittedly, there have been conversations about the ability to
conduct the business of the charity effectively with so many
involved at each monthly meeting. The Executive Committee,
however, with its smaller size, (its membership includes the
officers and the chairman) offers easy opportunities for detailed
discussions. And with analyses of the issues usually completed
by the appropriate Local Committee, Regional Committee, or
special subcommittee of the board (and, in some cases, by all
three), questions of policy can be clarified and simplified before

*Standing Committee chairmen
during the more than 17-year
tenure of Director Gordon
Abbott, Jr. From left, Preston
H. Saunders, Augustus P.
Loring, Abbott, Theodore
Chase, and John M. Woolsey,
Jr. Missing from the photo is
Thomas L.P. O'Donnell.*

they reach the Standing Committee, thus shortening the time needed to come to a decision. The joy of the larger meetings is that they provide a spirited and congenial forum for every member of the governing board who wishes to become involved.

The process of institutional management can be cumbersome. Its success depends upon reaching an intelligent consensus and this means, by necessity, the participation of an often large number of people. Leadership is critical, as is the ability to clarify issues, to rationalize them and to present them effectively. A key ingredient in the process is, as mentioned above, the committee or subcommittee, a small group composed of both volunteers and members of the professional staff, which can dissect a problem, research alternatives and recommend to the governing board solutions which are in keeping with the character and the mission of the organization. Fuel for the process (hopefully of high octane) must be provided by the Chairman of the Standing Committee and by the Director.

The Trustees of Reservations has been fortunate. Volunteers and staff members work well together and, frankly, find each others' company both stimulating and enjoyable.

2

The Mid-1950s: the Old Guard Retires

Although the institutional structure of The Trustees of Reservations has served it well in the last three decades, there was a time in the mid-1950s when things were different. Without specific terms and some limits on length of service, the Chairman of the Standing Committee, then Charles S. Bird, had been in office for 23 years and the President, Robert Wolcott, for 18.

Executive Secretary Laurence B. Fletcher had held his position for nearly three decades. Moreover, a series of annual operating deficits had been a nagging problem. It was decided by the Standing Committee that after more than 60 years, the structure of The Trustees of Reservations should be examined and brought up to date as necessary and appropriate.

A study group, the Committee on Nominations and Organization, was appointed in early 1955. Its members clearly represented the younger generation. David C. Crockett of Ipswich was named Chairman. Serving with him were Augustus P. Loring of Beverly, Maurice M. Osborne of Ipswich and John M. Woolsey, Jr., of Cambridge and Petersham. In October, committee members presented their report. It minced no words.

Although the number of properties acquired by The Trustees had increased significantly in the past 26 years, it declared, "financial support has not grown proportionately. The annual membership appeal brings inadequate returns, and the total of general purpose endowment funds has been increased by less than 15 percent (from $47,500 in 1929 to $54,515 in 1955)."

With "no assurance that conditions will improve appreciably in the future," the committee recommended a major program of decentralization. They proposed that much of the management responsibility for the organization's then 28 properties be transferred from the head office to Local Committees. They also recommended that six Regional Committees be appointed; that the Chairmen of each be a member of the Standing Committee; and that there be a Committee on Budget and a Committee on Public Relations "to promote a better understanding of the purposes of The Trustees of Reservations" and to help raise urgently needed operating funds.

The report also dealt directly with the question of longevity in office. Again, the committee went to the heart of the matter. To "introduce new blood into positions of prime responsibility. . . and to place the direct responsibility for operation of The Trustees' affairs on younger shoulders while still making available the experience and counsel of those who have served faithfully and wisely in office over the years," it urged that the Standing Committee be increased from 11 to 13 members, and it recommended that no Standing Committee member be able to serve more than two three-year terms without "an interval of one year out of office." The President and the Treasurer were excepted.

It was also suggested that an Advisory Council be established which would meet each month with the Standing Committee to provide opportunities for retiring officers and members of the Standing Committee to serve as "elder statesmen" for the benefit and advancement of the organization.

Finally, the report addressed the matter of Laurence Fletcher's impending retirement: ". . . time does not stand still," it observed, "and while the Secretary/Executive-Director has faithfully served The Trustees to [its] very great advantage during the past 25 years or more, he would be the last to say that he is prepared to do so for the next 25 years — nor would he make any indefinite promises as to an unforeseeable future! The fact is that he has earned relief from the arduous duties of office as The Trustees' executive officer. . . ."

Without administrative responsibilities, Fletcher stayed on as Secretary of the board, the last professional to do so, until his death in 1959. As Executive Director, the Standing Committee chose an able and well-respected friend, Arthur T. Lyman, whose term as State Commissioner of Natural Resources had just ended.

Lyman remained about a year until he entered public service again as Commissioner of Corrections. The Standing Committee then appointed Loring Conant Executive Secretary, a post he held until his retirement in 1968.

The Report of the Committee on Nominations and Organization was adopted by the Standing Committee on October 11, 1955. It put the younger generation firmly at the helm.

Robert Wolcott died in office in 1956 and was succeeded as President by William Roger Greeley. Charles Bird, who retired that same year, was presented with a scroll commemorating his years of service, as well as an antique sun dial for his garden at a special ceremony at the Annual Meeting. He was succeeded as Chairman by Maurice Osborne.

3

Character and Commitment

Few would disagree that with minor modifications, the institutional structure of The Trustees of Reservations has worked well since its beginnings in 1891. But it has been the quality and caliber of the people who have been involved in its activities which have made the organization what it is today. It is their values and their principles which have given it its rock-solid reputation for integrity and enabled it to serve the public so effectively for the first century of its existence.

They have been men and women of extraordinary character and commitment. Some have had outstanding records of public service, prior to or after their association with The Trustees as members of its governing board. These include, Charles William Eliot, of course, President of Harvard from 1869 to 1909 and President of The Trustees from 1905 to 1926; Herbert Parker, President from 1933 to 1938, who, it is said, as Attorney General for the Commonwealth, engineered the end of the Boston Police Strike which catapulted Calvin Coolidge into the vice presidency; Elliot L. Richardson, former U. S. Attorney for Massachusetts, who later served as Secretary of Health, Education and Welfare, of Defense, and of Commerce as well as U. S. Attorney General; Francis W. Sargent, former State Commissioner of Natural Resources, who served the Commonwealth as Governor from 1969 to 1975; Francis W. Hatch who, as a State Representative, was House Minority Leader for many years;

Also, J. Graham Parsons, a career diplomat who served as U.S. Ambassador to Laos and to Sweden and later became Assistant

Herbert Parker, President from 1933 to 1938

*Ambassador J. Graham
Parsons of Stockbridge was an
active member of the Standing
Committee for many years.*

Secretary of State for Far Eastern Affairs and for the first SALT talks; James Hoyte, former State Secretary of Environmental Affairs; and present Massachusetts Governor William F. Weld, who resigned from the board when he, like Richardson, was appointed U.S. Attorney for the Commonwealth. Finally, Frederic Winthrop, Jr., Director of The Trustees of Reservations today, served two Massachusetts governors, one a Democrat and one a Republican, as Commissioner of Food & Agriculture from 1975 to 1985.

Other members of the Standing Committee and the Advisory Council — lawyers, doctors, architects and landscape architects, educators, authors, scientists, financiers, full-time volunteers, and business men and women — have also won outstanding recognition in their own fields, although none perhaps more distinguished than the Nobel Prize awarded for Medicine in 1990 to Dr. Joseph E. Murray, former Advisory Council member and Chairman of the Local Committee for Cape Poge and Wasque.

Perhaps the least glamorous but among the most important offices of any charitable institution are those held by the Secretary and the Treasurer. Certainly The Trustees of Reservations is no exception. Charles Eliot himself served as Secretary for two years from 1891 to 1893. He was followed by John Woodbury, who held the office for a record three decades from 1894 to 1924. Woodbury also served as the first Secretary of the Metropolitan Park Commission. Others whose time in office exceeded a half-dozen years include Henry M. Channing, Secretary from 1926 to 1936; Laurence Fletcher, Secretary from 1937 to 1958; Arthur H. Phillips, Secretary from 1959 to 1966; and Henry R. Guild, Jr., Secretary from 1967 to 1979.

In the last three decades, the Secretary's lot has not always been a happy one, thanks to the all but surgical precision employed to address the minutes of each Standing Committee meeting by the man who has been called the "conscience" of The Trustees of Reservations, the late Charles W. Eliot II. Eliot, who served as Secretary himself from 1925 to 1926, for years examined the minutes, habitually and minutely, and invariably proposed a correction here, or a change in wording there, some of a substantive nature. For years the chair's calls for approval of the minutes was often directly addressed to Eliot, who was seldom without a response. Secretaries, however, for the most part, learned to maintain a sense of humor and perspective (although in the old days one did complain that his blood pressure was affected), realizing that Eliot's remarks were not only often useful, but were made with a genuine concern for the welfare of the organization as a whole.

Since its establishment in 1891, there have been but 10 Treasurers of The Trustees of Reservations. George Wigglesworth served for 29 years, from 1891 until 1920; John Ames for 18, from 1921 to 1939; Allan Forbes for nine, 1940 to 1949; Francis E. Frothingham for five, 1949 to 1954 (an investment banker and utilities expert, he died in office at age 83); and Augustus P. Loring for six, 1954 to 1961, with an extra year between Richard L. Frothingham's two terms of five and six years each, 1962 to 1967, and 1969 to 1974.

H. Gilman Nichols, former president of Boston's Fiduciary Trust Company, followed Frothingham, serving from 1975 to 1987. He in turn was followed by Norton Q. Sloan, now an executive vice president of State Street Bank, who held the office from 1981 to 1987. Peter C. Thompson, President of David L. Babson, & Co., Inc., investment counsellors, is Treasurer of the organization today.

Richard Frothingham, a nephew of Francis, must be credited with modernizing the financial activities of The Trustees of Reservations. A former Senior Vice President and Chairman of the Trust Committee of the New England Merchants National Bank, Frothingham loved the out-of-doors. He had summer places both in the Adirondacks and in southern New Hampshire, and upon retirement, devoted a major portion of his time to The Trustees, working directly on the organization's finances with Director Gordon Abbott, Jr.

Richard L. Frothingham, a member of the Standing Committee and Treasurer of The Trustees for 12 years

With the advice of auditor Cortland B. Bacall, the two established a Controller's Office at General Headquarters and moved bookkeeping and cash management from a contract arrangement with the Merchants Bank in Boston to new offices at the Pierce House in Milton. Again with Bacall's assistance, they also devised new systems of budgeting and accounting, most of which are still in place today. Initially, operating accounts were handled manually, but were put on computer in the early 1980s. By 1970, all of the organization's finances, both revenue and costs (with the exception of its endowment portfolio), were managed by a professional team at General Headquarters.

Treasurers of The Trustees of Reservations have also traditionally served as Chairmen of the organization's Investment Committee. During Richard Frothingham's era, endowments were pooled for management purposes (with the exception of The Mission House and Naumkeag, kept separate at Miss Choate's request, and the Budd Trusts, which are managed elsewhere) with income being assigned and allocated to appropriate properties and accounts according to the terms of the gift or devise. In recent years, as assets increased, Director Frederic Winthrop, Jr., appointed a Deputy Director for Finance and Administration. John Coleman, a graduate of Bryant College and an accounting specialist, came to The Trustees of Reservations with experience as the chief financial officer for several small businesses in the fields of educational development and computer programing. He was preceded by Controller Andrea T. Plate, who, with an MBA from Boston University, coordinated and directed The Trustees' move to computer bookkeeping, and by Charles T. Tacito, who was apppointed the organization's first Controller in 1970.

4

A Vital Asset: Special Skills, Generously Contributed

Long-time member of the Standing Committee Roland B. Greeley

Robert Livermore, Jr., member of the Standing Committee and Trustee of the Massachusetts Farm and Conservation Lands Trust

As important as the officers, in their own way, are those other individual members of the Standing Committee and of the Advisory Council who have so generously contributed their time and their special skills to help The Trustees of Reservations function more effectively.

Through the years there have been many: architects such as Daniel J. Coolidge, William R. Greeley, George R. Mathey and Charles S. Strickland; landscape architects Peter Hornbeck, Carol R. Johnson, Sidney N. Shurcliff and Fletcher Steele; planners Charles W. Eliot II and Roland B. Greeley; real estate specialists John M. Kunhardt and Robert Livermore, Jr.; and attorneys Theodore Chase, Thomas L.P. O'Donnell, Carolyn M. Osteen, John M. Woolsey, Jr., John C. Vincent, Jr., Preston H. Saunders and Herbert W. Vaughan.

Included also must be those with curatorial skills: Frances H. Colburn, Frances C. Forbes and Joseph P. Spang III, all members of the Committee on Collections; those with financial acumen: Jane C. Bradley, John P. Chase, John L. Gardner, Frederick S. Moseley III and Ralph B. Vogel, each of whom served on the Investment Committee; and, of course, countless other board members who have pitched in through the years to bring energy and intelligence to whatever decisions The Trustees of Reservations found itself facing.

No commentary on the role and importance of volunteers would be complete without mention of the organization's now Property Committees, and particularly of their chairmen, who have played such a vital part in the continuing management and protection of the reservations they have represented.

These have included Morgan G. Bulkley and John R. Downey, Bartholomew's Cobble; the Reverend Philip H. and Esther Steinmetz, Bear Swamp; John and Rosalie Fiske, Brooks Woodland Preserve; Oliver D. Filley, Edith W. Potter, and Elliot M. Surkin, Cape Poge and Wasque; Nancy A. Claflin, Coskata-

Coatue Wildlife Refuge; Sidney N. Shurcliff and Sheila U. Mathey, Crane; Carl V. Magee and James T. Wetherald, Crowninshield Island; Pamela Weatherbee, Field Farm; Elizabeth B. MacKenzie and Richard A. Waite, Glendale Falls; and Robert C. Hooper, Halibut Point.

Also, Martin B. Person, Jr., Holmes Field; Jane C. Saltonstall, Long Hill; Daniel Prowten, Long Point Wildlife Refuge; Wilfrid Wheeler, Jr., Lowell Holly; Walter D. Howard, Tyringham Cobble; John S. McLennan, McLennan Reservation; Madeline U. Chesney, Eleanor B. Crocker and Mary Waters Shepley, Misery Islands Reservation; Robert K. Wheeler, Monument Mountain; Andrew R. Mack and Rush Taggart, The Mission House; Elizabeth P. Corning, Stephen V. C. Morris and Beverly U. Hallock, Naumkeag; Harriet Davis Minot, Mount Ann Park; and Paul Horovitz, Noanet Woodlands;

Also, Eleanor F. Norris, Norris Reservation; Maudi U. Smithers, Notchview; Charles L. Ward and Jonathan M. Keyes, The Old Manse; Arthur M. Jones and William L. Plante, Old Town Hill; George S. Mumford, Jr., Pegan Hill; Richard R. and Marcia U. Graves, Petticoat Hill; Muriel S. Lewis, Rocky Narrows; Ellis N. Allen, Rocky Woods; Roland B. Hammond, Peter L. Hornbeck and Nancy W. Goss, Stevens-Coolidge Place; Charles C. Ames, Swift River Reservation; Dr. Rustin McIntosh, Douglas and Marion Leach, Tyringham Cobble; Frank T. Haynes and Wolfgang Lowy, Tantiusque; John W. Kimball, Ward Reservation; Thomas B. Williams, Whitney and Thayer Woods; and Samuel Wakeman,

Standing Committee member Ralph B. Vogel, concluding Chairman of The Trustee's first capital program. When it ended in 1986 the campaign had raised more than $8 million.

Officers and members of the Standing Committee at Long Hill. From left, Theodore Chase, Frances H. Colburn, Richard Prouty and David C. Crockett.

Paul C. Reardon, Henry W. Stokes, Laurence B. Stein, Jr., Anne L. Lincoln, and Edward B. Long, World's End.

For their lasting interest in the welfare of their properties, for their cheerful willingness to get involved in everything from the physical management of the land to local politics, and for their wise counsel, The Trustees of Reservations must be forever grateful.

Today, of course, there is no such thing as a typical member of the Standing Committee or of the Advisory Council. Men and women from every corner of the state, they bring a host of different talents and interests to the board. But each of them does share a dedication to the cause for which The Trustees of Reservations was founded and a loyalty to the principles and values which have enabled it to serve the public so effectively for more than one hundred years.

Despite the changes in society which have taken place during its century of existence, The Trustees has managed to retain the important qualities and characteristics given to it by those who served it in earlier eras — its sincere and continuing commitment to its mission, its high standards of performance, its graceful mix of innovation and tradition, its integrity and its rock-solid New England dependability.

Nowhere are these characteristics better described than in a eulogy for Charles S. Rackemann, a former President of The Trustees and, during the 1920s and '30s, a member of its Standing Committee. Rackemann was uniquely Boston as his friend and relative Ellery Sedgwick, editor and publisher of *The Atlantic Monthly* magazine, makes delightfully clear in a wonderful eulogy which appeared on the front page of *The Boston Transcript*, the Brahmin newspaper of the time, shortly after Rackemann's death in 1933.

Extraordinary volunteers and hard-working members of the property committee for Tyringham Cobble, Douglas and Marion Leach

"Massachusetts builds solidly," Sedgwick wrote, "and Charles Rackemann was of the type which has made the tough framework of her endearing character. Customs may change, but principles are unchanging. Thus he thought and thus he lived. Innovation, he was apt to scan with suspicion, if not distrust, and in a generation not incredulous of novelty, he was ever inclined to place the burden of proof on those who make the experiment. Yet he was no narrow-visioned Tory. Charles Rackemann had good reason to trust the old, for the old that he had known was very good. Never for an instant did he forget his boyhood training among the old-fashioned simplicities of Berkshire; and living memories of his own people who had gone before him to show him the way, left upon him an impression which remained bright and radiant through three-quarters of a century to the very day he died.

"His life was undramatic. Duty is not always glamorous and conveyancing, to which he gave a large measure of his professional career, is not the most exciting branch of the law. But his duties as a lawyer, a citizen and a man, demanded an exactitude which was part of his nature, and which in completest measure he was proud to give. No public service found him reluctant. For Belgian Relief (during World War I), for the extension and preservation of public parks, for the liberties bequeathed by the Constitution, he worked with a zeal and fire no one could have supposed could lurk under the modesty and friendly quiet of his demeanor. Many there are who loved him, for his affections were strong; but far beyond the circle of his intimates still radiates the influence of a man whose creed was kindness, prudence, loyalty, and who never faltered on his way."

Such are the kind of people who helped to shape The Trustees of Reservations.

10

Finances and Fundraising

1

From the Beginning: an Understanding of the Need for Funds

With his customary wisdom, Charles Eliot knew in the beginning that without adequate funding, The Trustees of Reservations would be hard pressed to accomplish its mission. Indeed, as he wrote, in part, in the Annual Report of the Standing Committee for 1891, "correspondents, anxious for the rescue of this or that interesting spot or structure, must not be discouraged when they learn that this Board possesses no magic powers. With all the other lovers of scenery. . . they must hasten to imitate those admirers of fine arts who have so liberally endowed the public art museums. Maintenance funds as well as purchase money will be needed. . . ."

By the following year, a constituency had been created that began to respond. More than 158 people and such institutions as the Appalachian Mountain Club contributed $1,859 to endow Virginia Wood, the organization's first property. And an additional 16 provided $1,353 for general purposes. Most subscriptions varied from $5 to $10. There was one gift of $1,000, a significant amount in those early days, which qualified its donor, Miss Ellen Chase, to become a "Founder." Other categories for givers included "Life Associate" and "Contributor."

The focus financially was upon the acquisition of funds for "future care," for the records show that each year a number of properties were refused because money was not available for their maintenance and continued protection. Included were parcels of land in Milton and Cohasset, but perhaps the largest was an expanse of more than 2,000 acres of land in Petersham which, in 1907, became the beginnings of the Harvard Forest.

At the time, Standing Committee members expressed concern about the difficulty of "securing a sufficient fund to provide adequate income for the maintenance of [such a] considerable tract," and recommended that it be acquired by the President and Fellows of Harvard University and operated by the Division of Forestry of the newly-established Graduate School of Applied Science.

The Trustees also experienced much the same kind of frustration in its dealings with historic houses which it was offered regularly in its early years. Again, restoring and maintaining the buildings, "often in a precarious condition of repair," would have only served as a drain upon existing resources, which were already insufficient.

In 1899, however, Miss Helen C. Butler generously gave Monument Mountain to The Trustees of Reservations with an endowment of $2,000. The principal, which was immediately invested in Chicago Terminal Transfer Railroad Company bonds, yielded an income of four percent. It was enough in those days to meet the property's annual operating needs. And time was to prove that endowments which accompanied gifts of land were, indeed, the best way to fund their future.

But while it may have been difficult to find money to maintain prospective properties, The Trustees of Reservations, unlike many land trusts in other states around the region and the nation, was and is spared the need to pay annual real estate taxes by the provisions of its charter. It was a blessing long to be appreciated, although sometimes challenged, even today, by a small minority of members of the state legislature who, anxious for revenue, question the tax-free status of charities everywhere throughout the Commonwealth.

As early as 1898, there was talk about the need for a "working (or general) fund," and the hope was expressed that "some benefactor or benefactors" would provide it. It was a dream that would continue for decades. As time passed and few contributions were forthcoming, Standing Committee members in 1914 agreed to "put the needs of the corporation in the form of an advertisement" in *The Boston Transcript*.

A month later, attorney John Woodbury, secretary of the corporation, wrote in the Annual Report, "it is too soon as yet, and perhaps present conditions are not sufficiently favorable, to expect any tangible results from such an appeal. It is to be hoped, however," he added, "that The Trustees individually will bring the needs of the corporation to the attention of those who are interested in the objects for which this body was created." Meanwhile, the balance sheet showed that the assets of the organization, including cash, totaled $25,168.

To be sure, it was a smaller world in those days. At the turn of the century, Boston's population was just more than one-half

million people. By 1915, the immediate constituency of The
Trustees of Reservations numbered seven members of the Standing Committee; 41 members of the corporation; 12 Founders
(annual gifts of $1,000 or more) and 40 Life Associates (annual
gifts of $100 or more).

Although this handful provided generous support, it seemed
that in the community at large there were priorities other than
open space conservation, a movement which was just beginning.
Museums, educational institutions, hospitals, libraries and the
city's symphony orchestra, were charities whose goals were better
understood and thus were more successful in their quest for
public support.

However, by the end of 1929, despite the legendary collapse
of the stock market, the finances of The Trustees of Reservations
had improved markedly. Restricted funds or reservation endowments, invested wholly in the bonds of America's most substantial
companies, totaled $21,000. The General Purpose Fund, which
amounted to $47,500 in bonds (and included a legacy of $25,000
from the Estate of Arthur F. Estabrook, a former member of the
Corporation), showed an income balance for the year, after
expenses, of $3,862. And, finally, contributions totaled $2,685.

*Frances Fairchild Bryant
(1797-1866) was the wife of
William Cullen Bryant and
grandmother of Minna
Godwin Goddard, who gave
the property to The Trustees of
Reservations. It was to benefit
Frances' health that the poet
restored the Homestead in the
mid-1800s.*

During the same year, the organization acquired the William
Cullen Bryant Homestead in Cummington. Bequest of the poet's
grandaughter, Minna Godwin Goddard, it included with it a
legacy of $10,000 which, with another $10,000 from the estate of
Julia Bryant, daughter of the poet who had died earlier, was to
serve as a very generous and welcome endowment, the largest for
any reservation received to date.

As if to celebrate, The Trustees of Reservations, also in 1929,
hired its first full-time employee, Executive Secretary Laurence B.
Fletcher, who was to make such important contributions to the
growth of the organization in the years that lay ahead. For it was
Fletcher's flair for public relations that expanded public understanding of The Trustees and added a growing number of new
names to its list of supporters.

By 1934, he had established a special Committee on Publicity;
a lecture series illustrated with colored lantern slides which he
estimated was seen by as many as 6,000 people a year; a much-
expanded Annual Report; and annual meetings which featured
an elegant luncheon for as many as 300 members and their guests
at the Hotel Somerset, the Copley-Plaza or the Parker House, as
well as a featured speaker and the always interesting presentation
of The Trustees of Reservations' Conservation Award.

The number of contributors had doubled to 320 by 1935 and
jumped to 455 a year later. The lecture series grew so popular that
it was decided to charge groups $15 for Fletcher to appear. The
word had finally begun to get around.

2

Deficit Budgets and the Courage to Take a Chance

Meanwhile, however, although operating expenses for the Head Office remained easy to control (they amounted to little more than $8,500 a year in 1936 including Fletcher's salary, rent, telephone and travel), expenses in the field were increasing as more people discovered The Trustees of Reservations and its then 16 properties.

At Whitney Woods, for example, expenses, including warden's services, general maintenance, two new fireplaces, repairs to the Civilian Conservation Corps Camp, and the purchase for $35 of a "used Ford automobile," had grown to $584 annually. Income from the property's endowment fell $94 short of meeting its needs, creating a deficit in the account which ultimately had to be charged to the General Fund. There were deficit balances as well in the operating accounts for Rocky Narrows and for Goodwill Park in Falmouth. And more than $1,900 was owed for special projects such as the purchase of Dinosaur Footprints in Holyoke.

But although finances were a problem that wouldn't go away, the Standing Committee continued its mission. Indeed, ever promotion-minded, Laurence Fletcher coined the idea of adding "Three New Places a Year" to the list of properties throughout the Commonwealth which, in full or in part, had been preserved by the activities of The Trustees of Reservations. Although he succeeded admirably over the next two decades, the organization's achievements in land conservation, even though many represented additions to existing properties, created an increasing drain on its financial resources. Few of the new areas received as gifts were accompanied by enough endowment to be able pay their own way.

There were others as well, high on the list for preservation, such as The Old Manse in Concord, which had to be purchased. This meant borrowing money for the purpose, usually, if possible, from the corporation's own limited capital resources until funds could be raised from public subscription at a later date which would, hopefully, also include money for endowment.

The result was that during the 1930s deficits grew, not alarmingly (at one point, including bank loans, they totaled $17,000), but enough to concern a number of members of the Standing Committee. Courageously, however, with confidence in the future, and, most important, in the wisdom of what it was doing for the environment, The Trustees of Reservations continued to press ahead.

All this, of course, was in striking contrast to the fiscal conservatism of earlier times. Then, as Charles S. Rackemann explained in 1923, "we would not accept a gift until [it] was sufficiently financed." But, remarkably, in the 1930s and 1940s, decades which included such climactic events as the Great Depression and World War II, things were different. The Report of the Committee on the Needs and Uses of Open Spaces, completed in 1929, had clearly presented not only the urgent need for action but a list of opportunities and The Trustees of Reservations was not to be stopped.

Looking back in 1951, Chairman Charles S. Bird had few regrets. "Some years ago," he said, addressing the Annual Meeting, "we adopted the slogan of 'Three New Reservations a Year.' For a few years we reached this goal, but in doing so we took chances and have, in consequence, been somewhat embarrassed [financially]. However, I do not think it has been a very serious embarrassment and I do know that because of our needs it has stimulated us to carry on some successful money-raising campaigns.

"Our Standing Committee is now more conservative, but it seems to me that it is far more important to save places of natural beauty and historic interest before it is too late, even if we do take chances on endowments, rather than lose opportunities because of fear. . . ."

Few today would disagree. Indeed, most would thank heavens that there were those such as he and others at The Trustees of Reservations who were willing to take the risks when they counted.

3

New Sources of Income: Admission Receipts and Those Important Bequests

As tourism and the demand for outdoor recreation began to increase after World War II, the management and accounting of admission receipts began to play a major role in the finances of The Trustees of Reservations. Most came from three properties: Rocky Woods in Medfield, acquired in 1942; The Old Manse in Concord, acquired in 1939; and Crane Beach at the Richard T. Crane, Jr., Memorial Reservation in Ipswich, acquired in 1945.

By 1953, for example, more than 14,000 people a year visited The Old Manse, providing receipts of $4,969. Activities at Rocky Woods generated receipts totaling $2,089. While at Crane Beach, an estimated 217,000 people arriving in 53,529 vehicles, paid a

total of $90,544 for use of the parking facility as well as for the
purchase of some 2,000 gallons of ice cream, 3,000 cases of soft
drinks, 5,000 bags of potato chips and 20,600 sandwiches. It must
be remembered, however, that because of the agreement which
settled the dispute over title, seven and one-half percent of gross
revenues at Crane Beach was legally due the Town of Ipswich.
Cash flow from admissions and other related fees were no guarantee that a propertry would be able to pay its own way, but they
certainly helped.

During the late 1950s, membership contributions continued to
seesaw between $12,500 and $13,900 a year. Some 1,200 to 1,500
people responded to the one appeal letter mailed annually.

Meanwhile, however, The Trustees of Reservations began to
receive significant new funds from bequests. Legacies from the
Estate of Louise Ayer Hathaway now totaled a wonderfully
welcome $200,000 in unrestricted money. And upon the death of
Miss Mabel Choate in 1958, the acquisition of Naumkeag meant
another $600,000 was added to reservation endowments.

Earlier, it had been decided by the Standing Committee that
20 percent of the income received from each reservation endowment account would be credited to the Head Office to help pay for
administrative and other services provided for the property
throughout the year. The decision was not only fair, but also
provided a more accurate method of accounting for reservation
operating expenses. And it was a welcome windfall to help stem
the drain on the General Fund which heretofore had picked up all
administrative and related costs.

During the next decade, bequests were to become a major
source of capital for The Trustees. In 1962, upon the death of Mrs.
Helen Stevens Coolidge, the organization acquired the Stevens-
Coolidge Place in North Andover with an endowment of
$901,000. Within a few years, this was increased to just over $1
million. And, finally, in 1966, with the death of Lieutenant-
Colonel Arthur D. Budd and the acquisition of Notchview, The
Trustees of Reservations became the residual beneficiary of the
Arthur D. and Helen Budd Trusts, which at the time of the gift
were valued at $3,746,429.

By 1970, the organization preserved a total of 53 properties, 31
of which could report some sort of endowment. A few were
sufficient to meet annual operating expenses. The great majority
were not, but there was little doubt that much progress had been
made thanks to slow but persistent efforts through the years.

The endowment for Agassiz Rock Reservation in Manchester,
for example, totaled $12,000; for Bartholomew's Cobble, $10,061;
for little Crowninshield Island, $10,000; for Lowell Holly, $9,994;
for Misery Islands (thanks to a major grant that same year),
$194,825; for Mount Ann Park, $21,851; for The Old Manse,
$40,245; for Rocky Woods (thanks primarily to the continuing

generosity of Dr. Goldthwait), $221,489; for Weir Hill, $52,210; and for Whitney Woods, $22,866. The difference between 1970 and 1940 was dramatic.

Part of the growth had come from additional contributions; part from the transfer, whenever possible, of accumulated income, including especially reservation receipts; and part, of course, from the management of investments. The arrival of income from the Budd legacy enabled the organization to view its deficit years as something thankfully in the past.

Indeed, then Director Gordon Abbott, Jr., was told by leading members of the Standing Committee, who were all but embarrassed by year-end surpluses, to expedite programs which would spend the money and expand the mission of the organization.

As Abbott knew, there was little doubt that if The Trustees of Reservations pursued its mission with imagination and courage, deficit budgets once again would be a part of its future. However, there was work to be done and worlds to conquer in the immediate years that lay ahead.

4

The Friends

The accelerated fundraising efforts connected with the acquisitions of World's End, Wasque, and the expansion at Bartholomew's Cobble in the late 1960s and early 1970s were in dramatic contrast to how The Trustees of Reservations had raised money for more than three-quarters of a century. For the first time, the organization had reached out to huge segments of the public at large and waged major regional campaigns, utilizing every modern technique, to acquire charitable gifts. To be sure, the world had changed as well. The green revolution had begun, and open space and the environment were now household words. But the success of the three ventures, admittedly insured by the generosity of Colonel Budd, astounded even the experts.

Some 1,800 people contributed $450,000 to the effort to preserve World's End. More than 840 had given a total of $170,000 to purchase and protect Wasque. And just over 700 had provided $167,500 to enlarge Bartholomew's Cobble and to acquire the Colonel John Ashley House. The total of 3,300 donors to the three projects already represented more people than gave yearly to the Annual Appeal. Obviously, the question now was how to maintain this new interest and support after the acquisition portion of the campaigns had ended. The answer was not long in coming.

As the campaign to preserve Wasque wound down, it was agreed that its local flavor had been one of its most powerful appeals. Funds were solicited by local people on a local letterhead. Even the return envelope had a local address. The treasurer of the campaign and its committee members were people locally known and trusted. Everything was done to reinforce the fact that money which came from island residents would remain to benefit the island's future. Much the same thing, of course, could have been said in Hingham and Cohasset with World's End or throughout Berkshire County with the Cobble campaign.

At a winter meeting on the Vineyard, after much discussion, it was decided that the best way to continue localized fundraising was to establish a new organization. It was to be entitled the Friends of Wasque Reservation and Cape Poge Wildlife Refuge. "The Friends," as it would come to be known, would, in effect, be a subcommittee of the Local Committee with the same members but different officers. Its responsibility would be solely to raise funds to benefit the two properties and to add urgently needed operating income annually to what little was received from a tiny ($5,000) endowment. The Local Committee would continue its traditional role in the area of property management. Officers of the Friends were also members of the Local Committee.

The annual appeal letter was to be written by the Chairman of the Friends, Harold B. Kelley, Jr., a well-known and widely respected island resident. The Friends also planned a cocktail party annually at which both the Chairman of the Local Committee, then Oliver D. Filley, Jr., and the Chairman of the Friends would report. For a while, the organization even had its own newsletter produced by General Headquarters in Milton.

A huge success its first year and every year thereafter, the Friends of Cape Poge and Wasque opened the door to a new era of fundraising for The Trustees of Reservations. With the enthusiastic support of the Director (who was in on its founding), an ardent believer in the success of local appeals, and the Standing Committee, it shortly became a model for other areas as well.

That same year (1974), with equal success, "Friends" organizations were established for Bartholomew's Cobble and the Colonel John Ashley House, as well as for World's End. Within months, they were followed by the Friends of Coskata-Coatue Wildlife Refuge, Nantucket; the Friends of Crane Wildlife Refuge, Essex and Ipswich; the Friends of Misery Islands, Salem Bay; and the Friends of The Old Manse, Concord. Later, the organization created the Friends of Long Point Wildlife Refuge, West Tisbury; and the Friends of the Charles River Valley, which benefit a series of properties owned by The Trustees of Reservations within the scenic corridor of the Charles River.

By 1983, nearly 3,000 members of The Trustees of Reservations' nine Friends organizations contributed a total of some $143,000 annually in operating income.

To be sure, there were drawbacks as well to the the concept of the Friends. With separate committees for each organization and with individual appeal materials such as folders and letterheads, the demands for service increased markedly. Quality and uniformity were insured by maintaining ultimate control at General Headquarters, where assistance was provide by the addition of the organization's first staff member added for development purposes, John C. Marksbury, former Director of Development at Beaver Country Day School in Chestnut Hill. Bright and personable, Marksbury helped The Trustees' Friends organizations grow into a powerful source of funds.

By 1980, as well, The Trustees of Reservations had established a full-fledged membership program with different privileges for each category. And every member of a Friends organization was a member of The Trustees as well and could carry a membership card to prove it.

Those in areas not served by a Friends organization or who wished to support the organization as a whole, were able to join as General Members. In 1983, for example, 990 General Members contributed a welcome $39,240.

As was the case with the Friends of Cape Poge and Wasque, The Trustees' first Friends organization, it was the chairman who carried the flag during each annual appeal, organizing the committee, and writing and signing, with others, appeal letters and

Members of the committee for the Friends of Misery Islands prepare letters for the Annual Appeal. From left, Florence Perkins, Rita Meyer, Mary Waters Shepley, Nat Brengle, Ruth McGreenery and Eleanor Crocker.

thank-you notes. Veteran Friends organization chairmen included such loyal and long-time volunteers as J. Graham Parsons and Arthur C. Chase, Bartholomew's Cobble and the Colonel Ashley House; Harold B. Kelley, Jr., Julia B. McRae, and Danwin M. Purdy, Cape Poge and Wasque; Alice W. Stewart, Charles River Valley; John V. Jamison, III, Coskata-Coatue Wildlife Refuge; Gale R. Guild, Crane Wildlife Refuge; Ann W. Brewer and Madeleine Chesney, Misery Islands; Paul Brooks, Mrs. Henry C. Laughlin, and Jonathan M. Keyes, The Old Manse; Barbara E. O'Hara and Elizabeth M. Jerome, Long Point Wildlife Refuge; Urs F. Dur, Old Town Hill; and Henry W. Stokes and Polly Cowen, World's End and Whitney & Thayer Woods.

During the early 1980s, impressive support for the Great House was provided by the Friends of Castle Hill, administered by the Castle Hill Foundation.

Alice Stewart, chairman of the Friends of the Charles River Valley

5

An Expanded Annual Appeal and the Need for New Capital

Efforts to enlarge the scope and results of the Annual Appeal were continuing. For a number of years during the early 1960s, a single appeal letter a year could be counted upon to raise $12,000 to $15,000 annually from an average of 1,500 subscribers. The figures remained the same for some time.

Then, in 1968, thanks to a more sophisticated approach, which included mailing to an increasingly larger list of prospects, a second reminder letter, and a better explanation of the organization's needs, the results began to improve. In 1970, the Annual Appeal raised $37,721. By 1976, it had reached $65,703; and by 1979, $79,059.

By 1980, members of the Standing Committee and the Advisory Council began to play a major role during the Annual Appeal, both as donors and solicitors. The Development Office was enlarged to included a new deputy director, Caroline D. Standley, former Director of Development at the Peabody Museum in Salem; an Assistant Director for Annual and Capital Programs; and, to service the growing number of Friends organizations and to produce the organization's quarterly newsletter, an Assistant Director for Information and Membership Services.

Wonderfully warm and outgoing, Caroline Standley set the tone for development activities. Her enthusiasm and good humor

Polly Cowen, chairman of the Friends of World's End and Whitney & Thayer Woods

Caroline D. Standley, Deputy Director for Development during The Trustees' first capital program

were contagious and volunteers across the state enjoyed working with her and her staff to increase the number of individuals whose generosity supported the activities of The Trustees of Reservations.

To encourage major gifts for operating purposes, *The 1891 Society* was created. It rewarded donors of $1,000 or more each year with a special luncheon or dinner held at a selected property of The Trustees of Reservations. The result, in 1980, was a new record for annual appeal giving: 412 donors contributed $101,889. And by 1983, gifts to the Annual Appeal had nearly doubled both in number and amount: 917 donors had contributed $198,049.

Following completion of the Report of the Future Policy Committee in 1977, The Trustees of Reservations, with an eye on rising operating costs as well as on new challenges, needs and opportunities in land conservation, planned a major program to raise capital funds. Its primary goal was to increase endowment. Only a portion of the organization's 67 properties had endowment enough to meet annual operating expenses. Twenty-nine had no endowment at all. Strategic financial planning indicated that a series of deficit operating budgets lay on the horizon and that unless new capital was raised, programs, both in the areas of property management and land conservation, would suffer.

A feasibility study was completed by The Trustees of Reservations' professional fundraising consultant. A Pooled Income Fund was established and a Campaign Steering Committee, led by former Standing Committee Chairman Theodore Chase, was appointed.

Leaders of The 1891 Society and the Annual Appeal. From left, Standing Committee members Albert M. Creighton, Jr., also a Trustee of the Massachusetts Farm and Conservation Lands Trust, Lee Albright and Arthur D. Clarke, both members of the Advisory Councl

Working closely with Caroline Standley and members of the Steering Commitee, Director Gordon Abbott, Jr., had drafted a statement presenting the purposes and goals of the campaign. With Steering Committee member Albert W. Creighton, Jr., Abbott had also written and helped produce an attractive color slide presentation which told the story of the campaign and its objectives. Policy memoranda explaining various methods of giving had been prepared and circulated. And members of the governing board were being solicited for contributions.

Most important, a goal of $10.1 million had been set to meet the organization's needs. However, a critical question remained. Despite the impressive growth in the number of donors now supporting The Trustees of Reservations annually, were there enough to provide sufficient capital to reach campaign objectives? Only time would tell.

6

The 1981 Capital Fundraising Program

Key, of course, to the success of any capital program is the leadership it receives. Here, The Trustees of Reservations was doubly fortunate. For Theodore Chase, a widely respected attorney and a former chairman of the Standing Committee, happily agreed to serve as chairman. Chase also had been chairman of the Future Policy Committee which had drafted the recommendations about setting the organization's course for the future.

Honorary chairman of the campaign was Thomas B. Cabot, a distinguished industrialist and legendary conservationist who had served as president of the Appalachian Mountain Club and, with Mrs. David Rockefeller, had founded the organization now nationally known as Maine Coast Heritage Trust. Cabot also had been a member of the Standing Committee of The Trustees of Reservations and had received its prestigious Conservation Award.

The first team of the Capital Fundraising Program was composed of the members of Chase's Steering Committee. They were Vice President Ann W. Brewer; Standing Committee members Frances Colburn, Albert M. Creighton, Jr., and Thomas B. Williams; President David C. Crockett; soon-to-be President Henry R. Guild, Jr.; and Preston H. Saunders, who in 1982 had taken over from Chase as Chairman of the Standing Committee.

The campaign itself called first for raising $3.7 million to maintain the quality of The Trustees of Reservations' management programs. The largest portion of this, $2.8 million, would be used for endowment to provide a guaranteed income to meet the growing costs of overhead, the maintenance of historic landscapes, museum houses and other structures, as well as to pay the salaries of essential field personnel.

Second, it was proposed that $1.5 million be raised to establish a Revolving Loan Fund for Land Conservation which could utilize new and imaginative techniques developed by The Trustees of Reservations to protect significant open spaces. In addition, the sum of $2.3 million would be raised locally, over time, to be used to acquire, or protect with conservation restrictions, "inholdings" and other properties not available through gift, whose continued existence as open space was vital to retaining the integrity of the organization's 69 properties.

Another $600,000 was proposed to endow programs for student interns in landscape architecture and resource planning, horticulture and park management, and forestry and wildlife biology, to assist members of the professional staff in the process of management and protection and to provide young environmentalists with hands-on experience in the field.

Finally, a total of $1.8 million represented the anticipated results of an increasingly successful Annual Appeal. If a goal of $200,000 could be reached in 1981, it was hoped that by 1985 the Annual Appeal would be able to raise $500,000. The significance of annual giving, of course, is enormous. That $500,000, for example, represented income equal to that received from endowment totaling $10,000,000, assuming a five percent return on invested capital.

During its first year, The Trustees of Reservations' Capital Program raised $2.5 million towards its goal of $7.8 million in new capital (the total goal of $10.1 million counted five years of annual appeals). The Annual Appeal yielded $234,000, while memberships, the bulk of which were received from Friends organizations, reached $150,893, a 24 percent increase in dollars and a 29 percent increase in numbers of donors over the year before.

By 1983, the Annual Appeal was on a roll. Led by Gale R. Guild, committee members increased not only the total amount raised some 24 percent to $291,000, but the number giving from 977 in 1982 to 1,324 in 1983. The following year, the amount was up more than 30 percent to $389,211 and the number of donors increased to 1,500. Corporate support, a brand new area for The Trustees of Reservations, also grew, as did the number of grants received from foundations.

The capital program, however, which by 1984 had reached some $6 million, soon began to run out steam. Despite the best efforts of everyone involved, the small constituency of The Trustees of Reservations was simply not enough to provide the funds needed within the time limit set for the duration of the campaign.

Two years later, things were different. By 1986, enough time had passed to enable the Campaign Committee, now headed by Standing Committee member Ralph Vogel, not only to reach out to new members who had joined in the previous 24 months, but, most important, to return to those who had been so generous earlier and to ask once again for their support. It was gladly given and by December, 1986, the 1981 Capital Fundraising Program had been completed. No gift to it had exceeded $250,000 and there was only one of these.

Abbott, meanwhile, had decided to retire in June 1984. As he wrote in a letter sent to every member, his reasons were two-fold. The first was personal. He'd long had his eye on a series of special projects in land use and open space conservation (one of which led to the establishment that same year of the Center of Rural Massachusetts at the University of Massachusetts at Amherst), and he hoped to return to school for further graduate study of the history of the environmental movement throughout the United States. (In June 1990, he received an MA in American Studies from the University of Massachusetts/Boston.) But the primary reason for his departure, as he explained, was that after nearly 18 years of one administration, he believed that The Trustees of Reservations needed a change in leadership to carry it successfully into the decades that lay ahead. Like all institutions, the history of The Trustees could be measured in a series of successive eras. Much had been accomplished, but much needed to be done to shape the organization for new and very different times.

"Gordon's retirement," said Sandy Sauders, then Chairman of the Standing Committee, "marked the end of an extraordinary era for The Trustees of Reservations. He came to the organization at a perfect time, as the environmental movement was emerging as a national concern and as land values were less inflated than they are today.

"He believed deeply in the mission of The Trustees; it was a natural extension of his own commitment to the out-of-doors. Years of sailing, skiing, hiking and canoeing in New England heightened his desire to preserve the landscape he loved.

"With Abbott's leadership, The Trustees achieved a professionalism that was second to none. He built a staff of dedicated individuals, who, within a well-designed management structure and the regionalization of authority, became intimately involved with the organization. They took a personal pride in their accomplishments and soon were as commited as Abbott was to the cause.

"He made them a part of the decision-making and policy-formation process with site visits, meetings and discussions. His

vision, his excitement for new ideas, and his charm were contagious. More than anything else, his enthusiasm for The Trustees of
Reservations and its activities inspired others, both staff and
volunteers, to join in and to have as much fun as he was having.
He made things happen and, most important, he successfully set
the stage for the next administration and the decades that lie
ahead."

First on the list of priorities for the future, Abbott declared,
were broadening the organization's base of support and raising
new capital."I continue to believe that the best way to do this," he
added, "is to do what we have been doing, seeking out and
preserving significant open spaces, and maintaining present
properties with a sensitivity towards details and with the highest
possible standards of management. But we must tell more people
what we are doing and we must play a greater and more visible
public role in doing it."

It remained for the next Director to do just that.

7

A Perfect Fit

Director Frederic Winthrop, Jr.

Frederic Winthrop, Jr., was the ideal man for the job. A former
Executive Director of Essex County Greenbelt Association, he'd
been involved in conservation as a professional. He'd grown up
with a tradition of sound land management values, and, as owner
and operator of Turner Hill Farm in Ipswich, he had personal
experience in the business of agriculture. On top of all this, he had
just completed a distinguished 10 years as the Commonwealth's
Commissioner of Food & Agriculture, where his abilities had been
such that he had been enthusiastically appointed by two successive Governors, one a Democrat and one a Republican.

A Harvard graduate, he'd served his country with the Marine
Corps Reserve and, prior to his appointment as Commissioner, he
had compiled a wonderfully eclectic collection of employment
experiences, both in this country and abroad, which gave him
valuable perspective on the world around him. Equally important, he was a cheerful, attractive and engaging human being who
had demonstrated an ability to work with others in congenial and
productive ways and who could provide the leadership skills so
necessary for the future.

Following a transition year during which the organization
was solidly managed and administered by Acting Director
William C. Clendaniel, who had served as Deputy Director since

1979, Winthrop took over the reins of The Trustees of Reservations in Janaury 1985.

His first year was a full one. It included successfully completing a long-term effort with the Massachusetts Division of Fisheries & Wildlife to conduct a controlled hunt at the Crane Reservation in Ipswich to reduce the size of the area's herd of white-tailed deer, as well as the acquisition of Powisset Farm in Dover and the use of a "limited development" project to protect some 139 of its 188 acres as open space and agricultural land.

In 1986, after 29 years in what had become unworkably cramped quarters at Milton, General Headquarters moved to the spacious luxury of Long Hill in Beverly. It was a major shift for staff members. Governor Michael S. Dukakis officially christened the facility with a ribbon-cutting ceremony in August.

Meanwhile, as well, trends were at work which would change the organization's directions. One was a dramatic rise everywhere in property values. Another was a revision of the Federal tax law. Combined, as Winthrop explained, they "reduced the frequency of major gifts of land and endowments, all of which had required new thinking and new approaches in our Land Conservation Program.

"More specifically," he added, "we have begun to concentrate less on fee acquisition and more on conservation restrictions and on outreach to landowners and land planners."

There were a few major properties in the pipeline whose future had been determined earlier. But even with these, between 1984 and 1988, The Trustees of Reservations acquired an impressive 1,533 acres of land in fee title and preserved an additional 1,806 acres with conservation restrictions. Acting as a consultant, it also helped both state resource agencies and town Conservation Commissions protect hundreds of additional acres of open space.

Among the properties the organization preserved were major additions to land already protected along the corridor of the Charles River and at Coskata-Coatute Wildlife Refuge, Nantucket; much of the western slope of Monument Mountain in Great Barrington; new reservations on the northern shore of scenic Goose Pond in Lee; Noanet Woodlands, Dover; Field Farm, Williamstown; and White's Hill in Essex.

But as the organization's 100th anniversary neared, Winthrop himself was wisely asking critical questions about the years ahead. "What kind of an organization will we be in our second century? Will our historic mission of preserving properties of natural beauty and historic interest still be pertinent and, if so, how well equipped will we be to carry it out? Will we be able to

afford the high level of property maintenance long associated
with our name?"

He continued: "Will The Trustees be viewed as an active
participant in shaping environmental land use policies statewide
as it was in 1891, or will financial constraints require a more
narrow focus? In an age when high land values make gifts increasingly rare, how will The Trustees remain the leader in
conserving land? Can The Trustees count on an ever-expanding
membership and on an ever-higher level of annual giving? To
whom should we look for support? Do we need to consider new
sources of revenue, and if so, what?"

The answers were to come from the Long Range Planning
Committee, the first of its kind for a decade. Its Chairman was
Stevin R. Hoover, a member of the Advisory Council. His commit-
tee included veterans of many years' service to the organization as
well as some fresh new faces: John Callahan, Gale R. Guild,
Richard Perkins, Hall J. Peterson, Susanne LaC. Phippen, Rush
Taggart, Ralph Vogel, President Henry R. Guild, Jr. and Standing
Committee Chairman Preston H. Saunders. Their report, prima-
rily written by Sandy Saunders, was presented to the governing
board in April 1988.

8

Looking Ahead: the Course for the Centennial and Beyond

Following the experience of the Capital Fundraising Program of
1981, it was clear to The Trustees of Reservations that a major
priority must be to broaden its base of support. This meant adding
new members.

It was also clear that if The Trustees was to expand its membership program, it would have to reach out to a broader constituency than that provided by the Friends organizations. Accordingly, in 1987, a new program was initiated. The Friends, which
had done their work so well for so many years, were retired and a
major effort began to increase the number of general members. It
was possible, still, in keeping with local loyalties, to credit membership contributions to selected properties. There was, and
always will be, a passionate feeling for the land next door.

Coordinated by newly appointed Deputy Director for Development Ann F. Powell (Caroline Standley had departed after six
years to administer a capital program at the Isabella Stewart
Gardner Museum), and Associate Director for Membership Susan

McGarvey, the new program blossomed. By the end of 1987, 5,474
members had provided a total annual revenue of $333,166, an
increase of 39 percent over the previous year.

Equally important, 1,737 donors had set a new record for the
Annual Appeal, raising $461,773, up 21 percent. The result was the
first surplus in the organization's operating fund, albeit a modest
$26,000, after two years of deficits occasioned by a dramatic drop
off in admission receipts at Crane Beach because of unexpected
bad weather. It must be also said, however, that even during those
two deficit years, The Trustees of Reservations, acting with
traditional prudence and care, considered it critical to fund the
Reserve for Depreciation and Extraordinary Repairs. To do less
was to ignore the future.

Meanwhile, the Standing Committee had enthusiastically
embraced the recommendations of the Long Range Planning
Committee. They included the establishment of a new information
and referral center to revitalize the organization's land conservation programs and provide adequate funding for its activities, a
major effort to increase the quality of The Trustees of Reservations' property management program with a special focus on its
historic houses, and new inititiatives to expand its educational
and interpretive efforts and its use of volunteers.

*Susan McGarvey, Associate
Director for Membership*

The report also proposed improving the system of governance
by increasing the effectiveness of volunteer committees and
reducing staff time used to service them. It urged the organization
to increase its involvement with public issues and its advocacy of
political programs in keeping with the mission of The Trustees of
Reservations.

And finally, it proposed establishment of "a vigorous development program that raises income and endowment to needed
levels. . . and fosters steady membership growth on a manageable
basis." A vital ingredient in the implementation of this latter
proposal was to be "a more aggressive public information
program. . . [to] heighten public awareness of The Trustees of
Reservations." They were words that had been repeated for nearly
a century. But now, finally, something was to be done.

9

A Productive Marriage: Membership and Public Information

It was obvious that what was being done with membership
programs and the Annual Appeal was working. By 1988, the

number of members of The Trustees of Reservations had jumped
to 7,067, up 29 percent from the year before, thanks primarily to a
series of specially targeted direct mailings.

The following year, the Annual Appeal also passed the half-
million mark to reach another record total of more than $557,000.
According to newly elected treasurer Peter C. Thompson (Norton
Sloan had become a vice president after six years in the office), the
operating statement of the corporation showed a surplus of
$40,000. The Trustees had also initiated a policy that set aside a
portion of its income each year to offset erosion of the real value
of its endowment by inflation. And it had assumed total responsibility for the management and administration of both property
and programs at Castle Hill in Ipswich, including the Great
House. Henceforth, the Castle Hill Foundation was to be involved
only in cultural activities with a prime focus on its popular
summer concert series.

What was making all the progress in membership possible,
besides aggressive mailings, was a remarkable marriage of
interests between the Associate Director of Membership, Susan
McGarvey, and The Trustees' new Deputy Director for Public
Information, Eloise W. Hodges. Editor and reporter for Essex
County Newspapers (a chain of small dailies on the North Shore)
for many years, Hodges had been brought aboard part time by
Director Gordon Abbott, Jr., to administer and coordinate the
organization's publications. She later produced The Trustees'
newsletter and provided publicity for its activities, events and
accomplishments. Then, in 1988, as planning for the centennial
celebration got underway, she accepted Fred Winthrop's invitation to become a full-fledged member of the staff at General
Headquarters.

*Eloise W. Hodges, Deputy
Director for Public
Information*

Susan McGarvey, a former program director for the Y.M.C.A.,
joined The Trustees of Reservations in 1985. She realized immediately that it was at the properties that visitors could be most easily
converted to members, and she met with every property manager
to develop a process of membership solicitation. The link between
membership growth and events at selected properties had long
been recognized, and, with a new emphasis on increasing public
understanding of the organization and its mission, as well as on
membership support, the number and variety of events was
accelerated.

In 1984, The Trustees of Reservations held 44 events on 20
different properties. By 1988, the number had grown to such
proportions that special booklets listing them were published for
the spring and summer seasons as well as for fall and winter, and
thousands of new visitors had been introduced not only to
specific properties, but to The Trustees of Reservations as a whole.
The 1992 calendar for spring and summer listed a total of 77
different events.

The annual favorites continued: garden parties at Naumkeag, the road race at Tyringham Cobble, and canoe trips on the Charles River. There were also a series of nature walks at World's End; garden parties and plant sales at Long Hill and at the Stevens-Coolidge Place; and the annual craft fair at the Bryant Homestead. Among the new events are rock climbing instruction at Chapelbrook; tours of the Colonel John Ashley House for children conducted by previously-instructed youngsters their own age — third, fourth and fifth grade students from nearby schools; and a day-long series of natural history safaris at Cape Poge Wildlife Refuge.

Meanwhile, planning had begun for what was to be an epochal event in itself, the celebration of the organization's first century in 1991. A Centennial Committee was appointed with Standing Committee member Judy Keyes as chairman. On its agenda was a trip to visit properties of The National Trust in England in September 1990; an exhibit featuring The Trustees of Reservations at the New England Flower Show in March 1991; a series of Discovery Days throughout the anniversary year at selected properties across the state; an appearance at Boston's celebrated Ellis Antique Show to display portions of the collections from many of The Trustees' historic houses; a special Centennial poster; a gala birthday celebration at Castle Hill in June 1991; and the grand finale, a formal ball, at Naumkeag in October.

One of the most exciting parts of the public information program for the Centennial was to be the production of a film which would tell the story of The Trustees of Reservations, its accomplishments in the past and its ambitions for the years ahead. The film, entitled *Saving Special Places*, was completed in 1990.

Finally, The Trustees of Reservations was poised, as Fred Winthrop wrote, "to launch a major capital campaign. Before our centennial year is over," he continued, "all of us will have an opportunity to make a special contribution to The Trustees of Reservations, to participate in building a strong foundation for our second century of preserving the very best of the Massachusetts landscape."

10

Raising the Profile

With one assistant, Eloise Hodges began to tackle the problem that had plagued The Trustees of Reservations since its beginnings: a lack of public awareness of the organization and its mission.

Annual Reports of the early years of The Trustees show clearly that the absence of "brand recognition" had frustrated Standing Committee members for decades. As the landmark report of the Committee on the Needs and Uses of Open Spaces issued by The Trustees in 1929 declared: "this group would be more effective if [its] purposes were better appreciated."

In 1933, the Massachusetts Landscape Survey put it this way: "The people of Massachusetts should know what The Trustees have done, and — more important — what they can do through cooperative effort." The battle for recognition had been waged but never won.

By the time Eloise Hodges had left in 1991, "The Trustees of Reservations" were not yet words on everyone's lips, but the organization was considerably better known than when she began. Perhaps the best testimonial to this was that by the end of its Centennial year, The Trustees could count more than 10,000 members thanks to the coordinated efforts of the membership department and of the department of public information.

Stories in newspapers and magazines, as well as television and radio coverage of the centennial and its events, reached out to readers, viewers and listeners in every corner of the Commonwealth. As Fred Winthrop explained, the "media campaign and events schedule have presented the organization and its properties to [more than] six million consumers." For Hodges and her assistant, Lisa McFadden (now, with Hodges's departure, Deputy Director for Public Information herself), it was a job well done.

At the gala at the Great House in June 1991, The Trustees received a special message from the White House. "I am pleased," the President wrote in a personal letter, "to extend warm greetings to everyone celebrating the 100th anniversary of The Trustees of Reservations.

"The United States has experienced tremendous growth and development during the past century — growth and development that have sometimes threatened our natural heritage. Fortunately, however, concerned individuals across the Nation have joined together to help protect lands of scenic, ecological, and historical value. As the pioneering achievements of The Trustees attest, their efforts are making a difference.

"One of the oldest privately supported land conservation organizations in the United States, TTOR (The Trustees of Reservations) has not only helped to safeguard portions of the rich Massachusetts landscape, but also served as a model for other voluntary land trust programs. TTOR-held beaches, woodlands, wetlands and gardens, have been enjoyed by thousands of visitors, and thanks to your outstanding work, future generations will share the opportunity to enjoy them as well. Your century of public service is highly commendable, and you have my heartiest congratulations on this important anniversary.

"Barbara joins me in sending best wishes. God bless you."

It was signed "George Bush."

For the more than 350 persons present that spring evening, it was a fitting way to christen The Trustees of Reservations' second century.

11

Increasing Endowment: the Key to New Revenue

It was clear from the very beginning that the road to financial stability had to be paved with new revenues. Costs had been cut to the bone with some pain and suffering along the way. As Fred Winthrop put it: "Further cuts in expenses would mean many missed opportunities for preserving important new properties and deferred maintenance on the 72 we already own. The only answer is to build a broader and stronger base of support. . . ." That had already been started.

In 1966, it cost $386,000 to operate The Trustees of Reservations for one year. By 1984, that had risen to $2.2 million and by 1990, the figure had all but doubled to $4 million.

Expenses were divided as follows: Property Management, 73 percent; General and Administrative, 13 percent; Development, seven percent; Land Conservation, five percent; and Public Information, three percent.

Revenues had risen dramatically in the 24 years as well. Income in 1966 totaled $387,135, in 1984, $2.2 million, and in 1990, nearly $4.1 million. By the centennial year, the Annual Appeal raised $731,000 and memberships contributed another $442,000.

The organization's endowment was still a major source of income, contributing 33 percent of annual revenues. Receipts from reservations added another 37 percent; contributions, 19 percent;

memberships, nine percent and other income, two percent. It was easy to see why fundraising programs focused on adding more capital to endowment.

As of March 31, 1991, the market value of endowment principal totaled a record $27.6 million. This compared to some $8 million (including the Budd Trusts) in 1966 and $14 million in 1984. Market appreciation, skilled portfolio management, and the 1981 capital program had been good to The Trustees of Reservations but additional funds were needed. They were to come from "The Centennial Campaign."

Its goals, understandably, were much the same as its predessessor: to acquire new capital, first, to help preserve and maintain The Trustees' existing properties, and, second, to provide for an expanded program to meet the challenges of the future.

Despite a downturn in the economy, both national and regional, it was not a bad time to seek additional capital. By early 1990, dramatic growth had seen the number of members of The Trustees of Reservations top 10,000. The Annual Appeal had kept up its winning ways as well. The number of donors to both had increased to nearly 13,000 people, providing a significantly larger constituency than had existed for the capital program nearly a decade earlier.

The development office had been expanded both in numbers and in talent. The board itself was considerably wiser and more sophisticated in the ways of raising money. And, with a drop in interest rates coming, the stock market was about to take off on a new and unprecedented rise in value.

The organization also continued to make its mark around the Commonwealth, protecting new and outstanding open spaces with the acqusition of fee title and conservation restrictions. In 1989 and 1990, in the North Shore community of Manchester-by-the-Sea alone, The Trustees preserved three parcels of land totaling some 176 acres. Other "special places" were protected in Chilmark, in Williamstown, in Warwick, and along the Palmer River in Rehoboth.

The new Land Conservation Center with Deputy Director Wesley Ward at the helm, was a demonstrable success. And the program to celebrate the organization's first 100 years was in full swing.

12

The Centennial Campaign: Blazing a Trail to the Future

Although the end of boom times and the beginnings of the national recession of the early 1990s slowed — and in places even eliminated — development patterns that earlier had devoured open space throughout the Commonwealth, The Trustees of Reservations was well aware that the threat still existed.

Farmers, particularly in the dairy business, pressed by a difficult economy, were having a hard time holding onto their lands. The number of great estates still remaining had shrunk dramatically as the curtain was slowly drawn on an earlier era. And a lack of comprehensive, regional land use policies still meant that dispersal of development rather than concentration was what was taking place in rural communities everywhere.

But the spirit to preserve the character of the landscape and its special places was more alive than ever. This was evident by the number of land trusts — which now numbered more than 100 from Berkshire County to Cape Cod and the Islands — and, most importantly, by the continued success of The Trustees of Reservations itself in acquiring new properties and conservation restrictions.

For decades, the land conservation efforts of The Trustees had struggled with insufficient funds. Now it was proposed to raise

A birthday cake helps The Trustees of Reservations celebrate its 100th year in 1991. From left, Hall Peterson, President; Charles Eliot, Life Member, Honorary Trustee and nephew of the founder; Director Fred Winthrop; and Chairman Wiley Vaughan.

$2,500,000 to endow the Land Conservation Center and an additional $500,000 to expand the Gordon Abbott Emergency Land Acquisition Fund, which then amounted to just more than $100,000. A revolving loan fund established to honor the former director upon his retirement in 1984, it demonstrated its worth by providing emergency money to protect critical properties threatened by sale, subdivision or development.

The Land Conservation Center itself was designed to coordinate and concentrate the efforts of both members of the the organization's staff and its volunteers engaged in the preservation of additional properties of exceptional scenic, historic and ecological value throughout the Commonwealth. As one of its major new initiatives, the Center serves as a catalyst for "Greenways for Massachusetts," a cooperative program to establish conservation corridors linking protected lands, as well as rivers and streams and other important open spaces, both public and private.

Clearly, The Trustees of Reservation's ability to continue to protect the quality of its existing properties was still of critical importance to its mission, as well as to its role as a fiduciary. And although previous efforts had added to endowment principal, a substantial majority of properties still lacked sufficient funds to provide even adequate maintenance services. Without any endowment at all, 20 properties still depended upon income from the General Fund to meet their annual operating expenses.

With increased membership came an increasing number of visitors and a new awareness that the organization's natural landscapes needed new attention. None had a higher priority than the dynamic areas of ocean shoreline known as barrier beaches where the struggle continued with even greater ferocity to balance public use with environmental conservation. Funds were needed as well to intensify management of The Trustees of Reservation's more formal landscapes, particularly its gardens and their plant material as well as other features such as drives and walkways, walls, terraces and statuary.

Finally, it was agreed that new recognition must be accorded the continuing needs of the organization's historic houses. Small in number (eleven in all) but each a distinguished example of America's heritage, they include three National Historic Landmarks as well as four others listed on the National Register of Historic Places. Eight of the houses also contain extensive collections of furniture, ceramics and textiles, and although much has been accomplished with current inventories and specific restoration projects, a more comprehensive approach is needed to protect and interpret historic and literary resources of vital interest and importance to the nation.

Accordingly, to provide for the restoration, management and continuing protection of its properties, The Trustees of Reservations also proposed raising a total of $7 million: $4 million to be used to increase reservation endowments; $1 million to endow an historic house fund; and $2 million to be spent for capital improvements.

Christened and launched in June, 1991, as a part of the organization's l00th anniversary celebration, the Centennial Campaign got off to a fast start. The results to date are exciting. As of July 31, 1993, $9.1 million of the $10 million sought had been raised. An appeal for the balance is underway in regional campaigns throughout the state and in an all-out effort to reach every member of The Trustees of Reservations.

The success so far of the Centennial Campaign is, of course, in large part due to the energies and commitment of the Steering Committee and its regional leaders. They are General Co-Chairmen Henry R. Guild, Jr., and Ralph B. Vogel; Hall J. Peterson and David W. Scudder, Major Gifts Co-Chairmen; Edward H. Ladd and Norton Q. Sloan, Corporate Co-Chairmen; Susanne LaC. Phippen and Preston H. Saunders; and Foundation Co-Chairmen Herbert W. Vaughan and Albert M. Creighton, Jr.

Regional leaders include Wyatt Garfield, Central; Flora Epstein and Dr. Joseph E. Murray, Martha's Vineyard; William Matteson and Donal C. O'Brien, Nantucket; James N. Esdaile, Jr., and Jonathan B. Loring, Northeast; Theodore Chase and Charles F. Kane, Southeast; and in the West, Joan McFalls and F. Sydney Smithers IV.

As Fred Winthrop declared: "Despite uncertain economic times, the tremendous response of our members and supporters

Surf rolls ashore at Halibut or "Haul-about" Point, Rockport, as a small sloop tacks to round the rocky headland. The Reservation was established in 1934. It borders Halibut Point State Park, site of a former granite quarry, which The Trustees helped the Commonwealth to acquire and protect.

to date makes us optimistic that we will reach our goal of $10 million. We must. Our second century depends upon it."

In the minds of those who know The Trustees of Reservations and what it stands for, there is no doubt that the Centennial Campaign will be a success. For it is not only a quest for funds, but a crusade for the future of the Commonwealth and the preservation of those rare and precious places which make living here such a pleasure not only for ourselves but, perhaps most important, for generations yet to come.

Afterword

When Charles Eliot proposed establishment of The Trustees of Reservations a century ago, he could not have imagined that his ideas would give birth to a movement which today is not only national but worldwide.

In 1992, according to the Land Trust Alliance, the national service organization for land trusts created in 1980, there were more than 889 land trusts throughout the United States and the number was still growing. (A land trust, according to the Alliance, is defined as a local, state or regional not-for-profit organization *directly* involved in protecting land for its natural, recreational, scenic, historic or productive values.")

Although, public resource agencies, Federal, state and local, have led the way in land preservation, the private sector has compiled a remarkable record of accomplishment in the century of its existence. By 1992, land trusts had helped to protect some 2.7 million acres of land throughout the United States, an increase of more than 630,000 acres since 1989, and an area about twice the size of the state of Delaware. The total includes some 440,000 acres owned by land trusts; some 450,000 acres which land trusts protect with conservation easements or restrictions; and 670,000 acres which were acquired by land trusts and transferred to other resource agencies or organizations.

1.14 million acres were protected as open space by land trusts which negotiated the transactions or raised funds for the purpose but did not end up actually holding the land. A portion of this figure also includes private lands managed by land trusts for conservation reasons. As negotiators and facilitators, land trusts have helped protect substantial acreage in such areas of unique national importance as Acadia National Park in Maine, White Mountains National Forest in New Hampshire, Redwoods National Park in California and Great Meadows Wildlife Refuge in Wayland and Sudbury, Massachusetts.

With the largest number of land trusts, New England accounts for 42 percent of the acreage preserved. Connecticut and Massachusetts have more than 100 land trusts each. And Maine, which in the early 1980s had some half-dozen, can list more than 70 land trusts today. The country's mid-Atlantic region ranks second with 17 percent of the total number of land trusts, followed by the Far West, the Great Lakes, the South, the Plains States, the Rocky Mountains, and, finally, the Southwest.

The land trust movement is growing in Canada, too, where 14 land trusts are now active from Prince Edward Island to British

Columbia. And, following the redoubtable example of Britain's National Trust which was modeled on The Trustees of Reservations, there are national trusts in Scotland, Bermuda, the Bahamas, Australia, South Australia, New Zealand, in India and in Greece. Similar organizations independent of government devoted to the preservation of significant open spaces exist in Europe, Asia, Latin America and in other parts of the world including Eastern Europe.

Following the establishment of The Trustees of Reservations in 1891, Charles Eliot's idea began, albeit slowly, to catch on elsewhere and the beginnings of a new century marked an awakening of the importance of preserving "beautiful and historic places." In New Hampshire, the Society for the Protection of New Hampshire Forests, founded in 1901, was soon followed by the Squam Lakes Association in 1905. Interest in protecting open space to preserve the character of New England towns began to grow as well, as village improvement societies acted to protect special places within their own communities. The Andover (Massachusetts) Village Improvement Society, for example, began its work in 1894. Today, it preserves some 1,000 acres of land. The first village improvement society in the nation, the Laurel Hill Society, was founded in Stockbridge, Massachusetts, in 1853. It, too, protects special portions of the town's landscape.

Organizations also were established to preserve shade trees and forest lands. The Connecticut Forest and Park Association was formed in 1895, and in 1898, it was followed by a Forest and Park Association in Massachusetts.

Audubon Societies, devoted to the preservation of birds and other wildlife, as well as to public programs in environmental education, got an early start. Maine Audubon, for example, was founded in 1843. Massachusetts Audubon and New Jersey Audubon followed the founding of The Trustees of Reservations in 1896 and 1897. Today, the habitat protection efforts of Audubon Societies everywhere encompass thousands of acres of land. Massachusetts Audubon Society, for example, now protects a total of some 24,000 acres.

As the century ended, there were early signs of an environmental awakening in the Far West as well. Concerns about the the protection of Yosemite spurred the establishment of the Sierra Club in 1894. In 1900, the Sempervirens Fund called for saving the area's majestic redwood forests. Marin County's Tamalpais Conservation Club was founded in 1912, and the Save-the-Redwoods League in 1920. But most of California's now more than 70 land trusts, like their sister organizations throughout the nation, were established in the 1970s and 1980s following a surge of interest nationally in the protection of the natural environment.

The first wave of concern came in the 1960s as the country turned the corner into a new era. The decade was marked with the publication of Rachel Carson's *Silent Spring,* which alerted the world that it was slowly poisoning itself with chemical pesticides. In *The Quiet Crisis,* Secretary of the Interior Stewart Udall warned that the beauty of the American landscape was being destroyed by unplanned commercial development and accelerating suburban sprawl. William H. Whyte's *The Last Landscape* talked about the need for open space in urban and exurban areas, "where people live," and described some of the techniques and devices, such as easements, preferential assessment and cluster development, which could be used to create more livable communities and help protect vital agricultural lands. Ian McHarg's landmark publication, *Design with Nature,* also urged the introduction of a reverence for the natural environment and an understanding of ecological relationships to the process of urban planning.

Land conservation in the United States reached a major milestone in 1962 with the report of the Outdoor Recreation Resources Review Commission. It recommended that Congress establish the Land and Water Conservation Fund with revenues from offshore oil leases. Thanks to its existence, nearly $6 billion worth of open space and recreation lands have been protected by Federal, state and local resource agencies and organizations around the nation. They include wilderness areas, wild and scenic rivers, hundreds of miles of seashore, as well as special places of scenic, historic, and natural value which otherwise might have been lost forever. In addition, the Fund has constructed thousands of recreational facilities in communities large and small. Many of these preservation projects have been initiated and facilitated by local, regional and national land trusts such as The Nature Conservancy, which has established a remarkable record since its founding in 1951.

Earth Day, 1970, marked another turning point as hundreds of thousands of people across the country expressed their desire to preserve open space within their communities, to safeguard precious water supplies, to prohibit the dumping of toxic wastes and to promote regulations which would guarantee clean air. In response to public appeals, the National Environmental Policy Act of 1970 called for environmental impact assessments of all major projects built on Federal lands or with Federal funds, thereby setting into motion a process which has proved its worth time and again for more than two decades.

Since the founding of The Trustees of Reservations more than a century ago, the expanding number of local and regional land trusts has mirrored an increasing concern about the impacts of growth and change, in communities large and small, upon the lives and livelihoods of their inhabitants. Indeed, suburban residents were among the first to realize that accelerating development of residential housing, dependence upon the automobile for primary transportation needs (which gave rise to the shopping center and later to today's huge regional malls), a lack of effective planning and counter-productive zoning, were dramatically changing the character of their towns and villages.

In many cases, their response was to establish a land trust to preserve rapidly disappearing open spaces. These were often old farms, symbols of an earlier and simpler way of life, as well as wetlands, watersheds, habitats for wildlife, and ponds, streams and brooks, often sources of such critical necessities as pure drinking water.

But it was the real estate boom of the 1980s which fueled the most dramatic growth in the number of land trusts around the nation. According to the Land Trust Alliance, "nearly one third of the land trusts in existence today were formed in the last five years; almost half were formed in the last decade." In general, it was largely a middle-class, suburban movement initiated in generally sophisticated communities by those who had moved out of the city to enjoy the pleasures of exurban life. It was characterized and at times criticized as being primarily white, Anglo-Saxon and Protestant. But in recent years, as the suburbs have changed, so land trusts have become more inclusive and broadly-based.

Many highly-effective trusts today reflect a serious concern for urban residents and a recognition of the environmental needs of minorities. In the East, the Boston Natural Areas Fund and Boston Urban Gardeners fight to protect areas of open space within the city limits. While in the West, The Trust for Public Lands and the (San Francisco) Peninsula Open Space Trust act to preserve special features of the landscape as cities in the region grow and expand.

Today, land trusts everywhere are coming to grips with a responsibility to meet the needs of society as a whole. The Westchester Land Trust in Westchester County, New York, for example, has facilitated the establishment of urban gardens in Yonkers, Greenburgh and Mt. Kisco. The Neighborhood Gardens Association, a Philadelphia land trust, using vacant land and lots, has created more than 1,000 community gardens where in 1987 some 4,000 families cultivated vegetables and other produce worth an estimated $2 million.

In Vermont, a coalition of land trusts and those interested in addressing the need for affordable housing, banded together and successfully urged the Legislature to create and fund a Housing and Conservation Trust which makes grants and low-cost loans available for the acquisition of open space and the construction of less-than-market-value housing. One Vermont property, protected as a working dairy farm, offers urban children, in groups of 20, supervised by teachers and farm employees, a chance to live and work in a rural environment. In the Delaware River valley, The Natural Lands Trust is involved in a effort by a south Jersey township to buy privately-held lands for recreation, and negotiations are underway with the landowner to tie the purchase to the owner's donation of property elsewhere which could be used as a site for affordable housing for senior citizens.

The Chicago Open Lands Project has created an imaginative program called "Neighborwoods" to encourage "reforesting Chicago through community participation in tree planting and care." To date, more than 2,000 volunteers have planted some 1,000 trees and shrubs in neighborhoods throughout the city. The Cultural Conservancy, founded in California in 1991, calls itself "the first land conservation organization dedicated to the preservation of traditional native cultures." It has helped establish a land trust in Maui, Hua 'Aina O Hana, which will work to protect lands traditionally used for hunting and gathering, as sites for worship and as sources of fresh water.

In northern Michigan, The Little Traverse Conservancy is involved in efforts to help Native Americans, members of the Amik Circle Society, preserve an historic settlement and sacred site on Beaver Island in Lake Michigan. The Conservancy has also been talking with the Odawa Indians about the protection of lands of natural and historic value. In Arkansas, the Menard-Hodges Mounds, site of the only Quapaw ancestral village identified by archaeologists, already preserved by the Archaeological Conservancy, was recently named a National Historic Landmark. In the state of Washington, the Indianola Land Trust teamed up with members of the Suquamish Tribe to protect land to be used as a softball field.

In Los Angeles, The Mountains Conservancy Foundation recently completed a planning project for the Los Angeles Transportation Commission which proposes a county-wide Urban Greenway. The plan identifies 85 miles of abandoned or declining rights-of way, owned or operated by the Commission, which could link natural resource areas, parks, university properties, and historic and cultural sites throughout the county. And in rural, western Massachusetts, the Monterey Land Trust is engaged in an affordable housing program which will help local, first-time homebuyers who might otherwise not find it financially feasible to remain in the community. Donations of properties, particularly with existing buildings, are being sought.

The philanthropic motivations which began the land trust movement a century ago are stronger today than ever. As Charles Eliot predicted, it has, indeed, been primarily "the munificence of public-spirited men and women" which has enabled land trusts to acquire and protect the properties they hold for the benefit and enjoyment of the public. Even where open space has been purchased, it has generally been accomplished with funds contributed for the purpose. More than three-quarters of America's land trusts have received gifts of land. And although 43 percent of the nation's land trusts have paid staff, either full or part-time, the fundamental strength of the movement is still its volunteers. The Land Trust

Alliance reports that more than 770,000 people are members of land trusts, a powerful and growing constituency throughout the country for open space preservation, for comprehensive community planning and for responsible land use practices.

Land conservation today is considerably more complex than it was even a decade ago. To be sure, gifts of fee title and conservation easements are still to be had and should be sought with vigor and imagination. But the concept of preserving open space is increasingly being used as a part of a larger matrix of town and regional planning. Land trusts can and should continue to play a major role in this new process by protecting natural resources such as wetlands and wildlife habitats as well as farm and forest lands. But only a portion of the land can be preserved directly. It is how we deal with the remainder that will determine how livable our communities are in the years ahead. We cannot buy up all the land we need to preserve. Nor can we expect landowners to donate more than a small part of it. Thus increasingly it is apparent that planning and land use regulation must, in the years ahead, play a greater role in protecting the character of our communities as well as their abilities to support human life effectively and economically.

One of the best examples of utilizing planning to preserve open space and natural resources while making way for new development, was assembled by the Center for Rural Massachusetts at the University of Massachusetts at Amherst.

The Center's publication *Dealing with Change in the Connecticut River Valley: A Design Manual for Conservation and Development* produced in 1988 and funded by the Massachusetts Department of Environmental Management, puts forth "practical planning standards which towns (everywhere) may adopt to protect their distinctive character, while at the same time accomodating economic growth." Utilizing what the Center calls "Rural Landscape Planning," it creates "new settings deliberately designed to suit new land uses such as residential subdivisions and shopping centers." The Design Manual illustrates how each of eight typical sites can be developed, first, following conventional zoning and subdivision practices, and second, using innovative techniques to help conserve their essential rural character. Each scenario assumes the same overall amount of new development. The difference is amazing.

For new shops and offices, "commercial nodes" and "setbacks" from roadways are proposed as alternatives to highway strip development. Carefully selected plant materials such as native trees, shrubs and wildflowers are used to reflect the natural beauty of the region "as opposed to the conventional junipers and bark mulch treatment so prevalent in suburbia." Standard zoning and subdivision practices, which in too many communities today are a blueprint for what should not be done, are modified, utilizing cluster or "open space" development practices. Building contractors find that the costs of constructing roads, as well as sewer and water systems, are reduced. Local governments save on snow-plowing and roadway maintenance. And homebuyers potentially pay less because of lower construction costs. In some cases, open space generated by cluster housing can be held by local land trusts.

In a rapidly changing environment, it should be clear by now that land use planning must comprehensively build a bridge between preserving the traditional character of a community and providing for its financial well-being. Open space preservation plays an important role in maintaining a region's environmental and economic viability, protecting not only its natural beauty, but its biodiversity, its water supplies, its flood plains and its opportunities for outdoor recreation. But jobs are important, too, as are the commercial elements of the community. And traditional industries such as farming, forestry and commercial fishing, shipbuilding, furniture-making or ranching, may have a special priority as they relate to the historic character of a town or of a region.

To be effective in the years ahead, many believe that land trusts must broaden their mission to include not only land conservation and land management but related activities as well. These include becoming more active advocates for land use planning and open space protection by educating their communities about the value of environmental quality, and by holding themselves to a high standard of creative stewardship. At Shelburne Farms in Vermont, for example, a model farm protected with an easement held by the Vermont Land Trust has become a new non-profit, emphasizing environmental education and the possibilities of combining limited development and active agriculture.

Land trusts also, many of them local, may wish to consider banding together to view their regions as a whole, for regional planning, whether it pertains to open space and resource preservation or to the provision of such essential municipal services as education, public safety, transportation, or health care, is the way of the future. As communities become more diverse socially, ethnically and racially, so, of course, should the membership and governing boards of local land trusts, thus enabling them to better reflect the needs of every resident.

In this complicated world, it is also becoming increasingly clear that partnerships between private sector organizations and government can often accomplish more than can either one working alone. Land trusts should be even more aware than they are at present of ways to bring both public and private programs together to accomplish desired goals. For example, the *Report of the President's Commission, Americans Outdoors* published in 1987 suggests that past experience in many communities demonstrates that alliances between the environmental sector and business enterprises such as building contractors, public utilities, and paper companies, as well as banks, small businesses, religious organizations, other non-profits and municipal departments, can be immensely effective.

The future, of course, belongs to the young, and it is imperative that we teach our children about the natural environment and the critical role it plays in their lives. With understanding comes respect, and respect for the physical world around them can bring to the next generation a new way of thinking which may be essential to survival here on earth. Many land trusts throughout the nation are seizing on the necessity of education and are using their own lands as a way to reach youngsters and their teachers to tell them more about the importance of nature and its relationship to everyday life.

Instead of being content with preserving specific features of the landscape as in the past, land trusts are also learning that what is most important is the protection of whole "natural units" or ecosystems with multiple values which range from water resources to rare and endangered species. Some of this more comprehensive protection may be provided with the renewed emphasis on Greenways, corridors of private and public open space (such as The Bay Circuit in Massachusetts) which can link communities together.

There will come a day also, as real estate markets recover, when land trusts will find that using "limited development" (permitting controlled, environmentally-sensitive development of a portion of a newly-acquired property in order to preserve the remainder) is once again possible. It is no panacea, but it is another option in the collection of those which can be considered to protect a specific parcel of land. And, as each case is different, every option may one day be useful.

Land trusts are learning, too, to emphasize that open space preservation makes good sense economically. For not only does it protect vital resources, but, by steering development away from flood plains and exposed shorelines, for example, it saves taxpayers, homeowners and municipalities unwanted costs and needless aggravation. Protecting open spaces also adds to property values in the community as a whole by making it more attractive and more desirable as a place to live. For as the report *Americans Outdoors* reveals, the need for recreation opportunities — as increasing numbers of Americans inhabit metropolitan areas — is "close to home where they can be a part of our daily lives." Finally, studies have shown as well that open space, particularly that devoted to agriculture and forestry, costs a town or village less than land that is developed.

The key to preserving open space and protecting community character to provide for more livable and environmentally sustainable cities and towns, is planning, both on a local and regional level. For only with planning can a community respond satisfactorily to needs and desires of its residents and effectively solve its problems. Since the real estate boom of the 1980s, there has been an increasing conviction among many that managing growth and change must be a major priority for both public officials and private citizens throughout the country.

As John M. DeGrove and Deborah A. Miness write in *The New Frontier for Land Policy, Planning and Growth Management in the States*, "Properly defined and understood, growth management, far from being a code word for no-growth or slow-growth efforts, has as central to its meaning a commitment to plan carefully for the growth that comes to an area so as to achieve a responsible balance between the protection of natural systems — land, air and water — and the development required to support growth in residential, commercial and retail areas." Land trusts can become important vehicles to assist and expedite this process through their efforts with education and directly through their actions in the public policy area at all levels. As the record shows, they can be enormously influential and effective.

Much the same kind of energy and commitment that is needed today went into the founding of The Trustees of Reservations in 1891. As Charles Eliot wrote in 1890, "as Boston's lovers of art united to found the Art Museum, so her lovers of Nature should now rally to preserve for themselves and all the people as many as possible of these scenes of natural beauty which, by great good fortune, still exist near their doors."

Despite the dramatic changes that the past century has brought to the landscape, "scenes of natural beauty" and areas of critical environmental value wait still to be preserved throughout the country. Time, however, is running out. Land trusts, which are local entities, sensitive to needs and desires of local areas and local people, may be in an ideal position to take the lead in a renewed effort to make the nation more aware of the need for effective environmental planning and of the importance of open space to maintain and improve the quality of life in communities across America.

G.A., Jr.

Bibliography

Abbott, Gordon, Jr. *Private Initiatives in Land Conservation — the New England Story.* A paper written for the 1987 Lincoln Institute of Land Policy Conference in Fairlee, VT, 1987.

Belcher, C. Francis. *A Century of the Appalachian Mountain Club.* Published by the Appalachian Mountain Club, 1976.

Beveridge, Charles E. *Moraine Farm in Beverly, Massachusetts.* Copy on file with The Trustees of Reservations, 1984.

Bradley, John M. *Everything Was an Adventure: Ralph Bradley Remembered in His Words and Ours.* Beverly, Massachusetts: Memoirs Unlimited, 1992.

Brown, Richard. *Massachusetts, A Bicentennial History.* New York: W.W. Norton & Company, 1978, in conjunction with the American Association for State and Local History.

Bulkeley, Morgan. "Our Berkshires," a series of columns appearing regularly in *The Berkshire Eagle,* 1960s and 1970s.

Bush, President George. Letter to The Trustees of Reservations upon the celebration of its Centennial in 1991.

Conant, Loring. Writings in the Twenty-fifth Anniversary Report of the Class of 1925 at Harvard College.

Crane, John C. "Story of the Bear's Den." Newspaper article in the *Orange Enterprise and Journal.* February, 1899.

DeGrove, John M., with Deborah A. Mines. *The New Frontier for Land Policy, Planning & Growth Management in the States.* Cambridge, Massachusetts: Lincoln Institute for Land Policy, 1992.

Drew, Bernard. *A History of the Arthur D. Budd Reservation.*

Eaton, Walter Prichard. *Wild Gardens of New England.* Boston: W.A. Wilde Company, 1936.

Edwards, Susan C.S. "The Mission House, Stockbridge, Massachusetts." *Antiques Magazine,* March, 1983.

Eliot, Charles W. *Charles Eliot, Landscape Architect.* Boston and New York: Houghton, Mifflin & Company, 1902.

Farley, John W. Daily logs of fishing experiences on the Mashpee River, 1915 to 1958.

Fedden, Robert. *The National Trust Past and Present.* London: Jonathan Cape, Ltd., 1975.

Fein, Albert. *Frederick Law Olmsted and the American Environmental Tradition.* New York: George Braziller, Inc., 1972.

Field, James Thomas. *Yesterday with Authors.* Boston: Houghton, Mifflin & Company, 1899.

Forbes, Alexander. "Twenty Years of the Westfield River," an article in *Appalachia,* the journal of the Appalachian Mountain Club, June, 1937.

Forbes, Stephen H. Memorandum about life at Nashawena Island, 1976.

Forbes, Stephen H. Writings in successive Reports of the Class of 1934 at Harvard College.

Garland, Joseph. *Boston's North Shore.* Boston: Little Brown, 1978.

Garland, Joseph. *Gold Coast: The North Shore.* Boston: Little Brown, 1981.

Geiger, James S. *Appleton Farms, 1638-1988: A Brief Agricultural History.* Ipswich: privately published, 1988.

Hart, James D. *The Oxford Companion to American Literature.* New York: Oxford University Press, 1953.

Harvey, Sir Paul. *The Oxford Companion to English Literature.* London: Oxford University Press, 1953.

Her Majesty Queen Elizabeth, the Queen Mother. Special Message for The Trustees of Reservations. Original on File with The Trustees of Reservations.

Hildebrand, Daniel (EIP Intern). *An Historical Survey of the Mill Lots in Virginia Woods, Middlesex Fells Reservation.* Prepared for the Metropolitan District Commission, August, 1988.

Hosmer, James K. *The Life of Thomas Hutchinson, Royal Governor of the Province of Massachusetts Bay.* Boston and New York: Houghton, Mifflin & Company, 1896.

Hull, Forrest P. "Castle Hill, Ipswich," an article in the *North Shore Breeze,* July, 1928.

Jacobson, Sebby Wilson. *Gardens of Steele.* Feature article in the *Rochester Times-Union,* April 27, 1989.

James, Henry. *Charles William Eliot, Volume II.* Boston and New York: Houghton, Mifflin & Company, 1930.

Karson, Robin. *Fletcher Steele, An Account of a Gardener's Life, 1885-1971.* Sagapress/Ngaere A. Macray with Harry N. Abrams, Inc., February, 1989.

Kimball, John W. Paper about the historical background of the Charles W. Ward Reservation, 1986.

Land Trust Alliance. *National Directory of Conservation Land Trusts 1991-92.* Washington, D.C.: Land Trust Alliance, 1991.

Members of the Federal Writers' Project of the Works Progress Administration for Massachusetts. *The Berkshire Hills,* with a new Forword by Roger Linscott. Boston: Northeastern University Press, 1987.

Morison, Samuel Eliot. *The Maritime History of Massachusetts, 1783-1860.* Boston and New York: Houghton Mifflin, & Company, 1921.

National Trust for Places of Historic Interest and Natural Beauty (The). Minute Books and Records, 36 Queen Anne's Gate, London, England, 1989.

Nelson, Albert, ed. *Who's Who in New England, A Biographical Dictionary of Leading Living Men and Women of the New England States,* Marquis First Edition. Chicago: A.N. Marquis & Company, 1909.

New England Forestry Foundation. "Friends of the Foundation, Miss Amelia Peabody." *News of the New England Forestry Foundation.* November, 1974.

Olmsted, Frederick Law. Selected letters to John C. Phillips, May, 1880 to March, 1882. Text on file with The Trustees of Reservations.

Platt, Helen Coate. *Naumkeag and Us,* a paper delivered at Naumkeag, June, 1973.

Polleys, Maidee Proctor. "Castle Hill, Ipswich," an article in the *North Shore Breeze,* April, 1924.

Porter, Rev. Edward G. *Memoir of John C. Phillips,* Cambridge: John Wilson and Son, University Press, 1888. privately printed.

Pratt, Richard. *David Adler, The Architect and His Work.* New York: M. Evans Co., 1970.

Regan, Jane V. Paper on the history of Wauwinet and Coskata, 1981.

Report of the President's Commission (The), Americans Outdoors, The Legacy, The Challenge. Washington, DC, and Covelo, California: Island Press

Richman, Michael. *Daniel Chester French: An American Sculptor,* with postscript by Paul W. Ivory. The Metropolitan Museum of Art for the National Trust for Historic Preservation.

Rothery, Agnes. *Family Album,* memories of Cataumet Neck, now Lowell Holly Reservation.

Scovel, Rev. Dr. Carl. Eulogy, Laurence Minot Channing, April, 1989.

Scovel, Rev. Dr. Carl. Eulogy, Sidney Nichols Shurcliff, January, 1981.

Sedgwick, Ellery. Eulogy for Charles S. Rackemann, *Boston Transcript,* March 29,1933.

Shands, Dr. Alfred R. *Our Twenty-first President, Joel Ernest Goldthwait, 1866-1961.* A manuscript written in 1971 for publication in the *American Orthopaedic Association News.*

Sherer, Stan, and Michael E.C. Gery. *Founding Farms: Five Massachusetts Family Farms, 1638 — Present.* Northampton, 1990.

Shurcliff, Sidney Nichols. *Upon the Road Argilla.* Privately printed, 1958.

Stavros, Mrs. Mary. Brier Neck, Gloucester, Massachusetts. Statement, notes on file with The Trustees of Reservations.

Tisbury Pond Club (The). Daily logs of gunning for waterfowl, 1920-1946.

Trustees of Reservations (The) Correspondence and reports (on file), 1892-1992; Minute Books and records of the Standing Committee (on file), 1891-1992; *Annual Reports of The Trustees of Reservations,* 1891-1992.

Whitehill, Walter M. *The Stevens-Coolidge Place in North Andover, Massachusetts,* a manuscript written for The Trustees of Reservations, May, 1978.

Who's Who in Massachusetts, 1940-41. Boston: Larkin, Roosevelt & Larkin, Ltd., 1940.

Wonson, Mary, and Roger Choate. *Downriver — Memoir of Choate Island.* Poems by Agnes Choate Wonson, photography by Roger Choate Wonson. Randolph Center, Vermont: Greenhills Books, 1983.

Woodbury, C.J.C. *Phillip Augustus Chase: A Memorial of the First President of the Lynn Historical Society,* 1903.

Yaro, Robert D., Randall G. Arendt, Harry L. Dodson, and Elizabeth A. Brabec. *Dealing with Change in the Connecticut River Valley, Volume One; Dealing with Change in the Connecticut River Valley: A Design Manual for Conservation and Development, Volume Two.* Massachusetts Department of Environmental Management and the Center for Rural Massachusetts, University of Massachusetts, Amherst, Massachusetts. 1988.

Articles, etc.:

—. "A Modern Massachusetts Farm," article from *Garden and Forest,* a weekly periodical, March 30, 1892. New York; conducted by Professor C. S. Sargent.

—. *Appleton Farms, Sunday Afternoon, August twenty-second, Nineteen Hundred and Twenty.* Booklet privately published for ceremonial dedication of a tablet in memory of Samuel Appleton.

—. Augustus P. Loring obituary, *The Boston Globe, The Beverly Times,* November 28, 1986.

—. Catalog for the Public Auction Sale, June 29, 30 and July 1, 1950, at Castle Hill, Ipswich. Parke-Bernet Galleries, New York.

—. Charles S. Bird obituary, *The Boston Globe,* May 14, 1980.

—. Charles S. Rackemann obituary, *The Boston Daily Globe,* March 29, 1933.

—. Chase obituary, newspaper clipping, Lynn Historical Society, 125 Green Street, Lynn, Massachusetts 01902, 1989.

—. Cornelius Crane obituary, *The Ipswich Chronicle,* July 12, 1962.

—. Dictionary of American Biography, Author's Edition. New York: Charles Scribner's Sons, 1937.

—. Ellen L. Parkinson vs. Board of Assessors of Medfield, Supreme Judicial Court, Commonwealth of Massachusetts; Appeal from a decision of the Appelate Tax Board, 1986.

—. Francis Edward Frothingham obituary, *The Boston Herald,* February 14, 1954.

—. *Gloucester Daily Times.* Articles in connection with a hearing on the burial of Cornelius Crane, July 13 and 14, 1962.

—. Harriet Backus obituary, *Nantucket Inquirer & Mirror.*

—. Information about the Rev. Jonathon B. Harrington, Albert G. Garneau, Historian, Town of Franklin, New Hampshire.

—. *Ipswich Chronicle (The).* Numerous articles about Crane Beach including its proposed taking by the Commonwealth. 1950s and early 1960s.

—. Isadore Smith obituary, *The Beverly Times,* December 2, 1985.

—. J. Graham Parsons obituary, *The New York Times,* October 22, 1991.

—. James N. Stavros obituary, *Boston Sunday Globe,* March 15, 1981, and the *Gloucester Daily Times,* March 14, 1981.

—. Leverett Saltonstall obituary, newspaper clipping, Newton Free Library, Newton, Massachusetts.

—. Lieutenant-Colonel Arthur D. Budd obituary, *The Berkshire Eagle,* September 27, 1965.

—. May Wakeman obituary, *The Vineyard Gazette,* April 6, 1984.

—. *Memorial for John Charles Phillips.* Cambridge: Privately printed at the Harvard University Press, January, 1939.

—. Newspaper clipping in connection with a child momentarily lost in the Manchester woods, *Beetle & Wedge,* August, 1877.

—. Newspaper clipping in connection with the auction at the Crane Reservation, *The Boston Daily Globe,* June 30, 1950.

—. Newspaper clipping in connection with the Wampanoag Indians' suit for land in Mashpee, *The Boston Globe,* October 2, 1979.

—. Richard T. Crane, Jr., obituary, *The Ipswich Chronicle,* November, 1931.

—. Shurtleff obituary, newspaper clipping, January, 1896. Connecticut Valley Historical Museum, Springfield, Massachusetts.

—. *The Narrative of the Captivity and Restoration of Mrs. Mary Rowlandson,* First Printed in 1682 at Cambridge, Massachusetts, & London England. Boston: Houghton Mifflin Company, 1930.

—. "What a Thing to Steal". Editorial in connection with the theft of dinosaur tracks. *Boston Transcript,* December 5, 1936.

—. William Ellery obituary, *The Boston Herald,* Monday, July 24, 1961.

—. William R. Greeley obituary, *The Boston Globe,* October 10, 1966.

Index

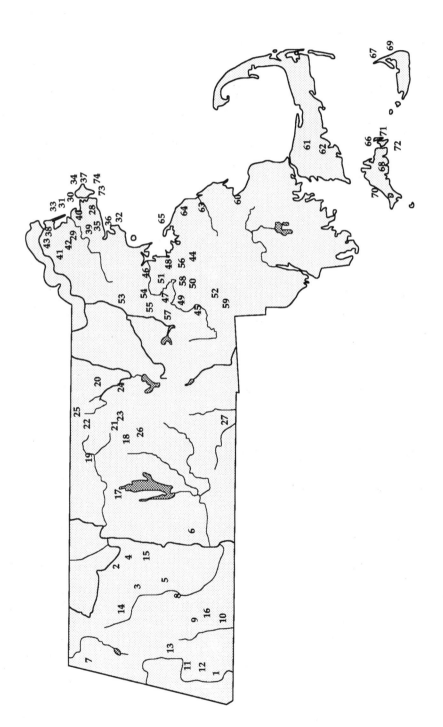

Map of Properties

1. Bartholomew's Cobble & Col. John Ashley House, Ashley Falls, 277 acres
2. Bear Swamp Reservation, Ashfield, 213 acres
3. William Cullen Bryant Homestead, Cummington, acres
4. Chapelbrook Reservation, South Ashfield, 143 acres
5. Chesterfield Gorge, West Chesterfield, 161 acres
6. Dinosaur Footprints Reservation, Holyoke, 8 acres
7. Field Farm, Williamstown, 294 acres
8. Glendale Falls, Middlefield, 60 acres
9. Goose Pond Reservation, Lee, 112 acres
10. McLenan Reservation, Tyringham & Otis, 491 acres
11. The Mission House Stockbridge, 46 acres
12. Monument Mountain Reservation, Great Barrington, 503 acres
13. Naumkeag, Stockbridge, 46 acres
14. Notchview Reservation, Windsor, 3000 acres
15. Petticoat HIll Reservation, Williamsburg, 60 acres
16. Tyringham Cobble, Tryingham, 206 acres
17. Bear's Den, North New Salem, 6 acres
18. James W. Brooks Woodland Preserve, Petersham, 510 acres
19. Doane's Falls, Royalston, 31.5 acres
20. Doyle Reservation, Leominster, 23 acres
21. Elliott Laurel Reservation, Phillipston, 33 acres
22. Jacobs Hill Reservation, Royalston, 135 acres
23. North Common Meadow, Petersham, 24 acres

24. Redemption Rock, Princeton, .25 acres
25. Royalston Falls, Royalston, 205 acres
26. Swift River Reservation, Petersham, 439 acres
27. Tantiusques Reservation, Sturbridge, 55 acres
28. Agassiz Rock, Manchester, 101 acres
29. Appleton Farms Grass Rides, Hamilton, 228 acres
30. Cornelius and Miné Crane Wildlife Refuge, Ipswich & Essex, 650 acres
31. Richard T. Crane, Jr., Memorial Reservation, Ipswich, 1398 acres
32. Crowninshield Island, Marblehead, 5 acres
33. Greenwood Farm Salt Marsh, Ipswich, 138 acres
34. Halibut Point Reservation, Rockport, 12 acres
35. Long Hill, Beverly, 114 acres
36. Misery Island Reservation, Salem Bay, 84 acres
37. Mount Anne Park, West Gloucester, 87 acres
38. Old Town Hill Reservation, Newbury, 372 acres
39. Pine and Hemlock Knoll, Wenham, 14 acres
40. James N. and Mary F. Stavros Reservation
41. Stevens-Coolidge Place, North Andover, 94 acres
42. Charles W. Ward Reservation, Andover & North Andover, 640 acres
43. Weir Hill Reservation, North Andover, 192 acres
44. Eleanor Cabot Bradley Reservation, Canton, 84 acres
45. Bridge Island Meadows, Millis, 82 acres
46. Charles River Peninsula, Needham, 29 acres
47. Fork Factory Brook Reservation, Medfield, 144 acres
48. Governor Hutchinson's Field, Milton, 9 acres

49. Medfield meadow Lots, Medfield, 133 acres
50. Medfield Rhododendrons, Medfield, 213 acres
51. Noanet Woodlands, Dover, 695 acres
52. Noon Hill Reservation, Medfield, 204 acres
53. The Old Manse, Concord, 8 acres
54. Pegan Hill Reservation, Dover & Natick
55. Peters Reservation, Dover, 89 acres
56. Pierce Reservation, Milton, 4 acres
57. Rocky Narrows, Sherborn, 157 acres
58. Rocky Woods Reservation, Medfield, 488 acres
59. Henry L. Shattuck Reservation, Medfield, 235 acres
60. Holmes Reservation, Plymouth, 25 acres
61. Lowell Holly Reservation, Mashpee & Sandwich, 135 acres
62. Mashpee River Reservation, Mashpee, 243 acres
63. Albert F. Norris Reservation, Norwell, 101 acres
64. Whitney and Thayer Woods, Cohasset & Hingham, 817 acres
65. World's End Reservation, Hingham, 251 acres
66. Cape Poge Wildlife Refuge, Edgertown, 509 acres
67. Coskata-Coatue Wildlife Refuge, Great Point, 112 acres
68. Long Point Wildlife Refuge, West Tisbury, 632 acres
69. Medouie Creek, Wauwiet, 5 acres
70. Menemsha Hills Reservation, Chilmark, 211 acres
71. Mytoi, Edgertown, 14 acres
72. Wasque Reservation, Edgertown, 200 acres
73. Coolidge Reservation, Manchester-by-the-Sea, 52 acres
74. Ravenswood Park, Gloucester, 600 acres

About the Author. . .

Gordon Abbott, Jr., was the first Director of the Trustees of Reservations. He served the organization from 1966 to 1984, seventeen and one-half years. A former schoolteacher and advertising copywriter, Abbott went on to become editor of two prize-winning daily newspapers on the North Shore of Massachusetts, *The Gloucester Times* and *The Beverly Times*. A 1950 graduate of Harvard College, he received a master's degree in American Studies from the University of Massachusetts at Boston. In 1984 and 1985 he was a Visiting Scholar at Harvard University's School of Design.

Gordon Abbott, Jr.

Active as a board member of many charitable organizations, he has been an elected director of the Harvard Alumni Association, a Trustee of Connecticut College and of Brooks School, and a director of Maine Coast Heritage Trust. A founder and former Treasurer of the Land Trust Alliance, he also proposed and helped establish the Center for Rural Massachusetts at the University of Massachusetts at Amherst, where he served as Associate Director of the Center and as Adjunct Professor of Regional Planning. He is a former member of the Planning Board and of the Harbor Committee in Manchester-by-the-Sea, Massachusetts, where he lives with his wife and family. An ardent sailor and skier, his activities and interests include writing and the problems associated with changing conditions in small communities throughout the country.

The Trustees of Reservations conserves for public use and enjoyment properties of exceptional scenic, historic and ecological significance throughout Massachusetts. The Trustees owns and manages 75 reservations across the Commonwealth, totaling 19,000 acres. Through the use of conservation restrictions, The Trustees protects an additional 8,000 acres of land.

The Trustees of Reservations has an active membership of more than 12,000. It is a private, non-profit organization and relies for support entirely upon income from membership dues, charitable contributions, admission fees, grants and endowment.

The Trustees
of Reservations

Conserving the
Massachusetts Landscape
Since 1891

572 Essex Street
Beverly, Massachusetts 01915-1530
508-921-1944 .